RETHINKING
HISTORY OF WALES

EARLY
MODERN
WALES

c.1536– c.1689

Series Editors:
Professor Paul O'Leary, Aberystwyth University
and Professor Huw Pryce, Bangor University

This series aims to stimulate fresh thinking about the history of Wales by introducing particular periods and themes in ways that challenge established interpretations. Whether by offering new perspectives on familiar landmarks in the historiographical landscape or by venturing into previously uncharted terrain, the volumes, each written by a specialist in the field, will provide concise and selective surveys that highlight areas of debate rather than attempting to achieve comprehensive coverage. The series will thus encourage an engagement with diverse understandings of the Welsh past and with its continuing – and sometimes contested – significance in the present day.

RETHINKING THE
HISTORY OF WALES

EARLY MODERN WALES

c.1536– c.1689

AMBIGUOUS NATIONHOOD

Lloyd Bowen

UNIVERSITY OF WALES PRESS

2022

www.uwp.co.uk

British Library Cataloguing-in-Publication Data
A catalogue record for this book is available from the British Library.

ISBN   978-1-78683-958-9
eISBN   978-1-78683-959-6

Typeset by Marie Doherty
Printed by CPI Antony Rowe, Melksham

This book is dedicated to Nicki, Tal and Osian
(because this is the only bit they ever read)

CONTENTS

Acknowledgements • ix
Abbreviations • xi
Map • xiii

CHAPTER 1
Locating Early Modern Wales • 1

CHAPTER 2
'They Value Themselves Much upon their Antiquity':
History, Myth and Identity • 19

CHAPTER 3
'Awake Now Thou Lovely Wales!':
The Reformation and its Legacies • 39

CHAPTER 4
Alternative Visions: Catholicism,
Puritanism and Dissent • 63

CHAPTER 5
'The Communion of One Tongue':
Language and Society • 91

CHAPTER 6
'A Prince of our Own Natural Country and Name':
Welshness, Britishness and Monarchy • 115

CHAPTER 7
Politics, Officeholding and Participation • 139

CHAPTER 8
Women and Gender in Early Modern Wales • 167

CHAPTER 9
'A Brittain by Nation Born': Welsh Diasporas • 195

Notes • 219
Select bibliography • 257
Index • 271

ACKNOWLEDGEMENTS

I would like to thank Huw Pryce and Paul O'Leary for the invitation (rather more years ago than I think we should dwell on) to contribute to this series, and for their encouragement as the volume took shape. Llion Wigley has, as ever, been a model of support, courtesy and accommodation at UWP, for which I am enormously grateful. I would also like to thank Adam Burns for designing the cover and tracking down an image of the coin from the Aberystwyth mint.

I am most grateful to the many archives and libraries that have made their collections available to me over the years during which the research for this volume was undertaken. Special thanks go to the staff of the National Library of Wales and The National Archives of the United Kingdom, the two repositories upon which this book draws most heavily. The Arts and Social Studies Library at Cardiff University, and particularly the staff who deal with Inter-Library Loans were also most patient with my many requests, particularly when the restrictions imposed by the Covid-19 pandemic made matters all the more challenging.

I would like to record my heartfelt thanks to my splendid colleagues in the History Department at Cardiff for being so supportive. These are, in no particular order (or are they?), Steph Ward, David Doddington, James Ryan, Keir Waddington, Kevin Passmore, Bronach Kane and Mark Williams. I would also like to record my debt to the late Professor John Gwynfor Jones who was always supportive of my work and was a fount of good humour and cheer as you encountered him on his slow ascent to the 5th floor. My heartfelt thanks go to Mark Stoyle for his encouragement and help, and also to our wonderful colleagues on the 'Civil War Petitions Project', Andy Hopper, Ismini Pells and David Appleby. I am also very grateful to Prof. Newton E. Key for generously assisting me with my discussion of the 1689 petition against the Council in the Marches.

Without my family this book would have been finished much more quickly. Still, they've demanded inclusion or they've threatened to injure the dog, so thank you to Nicki for your extraordinary support and patience; to Tal for your dedication to beating me in every board game; to Osian for also beating me in every board game; and to Gatsby, for getting me out of the house. You are an amazing bunch and I am enormously lucky to have you in my life.

My friends are, frankly, a spent force. Dar is consumed by the media wall; Dark Skies by 'Tympanist Monthly'; and Dids continues petulantly to spurn the group chat. Still, this was the year in which Trabzonspor brought us together. I'd like to thank the Black Sea Storm, Avcı, Hamsik, Denswil, Cornelius (of course) and all the boys for bringing the Lig back to the Medical Park after 38 years of hurt. Other friends who contributed their support in various ways and, who it is my delight to acknowledge, include Ray Purchase, Daniel John Garside Wynn, Beezus Fuffoon, Claire Macgourley, Hoop Kaaak and Cliff Praise. Juan Sweener, as always, was there when you needed him.

I'd also like to thank Brian Eno for 'Apollo: Atmospheres and Soundtracks' and R.E.M. for 'Fables of the Reconstruction', which were the constant accompaniments to the writing of this book.

ABBREVIATIONS

AC	*Archaeologia Cambrensis*
BBCS	*Bulletin of the Board of Celtic Studies*
Bodl. Lib.	Bodleian Library, Oxford
BL	British Library, London
CJ	*Journals of the House of Commons*
Davies, *Rhagymadroddion*	Ceri Davies (ed.), *Rhagymadroddion a Chyflwyniadau Lladin, 1551–1632* (Cardiff, 1980)
Dialogue	John Gwynfor Jones (ed.), *The Dialogue of the Government of Wales (1594)* (Cardiff, 2010)
Description	George Owen, *The Description of Penbrokshire*, ed. H. Owen (4 vols, London, 1892–1936)
EHR	*English Historical Review*
FMW	Geraint H. Jenkins, *The Foundations of Modern Wales, 1642–1780* (Oxford, 1987)
HMC	Historical Manuscripts Commission reports
HPO	History of Parliament Trust Online (all biographies and constituency articles can be found at *https://www.historyofparliamentonline. org/*; citations indicate relevant volume entries in brackets)
Hughes, *Rhagymadroddion*	Garfield H. Hughes (ed.), *Rhagymadroddion, 1547–1659* (Cardiff, 1951)
LJ	*Journals of the House of Lords*
ODNB	*Oxford Dictionary of National Biography*
NLW	National Library of Wales, Aberystwyth
NLWJ	*National Library of Wales Journal*

PoP	Lloyd Bowen, *The Politics of the Principality: Wales, c.1603–1642* (Cardiff, 2007)
RR	Glanmor Williams, *Renewal and Reformation, c.1415–1642* (Oxford, 1993)
SR	*Statutes of the Realm* (11 vols, London, 1810–28)
TCS	*Transactions of the Cymmrodorion Society*
TNA	The National Archives of the UK, Kew
TRHS	*Transactions of the Royal Historical Society*
Tudor Wales	Trevor Herbert and Gareth Elwyn Jones (eds), *Tudor Wales* (Cardiff, 1988)
WHR	*Welsh History Review*
WLBIR	Geraint H. Jenkins (ed.), *The Welsh Language before the Industrial Revolution* (Cardiff, 1997)
UBA	University of Bangor Archives

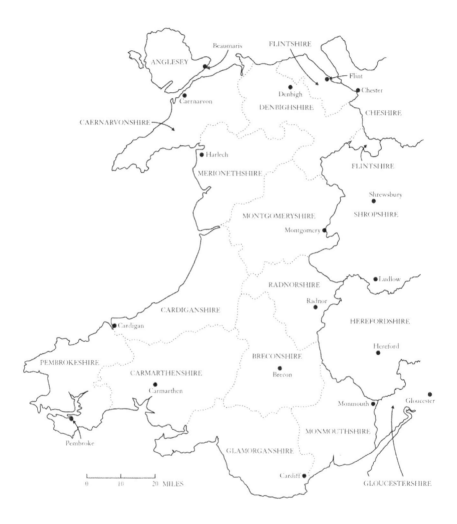

ANGLESEY

Beaumaris

FLINTSHIRE

Flint

Chester

Denbigh

CAERNARVONSHIRE

Caernarvon

DENBIGHSHIRE

CHESHIRE

Harlech

MERIONETHSHIRE

FLINTSHIRE

Shrewsbury

MONTGOMERYSHIRE

SHROPSHIRE

Montgomery

Ludlow

RADNORSHIRE

CARDIGANSHIRE

Radnor

HEREFORDSHIRE

Cardigan

Hereford

PEMBROKESHIRE

CARMARTHENSHIRE

BRECONSHIRE

Brecon

Carmarthen

Monmouth

Gloucester

Pembroke

MONMOUTHSHIRE

GLAMORGANSHIRE

0   10   20 MILES

Cardiff

GLOUCESTERSHIRE

WELSH COUNTIES AND COUNTY TOWNS
FOLLOWING THE ACTS OF UNION

1

Locating Early Modern Wales

I n 1573 the Dutch cartographer Abraham Ortelius published a
supplement to his successful 1570 atlas *Theatrum Orbis Terrarum*
(*Theatre of the World*). This publication included the first printed
map to show Wales as a distinct region. The map had been
drawn in his last sickness by the north Wales scholar and antiquarian
Humphrey Llwyd, who had died some five years before Ortelius's
supplement appeared.[1] The image Llwyd presented to his readers
was, however, a curious one. It showed the eastern border of Wales
as extending to the River Severn, although this incorporated into
'Wales' significant parts of the English counties of Gloucestershire,
Herefordshire, Worcestershire and Shropshire. The country was also
divided into the old medieval territories of Gwynedd, Deheubarth
and Powys, all of which had long been dismantled. Llwyd's beautiful
rendering of this distended country also possessed distinctive linguistic
features, with regional divisions and many place names displayed in
three languages: Latin, English and Welsh. Indeed, the map itself was
titled not 'Wales' but 'Cambriae typus', the name Cambria deriving
from Camber, son of the fabled first king of Britain, Brutus. Legend
had it that Camber had inherited this part of the island (England
and Scotland went to his brothers) many centuries before the birth
of Christ. In a commentary which was published around the same
time as Ortelius's volume, Llwyd laid out the methodology behind
his map. He wrote that he had represented the nation according to
an understanding derived from old 'chronicles', and noted that those
who now inhabited this space

> use the British tongue and are the very true Britons by birth.
> And although some do write that Wales doth not stretch forth

on this side the River Vaga, or Wye, this can be no fraud to us. For we have taken in hand to describe Cambria and not Wallia, 'Wales' as it is now called by a new name, and unacquainted to the Welshmen.[2]

Llwyd's map, then, was a historical and cultural composite rather than a faithful rendering of Elizabethan administrative realities.

Llwyd and his map provide a useful route into the central themes of this volume.[3] Born in 1527, Llwyd was the product of a Wales shaped by its formal assimilation into the English state through the 'Acts of Union', two landmark statutes which were engineered by Henry VIII's chief minister, Thomas Cromwell, and enacted in 1536 and 1543. This legislation drew a very different border between England and Wales than did Llwyd, but it also encouraged and facilitated Welsh participation in the wider cultural, social and political worlds of an expanded state. Llwyd took advantage of these opportunities, attending Oxford University before entering the service of a powerful English nobleman. Llwyd sat for a Welsh constituency in the national Parliament at Westminster and was himself crucial in the passage of another piece of legislation which had epochal significance for Wales and the Welsh: the 1563 Act authorising the translation of the Bible and the Book of Common Prayer into Welsh. A Welsh-speaker who was lauded by local vernacular poets (or 'bards'), Llwyd was also a humanist scholar and fascinated by history and antiquities. He travelled on the continent in 1566–7, and in Antwerp was introduced by another Denbighshire man to the cartographer Ortelius. Llwyd was captivated by the ancient history of Britain, a line of academic inquiry which lauded the Welsh as the original inhabitants of the island, and the heirs of its glories. His pride shines through in his reference to the Welsh as 'the very true Britons by birth' in his letter to Ortelius. Llwyd's posthumous works would provide an important intellectual underpinning for the development in the sixteenth and seventeenth centuries (along with another Welshman, the astrologer and magus John Dee) of what might be termed an early modern 'British imperial ideology'.[4] It was Llwyd who first coined the term 'British empire'.[5]

Llwyd's life and career touch upon important threads in the story of early modern Wales which will be elaborated in this book. These include the influence of the Acts of Union and Wales's incorporation in the English (and later 'British') polity; politics, patronage and the role of the Westminster Parliament; the Reformation and the shift from Catholicism to the Church of England after Henry VIII's divorce crisis; the significance and role of the Welsh language in an English-speaking state; the influence of Renaissance learning; Welsh mobility and movement in England and beyond; and the importance of history and myth for the Welsh during the sixteenth and seventeenth centuries. These are themes which have been considered in previous studies, but instead of providing another narrative of political and religious developments between the passing of the first Act of Union and the 'Glorious Revolution', this volume will endeavour to explore these ideas through the prism of Welsh identity. Moreover, rather than taking its subject of study as a given, the book argues for the uncertain and ambiguous nature of 'Wales' and 'Welshness' in the period following the Acts of Union and the Reformation crisis, when these categories were being reformulated and reimagined.[6] Llwyd's map of Wales offers some useful evidence in this regard, depicting as it does an enigmatic space shaped by history, myth and language as well as by political borders and geographical features. Professor Gwyn A. Williams's startling question 'When Was Wales?' remains a fruitful point of departure for a discussion of the sixteenth and seventeenth centuries, when any pretensions to an independent Welsh political identity had disappeared.[7] This volume argues that early modern Wales can be best understood and conceptualised not simply as a constitutional entity produced by the Acts of Union, but rather as an aggregate of cultural, linguistic and historical communities, some of which were highly localised and others of which spilled over the country's administrative borders rather in the manner of Llwyd's 'Cambriae Typus'.

The tension between the post-union status of Wales as part of the English state and the awareness of its inhabitants, as well as those outside the country, that it was decidedly un-English, is a central paradox which provides us with much of our material for addressing the issue of Welsh identity under the Tudors and Stuarts. The multivarious ways in which Wales and Welshness were fabricated by contemporaries (both through self-identification on the part of the Welsh and through negative identification by non-Welsh subjects, usually the English) provided a countervailing force against the erasure of a Welsh identity in the face of the expanding English state. Indeed, there is something of a tension here in that the institutions of that English state served to enhance rather than to suppress concepts of a particularist identity. Welsh men and women in the sixteenth and seventeenth centuries sustained something recognisable as 'Wales' by their acts of cultural, linguistic, historical, literary, social and imaginative association, and these acts were often facilitated by state bodies such as the Church and the monarchy. In the period covered by this book, then, Wales was a dominion of the English Crown and a region of the kingdom of England (and, after the accession of James VI of Scotland to the throne of England in 1603, of what can somewhat anachronistically be called 'Britain') but it was populated by individuals who conceived of themselves as a distinct national community, albeit not a separate polity. Indeed, ambitions of a separate constitutional existence belonged to a long-dead past; they were buried with Owain Glyndŵr. While the Welsh of the sixteenth and seventeenth centuries were proud of their heritage and culture, these impulses drew them into rather than away from the heart of Britain. Ideas of Welsh separatism and what we might describe as political nationalism were anathema. This is not to say that there was not a sense of Welsh 'patriotism', but it is rather to acknowledge that such energies, although directed rhetorically against the English on occasion, were far more likely to assume a kind of historicised ardour for Wales-within-Britain. The early modern Welsh were the Crown's most enthusiastic 'British' subjects, and this volume endorses and provides a sustained exploration of Gwyn A.Williams's contention that 'Welsh identity has constantly renewed itself by anchoring itself in variant forms of Britishness'.[8]

Although the idea of 'Wales' had a long heritage which encompassed the geographical area that was administratively demarcated and defined under Henry VIII,[9] this was nevertheless a place of profound internal divisions. Rees Davies's assessment of medieval Wales remains relevant long into the early modern period, describing the country as 'a land of contrasts, national, regional and local [and] in such a fragmented country it was the locality or district which was often the most meaningful and basic unit of loyalty and obligation'.[10] This fragmentation has significant consequences for any discussion of national identity. The first and most important of these divisions was geography. Wales was dominated by a central mountain range which effectively cut the country in two. This is a fundamental division and was of considerable significance in separating north and south Wales. Communication between these regions was difficult: the gentleman from Anglesey would have had little intercourse with the squire from Monmouthshire. Routes running east to west operated more readily than those running north to south. We might thus divide Wales into three broad territories whose urban foci lay in England: the route along the north Wales coast which was centred on Chester; the mid-Wales region which traded principally with Shrewsbury; and the south Wales corridor linking to Bristol.[11] Thus regional loyalties and affinities were important in shaping the mental boundaries of early modern society. It was common, for example, for gentlemen in Glamorgan to seek their brides from among the gentry of neighbouring areas, and this included counties like Devon and Somerset which were readily accessible by sea. It was rare, however, to find a marriage concluded between a Glamorgan squire and a bride from north Wales. It has been said with some validity that Wales cannot be conceived of as a truly unified country until the coming of the railways which helped overcome these basic obstacles of distance and environment and forge some sense of face-to-face community between Welsh men and women from widely separated parts of the country.

Even beneath the regional level Wales was a country dominated by contrasts resulting from geographical barriers and boundaries.[12] The county of Denbighshire, for example, was divided by a mountain range into eastern and western halves. Glamorgan was split between the prosperous lowland Vale region and a poorer mountainous northern area. The contrasts between these two districts were seen not only in terms of highly localised family contacts, but also in economic activity and social structures which in turn had a major impact upon cultural, political and religious developments. It is striking, for example, that most of the Glamorgan religious radicals, or puritans, who appeared during the seventeenth century came from the mountainous regions of the northern shire where parishes were generally larger and ecclesiastical control was more difficult to enforce. Another division which is important to consider is that of language, for several communities were largely English-speaking, in contrast to the majority of native Welsh-speakers, and these areas also adopted Anglicised patterns of settlement and economy. Southern Pembrokeshire, the

Gower Peninsula and the Vale of Glamorgan, for example, all had significant populations which spoke only English. We must be aware from the outset, therefore, that early modern Wales can be approached as a grouping of diverse communities as much as a unified country.

Yet despite these divisions, there were important integrative factors which pulled in the opposite direction, towards a more communal and collective sense of identity for the Welsh. These elements helped the early modern Welsh 'imagine' themselves as a nation or a people.[13] In the absence of separate political, dynastic or constitutional structures, it was central to the maintenance of a distinct identity that the people of Wales continued to conceive of themselves as something other than their neighbours. From the twelfth century, despite the division of Wales into small fiefdoms, the sense of a wider Welsh identity had been identifiable.[14] Illustrative of this was the fact that during this period the Welsh word for the localised 'kin-group' (*cenedl*) changed its meaning to something closer to the modern notion of 'nation'. It was by this act of associating with other Welsh people, usually through a common language, shared views of historical descent and a collective social, religious and cultural experience, that something called 'Wales' survived the country's incorporation with England.

Perhaps the most important factor sustaining this separate identity was Wales's distinctive language, a topic which is pursued at greater length in Chapter 5. Despite the regional divisions, the overwhelming majority of Welsh men and women, perhaps near 90 per cent, used Welsh as their first, and for most their only, language.[15] This cannot but have helped forge a sense of shared experience and mutual understanding among people from the various parts of Wales, despite various regions' dialectical differences. The authors of an authoritative essay on the Welsh language in this period have observed that 'in a country which possessed no separate institutions of nationhood, the native tongue was the most distinctive and widely recognized badge of the collective identity of the Welsh people and one of the few unifying factors within Wales'.[16] It is highly significant in terms of this discussion, that the Welsh word '*iaith*' meaning 'language', also signified 'national community'.[17]

The capacity of this language to enshrine a sense of nationhood had been acknowledged since the Middle Ages. The Welsh bards were trained poets and songsters, and constituted an important part of Welsh cultural life down to the mid-seventeenth century. These figures helped protect and promulgate a Welsh sense of communal history and continuity with the past in their vernacular poetry and songs. They also helped propagate the foundation myth of the Welsh people as the original inhabitants of the island of Britain, something which was amplified and broadcast by humanist scholars such as Humphrey Llwyd. As is discussed further in Chapter 2, the Welsh were deeply attached to these ideas of ancient origins to support their claims to distinctiveness and, indeed, to a kind of historical and cultural superiority. This Welsh view of their own history was not restricted to elites, however, and the sense of a distinguished past seems to have been present throughout society. Intertwined with this interest in the distant past was the idea that the Welsh were descended from the 'Ancient Britons', the original inhabitants and possessors of the island, and particularly from the legendary king and founder of Britain, the Trojan Brutus. This notion of common bloodlines fostered a popular interest in genealogy, which was a major feature of Tudor and Stuart society, especially among those who claimed social status as gentry or '*uchelwyr*' (lit. 'high men').

Another significant factor encouraging a sense of collective Welshness in this period was the close presence of the English. The enduring dominance of the Welsh language meant that a linguistic as well as administrative boundary remained between the two peoples throughout the sixteenth and seventeenth centuries. However, this boundary was blurry and ambiguous as we shall see in Chapters 3 and 9. There were, for example, significant Welsh-speaking communities in English counties such as Herefordshire, where one commentator in 1608 noted: 'the Welch tonge even to this daie is as frequent and as usuall as in other shieres in Wales'.[18] Nevertheless, it remained true that the Welsh were seen as a separate people by the English, 'the most familiar of foreigners', although they did enjoy a special status as 'honorary Englishmen' following the union. The prevalence of the Welsh language along with its upland economy and warlike past caused the English to remain somewhat suspicious of their western neighbours. Although the English marking of the Welsh as a separate people was often expressed through satire or mockery, there were times, such as the early days of the civil wars in the 1640s, when it shaded into darker territory of ethnic fear and mistrust.

For all my comments about the localised and fragmented nature of Welsh society, another important element in helping the Welsh conceive of themselves and their country was its defined territorial borders. On the north, south and west the sea provided a natural boundary. The eastern border with England was more fluid and dynamic with social, cultural and linguistic geographies changing over time, but even here the Acts of Union drew an administrative line (albeit one that would come to be contested – particularly by English border gentlemen wary of being branded as 'Welsh'), which demarcated Wales from England. Wales's geography, which did so much to fragment the country's economic, social and political life, paradoxically also gave it some unity of interest in that it occupied a compact region on Britain's western periphery. As such its counties were fairly uniformly distant from central government and correspondingly political power here was focused on the resident gentry class which enjoyed a more dominant position in Wales than in many other parts of the realm. Additionally, its geographical position meant that Wales was also uniformly concerned with the threat of invasion and the potential danger from Catholic Ireland. Defence and matters of security, therefore, also provided issues around which some sense of common purpose could be forged.

Framing and contextualising Wales as part of a wider British polity underpins one of the book's central arguments: that many previous accounts have been insufficiently sensitive to Wales's integration within an early modern British state structure that encouraged movement, connection and integration in many spheres of life and at all social levels. The status of Wales, and the activities of Welsh men and women beyond the borders of the principality, then, will be an important component of the volume. The economic migration of Welsh individuals into towns such as Bristol, Shrewsbury and Chester were hardly innovations of the early modern period, but the scale and intensity was of a different order in the sixteenth and seventeenth centuries. The growing Welsh presence in the kingdom's rapidly expanding capital was also a notable feature of the post-union period. London's status as the core of what might be described as an early imperial polity also encouraged Welsh men and women to participate in the wars and plantations that were a feature of English involvement in early modern Ireland. Llwyd's 'British empire' also translated into Welsh plans for settling the New World such as Sir William Vaughan's proposed colony of Cambriol in Newfoundland in the early seventeenth century. This volume thus looks to integrate some of the fruitful methodologies of 'transnational' history into its investigations of Welsh identities beyond the country's boundaries.

This book also draws on recent scholarship to argue for a reframing of the Acts of Union and Wales's subsequent incorporation into the British legal, political, religious and administrative spheres. It suggests that state building was not simply something imposed on Wales from without and above by the ruthless English Crown, but was rather a transactional process which co-opted (and in some ways made) local agents in Welsh counties and parishes. At the same time, however, it is argued that this integration within the broader polity also allowed for a restatement and even a strengthening of concepts of Welshness. The Acts of Union and the attendant religious Reformation empowered local elites, but these developments also helped produce a bureaucracy that, in sharp contrast to English policy in Ireland, was indigenous and responsive to the local cultural environment. Indeed, a case can be made for the Acts of Union defining 'Wales' administratively and politically for the first time, giving it a corporate identity which had previously been fragmented by long-standing institutional divisions, particularly that between the medieval Principality and the Welsh Marches.

This focus on the integration of early modern Wales into the British state contributes to another argument of this book – that loyalty to the monarch and to the Established Church were fundamental components of Welsh political and religious culture. During the sixteenth century the Crown and the Church were both rendered as thoroughly 'British' in origin, with the understanding that this anchored them in Wales's vernacular historical landscape. This 'inculturation' produced significant dividends for the Tudor and Stuart rulers, as seen in the absence of any serious backlash against the Protestant settlement in Wales and the strength of royalist feeling in the principality during the tumultuous years of the civil wars and interregnum in the mid-seventeenth century. The volume thus challenges modernising accounts of the era which have tended to focus on subjects such as the birth of religious nonconformity, parliamentarianism and the coming of industry, and to have heaped scorn on the nefarious role of the supposedly 'Anglicised' Welsh gentry in early modern society. Instead, the following chapters thoroughly historicise these subjects, and argue that political loyalism and religious conservatism best characterise the Welsh experience during this period. Moreover, the book resists the temptation to vilify the early modern gentry as the cultural traitors they have often been portrayed, as particularly in accounts dealing with Welsh literature and language. Although there were strong Anglicising tendencies among Wales's ruling class in the sixteenth and seventeenth centuries, many gentlemen patronised the bards, involved themselves in Welsh cultural pursuits, enthused about the country's particularist history and spoke Welsh well into the seventeenth century. The social and cultural differentiation of the gentry from their communities was a complex, protracted, variegated and piecemeal phenomenon, and the account given in this volume hopefully reflects this complexity and rejects easy caricature.

In exploring these themes, and in contrast with most synthetic treatments of early modern Wales, the book will attempt to discuss not only the gentry elites, but also the experiences of groups lower down the social scale, although the former will necessarily receive much more attention. As we consider topics such as religion, gender and Welsh diaspora, we will encounter those beneath this upper stratum of society. Sometimes our evidence for these constituencies is frustratingly scarce and incomplete. This problem is compounded by the relative lack of scholarship on subaltern actors in early modern Wales, particularly compared with the wealth of literature on their English counterparts. A similar set of problems also bedevils the analysis of women and gender in the early modern period, although this tide is beginning to change. An attempt is thus made in Chapter 8 to integrate some of this recent scholarship and to provide some reflection on and insight into the nature of another crucial component of identity in early modern Wales, and one that has been missing from earlier histories of this period, that of women and gender.

Pulling these threads together, the volume has an overarching thesis which looks to modify previous accounts of Wales in this era. The very notion of 'early modernity' invites a degree of anachronistic determinism and a sense that this is a period characterised by emerging shoots of the 'modern' world.[19] Discussions of Wales in the sixteenth and seventeenth centuries have often portrayed this as an era of 'transition', of tension between the traditional and the modern, or as the 'foundation' of something else, of a 'modern' Wales.[20] Such a trajectory assumes certain developments such as the growth of religious nonconformity, the social division of the gentry from their communities and the beginnings of a form of cultural nationalism. By contrast, the current volume contends that we should consider Welsh history between the early sixteenth and later seventeenth centuries as a distinctive period in its own right, divested of the baggage of modern priorities and preoccupations. Across the century and a half with which this volume is concerned, there were, as there would be in any comparable epoch, contrasting elements of continuity and change in Welsh social, religious, political and cultural developments. This was, however, a period characterised by Welsh integration within an expanding British polity, a process which produced significant tensions and problems, of course, but which also generated powerful impulses of loyalty to the Crown, assimilation within the expanded state system and devotion to an acculturated Church. These impulses might be somewhat in tension with the traditional lines of force in Welsh historiography, but that does not make them any less deserving of historical analysis and discussion. Like Humphrey Llwyd, then, we need to (re)locate early modern Wales to better understand it, and a necessary starting point is the Acts of Union.

The 'Acts of Union' is a modern term of art used to describe two pieces of parliamentary legislation concerned with Wales which were passed in 1536 and 1543. There is not the space here to go into the minutiae of these complex and still debated statutes, but in broad terms they represented King Henry VIII and his chief minister, Thomas Cromwell's, response to two related problems. The first of these problems was late medieval Wales's administrative and jurisdictional diversity, which many believed encouraged violence and social disorder (although it is likely that the prevalence and seriousness of this violence is overstated in surviving sources). The second problem was associated with England's break from Rome and the royal supremacy in the Church which followed the annulment of the king's marriage with Catherine of Aragon. The momentous issue of the Reformation is discussed further in Chapter 3; suffice it to say here that the break with Rome brought with it anxieties about the implementation of religious change and about security throughout the king's territories. The last thing Henry and Cromwell wanted was a region possessing a common border with England where the process of religious change and the enforcement of the king's authority might be impeded by jurisdictional discontinuity. Wales was recognised as a potential weak point in the realm's defences (it was, after all, the place from which Henry VIII's father had launched a successful coup in 1485) where continental Catholic powers might find sympathetic allies and perhaps launch an invasion against the heretic monarch.

Wales's diversity of legal and administrative jurisdictions, and the problems of disorder believed to arise from this diversity, had become pressing issues by the 1530s. The legacy of English conquest and colonisation in Wales over the previous four centuries meant that the country was divided into the Principality, the region ruled by the Princes of Gwynedd in the thirteenth century which lay primarily in the north and west, and the Marcher lordships (or Marches) which covered much of the country's eastern territory. Since 1284, and following Edward I's defeat of Llywelyn ap Gruffudd, the Principality had been 'annexed and united' to the English Crown and governed by direct royal control; its territory was divided into counties along English lines such as Caernarvonshire and Cardiganshire. The principal officials who ran the Principality were Englishmen; the Welsh were prohibited from holding office although they often did so at lower social levels. The Marcher lordships, by contrast, were held for the most part by absentee English lords and here diversity of government and fragmentation of authority were defining features. However, by the early sixteenth century the king had become the greatest Marcher lord, and this produced the unsatisfactory situation in which the monarch exercised different forms of authority in different parts of Wales. Contemporaries believed that the legal and administrative discontinuities of the Marches promoted misrule and endemic disorder, with criminals able to flee from one jurisdiction to another and evade justice. A 1534 legislative precursor to the union strikingly articulated these concerns, describing the people of Wales and the Marches as committing 'dyvers and manye folde theftes, murders, rebellyons, wilful burninge of houses and other sclerous deeds and abhomynable malefacts', and promising 'sharpe correccion and punyshmente' if these problems were not addressed.[21]

Initially the course of 'sharpe correccion' was pursued through the ruthless efforts of Bishop Rowland Lee, who was instituted as president of the Council in the Marches in 1534, and who boasted of bringing order to the Marches by hanging malefactors.[22] However, the regime soon settled on an alternative course and Henry and Cromwell determined to legislate the whole of Wales into the realm of England and to make it internally coherent and universally subject to royal authority. A keystone of Henrician policy in the 1530s was securing a 'unitary realm' in which, as Glanmor Williams observed, 'the whole structure of authority in the localities throughout England and Wales was to be uniform, coherent, and royal'.[23] Crown policy towards Wales was thus of a piece with Henry's efforts to extend and regularise his royal authority in other peripheral parts of his kingdom and was in keeping with the developing 'imperial' doctrine of the royal supremacy.[24] Under the provision of the first Act of Union (1536), then, all of Wales was divided into thirteen shires along the English model, with new counties such as Monmouthshire and Denbighshire created from old Marcher jurisdictions to sit alongside the older shires of the Principality. In these counties English government was instituted with commissions of the peace populated by resident Welsh gentlemen who also presided over the regular quarter sessions courts which administered the king's justice through the common law: the 1536 statute was entitled 'An Acte for Lawes & Justice to be Ministred in Wales in Like Fourme as it is in this Realme'.[25] Effectively, the union took the governmental apparatus of the Principality and made it universal throughout the territory which it now defined as 'Wales'.[26] The Welsh were to enjoy the same rights and legal freedoms as the English. In addition, and in recognition of the country's formal incorporation into the wider polity, these counties and their principal boroughs (the towns of Merioneth excepted) were empowered to elect Members of Parliament to represent their communities at the political centre. The Act also made the Welsh liable for all future taxes which Parliament levied.

The second Act of Union of 1543 dealt principally with the extension of English legal and administrative provisions in Wales. It created a unique legal body, the court of great sessions, which was organised into four circuits of three counties each (Monmouthshire would be attached to the Oxford assize circuit). The great sessions were cognate bodies of the English assize courts, although they had a broader legal jurisdiction than the assizes, and met biannually under the supervision of centrally appointed judges. These were criminal courts with a wide competence to try serious felonies, but, unlike their English counterparts, they also had a civil jurisdiction. The 1543 Act also gave statutory authority to another court, that of the Council in the Marches of Wales. This institution had its origins in the fifteenth century as a body which counselled and helped administer the territories of the Prince of Wales (and in the 1520s, Princess Mary). However, it came to assume a more permanent administrative and supervisory role in Wales and the Marches, usually sitting in the Shropshire town of Ludlow. The 1543 Act ensured that it now operated not only as a Crown prerogative court but also effectively as the western administrative arm of the king's Privy Council. It had jurisdiction not only over the thirteen shires of Wales but also over the English border shires. After the 1543 Act, then, Wales acquired a coherent and integrated system of law and administration which reached from the localities through Ludlow and into Westminster and Whitehall.

The Acts of Union integrated Wales into the Tudor realm; the kingdom of England now became 'the kingdom of England and Wales'. This assimilation was profound and enduring; the Acts of Union were only repealed in the 1990s, and this was only a couple of decades after the reorganisation of the thirteen counties which the Act had established. The union provides the framework within which this volume operates, and we will have occasion to refer back frequently to its provisions and to the legal and administrative bodies it established. The union also, however, had significant ramifications for ideas of Welsh culture and identity which are best discussed briefly here.[27] These issues remain controversial, in no small measure because they deal with the status of the Welsh language and what is seen by some as the 'colonial' exploitation of Wales by England. The nationalist politician Gwynfor Evans, for example, described the 'fundamental purpose' of the Anglo-Welsh union as being 'to assimilate Wales culturally, to destroy the nation's civilisation ... [and] language and delete the national tradition', and, ultimately, to turn the country into an English 'colony'.[28] This, however, is to see the legislation through the distorting prism of modern politics and to deracinate the Acts from their historical context. As Glanmor Williams sagely observed, 'it is important not to attribute to the sixteenth century conceptions of government, language, culture, and nationality, which formed no part of its mental furniture'.[29] The union certainly contained elements of what might be described as Tudor 'cultural imperialism', but these were also pragmatic initiatives and not the hammer blow to Welsh identity and culture which some have claimed. Moreover, we need to be alive to the gap between the rhetoric of the Act, which may have been a sop to some English MPs to get the provision through Parliament, and its implementation on the ground which often ignored, undercut or subverted the legislation's more 'imperial' flourishes.

There is no question that Welsh cultural deficits resulted from the union, and that these derived principally from the 'language clause' of the 1536 Act. This clause decreed that judicial and administrative proceedings in Wales needed to be conducted in English and that no individual 'that use the Welsshe speche or language shall have or enjoy any man[nner of] office … onless he … use and exc[er]cise the speche or langage of Englisshe'.[30] The issue of the Welsh language is discussed in greater depth in Chapter 5, but it is as well to acknowledge here that this provision enshrined English as the language of law and power, and decoupled Welsh from having any formal role in the state. One historian has vividly described this as the 'excommunication of the Welsh language [from] … public life'.[31] Over time the provisions of the language clause would have cultural consequences for the country's principal officeholders – the Welsh gentry – but this group did not turn its back on the Welsh language immediately, and the causal link between the language clause and the (protracted) 'Anglicisation' of the gentry is difficult to establish. Moreover, the legislation did not proscribe the use of the vernacular among the Welsh population, as Henry VIII would in Ireland,[32] and it certainly did not discourage Welsh officeholders from being bilingual. Indeed, it is inconceivable that the Henrician authorities would have imagined this settlement working *without* the efforts of a bilingual class of gentry leaders. And this bilingualism would also need to extend to the not inconsiderable number of clerks, scribes and lesser officials required to make the whole union apparatus function within the linguistic world of sixteenth-century Wales. We can argue, then, that the union settlement embedded a semi-official form of bilingualism into the governmental landscape. The legislative provision of 1536 in fact recognised the degree to which the Welsh gentry had *already* been acquiring English in the late medieval period,[33] and thus acknowledged that they had attained a sufficient degree of 'civility' (as understood by English governors) to exercise self-government under the auspices of the English Crown. Moreover, as the union was so deeply concerned with legal and administrative harmonisation and with the establishing of a single judicial and administrative system based on the English common law, a language provision such as that contained in the 1536 statute was understandable, even perhaps 'inevitable'.[34] That this did not lead to the requirement to use or understand English on the part of the average Welsh litigant is, in fact, an argument for the Cambricising of the union in its contacts with the lower social orders.

The union also had other implications for concepts of early modern Welsh identity which should be discussed briefly here. Firstly, we should be wary of thinking that the union was something simply imposed upon the Welsh without their consent (although, admittedly, they had no representation in the Parliament which legislated the 1536 statute). There is evidence that elements among the Welsh gentry had requested provisions such as the union from the Crown because they wished to have equal access before the law and also to remove customary Welsh practices such as partible inheritance (*cyfran* or gavelkind) which threatened to divide their estates across the generations. For example, a petition to the king which has been attributed to either Sir Richard Herbert or Sir John Prise (who is discussed at greater length in the next chapter) but which purported to represent the whole of Wales, requested that the Welsh 'be received and adopted into the same laws and privileges which your other subjects enjoy'.[35] Writing in the seventeenth century, meanwhile, the lawyer Edward Coke remarked that the union's 'just laws' were made 'at the humble suits of the subjects of Wales'.[36] Incorporation with England and her laws, then, was something evidently desired by a powerful stratum of Welsh society.

One of the chief ambiguities about the Acts of Union was that, although they denied Wales any special status as a separate polity, they treated the country as a unified whole and for the first time integrated it administratively, politically and juridically within itself. The 1536 Act was also novel in describing and schematising the political and administrative unit of 'Wales' (as opposed to Llwyd's historical one) clearly and authoritatively. Indeed, much of the Act was taken up with defining borders and boundaries for shires which would constitute the 'Dominion of Wales'. After this point it becomes easier to identify Wales as a recognisable national unit rather than the administrative gallimaufry of the late medieval period. As one commentator has observed, Wales for the first time acquired 'a legal definition of its political geography'.[37] Although essentially an administrative and legal space, the union also gave a degree of form and substance to the concept of 'Wales' which had long been part of the national imagination. The territory defined by the union would also in time come to acquire a visual presence through the production of maps which were rather more faithful to the settled boundaries of 1543 than was Humphrey Llwyd.[38] Cartographers like John Speed and Joan Blaeu produced images that acknowledged the integration of England and Wales as a coherent kingdom, as had Christopher Saxton in the 1570s, but simultaneously also offered up views of Wales as a distinctive territory in its own right.[39]

We should also recognise that the Acts of Union did not, in fact, produce the seamless judicial and administrative integration with England which appears in most textbooks, and that a degree of particularism in these spheres endured after 1543.[40] For example, it has recently been shown that elements of Welsh customary law survived the union and that a degree of legal pluralism in Wales continued down to modern times.[41] Moreover, a degree of institutional particularity also endured after the union. The courts of great sessions, for example, with their extensive criminal and civil jurisdictions, were unique to Wales. When they were abolished in the early nineteenth century, this form of 'decentralised judicature' was defended by many as an important and particularly Welsh institution. One journalist in 1829 argued for the court's continuation, asking: 'Why should we not be allowed to retain our individuality?'[42] The Council in the Marches of Wales was another institution established by the union which was peculiar to this jurisdiction, and, although welcomed in Wales for most of its existence, it became rather unpopular after being run by a crypto-Catholic Lord President in the 1670s and 1680s. In 1689 some 18,000 Welsh petitioners lobbied (successfully) for the Council's abolition, arguing that its continued existence meant they were 'debarred the benefit' of the Acts of Union which had promised legal parity between English and Welsh subjects.[43] English common lawyers were at pains to argue that the Council was something for Wales and not for the English Marcher litigants over whom it had power until 1641. Such arguments suggest an awareness among contemporaries that Wales continued to possess a degree of legal and jurisdictional separateness even after the union.

There were other ways in which Wales continued to be separate from England after 1543. The arrangements for electing MPs for many of its boroughs, for example, was different from the model which prevailed in England. In Wales a system of 'contributory boroughs' operated in which a county's 'ancient' towns helped to elect the sole borough Member (and also to contribute to his wages). In the Cardiff constituency in 1604, for example, the burgesses of Swansea, Cowbridge, Kenfig, Neath, Loughour, Llantrisant and Aberavon all contributed to the election of the Member, Matthew Davys.[44] Although these Welsh Members would pass parliamentary subsidy bills to tax their constituents, here too Wales had a rather different regime from the rest of England. Throughout this period Wales, unlike England, remained subject to feudal financial levies called 'mises', which were due when a new Prince of Wales was created (as in the case of Prince Henry in 1610) or when a new monarch ascended to the throne. These levies could be quite burdensome and, because of this, the Welsh would frequently obtain exemptions or delays in paying general taxation because of the protracted collection of these mises.[45]

The foregoing elements of post-union Welsh administrative and judicial difference suggest that we should rethink the common assumption that Wales was seamlessly incorporated within the English state after 1536. Although these instances do not constitute profound fissures within the unitary state, they nonetheless provide some basis for thinking about the ways in which the union itself, for all its emphasis on integration and congruence, in fact produced subtle forms of ongoing Welsh institutional distinctiveness. The union, then, despite the claims of some nationalist commentators, was not the death knell for concepts of Welsh identity, even institutional ones. The volume now turns to consider some of the other 'materials' which helped comprise ideas of Welshness in this period, and we begin with the subject that captivated Humphrey Llwyd: history and myth.

2

'They Value Themselves Much upon their Antiquity': History, Myth and Identity

History is central to a society's sense of itself, to its identity. The late Professor Rees Davies observed that 'above all a people must have a shared history if it is to be a people'. Writing about the medieval era, but with an argument that applies equally to Wales in the sixteenth and seventeenth centuries, Davies continued: 'for the Welsh … the cultivation of their own historical mythology was one of the few means that they could exploit to hang on to their identity as a people'.[1] When thinking about the nature of identity in early modern Wales, then, ideas of history and the country's relationship to its past are crucial. It seems significant in this context that the Latin word for history, 'historia', was rendered into Welsh as '*ystyr*', or 'meaning'; so 'the history of something explained its meaning, and its meaning was to be found in history'.[2] For the Welsh, therefore, much of their meaning as a people, the way they interpreted and understood themselves, came from ideas about their shared past.

The present chapter explores this historical culture, focusing particularly on the Welsh attachment to the idea of a 'British History'. Historical consciousness became a controversial and contested issue for the Welsh from around the same time as the passing of the Acts of Union, when their long-cherished mythology came under attack from new currents of Renaissance scholarship. The Welsh rallied around their treasured heritage, however, and the past became something of a focus for a patriotic defence of national identity within the expanded English, and later British, state. This discussion of history and myth had ramifications that reached far beyond academic debate and came to include questions of religious change and the nature of early modern politics. Claims to historicity and 'Britishness' were important in harnessing the emotional sympathies of the Welsh, and it was partly through appeals to and adaptations of history that Protestantism and a Briticised monarchy came to be crucial foci of Welsh loyalty and affinity in the sixteenth and seventeenth centuries. As Katharine Olson has astutely observed, 'religion, the past, and national identity were intertwined for the [early modern] Welsh'.[3]

In approaching ideas of history in early modern Wales, it is important to recognise that we are not dealing with a discrete academic subject with modern standards of evidential criticism. Although elements of a more critical approach to sources and evidence developed in this period, the bedrock of the Welsh sense of a common heritage was a foundation myth. This mythology-cum-history derived principally from a native Welsh narrative tradition known as the *Brut*, which can be rendered as the 'British History'. This set of traditions and stories emerged in the Dark Ages and emphasised the lineage of the Welsh as the first inhabitants of the island of Britain. These narratives were propagated by Welsh bards and poets who were charged with preserving, as part of the national memory, 'the history of the notable acts of the kings & princes of this land of Bruttaen and Cambria'.[4] The *Brut* celebrated the sovereign unity of Britain which supposedly existed before the invasions of the Romans, the Saxons and the Vikings; this was a time when the ancestors of the Welsh people were said to have possessed dominion over the entire island. The British history found its most enduring and influential formulation in the 1130s with Geoffrey of Monmouth's *Historia Regum Britanniae* (*History of the Kings of Britain*, which was rendered into Welsh as *Brut y Brenhinedd*).[5] Geoffrey's fanciful literary production maintained that an exile from the city of Troy, Brutus, came to Britain many centuries before the birth of Christ and ruled over the island, endowing it with his name. His descendants established a great empire, battled the invading Romans and, led by the British hero, King Arthur, eventually faced the incoming Anglo-Saxons. After much fighting and intrigue, in the seventh century the British, under their last native king, Cadwaladr, were eventually defeated and driven into the west. However, an angel delivered a prophecy to Cadwaladr that the British (or Welsh) people would return and recover the kingdom they had lost: the island of Britain.

This was clearly myth rather than history, but in the medieval and early modern eras such distinctions were not readily drawn.[6] Indeed, most medieval English as well as Welsh scholars accepted this narrative as an authentic account of the early inhabitants of the island. The Welsh clung to this story and their reasons for a passionate Welsh defence of the *Brut* tradition are not hard to discern. This history afforded the Welsh a glorious past. For a people so often defeated at the hands of the English, and who, since the thirteenth century, had lost any pretensions of meaningful political autonomy, the *Brut* provided a glittering assertion of their noble blood and lineage. The story also contained a good deal of evidence of Saxon (ancestors of the English, of course) treachery, which meshed well with established Welsh attitudes towards their neighbours. Importantly, the *Brut* also possessed an aspirational and prophetic element, 'a programme for action',[7] that the old Britons would one day regain dominion over the island under the guidance of a messianic leader, the '*mab daro-gan*' or 'son of prophecy'. This component of the narrative was often employed to justify Welsh aggression against the English in the late medieval period; Welsh bards used prophetic poetry drawing on the *Brut* to help justify Owain Glyndŵr's rebellion in the early fifteenth century, for example.[8] However, these prophecies largely lost their anti-English edge after the accession of Henry Tudor as Henry VII, who claimed a noble Welsh ancestry. Indeed, Henry's arrival was hailed by many Welsh bards as the fulfilment of the *Brut* prophecies, as a Welshman had indeed now regained much of the ancient British lands. This subject is discussed at greater length in Chapter 6. As Henry Tudor incorporated the dragon of Cadwaladr into his her-aldry, so the Welsh reoriented their loyalties to a dynasty of their own bloodline. The Welsh could comfort themselves with tales of prophe-cies fulfilled, albeit the political dividend, until the Acts of Union at least, was meagre indeed. Yet the union also played something of a Janus-faced game here, for the statute of 1536 proclaimed a form of imperial historical precedent in stating that Wales had always been part of the 'imperiall Crowne' of England; a claim which could only be understood by reference to a united British past of the kind which the Welsh advocated and promoted.[9] This paradox highlights some of the slipperiness of the idea of 'Britishness' in this period, which could be embraced by the Welsh as their own heritage, but which could, equally, be used by others to marginalise them as merely a junior partner within an emerging British state.

The British history was to come under attack, however, from scholars animated by new intellectual forces unleashed by the Renaissance. Renaissance humanism encouraged the investigation of the past, but it also demanded a more critical attitude towards history and its sources (or lack thereof), and this was to have important consequences for the Welsh. The most damaging criticism of their cherished past came from the pen of Polydore Vergil, an Italian scholar at Henry VII's court whose history of England was, ironically, instigated by the '*mab darogan*' himself. Vergil wrote his *Anglica Historia* in 1512–13 but the text was only published in 1534, shortly before the union of Wales and England. In this work Vergil questioned the evidential basis of the British history, especially as it was found in the work of Geoffrey of Monmouth. One of his central points was difficult to rebut: if the Britons had ruled such a mighty empire as Geoffrey claimed, why had none of the Romans who came to Britain mentioned it? Vergil argued that Geoffrey had elevated his own people, the Welsh, to too great a height in his story, 'feininge of them thinges to be laughed at'.[10] A principal objection was the lack of evidence for the British history and the shakiness of the foundations upon which great literary traditions had been built. Vergil wrote:

> Trulie ther is nothinge more obscure, more uncertaine, or unknowne then the affaires of the Brittons from the beginninge ... This silence was the cause whie good authors have not left in memorie verie manie thinges of the originall of this contriemenne [countrymen]; and manie on the other side have ben bolde to speake so largelie, and to make suche a straunge historie thereof, that in admiration of the common people (who allwais more regarde novelites then trewthe) theye seme to bee in heaven, whear with a good will I will leave them.[11]

This was a stinging attack on the *Brut* beloved by the Welsh, but Vergil was not alone in this sceptical historical mode. In 1529 the Englishman John Rastell published a book which also questioned where the evidence was for the early accounts of Britain, describing the *Brut* as 'more mervaylous than trewe', and 'a feyned fable' which Geoffrey, as 'a Welchman born', only propagated 'for the … preys of his co[un]ntreme[n]'.[12] The Scottish Hector Boece in his Latin history of Scotland (1527) also rejected Geoffrey's account, presenting instead a patriotic view of the Scots' origins as deriving out of Ancient Greece and Egypt.[13] It is noteworthy that these commentators recognised how the British history was tied particularly closely to the Welsh, and that they criticised Geoffrey for the patriotic blind spot in his historical vision.

The British history was not, however, simply a Welsh narrative. This was an esteemed past for many English men and women too, and the distinction between English and British history was not readily made.[14] Indeed, Vergil's intervention can be seen as an important step in the early modern separation of English and British national histories, a process which was accelerated by the trajectories of the Reformation in the two countries. It is not surprising, then, that Vergil's *Historia* prompted an angry response by a group which we may term 'Britanists' which included a number of English writers.[15] Among these was the antiquary and topographer John Leland, who wished to recover 'the old glory of your renoumed Britaine', and also Leland's friend and Protestant polemicist, John Bale.[16] The most impassioned backlash against Vergil's treatment of the *Brut*, however, came from the Welsh. Indeed, Vergil's broadside prompted a flowering of Welsh historical writing from the 1540s onwards as Welsh scholars looked to rebut the Italian's account by employing the same techniques of Renaissance inquiry as he had used. Importantly, unlike the circulation of manuscript versions of the *Brut y Brenhinedd* and other medieval manuscripts, many of these rebuttals adopted that quintessentially Renaissance technology of print to broadcast their arguments. These Welsh *littérateurs* thus engaged in a debate over British history and its meaning that was European in scope; which responded to sceptical scholarship from England in particular; which became enmeshed in the politics of the Reformation; and which, of course, was now situated within the framework of a united England and Wales.

One of the first to enter this vibrant but disputatious field was a man Leland described as 'a lover of antiquity', Sir John Prise of

Brecon.[17] Prise was a public man of the new stripe in Tudor Wales. An Oxford-educated lawyer and Protestant administrator, he was closely involved in the process of dissolving the monasteries. In 1534 he had married Thomas Cromwell's niece (at Cromwell's Islington home) demonstrating his proximity to the centre of Henrician power. Prise had encountered (and acquired) many medieval manuscripts dispersed from ex-monastic collections, and he put these to use in writing a scholarly refutation of Vergil's work. Adopting a patriotic and scholarly humanist approach, by 1545 Prise had drafted one of the most significant responses to Vergil's *Historia*, a text which also comprised an erudite vindication of the British history. This took the form of a Latin treatise entitled 'Historiae Britannicae Defensio' ('A Defence of the British History') which circulated in manuscript. Prise's method in this text was impeccably that of the Renaissance scholars he was seeking to emulate and refute. He argued that Polydore Vergil's scholarship was deficient; that he was lacking in specialised linguistic skills for the research he was undertaking; that he had not consulted enough sources; and that he had not read these sources with sufficient sensitivity. Prise maintained that he had access to crucial manuscripts which testified to King Arthur's existence and the prowess of the early Britons. He stressed his capacity to read Welsh bardic literature and to decipher its references to the British history. Although a humanist scholarly debate, then, it is also clear that Prise recognised that this, simultaneously, was a battle over cultural identity and national memory. He demonstrated a patriotic pride in the antiquity and beauty of the Welsh language which, he argued, had the capacity to enshrine and protect the country's past, and castigated Vergil as a man 'whose aim, in fact, is to bury in perpetual darkness and oblivion the course of more than a thousand years of governance here'.[18] Prise went to some lengths to portray the Welsh as an ancient collective; indeed, one scholar has argued, it was this 'common will to preserve and pass on their history' that bound the Welsh together as a people in the early modern age.[19]

Prise's work was a restrained and academic defence of the British history, but its impact was limited as it remained in manuscript during his lifetime, although in his will he directed his son Richard to 'put my booke in printe that I have made against Polidorus' storye of Englande'.[20] This did not happen until 1573 when the published *Defensio* entered a somewhat different Elizabethan historical environment. Perhaps the first printed sally on behalf of the Welsh version of the *Brut* was, in fact, made by an Englishman. This was Arthur Kelton of Shrewsbury, a convinced and active Protestant, who published a lengthy poem in 1546 entitled *A Comendacion of Welshmen*.[21] This composition accepted wholesale the Galfridian (that is, from Geoffrey of Monmouth) narrative and praised the Welsh as being 'of the bloud imperiall' through their lineage from 'most mightie conquerours' derived from Troy such as Brutus, Arthur and King Cadwaladr.[22] Kelton followed up this work a year later with another long poem on similar themes. In this latter work Kelton focused initially on the delivery of the Welsh through Henry VIII's union legislation, but then turned to the controversy over the British history. He bullishly declared the Welsh to be 'lineallye descended from Brute', and the text became a sustained rebuttal of 'Polidorus' who, 'in reproche of our country', had denied Wales's British heritage and tried to 'extinguishe' their name from memory.[23] Kelton went on to rehearse and defend the *Brut* story in all its essentials and accused Vergil of his own biases in glorifying his countrymen, the Romans, and he called on the Italian to 'recante your fayned fantasie'.[24] Kelton thus sought to turn the debate on its head and to suggest that it was Vergil rather than Geoffrey who had fabricated the past to glorify his own people. His intervention is fascinating as an Englishman defending the British history in the guise of a fellow 'Welshman'; he described Vergil's assault on 'our country' and spoke of the post-union nation as 'Now it is England, sometime called Wales'.[25] His text was also produced in English rather than in scholarly Latin, and, moreover, in an accessible (albeit second-rate) rhyme. Although something of an outlier, Kelton's publications do suggest a more popular literary response to the *Brut* controversy while also indicating the ways in which someone like him, an inhabitant of Shewsbury, could claim a common heritage, even aspects of a common identity, with the Welsh in the sixteenth century.[26]

Few of Kelton's texts survive today – the *Commendacion* is only known from a single copy – and this, along with the fact that no contemporaries besides John Bale engaged with his publications, suggests that his works were not particularly influential in what has been described as 'the first great historical controversy of the print age'.[27] Far more significant in this regard was the contribution of the polymath we encountered in Chapter 1, Humphrey Llwyd. As we have seen from his cartographical efforts, Llwyd was an enthusiast for an expanded historical view of Wales, or rather 'Cambria'. His scholarly pursuits were very much oriented around defending Welsh identity and prestige through advocating the British history. In 1559 he completed an important manuscript text, 'Cronica Walliae' ('The Chronicle of Wales') which, despite its Latin name (given to the manuscript by the famous English antiquary, Sir Robert Cotton), was, in fact, an English scholarly adaptation of the key medieval Welsh chronicle, the 'Brut y Tywysogyon' ('Chronicle of the Princes').[28] His text took the Galfridian vision of British history and grafted onto it an account of the Welsh princes after Cadwaladr, down to the death of Llywelyn ap Gruffudd and its aftermath in the 1290s. The 'Cronica' was another work that circulated in manuscript before it was adapted and published in the most influential history of Wales down to the modern era by David Powel, a book which is discussed further below. Llwyd was explicit as to his intentions in the 'Cronica', noting 'I was the first that tocke the province [of Wales] in hande to put thees thinges into the Englishe tonge. For that I wolde not have the inhabitantes of this Ile ignorant of the histories and cronicles of the same'.[29] Notably, then, this was intended for readers in England as much as for those in Wales. The breadth of his intended audience is reflected in the fact that Llwyd's was no narrow Welsh historical nationalism, but rather a capacious and inclusive British vision encompassing the whole of the island. Llwyd aimed to build on the political union of Wales and England and to show that the British history was a central plank for the *collective* identities of all those inhabiting southern Britain (Scotland was something of a problem), although Wales could take pride in its centrality in this story. Indeed, there was something of a tricky balancing act to be struck here as men like Llwyd looked to counter Polydore Vergil's deconstruction of the *Brut* (according to Llwyd, Vergil was 'ignorante in the histories of this realme as of the diverse tonges and languages used therein'),[30] while producing a history that did not assert or glorify Welsh separatism or independence. This was a kind of *British* patriotism before the existence of Great Britain itself, which would come about with the 1707 Scottish union.[31] Nonetheless, Llwyd acknowledged that Edward I's defeat of Llywelyn ('the laste of the Britishe bloode that had governaunce in Wales') 'brought the whole countrey [of Wales] in subjection to the crowne of Englande to this daye'.[32] Any reading of this kind of historical patriotism for a potentially separatist view of Welshness was undercut, however, by Llwyd's continued evocations of a common British past around which even the ethnically diverse heritages of England and Wales could come together. Whether the English wished to get on board with this project would prove another matter entirely, however.

Llwyd made another important contribution to the debate over the British history with a Latin work he communicated to Abraham Ortelius along with his map of Wales in 1568. This was the treatise *Commentarioli Britannicae Descriptionis Fragmentum* (*Fragment of a Commentary on the Description of Britain*) which Ortelius had published in Cologne in 1572. Importantly, this was then translated and republished as *The Breviary of Britayne* by the English physician Thomas Twyne.[33] This brief work was an account of the island's geography and history that emphasised its British and Welsh origins. The text also followed Prise's lead through its refutation of Polydore Vergil and assertions that Welsh sources and linguistic competencies were needed to unlock Britain's deep memory. Llwyd follows a Galfridian course in his account of the country, maintaining that Geoffrey was merely translating an ancient and authentic British (read 'Welsh') text rather than fabricating an account of his own as some alleged. This once again was careful, source-sensitive Renaissance scholarship, but it was also a patriotic volley against Vergil and Boece, the first of whom Llwyd described as seeking 'not only to obscure the glory of the British name, but also to defame the Britons themselves with slanderous lies'.[34] Llwyd was ultimately concerned to reject these kinds of narrow national histories and instead sought to reassert the truth and pre-eminence of a genuinely British perspective on the past. That this was a history which redounded to the glory of the Welsh, the inheritors of this British mantle, was, of course, all to the good.

The culmination of these trends by which defenders of the British history produced forms of patriotic Welsh historical writing came with the publication in 1584 of *A Historie of Cambria, Now Called Wales* by David Powel, an Oxford-educated cleric of Ruabon in Denbighshire. Importantly, Powel was chaplain to the Lord President of the Council in the Marches, Sir Henry Sidney, who commissioned the work. It is possible that Sidney did this to help bolster the authority of the Council during a rather turbulent period in its history.[35] The commission resulted in two publications, the most important of which was Powel's *Historie*.[36] This impressive text incorporated a version of Llwyd's 'Cronica Walliae', but Powel added his own commentary and expanded the text with additional material. This was to be a compendious, high-status and impressive production which reflected Sidney's patronage and influence, something that also endowed the text with a degree of authority and authoritativeness. The volume's elaborate frontispiece incorporated the royal insignia as well as the prominent text, 'Cum Privilegio', or 'With Privilege', to indicate that the book had been licensed by royal authority, something which added to the impression that this constituted something akin to an authorised history of Wales. Like Llwyd, Powel drew on Welsh sources to augment his research base, and he combined these with English and Latin chronicles to produce an impressive scholarly volume.

Powel maintained that his intention in producing the *Historie* was twofold. On the positive side he wished to add a Welsh voice to the national conversation as the 'politike and martiall actes of all other inhabitants of this iland in the time of their government' were being discussed by numerous writers, but 'the whole doings and government of the Brytaines, the first inhabitants of the land ... [were] nothing spoken of nor regarded of anie'.[37] More negatively, he wished to address the 'slanderous report of such writers [whose] ... bookes do inforce every thing that is done by the Welshmen to their discredit'. By this he meant that English chronicles and histories generally described forces being sent to subdue 'the rebellious attempts, the proud stomachs, the presumptuous pride, stirr, trouble and rebellion of the fierce, unquiet, craking, fickle and unconstant Welshmen', but that no account explored why the Welsh were rebelling in the first place.[38] In other words, he wished to tell the Welsh side of the historical story, 'the cause and circumstances of most of those wars', many of which, he claimed, were effectively actions taken in self-defence. Powel's efforts were thus designed to place Wales *within* Britain rather than *against* it. As such he praised effusively the 'uniting of that countrie to the crowne of the kingdome of England' whereby 'uniformitie of government' had produced peace and quietness.[39] As his comments about the 'slanderous reports' of other writers indicated, however, this was also an intervention in the 'battle of the books' over the status of the British history, and on this point Powel's patriotic passions could run high. In one passage describing the supposed discovery of the remains of King Arthur in the twelfth century, Powel wrote:

> therefore let … Polydore Vergil with [his] … accomplices stop their lyieng mouthes and desist to obscure and darken the glistering fame & noble renowme of so invincible and victorious a prince, with the envious detraction and malicious slaunder of their reprochfull and venomous toonges, thinking that they may cover with the cloud of oblivion and burie in the pit of darkenesse those noble acts and princelie deeds by their wilfull ignorance and dogged envie.[40]

This bitter passage suggests how questions of history and national origins were not simply issues of polite academic discourse but were rather matters which struck at the heart of a sense of Welsh identity.

Powel's volume became the standard Welsh history of the period. It was revised by William Wynne in 1697 and continued to be reprinted down to the nineteenth century. Powel, along with Llwyd and Prise, established and consolidated what might be described as the foundations of the Welsh understanding of their origins and historical identity in the early modern period. It is important to recognise that the historical consciousness described and elaborated in these works underwrote an integrative rather than a separatist sense of Welsh nationhood. All of these writers were Protestants and, as we shall see, the supposedly British origins of Protestantism were important in securing the country for the reformed faith in the sixteenth and seventeenth centuries. All supported the Anglo-Welsh union too, and the positive responses to the Henrician settlement also helped inform these works, which stressed the incorporative Britishness of Welsh history. Importantly, too, these histories endorsed the British lineages of the ruling house, naturalising the Tudors, and indeed later the Stuarts, within a Welsh milieu. More is said about this in Chapter 6. The significance of the British history which was fashioned and publicised by these scholars was an important authorising discourse for many aspects of early modern Welsh religious, political and popular culture, and will be a recurring theme throughout this book.

As suggested by the long life of Powel's volume, the 'British history' endured in Wales largely unchallenged throughout this period. Important in its longevity was the fact that the idea of 'Britain' and its splendid history gained a new significance and currency following the accession of James VI of Scotland to the throne of England as James I in 1603.[41] As the ruler of two kingdoms, James wished to adopt the title of 'King of Great Britain' to reflect his status and help unite his subjects. Although his ambitions in this regard had little to do with supporting any Welsh connections, nevertheless his project sparked a new enthusiasm among the Welsh who praised him as the rightful inheritor of the British title. The Welsh were also particularly animated by the fact that James's accession had physically united the lands of Britain once more; in this sense he had revived the ancient kingdom of Britain.[42] In the early seventeenth century the Radnorshire lawyer, John Lewis, wrote a spirited manuscript defence of the Galfridian tradition and praised King James as 'the absolutest Kinge of Brytaine syns Brutes tyme', describing how he had 'conjoined and united' the historic lands of Britain.[43] Similar sentiments were expressed by a Pembrokeshire cleric, Robert Holland, while shortly after the King's accession in 1603 Holland's associate, George Owen Harry, composed a genealogy which demonstrated that James was descended from kings of ancient British origin.[44] Around the time of James's coming to the throne, Thomas Salisbury wrote a preface to Wiliam Midleton's Welsh translation of the Psalms which praised God for sending the Welsh 'a king ... who is lineally descended from ancient Brutus, to the unspeakable comfort of al true hearted Brytaines'.[45] Another Welsh author, Dr. John Davies of Brecon (Siôn Dafydd Rhys), also wrote a tract on James's Welsh antecedents around 1604, as well as a defence of the *Brut*.[46] Such contributions show not only how James's accession stimulated further exploration of the British myth among Welsh men of letters, but also how closely tied this historical vision had become with the British monarchy.

Welsh defences of the British history continued to be written into eighteenth century and beyond, but it is true to say that English and Anglophone scholarship became increasingly uncomfortable with the Galfridian roots of the 'British' past, although even here responses to the British history remained rather more complex and accommodating than many accounts of its rapid rejection would lead us to believe.[47]

English historians such as the great William Camden, for example, had little place for Geoffrey's 'fabulous story' in their works. In the early seventeenth century Camden settled on an indulgent but ultimately dismissive approach, saying, 'let Brutus be taken for the father and founder of the British nation; I will not be of a contrary mind', but then added a telling admonition that 'antiquitie' should be 'pardoned' for 'entermingling falsities and truthes' in the attempt to make 'the first beginnings of nations ... more noble ... and of greater majestie'.[48] Following such barely-coded warnings, many English antiquarians became wary of venturing too far past the Norman conquest. Such reluctance is perhaps not surprising as the historical discourse of Britishness was increasingly recognised not as the origin story of all inhabitants of the Tudor and Stuart kingdoms of Britain, as someone like Llwyd would have hoped, but was rather seen as the preserve of the Welsh alone. In 1684, Bishop William Lloyd of St Asaph acknowledged the tenacity with which the Welsh adhered to their origin myths despite a wealth of scholarship to the contrary.[49] 'Briton' and 'Welsh' would become readily available synonyms in both popular and elite English culture.

Despite these currents in wider academic circles, a patriotic but nonetheless scholarly and critical Welsh historical culture endured. In the mid-1650s, for example, the antiquarian Robert Vaughan of Hengwrt wrote to Rowland Vaughan of Caergai who had cast doubts on the Galfridian tradition, requesting that he 'be ... pleased to embrase the British history, which hath been received as most true and authentic by both universities & by the 3 states of ye kingdom in parliament untill you doe produce unto us a more true & certaine history of our ancestor, supported with better authorities'.[50] His emphasis on authorities and evidence is telling of the fact that Welsh authors remained committed to the British history but were not simply credulous buffoons relying on an outdated myth. Rather they considered it as a valid and authoritative view of distant history until better evidence and interpretation could convince them otherwise. Robert Vaughan's letter also shows how, simultaneously with defending a scholarly tradition, attachment to the *Brut* was also seen as a means of defending and protecting a sense of Welsh identity; challenges to the British past were causes of genuine anxiety and concern. The antiquarian William Maurice of Llansilin expressed such worries in a tract of January 1662 which showed that the passion which had animated Powel's denunciation of Polydore Vergil in the 1580s had not diminished over the intervening decades. Maurice described 'our much persecuted & most envyed *Historia Britannica* who, but baser dounghill entities of malice and livid prejudice cann but wonder that our chronicles should preserve never so little of ye memories of so outworn and remote a time after so many revolutions of ages and state'. He praised God, however, for preserving the *Brut* 'from those that sought to destroy us root & branch, and raze our name besides'.[51] Attacks on the British History, then, were long understood as assaults on a key component of Welsh identity.

The seventeenth century witnessed a continued and vibrant interest in what we might describe as Wales's vernacular history. This remained focused on ancient and medieval Wales as can be seen in works such as Percy Enderbie's *Cambria Triumphans* (1661), Rowland Vaughan's *British Antiquities Revived* (1662) and William Wynne's *History of Wales* (1697), which all largely revamped and reinterpreted Powel's *Historie*. Brutus remained an important origin figure while the modern Welsh were understood to be his descendants and thus 'the very Brittains indeed'.[52] Despite their attachment to what modern scholarship would recognise as myth, these authors were careful, scholarly and fairly exacting in their deployment of sources and construction of argument.[53] Wynne, for example, prefaced his edition with a careful dissection of the historical controversy surrounding the British history, and acknowledged that there were serious problems with the full-blown version of the Galfridian narrative, parts of which he described as 'absolutely fabulous and unsincere'.[54] However, he also thought that those who rejected the totality of Geoffrey's narrative were mistaken and, on the basis of some close linguistic analysis, argued that 'there is some real foundations lodged in the ruins of the story of Brutus'.[55] Yet even though his was a particularly judicious presentation of the evidence, he nonetheless had a patriotic vision behind his reworking of Powel's *Historie*, seeing a 'very great necessity of reviving what to the generality of the kingdom is almost lost … which in the English histories are either totally omitted or but partially interwoven'. He added that if he was able to 'render our history more generally known, I have my aim'.[56]

Down to the end of our period, then, a particularist version of Welsh history, especially that focused on the essentials of the *Brut*,

prevailed in the nation's consciousness. This origin story was considered to be a crucial element in sustaining a vision of the Welsh past
that helped maintain and bolster a sense of nationhood and identity in
the early modern present. The historical culture of the late seventeenth
century was not radically different from that which had emerged in
the mid-sixteenth, with groups of like-minded men collecting and
sharing books and manuscripts with one another. These were texts
that gave hints of the earliest histories of Britain and supported a
patriotic vision of the Welsh as the 'Ancient Britons'. The man to
whom William Wynne dedicated his *History* was the bishop of Bangor,
Humphrey Humphries, someone who encouraged and sponsored this
kind of antiquarian activity in north Wales.[57] Among his circle was
Thomas Mostyn of Gloddaeth, whose library became a renowned
repository for Welsh historical texts.[58]

Far from undermining Welsh historical difference, then,
Renaissance scholarship and historical inquiry from the early sixteenth
century stimulated a renewed interest in a distinct Welsh historical
culture which endured throughout the early modern period. This
interest manifested itself in a new awareness of the material evidence
of the past, which needed to be collected, preserved and analysed, and
also a desire to publish the fruits of the resulting scholarship. And
it is in print and publication that we encounter a crucial difference
from the Welsh historical cultures of the medieval period, as these
texts became much more readily available than expensive manuscript
treatises and entered a scholarly space that was European rather than
simply Welsh or British in scope. Although these works did not make
an enormous impact on the wider republic of letters, they are nonetheless important cultural artefacts of an impulse that ran deep in
early modern Welsh society: to explore, memorialise and celebrate a
distinguished and distinctive national past.

That this was not simply an impulse to be found only among academic authors and antiquarians appears to be confirmed by scattered
evidence from other sources, although any attempt to evaluate Welsh
historical consciousness beyond the letter-writing and publishing elite
is fraught with difficulties. Nonetheless, it does seem that an attachment to the notion of the *Brut* and to a historicised 'Britishness' was
not confined to academics. Indeed, the evidence suggests that their
works reflected a popular Welsh historical consciousness rather than

something separate from it. Indeed, we should perhaps consider the likelihood that popular attachment to origin stories and historical mythologies would have been slower to erode than elite discourse which responded to academic trends and fashions in Latinate and Anglophone scholarship. At the popular level we should also recall that a good deal of the vernacular oral tradition of late medieval Wales concerned historicised forms of genealogy and that this continued into the early modern period. These types of 'oral histories' were frequently concerned with the *Brut* and with tracing bloodlines back to the glorious figures of early British history. It seems likely, then, that aspects of the British past circulated orally and entered the mental worlds of subjects who could not appreciate the subtleties of Sir John Prise's Latin text.

An extraordinary survival from Carmarthen in the early 1550s offers some important evidence about this more demotic historical awareness. This survival takes the form of depositions which were given against the bishop of St David's, Robert Ferrar, a Yorkshireman and future Protestant martyr under Mary I, who became caught up in a long-running dispute which caused a group of local canons to present to the Privy Council a series of accusations against him.[59] The accusations concerned a sermon he had delivered in the town around 1551. Ferrar, the English reformer, was supposedly 'evell beloved in that countrey', and so sought to ingratiate himself with his Welsh auditors. He thought the best way to do this was by praising them as being 'more gentle' than the English. However, he added that this was 'no marvayle for sumtyme ye wer[e] Britannes and had this realme yn govern[an]ce; and yf the prophesye of Merlyn be true, ye shall so have it agayne'.[60] Another deponent related the bishop as also saying: 'ye shall be Brytanes agayne and this land shalbe callid Great Brytayne'.[61] This is a fascinating glimpse into a hidden world where Arthurian prophecies (Merlin was said to have a connection with Carmarthen as seen by its Welsh name, *Caerfyrddin* or 'Merlin's Castle'), and simplified Galfridian ideas of ancient glory and aspirations to future rule through forms of Britishness circulated among the people and constituted a set of beliefs which Ferrar evidently expected to be well received. We find an echo of such attitudes in a letter of 1567 from the bishop of Bangor, Nicholas Robinson, to a man deeply interested in the distant past, Matthew Parker, archbishop of Canterbury. Robinson noted there were no monuments of antiquity left in his part of north Wales except 'certaine fabuloyse histories', the laws of Hywel Dda and 'ye life of a troublesome prince or tow which were subdued since ye Conquest'. Yet despite this relative evidential paucity, Robinson continued, 'the people here will talke of many [historical] thinges which appeere no where' in the written record; the letter goes on to discuss Robinson's researches into the 'doynges of ye olde Brittains', and it seems probable that this was the subject of the common people's 'talke' to which he referred.[62]

Evidence from English commentators also suggests that a form of particularist historical consciousness circulated at less elevated social levels among the early modern Welsh. For example, an anonymous report on the state of north Wales given around 1600 to Queen Elizabeth's chief minister, Sir Robert Cecil, reported that 'multitudes of all sorts of men and women and children' would meet on Sundays and holy days accompanied by harpers who would, 'sing them songs of the doings of their ancestors. Namely their wars against the kings of this realm and the English nation, and then do they rip up [discuss] their pedigrees at length, how each of them is descended from those their old princes'.[63] The Elizabethan courtier from Montgomeryshire, Lodowick Lloyd, informed Cecil around the same time that no culture was as attached to auguring the future as the Welsh, for 'many in my countrey ar geven to the prophecies of Merlin', which the 'bardi Brytannorum [British bards]' circulated among the people.[64] Yet despite Lloyd's willingness to burn the Welsh books of prophecy which he considered potentially dangerous to the Crown, he too saw the *Brut* as a legitimating idea: he provided commendatory verses for the English translation of Llwyd's British history and wrote a ballad praising Queen Elizabeth as descended 'From Brutus' blood' and 'Cambria's soil'; he also lauded her successor, James I, as 'the second Brutus'.[65]

In the sixteenth and seventeenth centuries, the Welsh were also satirised by the English for their devotion to genealogies and their British origins in a manner which suggests that such ideas were commonplaces in Welsh society. Dramas of the period had Welsh characters who frequently made reference to their ancient descents and sometimes explicitly to the British history. George Peele's 1593 play *Edward I*, for example, has Llywelyn ap Gruffudd describe himself as 'Sprong from the loins of great Cadwallader / Discended from the loines of Trojan Brute'.[66] During the civil wars, cheap pamphlets mocked the Welsh as 'Trojans' and 'Ancient Britons', a tradition carried on in a scurrilous volume by William Richards in the 1680s which described the 'Cambro-Brittons', or the Welsh, as 'much honour[ing] the memory of famous atchievements'.[67] Such satirical treatments should not be taken as accurate representations of reality of course, but we must equally recognise that they would fail to be satires if they did not pick up on and explode for comic effect traits widely recognised among the Welsh.

Further evidence for a popular attachment to a version of the British history appears towards the end of our period. The Welsh ethnographer and linguist Edward Lhuyd was interested in local antiquities and folklore and solicited correspondents to provide him with information about such matters in their villages and parishes. He received one such letter (in Latin) in 1695 from a William Rowlands in north Wales. Rowlands mentioned how William Camden's great historical text *Britannia* was disliked in Bala partly because it was sceptical about the Brutus story which had given Britain its name.[68] A decade earlier in one of the cheap Welsh-language almanacs published by Thomas Jones in Shrewsbury, the clergyman Elis ap Elis produced a short verse entitled 'Hanes y Cymru' ('History of the Welsh') which rehearsed an unreconstructed view of the *Brut*, praising the interpretations of Sir John Prise, Humphrey Llwyd and David Powel, but dismissing the 'libels' against the British history produced by Polydore Vergil and Hector Boece.[69] This vernacular publication was designed for popular consumption and is suggestive of the historical sympathies among the non-elite Welsh whom ap Elis and Jones were trying to reach. The bishop of St Asaph, William Lloyd, was probably referring to this kind of popular culture, when, around the same time ap Elis's poem was published, he described how 'printing' had brought new knowledge and caused 'our neighbouring nations' to send 'their Trojans to the poets from whence they came'. Lloyd continued, however, that 'if we are resolved to keep ours, we must do it in sight of all true History'.[70] His comments suggest that he too recognised the tenacious hold of the Galfridian story among the Welsh populace, perhaps particularly in his diocese in north-east Wales. That this general attachment to the *Brut* continued to prevail in Wales throughout the early modern period is also indicated by the observations of Daniel Defoe, who toured north Wales in the early eighteenth century. Crossing into Wales, Defoe noted: 'They value themselves much upon their antiquity: the antient race of the houses and families and the like; and above all upon their antient heroes'.[71] Defoe registered that he had entered a different country partly because he had entered an environment with a popular historical tradition different from that of England.

Despite the waning fortunes of the *Brut* in English academic circles, then, throughout the early modern period a form of shared historical literacy based on a common origin narrative was a powerful cohesive bond holding the Welsh together. The writing of history was, in many ways, the writing of early modern Welsh identity. And it seems that this was a sense of the collective past that held not simply for the learned elites, but which also penetrated the social bedrock and formed what can be described as a shared vernacular memory. As Defoe registered, this was a historical culture distinct and separate from that of England, and was important during the sixteenth and seventeenth centuries in maintaining the sense of the Welsh as a separate people. This sense of a distinct past had the potential to be mobilised as the ideological basis for some form of Welsh nationalism or separatism. After all, much of the British history concerned Welsh loss, English treachery and the resurgence of the Britons under a charismatic leader. However, these potentialities were never pursued, largely because of the ways in which such historical ideas were used to strengthen and reinforce the monarchy and the Established Church. The accession of the 'Welsh' Henry VII, the Anglo-Welsh Union, the advent of the Reformation, and King James I's vision of a Great Britain incorporating Wales, England and Scotland, all appealed to and were reinforced by the integrative propensity of Welsh historical sensibilities. The Welsh cherished their role as 'Britons', and their historical patriotism was directed not towards any form of political separatism but rather helped cement them at the emotional and mythical heart of the British state.

The tenacious hold of this history on the Welsh imagination was partly because it was shared across the social orders and across the geographical boundaries of early modern Wales. It would become reinvigorated and reformulated in a 'Romantic' vision of bards and druids in the eighteenth century after the political vision of Great Britain was realised in 1707.[72] A crucial aspect of its longevity and cultural significance, however, was the use to which religious reformers put the idea of a distinctly Welsh spiritual history. The next chapter considers the Reformation in Wales and the ways in which Protestantism became reframed as the rediscovery of an ancient British faith.

3

'Awake Now Thou Lovely Wales!': The Reformation and its Legacies

The Reformation was perhaps the most seismic upheaval in European history. Its shockwaves propagated through all Europe's nations (and beyond), where they were refracted through and changed by their interaction with local cultures. In some areas the challenge to the universal Catholic Church produced upheaval, war and rebellion as well as new visions of politics and society. Elsewhere the Reformation's influence was more muted, and the status quo, albeit never entirely unchanged by the encounter, endured. In some senses, then, all histories of the Reformation are local histories. This can be illustrated by looking at the different trajectories of religious change in the kingdoms of Britain and Ireland. England and Wales's Protestant Reformation was the product of Henry VIII's desire to annul his marriage to Catherine of Aragon. Initially a political and constitutional as much as a religious change, the confessional Protestant reaction against Rome intensified markedly during the brief rule of Edward VI before suffering a reverse under the Catholic Mary I. Elizabeth I's long reign achieved a moderate Protestant settlement which was broadly accepted throughout the kingdom, although its compromises and contradictions produced ongoing tensions and antagonisms which fed into the civil wars and political upheavals that blighted the country from the mid-seventeenth century. The kingdom of Scotland, meanwhile, remained faithful to the Catholic Church under James V, the infant Mary, Queen of Scots, and her French regent, Mary of Guise. In 1560, however, an aristocratic coup in the face of royal authority led to the rejection of papal authority and the adoption of a Reformed Confession of Faith.

This settlement assumed a more radical and thoroughgoing course of Protestant reform than was to be found in Elizabethan England and Wales. The Calvinist Presbyterianism of the Scottish Church (or Kirk) would remain a core element of Scottish identity and culture down to modern times, and would also become the source of a good deal of friction and instability when the native ruling house inherited the English throne in 1603. The third territory of Ireland was claimed as a kingdom by Henry VIII in 1542, partly to ensure that his title there, which rested on papal authority, would not be challenged by his excommunication from the Catholic Church. English monarchs (Mary I excepted) attempted to impose Protestantism in the country, but their efforts met with only very limited success among the native population and among long-established Anglo-Norman settlers. Indeed, Ireland's resolute attachment to the Old Faith and its (often violent) rejection of a foreign, English, confession became a vital component of early modern Irish identity and patriotic pride.

As this very brief and partial summary shows, the narrative of the Reformation is a complex one even within the small territory of Britain and Ireland. However, this characterisation still does not do justice to the kaleidoscopic intricacies of early modern religious change. The adoption of Protestantism was, for example, much smoother and more rapid in a county like Essex than it was in Lancashire. Moreover, we must add to this multifaceted and many-layered narrative historians' increasing recognition that we are dealing with what is best described as a 'Long Reformation': a process of religious adaptation which played out over many decades.[1] It is also the case, of course, that religious change in this period rarely involved a dramatic conversion of individuals or groups from Catholicism to Protestantism, to say nothing of the various shifts and movements between confessional groups within Protestantism itself. The development of more radical Protestants called 'puritans', from the mid-sixteenth century onwards, to some degree destabilised the Church of England, while the problem of heterodox ideologies within British Protestantism became a governing crisis and then a constitutional collapse during the civil wars of the mid-seventeenth century. What remains clear through all of these complexities, however, is that religion was the most important cultural referent for and component of personal, local and national identities throughout the early modern period.

Where does all this leave an account of the Reformation in Wales? It firstly provides this author with something of a 'get out clause', in acknowledging that a short synthesis cannot do justice to the complexity of the lengthy and convoluted process of religious change between the 1530s and the 1680s.[2] We are forced, then, to acknowledge that a particular path must be taken through this mazy and tangled terrain; we must choose to follow one narrative of the Reformation and its legacies from the many available. The position adopted here, in keeping with the overarching focus of the volume, is to consider the relationship between Reformation and concepts of early modern Welsh identity. This chapter argues that Reformation Protestantism developed a symbiotic relationship with particularist forms of history, language and monarchy to produce a resilient and enduring form of Welshness that is central to understanding the political and cultural as well as the religious histories of this period. The nature of this investigation demands a somewhat imbalanced focus on the Protestant reformers of the sixteenth century and the legacy of their efforts. Attention is given to the Catholic and nonconformist populations of early modern Wales in the following chapter, once again with particular notice given to the ways in which they sought to articulate and embody notions of Welsh identity, notions which were often elaborated in opposition to the Established Church.

One of the key points to acknowledge at the outset about Wales's experience of the Reformation was that it produced no revolts or rebellions as it did in many other parts of the realm. There were no events such as the Pilgrimage of Grace in northern England in 1536 or the 'Prayer Book Rebellion' in the counties of the south-west in 1549. Most scholars would agree that by the beginning of the seventeenth century, Wales had become a largely Protestant country and that the Church of England (in its Welsh guise) was the source of genuine loyalty and affection.[3] A conundrum which needs explaining, then, is how one of the most culturally and linguistically distinct parts of the Tudor and Stuart realms showed so few signs of outward disaffection in the face of fundamental religious change. It appears that the key to this puzzle lies in what can be described as the 'inculturation' of the Reformation in Wales, which is to say the naturalisation of an *English* Reformation within a *Welsh* cultural milieu. This was achieved principally by the subversion of the imperial English ambition articulated in both the

1536 Act of Union and in the initial propagation of the Reformation in Wales. Through a protracted process of cultural adaptation across the sixteenth century, the Reformation message was rendered into the Welsh language and, moreover, was recast not as an innovation from England but rather as the rediscovery of the original faith of the Britons (read, 'the Welsh'). It is also the case that the articulation and enforcement of the Reformation was left in the hands of Welsh elites rather than of English administrators and placemen, and they executed their task with an ameliorative mixture of leniency, indulgence and cultural sensitivity. The close association of Protestantism with the Crown also facilitated this assimilation of the new faith, as the Reformation's magisterial authority was another element that came to be rendered as particularly Welsh, something that is examined further in Chapter 6.

Before examining this process of naturalising the Reformation in greater detail, however, a few words should be said about the place of the Reformation and early modern religious history more generally in the canon of Welsh historical scholarship. Wales emerged into the modern world as a nonconformist nation; its political and cultural identity was inextricably tied up with its religious character.[4] This was also the period in which the nation's historical scholarship came of age, and the country's religious environment imparted a distinctive character to the study of Welsh early modern history.[5] A good deal of this scholarship, then, focused on the emergence in the mid-seventeenth century of the nonconformist sects which would, albeit in rather different guises, become so central to Welsh life in the modern period.[6] This served to impart a rather celebratory, somewhat narrow and determinedly Whiggish cast to a good deal of Welsh early modern religious history. Although these priorities have left us with many fine studies, we should be wary of the tendency for these narratives to stress the smooth inevitability of Protestantism's triumph. We need to remember, for example, that the propensity of some scholarship to stress the apathy and ineffectiveness of the late medieval Church in Wales was, in part, the product of a modern desire to reject Catholicism as somehow 'un-Welsh'. Similarly, we should acknowledge that throughout the period covered by this volume, puritanism, dissent and forms of Protestant nonconformity were very much minority sports in Wales, although their preponderance in the academic literature might cause us to think otherwise. Indeed, the focus on nonconformity has been shot through with a sense that the Church of England, against which seventeenth-century dissenters positioned themselves, was somehow alien, ineffective, corrupt and unreflective of Welsh sensibilities. This chapter argues otherwise and suggests that the Church of England in Wales during the later sixteenth and seventeenth centuries was emblematic of a form of inclusivist Welsh, and indeed British, patriotism. So we should be alive to the fact that the process of religious Reformation, far from being sure, smooth and predestined, was piecemeal, local, spasmodic and protracted. Nonetheless, this narrative is a success story, but it is less about the success of the dissenting sects and more about the slow and sometimes painful construction of a state Church which, in its local cultural confession, became a potent focus for Welsh national identity.

Although historians once saw the late medieval Church in Wales as decrepit and ineffective, recent scholarship has revived its reputation and recognised that it was generally a popular institution with strong cultural roots. A spate of rebuilding and redecoration of churches in the fifteenth century suggests that the Church was popular with the laity who had to provide the funds for the new towers, stained glass and stone carving which appeared in many parts of the country.[7] Significant problems still bedevilled the Church in Wales, however, principally its poverty and the associated evils of a poorly supported clergy and of largely absentee (and English) bishops. Despite these issues, there is very little evidence for any groundswell of dissatisfaction with the Church in Wales on the eve of the Reformation, and certainly no significant presence of reformist groups such as the Lollards as was to be found in parts of England. This was not, then, an institution primed to fall when the break with Rome and the Reformation crisis engulfed the country in the 1530s.

The timing of the Reformation in Wales is significant for understanding initial responses to the course of religious change, for Henry VIII's break with the papacy coincided with the country's assimilation with England. The union brought significant dividends for the Welsh gentry and these would not be thrown away lightly by open opposition to the regime. The co-option of the gentry through the union settlement was also important for the nature of religious change in Wales, however, as it was this group which would oversee and police the implementation of religious policy in concert with the local bishops and clergy.[8] It was also the case that much of the landed capital released by Henry VIII's dissolution of the monasteries in the late 1530s flowed into the coffers of the gentry, helping to cement their positions atop the pyramid of local society.[9] These gentlemen were part of the local community rather than separate from it, and, in general, they resolved to proceed slowly and cautiously in the implementation of the Protestant settlement in Wales, in no small measure because often they themselves were hardly enthusiastic supporters of the new faith.[10] In 1570 the bishop of St Davids lamented that such men were insufficiently bullish in their promotion of Protestantism, and that this was a serious problem, as their 'authoritie and ponishment the people gretly regarde and whose affection towardes religion they note, and are the redier to drawe forwarde or backwarde as they shall perceive the temporall magistrate to be affectede'.[11] It was important too that the gentry shared the cultural sensibilities of their communities and were aware that rigorous imposition of an unmediated English Protestantism would likely prove difficult and counterproductive. It is also the case that local clergy provided a complementary strand of continuity and flexibility across the early Reformation period. There was no wholesale purge of Catholic clergy, and the Reformation was, in large measure, accommodated through a pastorate with which local populations were familiar.[12]

This is not to say, however, that the shift to a Protestant Church of England across the sixteenth century was not met with recalcitrance, grumbling and some outright resistance from the laity. A frequent refrain from more committed Protestants was the glacial pace of religious reform in the principality.[13] Although this was, in part, a product of the gradualist and cautious approach adopted by most clergy and gentry in Wales, there is no question but that, while Wales had become officially Protestant, matters often looked distinctly *un*reformed at the parish level.[14] For example, Nicholas Robinson, bishop of Bangor, wrote to Queen Elizabeth's chief minister, William Cecil, in 1567 describing the spiritual condition of his diocese. He found that the people were obedient and 'faithfull subiectes', but added that 'ignorance contieweth many in ye dregges of superstition'.[15] He described a landscape filled with the apparatus of Catholicism which had officially been proscribed for years: 'images and aulters standing in churches undefaced, lewed and undecent vigils and watches observed, much pilgramege goyng, many candels sett up to ye honour of sainctes, some reliques yet caried about, and all ye cuntre is full of bedes and knottes [i.e. rosaries]'. A decade later in south-west Wales, the bishop of St David's, Richard Davies, similarly lamented an environment in which some 'defende papisterie, supersticion and idolatrie, pilgrimages to welles and blinde chappelles, [and] procure the wardens of churches in tyme of visitacion to periurie [perjury] to conceale images, roode loftes and aulters'.[16] Davies was describing a culture of deliberate disobedience and avoidance as local clergy and laity hid their images and altars from the diocesan visitors who were charged with ensuring that such Catholic remnants had been removed. Like Robinson, Davies reported in 1570 that there were none in his diocese that refused obstinately to attend Protestant church services as required by law, the subjects were 'faithfull' in that sense, but he nevertheless described a 'great nombre to be slowe and cold in the true service of God. Some careles for any relygion, and some that wysshe the romyshe relygyon agayne'.[17] Katharine Olson has recently drawn attention the commonplace book of a mid-sixteenth century Denbighshire individual of modest means, Ieuan ap William ap Dafydd ab Einws.[18] This text, compiled from the early 1540s, was intended for wider circulation, and it was used to this end until the 1580s. However, this was essentially a compilation of late medieval rather than reformed early modern piety, with vernacular poetry on Mary and the Passion, the lives of saints (including the Welsh Bueno and Collen), biblical stories and other devotional texts. Such survivals underline graphically how 'Reformation' was a protracted process in Wales, and that the gap between policy on the one hand, and practice on the ground on the other, could be wide indeed.

This, then, was not a country whose inhabitants were doctrinally Protestant even down to the latter parts of Elizabeth I's reign, although the same might be said for many areas of England too. There was clearly a survivalist culture in which traditional Catholic practices such as vigils before funerals and pilgrimages to the holy sites of indigenous Celtic saints, which were an important component of late medieval Welsh piety, continued to be popular. However, there was very little sense that the Welsh were willing to rebel or revolt to restore Catholicism. Indeed, a common refrain in the many dismal reports on the reformed nature of popular piety was Welsh loyalty to the Crown.[19] It appears that there was something of an unofficial indulgence of survivalist practices in the ceremonies of the Church in Wales, while governors sought to build slowly on Welsh loyalty as a means of consolidating confessional allegiance. Ultimately, the Welsh came to associate with the Protestant Church as part of a particularist confession, a collective mentality built around a vision of self-identification.[20] The development of a distinctively Welsh reformed identity was a process that gathered pace across the sixteenth century, and which was largely the product of a humanist attempt to reconcile the English Reformation with Welsh cultural sensibilities. As the evidence cited above indicates, this was a protracted process which met with a good deal of sullen resistance, but ultimately it was remarkably successful.

An important component in this construction of a distinctive reformed Welsh identity was the marrying together of print, Protestantism and the Welsh language. One of the most serious obstacles facing the reformed faith in Wales was the cultural disconnection between an English-language Reformation and a largely monoglot Welsh population. The Welsh language had a significant presence in the late medieval Church, but the early Reformation of the sixteenth century paid little heed to cultural differences within the Tudor state. The English Reformation soon began to be promulgated in the English tongue with Tyndale's unofficial translation of the Bible in the mid-1520s, the appearance of an 'authorised' Bible in 1539, and a royal proclamation of 1541 which ordered that the authorised volume be placed in every parish church in the kingdom (including those in Wales, of course).[21] The English-language reformation of the Church gathered pace in 1549 with the production of the Edwardian Book of Common Prayer, the text which detailed the services for administering the sacraments and ceremonies of the Church of England. There existed what Peter Roberts has described as an 'underlying principle' of government during the reigns of Henry VIII and Edward VI, which was never explicitly stated, that 'there should be only one law and one faith under the sovereign prince, whose subjects should also speak a common language'.[22] The reforming Bishop William Barlow of St Davids articulated something along these lines in his correspondence with Thomas Cromwell in the 1530s. Barlow wished to establish a school for encouraging scriptural study in south-west

Wales, and hoped that through these means 'the Welsch rudenesse wolde sone be framed to English cyvilitye', and lamented the fact that 'the Englishe tongue [is] nothinge preferred after the acte of parlemente', referring to the 1536 language clause.[23] The potentially damaging cultural ramifications of such a policy can be seen in the so-called 'Prayer Book Rebellion' of 1549, when Cornish-speaking rebels refused the new service book 'whereof certen of us understande no Englysh [and] utterly refuse thys newe Englysh'.[24] However, no such violent reaction occurred in Wales, probably because the prayer book was less strictly enforced by the indulgent clerical and lay elites, and also because there were signs of clerical tolerance of the Welsh language in local Protestant worship.[25] However, the relative Welsh quiescence was also attributable to the fact that the imperial drift of policy articulated in the 1536 union legislation was ultimately subverted by the efforts of native reformers. These reformers, while paying lip service to the government's English-language preferences, managed, in fact, to secure the vernacularisation of the Reformation into Welsh. And an important figure in this process was the humanist and precocious defender of the 'British history' discussed in the previous chapter, Sir John Prise.

In 1546, Prise produced (anonymously) the first book to be printed in the Welsh language, a signal event in the nation's cultural history. It is known to posterity as *Yny lhyvyr hwnn* (*In this book*) as the slim volume did not possess a title *per se*, but these are the first words on its frontispiece.[26] The volume was a primer which reproduced Welsh versions of the Creed and the Lord's Prayer, which were already available in manuscript, along with the alphabet and instructions on how to read Welsh. Prise was thus providing his fellow countrymen and women with the basic texts for reformed worship and also the rudimentary tools for their acquiring literacy. This was a major breakthrough in harnessing the Welsh language to the influential technologies of printing. Indeed, Prise argued in the volume that 'God has given us the printing-press in our midst to multiply knowledge of his blessed words', and maintained that there were many people who could read Welsh but who did not understand English or Latin, and so such works were required to save Christian souls. Perhaps in a nod to the Anglicising policy of the Tudor regime, he noted that this book was intended for the salvation of those 'who cannot obtain better guidance through the medium of other tongues'. Such translations of religious works were a necessity, Prise claimed, for 'a large part of my nation, the Welsh, are lost in untold darkness for want of knowledge of God's words and His commandments'.[27] Even at this early stage of Welsh printed literature, therefore, we find a concern for Wales's spiritual wellbeing resonating with wider patriotic themes; Prise said he had undertaken the translation 'for the love I have of my country'. There is also the sense of a national project here, of connecting the reformation of the self to a wider spiritual reconfiguring of the nation, and that in making individuals Protestant, this project would, in stages, construct something novel: a 'Protestant Wales'.

The year after Price's work appeared, another Oxford-educated Welsh humanist, William Salesbury, published a collection of Welsh proverbs. Salesbury would become a more influential figure in the Welsh Reformation 'movement' than Prise, and he was also a much more zealous Protestant.[28] His 1547 publication, *Oll Synnwyr Pen Kembro Ygyd* (*The Whole Wisdom of a Welshman's Head*), linked together language and religion as Prise had, but Salesbury was riding a wave of Edwardian reforming zeal and was more direct and explicit in his mobilising call to readers. Addressing the Welsh people directly in the preface to his volume, Salesbury called on them (in Welsh) to 'go barefoot like pilgrims to … the King and his Council, to get permission to have the Holy Scriptures in your language, for the sake of those among you that cannot or are unlikely to learn English … get the Scriptures in your own language'.[29] This was a remarkable request for the direct lobbying of government for provision of the Scriptures in Welsh. Salesbury was convinced that the Welsh needed truly to understand Christianity in their hearts if they were to be saved, and, although he acknowledged the Tudor policy of encouraging bilingualism (he also published an English–Welsh dictionary in 1547 which lauded the 'communion of one tongue'), he was nevertheless a passionate Welsh patriot who felt that thousands of souls would be lost to ignorance and damnation if the authorities waited for whole generations of Welsh people to learn English, something which had been the thrust of the union settlement.

Salesbury was involved in other vernacularising initiatives, including a translation of the epistles and gospels into Welsh in a 1551 publication entitled *Kynniver Llith a Ban* (*As Many Lessons and*

Articles). This seems to have been his response to the authorisation of the 1549 English Book of Common Prayer as the exclusive text for use in church services, something which imperilled the religious status of the Welsh language. Such reformist initiatives stalled during the reign of the Catholic Mary I (1553–8), of course, when the distinctly un-Protestant majority in Wales appeared content to have the Old Faith once more.[30] This very acquiescence in the Catholic restoration, however, probably helped spur on reformist initiatives for the principality under Mary's Protestant sister, Elizabeth I. Her religious settlement of 1559 was a moderate one, which attempted to walk a careful path and accommodate the wide spectrum of her subjects' religious proclivities. Hers was a Protestant state, however, and Wales did not look like a particularly Protestant part of it. In no small measure this was because no concessions to Welsh cultural differences were forthcoming; the 1559 settlement, for example, required all churches to possess a Bible and common Prayer Book, but the only ones available were in English. It seems, however, that English governors, lobbied by Welsh reformers like Salesbury, came to recognise that a degree of linguistic pluralism in the state was required if a common faith was to be established in England and Wales. This recognition resulted in a momentous Act of Parliament (apparently shepherded through the legislative process in part by the antiquarian Humphrey Llwyd, MP for Denbigh boroughs),[31] which provided for the Bible and the Book of Common Prayer to be translated into 'the Welshe tongue', and to be made available in churches throughout the country.[32] It is worth noting that the measure was a private rather than a public bill, and so was not an initiative emanating from the regime. Initially it appears only to have been designed to produce a Welsh Prayer Book and the provision for translating the Bible was added as the measure progressed through Parliament.[33] The act maintained that translation was required as English 'ys not understanded of the most and greatest noumber of her Majesties most lovyng and obedient subjectes … [in Wales] … who therfore arre utterly destitute of Gooddes Holy Woorde and doo remayne in the like or reyther more darcknes & ignorance than they were in the tyme of papistrye'.[34]

In many ways this was a remarkable turn of events, for the imperial implications of the Tudor union were here subverted, as the government endorsed the transmission of the Protestant faith in a tongue other than English within the borders of the unitary state. The act did, however, contain a proviso that English Bibles and Prayer Books should be placed alongside the Welsh texts in parish churches, so that the Welsh, 'by conferring bothe tongues together, [may] the sooner attayn to the knowledge of the English tongue'.[35] The goal of bilingualism leading to an Anglophone confession was still voiced, therefore, but it now smacked of wishful thinking rather than a determined piece of cultural or linguistic imperialism. We may speculate that this provision was included as a sop to elements within Parliament who were uneasy about attenuating the concept of English cultural superiority. Nevertheless, despite this hangover from the union's linguistic provisions, this legislation represented a sharp contrast to the policy the regime pursued in regions such as Ireland or Cornwall, where English was determinedly and decisively made the language of the Protestant faith. Indeed, this dispensation meant that Welsh would be the only non-state language of Protestant Europe to be the medium of a published Bible in this period.

The translation process was undertaken primarily by William Salesbury and Richard Davies, the bishop of St David's, who had fled to the safe Protestant haven of Frankfurt during Mary I's reign. The products of their labours appeared in 1567 in the form of a new Book of Common Prayer and a translation of the New Testament only; the production of a full Bible was evidently too mammoth an undertaking in the time available. These were critical texts for shaping a Protestant Welsh identity and it is noteworthy that Salesbury and Davies made concerted efforts not just to provide for the service and the gospels in the vernacular, but that they also produced a set of historical arguments and justifications for a naturalised Protestantism too.[36] These arguments were articulated in the lengthy 'Epistol at y Cembru', or 'Letter to the Welsh People' which prefaced the New Testament, which was largely Davies's work, although Salesbury contributed some of its most striking passages. This address was the means through which the translators hoped to convince Welsh parishioners that Protestantism was not the imposition of some kind of alien religion, 'ffydd Sayson' or 'faith of the Saxons', as one Catholic Welsh bard dismissed it, but rather that it was the rediscovery of the pure faith of the original Britons.[37] In so doing, they were building on the kinds of historical patriotism discussed in Chapter 2, and were helping to forge a powerful

composite of faith and fatherland which, while unimpeachably operating within the Church of England, was nonetheless rooted in Welsh
cultural concerns. They were also bringing together and systematising
arguments of long standing about the precocious and pure Christianity
of the Ancient British. In his *Defensio*, for example, Sir John Prise
maintained that the Britons were 'among the first to be received as a
body into the faith and to embrace Christian worship'.[38] In his 1547
publication *Oll Synnwyr*, Salesbury made a polemical argument for
translating the Scriptures into Welsh and married this with a claim
that 'your fortunate ancestors, the ancient British' had once possessed
a vernacular Bible, and their descendants were merely asking for its
recovery. He continued that the loss of the translated Scriptures was
part of God's curse 'since the time of Cadwaladr the Blessed', and that
if his readers did not request knowledge of Christ in the vernacular
then 'none of you can claim connection with British patriotism, nor
be related to its various achievements and good qualities'.[39] Drawing
on these traditions, Davies and Salesbury presented their translation
to the Welsh people as the *restoration* of a faith which had flourished
in the Welsh Church of the Dark Ages. Rather than an English confession, and therefore Protestantism was presented as the rediscovery
of a distinctively *Welsh* faith. This work, Salesbury hoped, would be
the means 'for the delivery of many thousandes of my countrey folkes
from the spirituall blyndnes of ignoraunce and fowl infection of olde
idolatrie and false superstition'. By granting the Scriptures, 'the verye
remedie & salve of our gostly blyndnes and leprosie [is] to be had in
our best knowen tongue'.[40]

The 'Epistol' opens with a startling address to the country itself:
'Awake thou now lovely Wales … do not denationalise thyself, do not
be indifferent, do not look down, but gaze upwards to the place thou
dost belong'.[41] The themes of national patriotism, but also of awaken-
ing from a slumber of ignorance and the rediscovery of the country's
rightful place through its rightful faith, were thus established from
the outset. In this technique of direct address, the translators looked
to achieve a sense of connection with the reader, but they were also
seeking to create communities among these readers and auditors (it
was almost certain that the 'Epistol' was read out in churches) who
were bound together not only by a common language and history
but also by a common faith. The translators went on to provide a

compelling narrative of how a pure form of early Christianity had been introduced into Britain soon after Christ's crucifixion by Joseph of Arimathea. The Britons, they said, 'received the undefiled and perfect religion of Christ'. These Britons had resisted the corrupt Roman Catholic faith which was introduced by Saint Augustine in the seventh century, and retained their pristine religion, now reinterpreted as Protestantism, while the Saxons fell victim to the errors of Rome. Eventually, however, the Welsh were forced to accept the abominable heresies of Catholicism as imposed by the Saxons at the point of the sword. They thus lost the Scriptures in their own language and fell into a Catholic dark age which was redeemed by Henry VIII's delivery from spiritual (and governmental) bondage.

The translators thus turned Catholicism into the foreign faith imposed upon an unwilling people, and transmogrified Protestantism into the rediscovered religion of the ancient British. They were seeking to graft a confessional dimension onto a linguistic and historical community; to create a Protestant Wales. Towards the end of the 'Epistol', Davies again addressed the reader/auditor in the following terms:

> I have shown to thee thy pre-eminence and thy privilege of old …
> Therefore thou shouldest be glad and frequent thy thanksgiving
> to God, to her grace the Queen and to the Lords and Commons …
> who are renewing thy privilege and honour … Take it [the New
> Testament] in thy hand; grasp it and read it. Here shall thou see
> thy former condition, here wilt thou acquaint thyself with thy old
> faith and the praiseworthy Christianity thou had before.[42]

This, then, was a programme which amalgamated history, language and faith into a patriotic vision that, it was hoped, would appeal to Welsh sensibilities and help inculturate as well as vernacularise the reformed faith in Wales. It is worth stressing that this patriotic appeal was not articulated in terms of a narrow nationalism of the modern variety, of a form of separatism or division. The Welsh reformers emphasised the blessings bestowed by the Tudor line and deployed arguments of unity, Britishness and participation in a common confession with their fellow English subjects. The vision offered up in the 'Epistol' would prove influential and enduring. Although the introduction of these texts into Welsh churches certainly did not make the country quickly adopt the reformed faith, this was nevertheless an enormously important step on the road to the creation of a reformed Wales.

Despite the publications of 1567, the translation of the Scriptures into Welsh remained unfinished, and quarrels between Davies and Salesbury (allegedly over the translation of one word!) hindered the project's completion. Their work, however, was taken up, unofficially, although with the encouragement of Archbishop John Whitgift, by William Morgan, a native of Caernarvonshire and the incumbent of Llanrhaeadr-ym-Mochnant in Denbighshire. Morgan was a Cambridge-educated clergyman and knew Richard Davies.[43] He was also a humanist scholar of towering ability and linguistic sensitivity who undertook the translation process by examining the Scriptures in Hebrew, Greek, Latin and English. He published a completed translation of the entire Welsh Bible in 1588, an event which has retained an especial significance for the defenders of the Welsh language down to the present day. Morgan's efforts were to be particularly welcomed as he revised the New Testament as well as translating the Old, and thus addressed problems with Salesbury's original, as the latter's approach to translation was highly idiosyncratic and caused serious difficulties in the ready use and understanding of the 1567 text. Morgan's Bible, by contrast, was hailed as a remarkable rendering into a powerful and commanding Welsh idiom, and many thought that it reinvigorated the language and demonstrated its potential for expressing the most profound spiritual ideas in an accessible form.

In his Latin dedication to Queen Elizabeth, Morgan acknowledged that some had cast doubt on the need for the translation, preferring rather to promote the use of English among the Welsh, but he countered their arguments with the claim that souls would be lost if generations passed in ignorance waiting to learn English. He referred explicitly to the fact that 'unity is more effectually promoted by similarity and agreement in religion than in speech'.[44] Rather than the Anglicising vision of the union settlement, Morgan instead propounded the view of two distinct cultural groups, the English and the Welsh, who were inwardly united by a common religious commitment to the ancient British faith. It was, then, through the vernacularisation of the Reformation that the Henrician ideal of unity of language, as well as of government was subverted and ultimately abandoned. Consequently, the languages, cultures and identities of England and Wales progressed along parallel rather than convergent courses for centuries to come.

Morgan's translation provided a linguistic standard which helped secure the future of the Welsh language from the challenges produced by closer political, economic and social integration with England. The bard Huw Lewys, for example, declared that Morgan had restored 'the respect and dignity of a language which was decayed and which had more or less collapsed'.[45] Indeed, Glanmor Williams, the principal historian of the Welsh Reformation, has written that the provision of the Bible and other texts like the Prayer Book in Welsh, was, 'in the long run, the most crucial single factor in ensuring the survival of the language'.[46] If English had continued to be the medium of worship used in Welsh parish churches, it is likely that it would have become a focus for familiarising the people with that language, and Welsh, along with its attendant sense of national identity, would have been dramatically weakened, and possibly even destroyed.

Morgan's Bible was followed by a number of Welsh religious works from authors who wrote original texts but who, more frequently, translated popular English-language material into the vernacular.[47] Nearly all of these publications were concerned with raising basic levels of religious understanding among Welsh parishioners and with helping Protestantism establish firm roots in Welsh-speaking communities. Important here was the 1620 Welsh revision of the Bible which followed the 1611 'King James' English translation, and which was undertaken by Bishop Richard Parry of St Asaph and the grammarian Dr John Davies; this was a very popular work and remained in use in Welsh churches until 1988. Parry's Bible was followed a year later by his revised Prayer Book, which also remained a feature of Welsh churches for centuries. Importantly, this work also incorporated the archdeacon of Merioneth Edmwnd Prys's metrical version of the Psalms, a work which became an enormously popular component of Welsh popular piety.[48] The congregational singing of these psalms was, of course, designed to appeal to non-literate parishioners, and Prys used a popular metre intended to appeal to 'children, servants and uneducated people' so that 'all be bound to spend their talent for the best'.[49] Also noteworthy in this raft of Welsh publishing was the

1595 Welsh translation of John Jewel's popular *Apology of the Church of England* by Morus Kyffin (a man who praised Elizabeth I's British ancestry), which appeared as *Deffynniad Ffydd Eglwys Loegr*, as well as the 1606 Welsh version of the Book of Homilies by Glamorgan's Edward James. Many of these texts were, of course, directed towards clergymen and literate heads of households who could afford and read these works. The vernacularisation of orthodox Protestantism down to the civil wars is principally a narrative of providing the texts, tools and an ideological framework within which the parish clergy and substantial householders could work to reform and instruct their communities. Bibles remained too expensive for most individuals to purchase, and would usually only have been seen in the parish church. It was not until a cheaper, more popular text for personal use, *Y Beibl Bach* (The Small Bible), was produced in 1630, through the efforts of Rowland Heylin and Sir Thomas Myddelton, that such materials might have been available to the ordinary parishioner. However, even after its publication, many complained about the shortage of bibles in Wales.[50] It is likely, however, that some of the problems of accessing works in Welsh were offset by the regular production of vernacular catechisms which were designed for the religious instruction of the ordinary parishioner in the basics of the faith, and some eight editions of these were published before the civil war.[51]

Low literacy levels and the lack of cheap texts of religious instruction, however, do not seem to have hampered too severely the assimilation of Protestantism within Welsh popular culture by the early seventeenth century. Important in this calculus was the fact that, contrary to late medieval practice, the Welsh episcopate down to the civil wars and for a good period beyond, was populated largely by Welshmen who were resident in their dioceses. Some of these, such as Richard Davies, William Morgan and Richard Parry, were in the vanguard of the vernacularisation effort. Moreover, an expectation was established, partly through the 1563 Elizabethan legislation, that clergy would be Welsh-speaking in those parishes where this was required. In 1593, for example, two churchwardens felt able to bring a case against the incumbent of St Mary's Swansea, John After, because he failed to conduct services in the Welsh language.[52] Bishop William Lloyd of St Asaph reported in 1686 that he needed to suspend a bar on ordaining those who were not graduates as it was 'not practicable in our Welsh dioceses ... most of ye people understanding nothing but Welsh, we cannot supply ye cures with any other but Welshmen'.[53] A revealing example is to be found in a petition to the archbishop of Canterbury from the parishioners of Llandaff and Whitchurch near Cardiff in 1688. The petitioners noted that only about one in ten of the parishes' communicants understood English, but that the arch-deacon and prebendaries had nevertheless selected a man to officiate over them who was 'a meer stranger to the Welsh=tongue'.[54] That they considered such proceedings 'unreasonable and arbitrary' is sug-gestive of their expectation that the Church speak to the people in their own language. Indeed, some clergy needed to overcome serious logistical difficulties to do just this, as in the case of Richard Pigott in Denbighshire, 'a preacher of Gods worde in the English and Welsh languages', who in 1615 was forced to 'explaine the chapters in Welsh upon the English bible every sabaoth day ... because there was no Welsh bible in the church'.[55]

Such allegiances are most visible among the elites, but there were indications that the Church of England had become a cherished insti-tution among ordinary layfolk also. The survivalist nature of piety endured, however, and to many of the hotter sort of Protestants, the country appeared only semi-reformed. This remained a culture in which ceremony, imagery and communal festive piety flourished, and part of this ceremonial attachment probably stemmed from the rela-tive absence of preaching clergy alongside the availability of the Prayer Book and liturgy in Welsh. Indeed, the Welsh liturgy integrated itself powerfully within the landscape of Welsh popular culture, with the Welsh becoming proverbially attached to a text that was looked on with suspicion by many puritans.[56] The general tenor of Welsh reli-gious culture meshed well with the conservative Protestantism of the early Stuart monarchs. The campaign of church beautification and emphasis on the rites and liturgy of the Church under Archbishop William Laud in the 1630s, for example, raised hackles in many parts of England, but appears to have been accepted almost without demur in most of Wales.[57] A striking manifestation of these High Church principles can be seen in the chapel at Rûg, Merioneth, built in 1637 by the future royalist governor of Denbigh, William Salesbury. The building contained a good deal of painting and architectural decor-ation which was focused on a communion table that was set up, in line with Laudian directives, as an altar.[58] Hotter Protestants would view this as an abomination, but it raised no outcry in traditionalist Merioneth.

The successful assimilation of the Church of England with Welsh popular culture can perhaps be most clearly seen in the powerful royalist and pro-episcopalian response in Wales to the crisis of the mid-seventeenth century civil wars. The parliamentarian challenge to King Charles I arose in no small measure from puritans who were horrified at what they saw as the Romeward direction of Church policy in the 1630s. The 1640s and 1650s are crucial for the emergence of a nonconformist religious element in Wales, and this will be considered in greater depth in the following chapter. What is striking, however, is the degree to which much popular opinion in Wales appears to have been behind the king and his Established Church. Some examples will serve to illustrate the argument. As the parliamentarian challenge to King Charles gathered pace in the early 1640s, attacks by puritan groups began to rain down on the episcopate as a Catholic remnant responsible for the corruption of the true Church. Loyalist constituencies across the kingdom rallied behind their bishops through petitions, which were also expressions of concern about puritan plans for radical reform of traditional worship.[59] One of these petitions was presented in the name of the six counties of north Wales in March 1642. It claimed to have the subscription of 30,000 hands, although this was almost certainly an exaggeration, and to be the 'unanimous and undevided request and vote of this whole country'. The petitioners maintained that the 'meere report' of altering church services in their counties had produced 'no good effect'. Interestingly, the petitioners defended episcopacy by claiming that it was the 'forme which came into this island with the first plantation of religion heere, and God so blessed this island that religion came earlely in'.[60] This was the 'British' historical vision articulated by Richard Davies in his 'Epistol', and suggests the kind of Welsh-specific understanding of the Established Church which had grown up in the intervening decades. Indeed, it is telling that a single-sheet printed broadside version of this petition is surmounted by the insignia of the Prince of Wales, anchoring its message even more firmly in a context that combined Welshness, royalism and religion.[61]

Although by no means universal, the strong Welsh attachment to the royalist cause was a striking manifestation of a collective political mobilisation, and it was one that appears to have rested largely on a common 'Anglican' identity. The parliamentarians satirised their Welsh enemies as credulous and benighted for following the king, but recognised that their political loyalties had a deep religious dimension. One parliamentarian pamphlet, for example, averred that the Welsh 'have no religion yet but litanies', while another commented that it was 'no wonder' that the Welsh followed the king 'for they have scarce had any more reformation than the common prayer book'.[62] Some episcopalians tried to combat the parliamentarian canard. One of these was the Breconshire minister Alexander Griffith, who challenged his enemies' characterisation of Wales as 'a land of darknesse', something that he described as 'a frontless untruth in it selfe and a shameless aspersion on the whole nation'. Instead, Griffith countered, 'not onely our nation was converted to Christianity as soone almost as our saviour suffered, but also the countries of Wales are by the blessing of God and the light of Christ Jesus civilised in a very good measure and in equall degree to diverse places in England'.[63] Griffith's reference to the 'British' interpretation of the early Church is again suggestive of the pride felt for what was understood as a naturalised Welsh institution, and also of the successful nature of the sixteenth-century reformers' historicising project. It is also telling in assessing the degree to which the Established Church had become a genuinely popular institution within Wales, that a number of Anglican clergymen from England and Ireland fled there during the years of persecution in the 1650s. It was evident that they felt they were escaping persecutory cultures in England and coming to something of a haven for Anglicanism in Wales.

The deep connections between the Established Church and Welsh culture in the mid-seventeenth century can also be seen in the vernacular political poetry of men like John Griffith of Llanddyfnan and Robert ap Huw of Anglesey. In its hour of persecution, Griffith penned a lament entitled *Bustl yr Eglwys, sef erlidiaû Eglwys Loegr Anno 1653* (*Bile of the Church, namely persecutions of the Church of England, 1653*), while ap Huw composed a verse entitled *Hiraeth am yr Eglwys Lân 1651* (*Longing for the Pure Church, 1651*). Huw Morys of Pontymeibion similarly lamented the tribulations of his beloved Church and country in allegorical verse which became more explicit and biting when the shackles were off after the Restoration of

King Charles II.[64] Many ordinary parishioners in the 1650s sought to continue clandestinely with the ceremonies of the treasured (Welsh) Prayer Book which the parliamentarian authorities had outlawed, sometimes being forced to undertake marriage services in the houses of sympathetic gentlemen 'by candlelight'.[65] A striking example of the attachment to the Book of Common Prayer can be found in the parish of Clynnog, Caernarvonshire, where one parishioner snatched away the Bible of Grace ferch Ffrancis [Grace, daughter of Ffrancis] in December 1660, saying 'mi a fynnwn weled llosgi y Bibles fydd heb y Common Prayer ynddynt' ('we demand that bibles which do not contain the Common Prayer be burnt').[66]

It is unsurprising, then, that the Restoration of King and Church in 1660 was greeted ecstatically in Wales. Orthodox religion had suffered a tremendous shock in the 1650s which had fractured the hegemony of the Church in Wales and opened the door to alternative religious visions of the country: the religious impact and legacies of the civil wars are considered in the following chapter. In addition to this 'psychological' blow, the Church also continued to suffer endemic problems of poverty and the difficulty of acquiring sufficient clergy and preachers of quality to minister in Welsh livings. These problems, however, can be (and often have been) overstated. In addition to highlighting what they consider to be structural weaknesses of the Restored Church, historians have also identified this period as one of cultural abandonment with the appointment of English bishops who were often non-resident and dismissive of Welsh cultural concerns. However, we should be careful on this point as such issues only became serious problems from the early eighteenth century, and we should not read the troubles of this latter era too readily back into the post-Restoration decades. In 1703 an anonymous Glamorgan cleric wrote to the archbishop of Canterbury about having recently had bishops in Welsh sees 'that could preach in Welsh and ... ye generality of ye people did keep ye unity of ye Church'. He added that it was only 'now *of late*' that the practice had changed to the appointing of 'perfect strangers to our country and language [who] ... seldom see us'.[67] Indeed, an argument can be made that the authorities made a conscious decision in the years following the Restoration to appoint predominantly Welsh and Welsh-speaking bishops and clergy to consolidate the Anglican Church's place in people's affections.[68] This was, for example, in sharp contrast with the puritan experiments such as the Commission for the Propagation of the Gospel in Wales in the 1650s, which struggled to secure Welsh preachers to fill cures.

Although it faced new challenges from dissenters and clusters of obdurate Catholics who came under increased suspicion in the 1670s and 1680s, the Established Church weathered the storms of the mid-seventeenth century comparatively well. It remained a critical focus for Welsh loyalties although it did not command this field unchallenged. It continued to be regarded by Welsh men and women as the 'British Church' and to have a claim of precedence on their loyalties.[69] The clergy remained active as supporters of Welsh culture and Welsh history, and although the Church in Wales suffered from its fair share of lazy drones, pluralists and non-residents, it was largely populated by men who cared deeply about the spiritual welfare of their flocks.[70] At his appointment to the see of St Asaph in 1680, Bishop William Lloyd ordered a census of his diocese, with local clergy returning 'notitiae' of the state of their parishes. There were smatterings of Quakers, Independents and Catholics who refused to attend church, although there were some places where their influence was more problematic than others. The incumbent of Ysgeifiog in Flintshire, for example, asked for something to be done about the Quaker Thomas Wynne and his 'wicked brethren', for he was worried 'least they seduce any of my flock after them'.[71] The census reported problems of poorly maintained church buildings, indulgent curates and parishioners flocking to the maypole rather than the church pew on a Sunday. However, the general impression is one of a committed pastorate doing its best for local congregations. Among these we can count Philip Rogers at Llanwyddelan, Montgomeryshire, who requested advice from the bishop on 'the most effectuall way to bring the youth of the parish to be catechized', and asked how best to encourage those 'negligent people … who seldome come to have the Word of God read or preached'.[72] We might also highlight William Williams at Bodfari in Flintshire, who had found some 'poor children' in the parish who were defective in their catechism, although they were able to recite the Lord's Prayer, the Creed and the Ten Commandments (the contents of the first Welsh book, of course). Williams requested help to 'looke after these poor children to instruct them in the rudiments of religion', but noted that he would 'set apart a day or two every weeke' to achieve this if no assistance could be found.[73] It was because of a parochial face such as this that the Established Church remained a vital force in seventeenth-century Wales. The Church's claims on Welsh affections can be seen in devotional tracts and works of historical scholarship, but it can also be found in administrative documents such as the 'notitiae'. It is clearly articulated, for example, in the return of the rector of Llangar, a Welsh-speaking parish in Merioneth of some 184 souls, who in 1681 reported proudly to Bishop Lloyd that 'there be noe popish recusants nor dissenters in the parish … for wee are all rightly fixed, being sons and daughter[s] of ye Church of England'.[74]

The Established Church was at the heart of Welsh society during the seventeenth century. The country's orientation away from the Catholic faith following the break with Rome, however, had been protracted and difficult. The hallmarks of early modern Welsh Protestantism were of a distinctly conservative stamp, as the popular ceremonies and traditions of late medieval piety long continued to have a visible presence within Welsh religious culture, something that troubled many reformers. Indulgence of such survivalism and the absence of a persecutory strain among most lay and clerical governors, however, may ironically have helped smooth the country's path towards its ultimate adoption of the reformed faith. Even more significant on this path towards a Protestant Wales, however, was the vernacularising programme from the mid-sixteenth century that intertwined language, history and faith, fostering the growing conviction among clergy and laity that the Welsh were among God's chosen peoples. The translation of the Bible and Prayer Book probably saved Welsh from the fate of its sister tongue, Cornish, which was destined to contract and wither in the face of overwhelming Anglicising forces and in the absence of a vernacular Bible and liturgy.[75] Welsh, however, maintained a critical presence in the nation's cultural life because it was conjoined with the Established Church, and this was enormously significant in sustaining a distinctive identity in the centuries following the Acts of Union. As Glanmor Williams observed, this successful marrying together of religion, language and nationality 'served as a most potent and active leaven in the Welsh consciousness'.[76] The Established Church did not hold the field unopposed, however, and the next chapter considers the challenges it faced in the sixteenth and seventeenth centuries from Catholicism and Protestant nonconformity.

4

Alternative Visions:
Catholicism, Puritanism and Dissent

The previous chapter described how the Established Church not only became a cherished institution in early modern Wales, but also how it came to embody an important aspect of Welsh consciousness and identity. The relatively slow adoption of the reformed faith, however, opened up spaces for alternative confessional visions of the country in the sixteenth and seventeenth centuries. On the one hand there was the opportunity for Catholicism to endure and, in some parts of the country even to flourish, as Protestantism struggled to put down roots in Welsh soil. On the other hand, the traditionalism and conservatism of much Welsh religion provided fuel for a critique from puritans who pressed for a more thoroughgoing Reformation in the country to save its inhabitants from the mire of popery and corruption. This chapter will explore both of these confessional strands, paying particular attention to the ways in which each claimed to embody and represent an authentic form of Welshness over and against that elaborated by the Established Church. Familiar themes resurface in this chapter, as we consider how Catholicism and puritanism/dissent both sought to utilise the technology of the press; to make arguments about the antiquity and historicity of their confession; and to connect their causes with the Welsh language. We begin by considering the Catholic community.

CATHOLICISM

As discussion of the Reformation in Wales has shown, Catholic beliefs and practice remained vibrant features of the Welsh religious landscape for many decades after the break with Rome. Indeed, modern scholars fixated on accounting for the apparently inevitable triumph of Protestantism in Wales have probably *underestimated* Catholicism's vigour and dynamism in early modern society. Although there was no Welsh religious revolt or uprising in the sixteenth century, we should nevertheless recognise the strength of Catholic sentiment here and the pervasiveness of its rites and rituals. In his preface to the 1567 translation of the New Testament, for example, Richard Davies observed of the 'Romish religion' that his countrymen were 'loth to forsake the same'.[1] Popular piety in early modern Wales frequently incorporated the practices of late medieval Catholicism with the use of rosaries, crucifixes and altars rather than communion tables. One English royalist coming through south Wales in the mid-1640s was surprised to find how 'almost in every parish the crosse or sometime two or three crosses [are] perfect in Brecknockshire, Glamorganshire, & c'.[2] These were elements of Catholic worship which should have been swept away many decades before. Also in the mid-1640s, one Welsh parliamentarian was scathing about the 'swarme of blinde, superstitious ceremonies that are among us, passing under the names of old harmles customs'.[3] One explanation for this survivalism was offered by a clergyman in the 1670s, who suggested that there was a tendency to retain Catholic rites among the Welsh 'which are tolerated by their guides, least they should be unsettled and scandalized in their more ancient and Catholick observations by abrupt disuse, till by knowledge they come to leave them off, according to their own accord'.[4]

In this environment, then, it is difficult to tell where Catholic practice ended and a traditionalist form of Protestantism began. Clearly the situation on the ground, particularly in the Tudor era, was fluid and characterised by a good degree of indulgence and pragmatism on the part of the authorities. We should resist the temptation to see post-Reformation society as being split into two opposing confessional camps which had little to do with one another. The reality was much messier and more complex, with Catholics attending Protestant churches as they were required by law while Protestants conformed but still sought the spiritual refuge of Catholic rites and doctrine. Indeed, one might attend Protestant services and welcome a vernacular service but still see the value in relics, shrines, pilgrimages and the other impedimenta of the Old Faith. The very labels we use of 'Catholic' and 'Protestant' are perhaps unhelpful in recovering the shifting religious identities of the period and the dynamism of a culture in which such positions were in flux and subject to ongoing definition and redefinition. The realities of simply 'getting along' meant that the boundaries between confessional communities in many Welsh parishes remained blurred in something of a conformist consensus.[5] Certainly, there seems to have been little of the appetite for persecuting Catholics in Wales that can be found in some parts of England, probably because local magistrates in the principality were themselves rarely zealous Protestants.

The line between acceptable and unacceptable religious traditionalism became somewhat sharper following the papal bull *Regnans in Excelsis* of 1570 which excommunicated Elizabeth I and asserted that any subject who continued in obedience to the heretic monarch would also be excommunicate. The growing identification of Catholics with foreign threats and treason after the Armada of 1588 and the Gunpowder Plot of 1605 also heightened confessional awareness and sensitivities. It is nevertheless the case that the institutional power of the Established Church, coupled with the state's apparatus for enforcing Protestant conformity through fines and imprisonment, over time eroded the numbers of Welsh recusants (those Catholics who refused to attend Protestant services) and reduced the strength and visibility of local Catholic cultures outside a few key areas, particularly those in Flintshire and Monmouthshire. Throughout the early modern period, however, the historian is left with the conundrum of dealing with the many 'church papists' in local society: those parishioners who outwardly conformed by attending their Protestant parish church, but whose hearts and spirits remained committed to the Old Faith.[6] That there were such individuals and communities is undeniable, but we struggle to identify and understand them because, by their very nature, they left few traces in the historical record. Moreover, when they do surface it is often through the hostile gaze of their enemies who are given to mischaracterise and demonise their opponents. This can give the problematic impression that Welsh Catholics comprised largely plotters and potentially treasonous fifth columnists. In fact, it is likely that in many areas a form of ecumenical coexistence meant that Catholics were part of the parish community rather than separate from it. We should also note that women were important in this calculus, as they comprise a good proportion of those who were presented to the authorities as recusants. It seems that these women became the 'public face' of much Catholic recusancy, while their husbands conformed, allowing the latter, for example, to hold local office.

Quietist Catholics working within but not against a Protestant state were probably majorities within most Welsh parishes down to the middle of Elizabeth's reign, if not later. These were men and women who conformed to the state religion and who saw little that was harmful in supporting the Protestant prince, but who nevertheless kept their rosaries, invoked their local saints and visited their shrines on holy days. These were forms of popular Catholic belief which are often dismissed as merely residual or emotional legacies of pre-Reformation culture and are largely emptied of meaning and significance. Such a view seems mistaken. It is telling that in 1632, John Dunn, the dying incumbent of Cwmdeuddwr in Radnorshire, communicated his concern over the prevalence of potentially Catholic rites which might accompany his interment. He left directions that he be buried 'according to Christian manner without watching in the night, without lighting of candles over my dead corpse or giving me ale over the bier or any pomp and superstitious ceremonies'.[7] That this was a Church of England minister discussing the likely practices of his congregants a century after the Reformation suggests the obduracy of ceremonial Catholic piety and affections in Welsh religious culture. In this context, we should also recall the commonplace book of Ieuan ap William ap Dafydd ab Einws mentioned in the last chapter. This work, which was used from the 1540s to the 1580s, was essentially a manuscript volume of Welsh Catholic piety, but was clearly being employed as a spiritual resource within a supposedly Protestant milieu.[8] Multiple examples could also be cited of men and women who 'in heapes goe one pilgrimage to the wonted wells and places of supersticion' where miracles were still proclaimed.[9] Particularly popular was St Winifred's Well at Holywell in Flintshire, which sat at the heart of the county's substantial Catholic community.[10] This site was such a significant landmark that John Speed included an inset representation of the building on his 1610 map of the county. A hostile account of religion in north Wales in the 1590s described people flocking to pilgrimage sites like Holywell and added that the commonality there maintained 'the absurdest poincts of popishe heresie, according to which knowledge … the greatest number of them doe frame theire lives'.[11] A note of 1629 recorded that some 'fowerteene of [*sic*, 'or'] fifteene hundreth' people had flocked to the well on St Winifred's feast day in November of that year, including Catholic peers and knights of the realm.[12] This was evidently something more significant than simple 'superstition' or a population's residual affection for old forms and certainties.

The general impression of confessional communities getting along without too much friction or opposition seems to describe the everyday reality for most. However, we should not allow this picture to become too cosy.[13] Political and religious pressures generated conflict and suspicion between Catholics and Protestants, particularly at times of crisis. Moreover, Welsh Catholicism from the early days of the Reformation also possessed a harder edge, a more militant and confrontational aspect. In 1534 Eustace Chapuys, the imperial ambassador in England, informed Emperor Charles V about the 'indisposition of the people of Wales', remarking that they were 'very angry' about 'what is done against the faith, for they have always been good Christians'. He further suggested that the people of Wales would support a Catholic invasion to restore the faith, and that 'the people only want for a chief to take the field'.[14] We can see the simmering resentment that Chapuys identified in some of the vernacular poetry of the period. In the 1540s, for example, Glamorgan's Tomas ab Ieuan ap Rhys composed verses which lamented how the Welsh had been 'turned by the faith of the Saxons … [the] churches everywhere are nothing but empty corners … Destroying the altars once so privileged … despoiling God and his house'.[15] Similar sentiments were articulated around 1553 in north Wales by Catrin ferch Gruffudd ap Hywel, who was angered at the 'Stealing [of] the chalice of Christ, stealing church and chancel / Without any gain but arrogance and exploitation'.[16] Hers is a valuable (and rare) female perspective on religious change in this period, and her marriage to a Catholic priest helps account for the bitterness of her comments. From the early Reformation era, we should also note the opposition to Henry VIII's religious policy represented by Pembrokeshire's James ap Gruffydd ap Hywel, the first layman to go into exile for his opposition to the break with Rome and an inveterate intriguer against the throne.[17] The Tudor authorities were deeply concerned about the potential for Catholic resistance from Wales, even if no major revolt actually materialised. Moreover, it was widely recognised that Wales was a vulnerable point in the kingdom's defences, which might be exploited by hostile Catholic powers.

A critical period in the Catholic reaction in Wales comes in the 1570s and 1580s. Ardent Catholic exiles on the continent trained missionary priests for reintegration into British society at the new seminary of Douai in northern France. These exiles included men like Morys Clynnog of Caernarvonshire and Owen Lewis of Anglesey who saw Wales as a region that was sympathetic to their cause. Indeed, Clynnog developed a plan for fomenting a Catholic uprising in Wales supported by a foreign invasion to overthrow 'that woman who has usurped the kingdom of England'. In support of the scheme, he advised the authorities in Rome that '[Wales is] most devoted to the Catholic faith, and most inclined to welcome aid from abroad for the restoration of religion'.[18] Clynnog claimed in 1572 that, as the Israelites awaited the Messiah, so the Welsh awaited a Catholic restoration. About one-fifth of those trained at Douai in its first decade came from Wales. Several of these priests were sent back into the country as part of a design for reconverting the kingdom to the Old Faith, and an early focus was on north Wales. One centre of activity was the Llŷn Peninsula in Caernarvonshire, where an underground Catholic network supported by local gentlemen fostered missionary activity. Thomas Owen of Plas Du sheltered six priests while his brother, Hugh, was a prominent lay conspirator on the continent who was implicated in several plots against Elizabeth I and allegedly had a role in fomenting the Gunpowder Plot. A case in Star Chamber between 1578 and 1581 lifted the lid on this clandestine activity, which included potentially treasonous correspondence (some of it in Welsh for the purposes of secrecy) between north Wales and the continent.[19] In the Flintshire parish of Overton in 1581, a young girl, Elizabeth Orton, claimed to have experienced ecstatic visions of Christ, the Virgin and Mary Magdalene which caused her to denounce 'the religion of the Protestauntes' and 'their wicked and accursed Churche', and which convinced her to become a recusant.[20] She condemned those who temporised by attending Protestant services although their convictions lay with the Catholic Church. Accounts of her visions circulated among the Catholic underground in north

Wales and beyond as part of a drive for Catholic renewal in the area. This was a dangerous moment with the arrival of the Jesuits Robert Persons and Edmund Campion on a mission to convert England a year before, as well as a Catholic revolt in nearby Ireland and circulating rumours about the queen's fitness to rule. There was an upsurge in local recusancy cases following Elizabeth's visions, and her case was followed by a repressive local, and indeed national, campaign against Catholics, which culminated in a draconian Act of Parliament that imposed swingeing fines on recusants. As the historian of this episode has noted, these events:

> underline the point that Wales was no sleepy backwater remote from the international politics of the European Counter-Reformation. Riddled with latent conservative sentiment and overt Catholic allegiance, it was a gateway through which a violent reconversion of the queen's realms with the aid of a foreign power might have been launched.[21]

Supporting these reconversion plans was an attempt by the Welsh exiles and missionaries to reach out to their countrymen and women through a culturally-sensitive propaganda effort which stressed the essential Welshness of the Old Faith, and which sought to counter the arguments of reformers like Salesbury and Davies. The Anglesey exile Dr Owen Lewis wrote in 1579 to an Italian cardinal requesting support for a programme of Catholic printing in Welsh. He argued that this was necessary as 'the English have seen to it that their heretical books … have been translated into Welsh, in order to contaminate with heretical disgrace these thirteen shires, which hitherto have been kept in a more healthy state through their ignorance of English heresies written in English'.[22] Despite his entreaties, the Catholic hierarchy paid rather more attention to the reconversion of England than of Wales, and the calls for a coordinated campaign in the vernacular were not heeded. More *ad hoc* schemes were thus launched to try to influence Welsh public sentiment. Some vernacular Catholic texts were produced but these usually required publication on the continent, such as Morys Clynnog's catechism, *Yr Athravaeth Gristnogawl* (*Christian Teaching*), which was published in Milan in 1568. This volume certainly entered the principality as it received a printed response (which no longer survives) in 1571 from the Protestant controversialist and client of the Earl of Leicester, Lewys Evans, who described Clynnog's text as being 'lately spread secretly abroad in Wales'.[23] The most noteworthy example of such Catholic printing in Welsh, however, is *Y Drych Cristianogawl* (*The Christian Mirror*) probably written by the Douai missionary Robert Gwyn.[24] This was the first book ever to be printed on Welsh soil in 1586/7, although it needed to be published secretly in a cave near Llandudno. This fascinating text sought to answer Davies and Salesbury's Protestant challenge partly by addressing the Welsh people directly (as 'the beloved Welsh') and partly by adopting their tactic of linking together faith and history. The *Drych* argued that their ancient Welsh language was being betrayed by the country's Protestant rulers, the gentry, who, it claimed, were being seduced by English wealth and power and were thus abandoning their native tongue and heritage. The text presented Catholicism as the natural faith of the Welsh people descending in an uninterrupted line from the Britons' original conversion soon after the crucifixion. The volume, moreover, sought to be an inclusive text in providing spiritual succour for all social classes through its adoption of what it described as 'the most common and vulgar language now used by the Welsh people'.

Y Drych was an interesting, if isolated, attempt to adopt the technologies of domestic printing for disseminating the Catholic message to the Welsh in their own tongue. Moreover, it represents a fascinating insight into the battle for Welsh souls as well as for the soul of Wales with its arguments that the Old Faith was an integral part of Welsh history, consciousness and identity, an argument which had real resonance in the semi-reformed heartlands of north Wales in particular. Yet *Y Drych* also illustrates the problems Catholics faced with reaching their audiences.[25] The volume was the only part of a much larger manuscript which managed to get into print, probably because of the logistical problems presented by the need to use a secret press. There was little prospect of greater access to domestic publishing networks, and the authorities were primed to seize Catholic material (as they had in the Llŷn recusancy case). In 1581, for example, magistrates ordered that churchwardens in Denbighshire be examined 'touching recusants', and also that they be asked whether they knew of 'any seditious people callinge theim selves Jesuits … and what bookes they

use'. These churchwardens were also to be examined as to whether
they knew of 'any that keepeth any bookes repugnant to the doctrine
now allowed & sett furth', or of any 'that useth eyther by proff[esie]s
or rymes any words agaynst the service nowe appoynted & allowed'.[26]
Following his arrest in 1580, the Welsh Catholic priest Richard White
(or Gwyn) was asked whether he carried or 'reade any bookes of service sett out by the authoritie of the byshope of Rome?'[27] It was a
dangerous business to produce, distribute and possess illicit Catholic
texts, and this helps explain the prevalence of manuscript circulation
in their religious culture.[28] Indeed, Robert Gwyn was explicit in one
of his writings about keeping the tract short so that it could readily be
carried in secret by the faithful.[29]

Gwyn did not restrict himself to the printed text. Before he arrived
in Wales from Douai, he wrote letters in Welsh back home (at the
encouragement of William Allen, head of the Douai seminary) encouraging friends and family to remain true to the Catholic Church. We
know that he wrote at least three of these epistles, although only one
has survived, the lengthy 'Na all fod un ffydd onyd yr Hen Ffydd'
('There can be no faith save the Old Faith') which he completed at the
end of 1574. We also know that this text was copied and redistributed
through scribal networks for the support and edification of the local
Catholic community, and that it spread into south Wales too. Gwyn also
circulated other manuscript tracts in Welsh, describing one of them as
being for the 'unlearned' and for 'every common man' who wished to
prosper in the Catholic faith. He also produced (while back in Rome)
a manuscript entitled 'Gwssanaeth y Gwyr Newydd' ('The Service of
the New Men'), which argued vociferously against Catholics attending Protestant services.[30] This tract is interesting for its presentation of
Protestantism as an alien, English faith and no part of Welsh culture.
He described the reformers as 'gwyr newydd o loyger' or, 'the new men
of England', but even applied this label to those within Wales itself,
referring to the 'gwyr newydd o Loyg[e]r, ie, a Chymru hefyd' ('new
men of England, yes, and [of] Wales too').[31] Gwyn thus sought explicitly
to position the reformed faith as something novel, alien and fundamentally un-Welsh, and attempted to wrestle concepts of Welsh religious
identity from the hands of Protestants like Salesbury and Davies.

Robert's namesake, Richard Gwyn, also known as 'Richard White',
also sought to mesh Welsh culture and Catholic popular piety by

composing metrical Welsh verses against the Protestants and their faith which circulated orally.[32] One of his poems summarises for a popular audience Robert Gwyn's (and also Robert Person's) arguments against attending Protestant services, singing that 'the English Bible is a whim-wham, / Full of crooked imaginings', while the Protestant minister was characterised as one 'who destroys the saints'. Elsewhere, White called William Salesbury 'the dirty-nosed translator' who was bound for hell. White was Elizabeth Orton's schoolmaster, and was arrested in 1580, tortured and finally executed at Wrexham in October 1584, becoming Wales's first Catholic martyr.[33] The kinds of connections between popular culture, vernacular poetry and Catholicism found in White's verse can also be seen in a more vicious *awdl* or strict-metre poem by Edward Dafydd which came to the authorities' attention towards the end of Elizabeth's reign. Part of the verse ran: 'Rout! Rout out the spurious priesthood, / The illiterate drunken cures ... Rout them with sword you Welsh of British blood: / The murder of Jesus lies in the hearts of the Saxons!'[34] The effort to combine Catholic opposition with a kind of patriotic Welshness had a degree of lingering sympathy in local society, but such calls for violent resistance never managed to animate anything more than a tiny minority into some form of action.

The Catholics' use of manuscript and oral cultures was often deft and, moreover, it meshed with the familiar vernacular cultures of late medieval Wales when religious transmission through such forms was the norm.[35] Indeed, manuscript texts may have retained a status and prestige in sixteenth century society which printed volumes could not match. However, the Catholics remained at a significant disadvantage in the battle to reverse the Protestant tide and win the argument about the 'true' religious heritage of the Welsh people. As an outlawed faith in a land where public servants were required either silently to draw a veil over their Catholic sympathies or actively to root it out from their communities, Catholicism increasingly existed on the margins, divorced from the structures of power which supported and promoted the Church of England. The Elizabethan period of political intriguing and missionary activity never flowered into a more militant and aggressive collective movement in Wales. There were, however, several instances of Welsh involvement in high-profile plots which highlighted the zealotry of individual Catholics. Notable here was the participation of the leading Denbighshire gentleman Thomas Salusbury of Lleweni in the Babington Plot of 1586. This involved a plan to assassinate Elizabeth I and put Mary, Queen of Scots on the throne, but it was foiled easily by the Elizabethan authorities. Salusbury, along with an associate, Edward Jones of Plas Cadwgan in Denbigshire, was apprehended and put to death on Tower Hill.

Efforts at policing local Catholics intensified around times of crisis, when recusants would be presented in greater numbers to the local courts (they were always there, of course, but the order to 'round up the usual suspects' probably went out at such moments) and directives for more rigorous enforcement arrived from the political centre. Missionary activity continued at a reduced level in the later sixteenth and early seventeenth centuries, and anxiety about the pervasiveness of Catholic sympathies in parts of Wales periodically resurfaced.[36] However, with the embedding of the Protestant settlement and the growing acceptance of the narrative, drawn from official propaganda and examples such as Thomas Salusbury, that Catholicism should be equated with treason and foreignness, recusancy contracted during the seventeenth century to heartlands in Flintshire and Monmouthshire. This is not to say that individual gentlemen were not locally significant in sustaining enclaves of sympathy for 'Yr Hen Ffydd', however. For example, the Barlows of Slebech in Pembrokeshire were obdurate Catholics across the generations and hostile observers reported that they fostered a culture of recusant activity in the area.[37] The same was true of the Turbervilles of Pen-llin in Glamorgan, the Edwardses of Chirk in Denbighshire and the notorious Morgans of Llantarnam in Monmouthshire. It was, however, the north-east and the south-east of the country that saw the most significant levels of Catholic activity during the seventeenth century.

The political earthquake of the Gunpowder Plot in 1605 threw some unwelcome light on these enclaves, although they remained quiescent and Welsh connections with the plot were tenuous.[38] Perhaps the most notable development of the Jacobean period was the establishing of a Jesuit mission, the College of St Francis Xavier, at Cwm near Monmouth in the 1620s.[39] It is unsurprising that the college was established in this area as Catholic numbers, under the protection of local families and Jesuits such as George Morgan, had swollen in the early seventeenth century. The Cwm college oversaw a missionary district which covered the whole of Wales, until it was divided into northern and southern units in the 1660s. Secular support for the college was probably given by the wealthy Earls (later Marquises) of Worcester at Raglan Castle in Monmouthshire.

The political breakdown of the early 1640s derived in no small measure from concerns about the influence of Catholicism at all levels of society. As civil divisions spread, anxieties about possible Catholic control of county armouries and magazines intensified, and Parliament tried to disarm leading Catholics such as the Earl of Worcester, and in Montgomeryshire Sir Percy Herbert and Lord Powis, as rumours flew of a 'Welch popish armie' in jaundiced London propaganda sheets.[40] One publication even claimed that Worcester had thousands of Catholic troops ready to mobilise at Raglan, and posed the question which was probably on many minds at this time: 'whether there be not more such evill affected plotters in Wales besides [Worcester himself]?'[41] A later tract recalled the 'base and scurrilous pamphlets cryed up and downe the streets and dispersed in the countrey ... [that] there were subterranean invisible [Catholic] troops mustered underground in Wales'.[42] Catholics like Worcester were prominent supporters of King Charles I's cause, but they earned more opprobrium from their enemies than they did honour for supporting their doomed monarch. After the royalist defeat in the civil wars Catholics in Wales as elsewhere were subjects to fines and sequestration – having their estates seized and their incomes appropriated by the enemy. It was no coincidence that when the arch-opponent of Catholics Oliver Cromwell was rewarded with lands and monies by a grateful Parliament in 1648, he took over a large part of the Earl of Worcester's sequestered estates in south Wales.

The Restoration of 1660 saw the Catholics battered and bruised by the anti-popish drives of the republican years, but there was also scope for expansion as some Anglicans had converted to the Old Faith while the Church of England lay in ruins; such dynamics seem to have been significant in Monmouthshire.[43] Although these Catholic communities eschewed the violent intriguing of the Elizabethan period, they nevertheless remained objects of suspicion; and shifting political winds could turn such suspicion into fear and frenzy. We can see such a dynamic in 1641–2, for example, when a rebellion in Ireland generated flying reports about Catholic infiltration and possible invasion in places like Anglesey and Pembrokeshire. The most spectacular example of anti-Catholic hysteria, however, came with the so-called 'Popish Plot' of 1678–80. The 'Plot' was a fantasy dreamed up by Titus Oates, a former Catholic priest, who maintained that there was a Jesuit conspiracy to assassinate King Charles II and place his Catholic brother James, Duke of York, on the throne. From late 1678 the plot gripped the imaginations of MPs who began to investigate Jesuit activities in the country, and their spotlight soon fell on Cwm and the Catholics of Monmouthshire and Herefordshire.[44] Their interest in this area was perhaps unsurprising for earlier in the decade the Monmouthshire MP, Sir Trevor Williams, had disingenuously claimed that half of the county's population was Catholic, while 'a world of stories of Popish Plots' centring on Monmouthshire was being reported as early as May 1676.[45]

Even more damaging, however, was the way in which the Plot gave oxygen to the anti-popish vitriol of Williams and especially John Arnold of Llanfihangel Crucorney, a man described by one contemporary as 'a vile fellow' possessed of a 'violent and virulent temper'.[46] Arnold had fallen out with Henry Somerset, third Marquis of Worcester (a Protestant but widely suspected of having Catholic sympathies) and, at Parliament's invitation, in the spring of 1678 he gave evidence before the Commons about the shocking prevalence of Catholicism in Monmouthshire.[47] He alleged that masses were said openly in the county and that the college at Cwm had a nefarious influence in local society. The Popish Plot thrust Arnold onto the national stage, and he became a lightning rod for anti-Catholic sentiment, a role he appears to have relished. Arnold offered £200 reward for each priest that was captured and, in alliance with Herbert Croft, bishop of Hereford, led a raid on Cwm in December 1678, seizing its library and effectively closing the mission. As priests were executed in the area because of his activities, in April 1680 Arnold presented himself to the world as the victim of a would-be assassin who had tried to murder him in revenge for his pursuit of Catholics. Arnold claimed that his assailants had cried 'damm you dogge Arnold, now pray for the soule of Captain Evans [an executed Welsh Jesuit] if you have breath'.[48] It seems likely, however, that Arnold fabricated the episode for his own self-promotion, apparently drawing a razor blade lightly over his throat to produce a shallow wound and leaving him with the nickname 'cut-throat Arnold'. Plots bred counter-plots, and fictions nurtured fantasy. Arnold also supposedly bribed a Portuguese Jew with £300 to tell Parliament that he had seen the Marquis of Worcester at mass, while Arnold himself allegedly said that Charles II was a Catholic and should be executed as his father had been, '& then [we] ... shall ... play football with the bastards he leaves behind him'.[49] Arnold was later pursued for his attack on Cwm and ended up in prison after £10,000 damages were awarded against him in a lawsuit for impugning Worcester's reputation.[50] Arnold had supposedly said that Worcester was 'a papist and as deeply concerned in the Popish Plot and as guilty of endeavouring to introduce popery and the subversion of the Protestant religion as any of the Jesuits that justly suffered for it'.[51]

If the period of the Plot was one of delusion and hysteria, however, it nevertheless had lethal consequences in south-east Wales. There was an intense pursuit of Catholics and Jesuits: of the twenty-four martyrdoms in the kingdom between 1678 and 1680, seven occurred in this area. Fathers Philip Evans, John Lloyd and David Lewis were all executed in south-east Wales in 1679 alone. Others were hounded to their deaths, 'being martyred by the misery and sufferings of their hiding places on mountain tops ... and dens and caves of the earth'.[52] The Jesuit mission was virtually destroyed, with one north Wales recusant describing it in 1679 as 'totally rooted up', and adding that the Catholic community around St Winifred's had 'fared a little better ... but God knows how long it is to last, for we live in constant fears and perils'.[53] The collapse was not complete, however, and although Monmouthshire's Catholics suffered a severe blow over the Popish Plot, they endured, recovering by the early eighteenth century and continuing to be an important part of the local confessional landscape.[54] Catholicism had a brief vision of toleration, and even of influence and power, in James II's short reign (1685–8), but this was quickly snuffed out by the 'Glorious Revolution' and the accession of William and Mary.

The fortunes of Welsh Catholicism chart something of a paradox but one which points to the highly regionalised and variegated nature of early modern Wales. The paradox is Catholicism's steady decline through most of the principality combined with its vigorous, almost open and public, presence in the north-east and south-east of the country. This points to the significance of regional confessional cultures which had important ties to England, but which were none-theless enduring features of the Welsh religious landscape. Although Catholicism did not have the resources to match the propaganda efforts of the Established Church, it nevertheless made strenuous efforts to present itself in print, in manuscript and in verse as the authentic embodiment of Welsh cultural values. Glanmor Williams accused Catholic leaders of failing to appreciate the 'national sympathies of the Welsh or the critical need to appeal to them through the medium of the Welsh language'.[55] Such a judgement is problematic, given the efforts of figures such as Robert and Richard Gwyn, but it also fails to appreciate the fact that the Jesuit mission in Wales would not have been so visible and successful in Flintshire and Monmouthshire by the late 1670s were it not for missionaries who could minister to the faithful in their own tongue and also make credible claims to represent an acculturated form of a national faith.[56] These areas represented some of the largest and most significant Catholic enclaves in the Stuart kingdoms outside Ireland, and their relative success seems a testament to the capacity of the Counter-Reformation to integrate with and sup-port Welsh cultural interests. This chapter now turns to consider the other religious nonconformists of early modern Wales: the puritans and dissenters.

PURITANS AND DISSENTERS[57]

As was mentioned in Chapter 3, puritanism and Protestant noncon-formity have been disproportionately influential in the historiography of early modern Wales. The fact that religious nonconformity was a central element of Wales's national identity in the nineteenth and early twentieth centuries, coupled with the origins of this tradition in the sixteenth and seventeenth centuries, has produced a sustained interest in those Protestant men and women who rejected or criticised the Established Church and pursued a more thorough reformation of faith and society. The origins of this historical interest, then, means that we need to be wary of anachronism in our accounts of early nonconformity in Wales and to ensure that we properly contextu-alise the phenomenon and avoid whiggish readings that overstate its contemporary influence and significance. Despite these caveats, however, the story of puritanism and dissent in early modern Wales is a fascinating one which, as is the case with Catholicism and the Established Church, is tied up with questions of language and national identity, and which has important connections with English and continental developments.

The first thing to say about Protestant nonconformity in early modern Wales is that, like Catholicism, it only involved a small minority of the population and that it was geographically quite restricted. It should not surprise us that Wales was hostile territory for early puritanism because, as we have seen, the Reformation itself was a slow and protracted process in the principality. Moreover, puritanism was a complex strand of piety which emphasised scriptural study and the individual's relationship with God. For most Welsh men and women, however, access to a vernacular Bible was difficult, even if they had the capacity to read it, which most, of course, did not. The 1588 Bible and its 1620 successor were expensive texts which were largely controlled and accessed through the Established Church.[58] There was little scope, then, for the kinds of individual and household-based study of the scriptures before a more affordable version was produced. Two puritanically inclined and London-based gentlemen, Sir Thomas Myddelton of Chirk Castle in Denbighshire and Rowland Heylyn of Shrewsbury, determined to rectify this situation.[59] In 1630 they published around 3,000 copies of a quarto-sized Welsh Bible bound with the Prayer Book and Edmwnd Prys's translation of the psalter, an edition which has become known as *Y Beibl Bach* (*The Little Bible*) and which cost around five shillings. The volume's introduction addressed Welsh householders, telling them not to use it only when they visited the church, but rather that 'it must live with you as a friend … like a dear associate and best companion'.[60] One Welsh cleric advised his congregation to sell their shirts to buy a copy as it was more valuable to them than gold. This small text also inspired a sympathetic Welsh puritan, Oliver Thomas (who received 50 of the Bibles), to produce a treatise in 1631, *Carwr y Cymry* (*Friend of the Welshman*), which praised Myddelton and Heylyn, and earnestly encouraged the clergy and laity of Wales to read their Bible daily and to inculcate its message.

Clearly the arrival of a portable vernacular Bible was the cause of much celebration in Wales, but this celebration also highlights the absence of such a text until nearly a century after the break with Rome (distribution of the volume was also slow and was tied up in legal problems), and throws into relief the difficult terrain that puritanism had to navigate in Wales. Two decades after *Y Beibl Bach*'s appearance, one Welsh puritan could still lament that there was hardly one bible to be found among twenty families.[61] Indeed, it is fair to say that the puritan impulse was distinctly muted in the rural and traditionalist principality until shortly before the civil wars. A notable exception to this trend, however, and a remarkable individual who, as much as anyone, represents the beginning of the Welsh nonconformist narrative, was John Penry.[62] Penry was born in the early 1560s to a minor Breconshire gentry family. Although advanced Protestantism was not a feature of this area, Penry went up to Cambridge University in the 1580s, entering one of the centres of English puritanism. He clearly came into contact with forward Protestant thinking there and, although he seems to have begun training for a career in the ministry, instead followed a very different path: that of a radical controversialist and puritan pamphleteer. Penry became convinced of his (and the world's) sinful nature, and also that the Bible offered a template not just for pure living but for the government of the Church and the correct forms of worship a reformed Church required. These convictions would ultimately lead him to the gallows.

In 1586 Penry wrote a lengthy tract regarding what he considered to be the abject condition of the reformed faith in Wales, entitled *Aequity of an Humble Supplication*. In February 1587 Penry persuaded Carmarthen's MP, Edward Donne Lee, to present the publication to Parliament, where it received the enthusiastic support of the Warwickshire puritan and pamphleteer, Job Throckmorton. Penry's text was an impassioned plea for a preaching ministry to be planted in Wales, something which he considered to be a fundamental requirement for advancing true religion there. Penry and like-minded reformers believed that a preaching ministry would awaken people's spirits to the truth of God's Word, and that a sustained effort to support a ministry that expounded regularly on the Scriptures would provide a route to the people's salvation. Contrariwise, the ceremonies and sacraments of the Established Church were seen as tainted and corrupting remnants of the Roman faith which needed to be expunged. Penry's *Aequity* was a fiery denunciation of the Church in Wales which lambasted the 'idle drones now in our ministrie'.[63] This was a patriotic treatise as well as a religious one, and Penry articulated his wish to save 'my deare countrimen' from spiritual desolation. Furthermore, he expressed a conviction that the Welsh were a proud and ancient people and were worthy of greater consideration in matters of religion than they had hitherto received from Parliament or the Crown. Interestingly, Penry drew upon the idea of early British Christianity in the *Aequity*, noting that 'it might greeve us [the Welsh] the lesse to be denied the gospel, unlesse the same were the inheritance which our fore-fathers the Cambrubrittons many hundred yeares agoe possessed in this lande'. Drawing from the same cultural and historical well as Richard Davies in his 'Epistol' of twenty years before, Penry averred that the 'impes of that lifeless and brutish stock of Rome', under the missionary Augustine, had corrupted the pure faith of the Britons. He argued that because the Welsh language had no oaths 'upon the mass' as did English, this was proof that Catholicism came 'but yesterday' into the principality. He continued: when 'ignorance and idolatrie … tooke such deepe roote in England, then it ran over our land also'. A preaching ministry, he thus reasoned, was 'but the possession and inheritaunce of our fathers … restored unto us'.[64] Penry presented the image of the Welsh as a chosen people possessed of a spiritual receptiveness that demanded parliamentary action. This was a similar rhetorical strategy to that of the 1567 translators, but Penry was appropriating the idea of the pure Christian heritage of the Welsh for a much more thoroughgoing vision of country's reformed future.

Penry's bullish criticism of the current state of the Church and the rather intemperate way it was expressed, brought him (and Donne Lee) into trouble. The *Aequity* was seized, and Penry was charged with treason and heresy. Despite the seriousness of the accusations, however, he spent only a month in gaol. He was not cowed by his experience and now embarked on another round of publishing. In 1588 he produced, on a secret press, a pamphlet entitled *An Exhortation*, which he directed to the Lord President of the Council in the Marches, the second Earl of Pembroke. Once again he earnestly requested the establishing of a preaching pastorate in Wales, but called the country's governors, like Pembroke, to account for the country's spiritual shortcomings in an intemperately forthright manner. Penry was drifting far from acceptable discourse and the mainstream of ecclesiastical politics. In 1588–9 he was probably managing the secret press which produced a series of controversial pamphlets that have come to be known as the

'Martin Marprelate' tracts, although it does not appear that he wrote any of the texts it produced. These were satirical diatribes targeting the Church hierarchy. The publications zeroed in on the government of the Church of England by bishops, the institution of episcopacy, which Penry and his associates believed was not only a crypto-Catholic survival from the Roman Church, but was also responsible for the religious corruptions and failings which, Penry claimed, were so debilitating in Wales. Indeed, in *An Exhortation* he described the Welsh bishops as 'the verye ground-worke of … our miserable condition'.[65] The ecclesiastical authorities (or 'ungodly and tirancial Lord Bishops' in Penry's rendering)[66] hunted Penry and his associates down, and he was apprehended in Stepney in March 1593. Although initially charged with inciting insurrection, Penry was ultimately found guilty of publishing scandalous writings against the Church. Rejecting any accusations that he had compromised his allegiance to the queen, Penry appealed to Lord Burghley for clemency as 'a poore young man borne & bredd in the mountaynes of Walles' who had laboured to 'have the blessed seed [of the gospel] … sowen in these barrayne mountaynes'.[67] But to no avail. Penry was executed in May 1593 aged only thirty and left behind him a wife and four small daughters; their names were Deliverance, Comfort, Safety and Sure-Hope.

Penry presented a view of Wales which has proved seductive and compelling for historians. The image of an Established Church which was slothful, corrupt and incapable of meeting the needs of the Welsh people has been an influential one. However, this image was soon challenged. The Elizabethan commentator from Pembrokeshire, George Owen, spoke of a 'store of good and godly preachers' in Wales, which he wished to publicise 'to confound a shameless man [Penry] that of late years to slander all of Wales' had printed 'slanderous' pamphlets misrepresenting the Welsh pastorate.[68] The incumbent of Montgomery in 1618 similarly decried those 'schismatically-rash censurers', citing Penry specifically, who 'layd an heavie aspersion of a Galilaean barrennese upon this countrie', rejecting such complaints as 'causelesse'.[69] His dismissal of Penry's arguments was rather too glib, however, and the lack of a preaching ministry, coupled with the systemic deficiencies of an underfunded Church meant that the ecclesiastical establishment in Wales remained a target for puritan criticism throughout the early modern era. This criticism often came from English commentators, however, and there was little evidence of an indigenous reformist strain in Wales before the 1630s. In many ways, Penry is a compelling and striking individual in early modern Welsh religious history because of his uniqueness: he did not spawn a thriving movement, and puritanism remained a rare phenomenon, perhaps because of the linguistic barriers to forward Protestant ideas and the issues of ready access to the vernacular scriptures.

By the end of the 1630s, however, we encounter puritan enclaves establishing themselves, particularly in bilingual towns of the east and in rural enclaves on the Anglo-Welsh border. Critical here was the community which sprang up around William Wroth in Llanfaches, Monmouthshire. Wroth was a minister and sometime pluralist who had undergone a conversion experience at some point in the 1620s. A beneficiary of the patronage of Sir Edward Lewis of Y Fan near Caerphilly, Wroth's reputation as a 'very godly & sincere' man grew quickly after this time.[70] He became increasingly out of step with the clerical authorities, who questioned him for some type of nonconformity in 1635. Wroth abandoned his living in 1638 and shortly thereafter formed the first separatist church in Wales at Llanfaches; that is to say, he established a congregation which operated outside the Established Church and did not observe its rites or recognise its authority.[71] This was a radical departure and was the first appearance of the form of 'congregationalist' nonconformity which would become influential in Wales in the coming decades. Wroth's church was a key focus for the first wave of Welsh nonconformity and he gathered around him a substantial number of followers and acolytes. Among these were individuals who would become highly influential in the Welsh nonconformist movement over the following two decades, including William Erbery, Henry Walter and Walter Cradock. These men formed the nucleus of a group that saw the meeting of the Long Parliament and the end of Archbishop William Laud's nefarious influence in the Church as a critical moment for their reformist ambitions.[72] They organised petitions to Parliament in December 1640 and February 1641 which lamented the lack of preaching in Wales and called for a 'seconde reformac[i]on' through the abolition of the Book of Common Prayer and the institution of episcopacy, as well as requesting the planting of an able preaching ministry to meet the people's needs.[73] The second petition was a substantial effort, with some

300 names attached. It survives among the papers of the Herefordshire puritan Sir Robert Harley, a man who gave support, succour and protection to many of this generation of Welsh puritans.[74] The positions articulated in these petitions, then, were truly radical, and they aligned the Welsh reformers with some of the more advanced puritan positions in England. Indeed, the Welsh radicals of the 1630s and early 1640s had close ties with English puritans, particularly those in the city of Bristol. This points to the fact that puritanism was, in many respects, not indigenous to Wales but rather drew on wider intellectual and confessional trends for its initial inspiration and support. It would, however, come to be changed and naturalised by its encounters with Welsh culture and language over the coming decades.

The civil war and the principality's dominant royalism dashed the hopes of the Llanfaches group in the short term. They were scattered abroad – as a chaplain in the New Model Army in the case of William Erbery, or as a preacher in Bristol and then in London in the case of Walter Cradock – but they retained hopes for return and for the religious refoundation of their homeland. Wroth died in 1641 but his spiritual inheritors continued to press for reform in the principality, especially after Parliament emerged victorious from the civil wars in 1646 and looked for friends and sympathisers upon whom it could rely in a hostile ex-royalist territory. Although in a minority, then, these early puritans now had a significance and an influence out of all proportion to their numbers. And they made the argument that the *political* re-education of Wales away from its traditions of royalism would require a thoroughgoing *religious* transformation. The critical moment in this project came in the aftermath of Charles I's execution when, in February 1650, the Rump Parliament established a powerful body to effect the country's spiritual remodelling: the Commission for the Propagation of the Gospel in Wales.[75] This initiative had come about partly in response to a petition from the godly of north Wales which requested assistance for 'our poor brethren and country men' by the removal of 'ignorant and scandalous ministers' and their replacement with 'pious, sound and able men'.[76] This petition probably emerged from the north Walian regicide Colonel John Jones and those associated with the Wrexham congregation of Morgan Llwyd, a man who had been converted by Wroth's protégé, Walter Cradock.[77] The Propagation Commission formally existed from 1650 until 1653, but the enormous influence wielded by its personnel and supporters in the country continued throughout the 1650s.

The parliamentary legislation empowered a group of some seventy-one commissioners to examine clergymen in Wales and dismiss them if they were found unworthy, unsound in doctrine or politically suspect.[78] In their place the commissioners were to install godly ministers to a settled living, or to institute them as itinerant preachers. The commissioners named in the parliamentary ordinance included individuals who had petitioned parliament in 1641 alongside William Wroth, such as Walter Cradock, Ambrose Mostyn, Henry Walter and Richard Symonds. It is worth noting, however, that the propagation commissioners included a significant number of Englishmen, while the Welsh commissioners were drawn largely from the centres of puritan nonconformity such as Cardiff and Wrexham. Welsh cultural heartlands such as Caernarvonshire or Merioneth thus had very little representation on the body. This imparted something of an English cast to the Commission's business which was perhaps reflected in the fact that, although it established schools in Wales for the godly education of young people, these were to operate through the medium of English only.[79] We would be mistaken in assuming that the influence of English personnel was dominant on the ground, however, for the everyday functioning of the Commission's business relied on native Welshmen who were passionate about the spiritual welfare of their fellow countrymen and -women. Prominent among these was Vavasor Powell, a native of Cnwclas in Radnorshire who had been an acolyte of Walter Cradock.[80] Powell had become a follower of the Fifth Monarchy Men, the extreme sect whose members were convinced that the end of days as foretold in the Book of Daniel was at hand. Powell's seventeenth-century biographer portrayed him as a tireless preacher under the aegis of the Propagation Commission, roaming the eastern counties of Wales preaching in both English and Welsh two or three times a day, and for hours at a time.[81]

During its short lifetime the Commission ejected some 278 ministers, a significant proportion of Welsh parishes, and these ejections were concentrated in south Wales. Opponents claimed that commissioners were unable to fill the vacancies caused by their ejection of episcopalian ministers because of the structural weaknesses which had also troubled the Established Church: the relative poverty of Welsh livings; the need to operate through the medium of Welsh; and the upland and dispersed nature of Welsh parishes. Commissioners attempted to address these challenges by falling back on a system of itinerant preaching where individuals moved between parishes which lacked incumbents, giving sermons and instructing the parishioners. However, there were more vacancies than there were itinerants, and even Vavasor Powell himself, dubbed 'the metropolitan of the itinerants', acknowledged that the Commission struggled to recruit enough men who could speak Welsh.[82] Reports circulated of churches left empty and of congregations abandoned by this radical experiment which, to many, seemed more interested in persecution than in reform. Partly because of Powell's visibility amongst the propagators, the Commission also garnered a reputation for nurturing sectarians of the most extreme type who alienated Welsh sensibilities rather than harmonising with them.[83] Concerns about such extremism were hardly assuaged when Powell moved into open opposition against Oliver Cromwell, who had been a conspicuous supporter of the Propagation Commission, when he assumed the role of Lord Protector in 1653. Powell considered this to be a move that betrayed the Commonwealth and the godly principles upon which it had been founded.

For all the problems that the Commission encountered, however, it is clear that it was a critical bridgehead for Protestant nonconformity in Wales, and that the mid-seventeenth century was a crucial moment in the fortunes of Welsh dissenting religious culture. In the Restoration era, for example, the bishop of St Davids observed that the propagation period had advanced heterodox religious ideas in his diocese, or as he described them, 'evill principles ... instilld during ye late rebellion ... [when the people] were governed by itinerants'.[84] More positively, Vavasor Powell noted that the only separatist church in Wales at the outbreak of war was that of Llanfaches, but that by the Restoration there were perhaps twenty such congregations in the country.[85] Many nonconformist denominations gained a presence in the principality in the 1640s and 1650s. Baptists, for example, appeared on the Anglo-Welsh border near Hay-on-Wye and also established a community on the Gower peninsula. Presbyterians also established themselves in some areas, such as the ministry of Philip Henry at Worthenbury in Flintshire. The precocious radical William Erbery has been seen as a 'Seeker', one who rejected all forms of church membership and association.[86] In fact he might be better characterised as following the course of one of the most disturbing religious groups to emerge at this time, the Quakers (certainly this was the path taken by his wife and daughters). In 1652 Erbery asserted that the Welsh were 'pure Britaines', and argued that as they had been the first to accept Christ's gospels, so they would be the first to be blessed with a new liberty of worship: the abolition of all church forms.[87] Another individual who professed religious opinions that had close connections to Quaker ideas about inner spirituality was Morgan Llwyd of Wrexham, and we should spend a moment with this fascinating individual as he was perhaps the most articulate of the Welsh religious radicals from this era.

Llwyd was a native of Merioneth and was converted to a more puritan theological position by Walter Cradock before the outbreak of the civil war.[88] Llwyd thus became associated with the Llanfaches community under Wroth and later served in some capacity with the parliamentarian army. He then settled in Wrexham and ministered to a congregation which became the most significant Independent church in north Wales (described by a royalist in 1661 as 'our Amsterdame ... the [most] faktious town in England' [sic]),[89] although he evangelised throughout the principality's northern counties.[90] Llwyd was a well-connected individual who corresponded with a wide range of English ecclesiastics and was also influenced by the mystical writings of the German theologian Jacob Böehme. Llwyd is also noteworthy because he was the most prolific publisher among the Welsh puritans of this period, and also because he did the most to connect radical ideas about reformed worship to concepts of Welshness. Unlike many of his contemporaries, Llwyd published bilingually, producing eight texts in Welsh and three in English, as well as a corpus of unpublished poetry in both languages. His works were determined efforts not just to explain the critical importance of a godly life to his readers, but, more ambitiously, to suggest a remaking of Wales itself as a spiritual collective, a new puritan nation.[91] As the modern authority on Llwyd observed, he 'laboured to make Wales puritan by first making puritanism Welsh'.[92] Llwyd implored the people of Wales to open their eyes to a life of the spirit which, he claimed, was their destiny. In his 1653 work *Gwaedd Ynghymru yn Wyneb Pob Cydwybod* (*A Cry in Wales in the Face of Every Conscience*), he addressed the Welsh people directly (as Richard Davies had done in 1567): 'O people of Wales! My voice is to you ... I shout at you! The dawn is broken, the sun is rising on you ... Awaken (O Welshman)! ... Behold, the world and its pillars are shaking'.[93] As with his sometime allies, the Fifth Monarchists, Llwyd believed that recent political events demonstrated that the kingdom of Christ was at hand; and he believed that the Welsh people, properly reformed and enlightened of course, were critical to the establishing of godly rule on earth. He thus elaborated a vision of the national community new-made, refashioned by the truths which had been revealed through the shattering of the Established Church's ecclesiastical control. This was not just a liberation of the individual spirit; he foresaw his nation's liberation from spiritual bondage.

As we have seen other authors attempt before him, Llwyd also drew on patriotic ideas of Wales's long and prestigious religious heritage to naturalise his conception of a spiritually emancipated nation. In perhaps his most famous composition, *Llyfr y Tri Aderyn* (*The Book of the Three Birds*) of 1653/4, he connected the early British church to Wales's current spiritual condition.[94] Llwyd maintained that the Welsh had been 'steadfast unto death in behalf of the true faith', and offered them up as one of God's chosen peoples who would have a crucial role in realising the establishment of a New Jerusalem. He dilated on this idea in *Gwaed Ynghymru* too, stating:

> O you, the race and descendants of the Ancient Britons! Listen to the history of your ancestors and remember how it once was, so that you can understand how it is now, that you can know how it will be, so you may start to prepare yourselves.[95]

Llwyd saw part of his mission to be opening Welsh eyes to the wonder of God's message and the imminence of His judgement. As they had once been the first to receive the God's Word in Britain, so the Welsh would now be the first to assimilate and spread the pristine truth that the Lord was revealing through His awesome power in these, the end of days. Allegorical and elusive, Llwyd's texts were superb pieces of imaginative prose which remain an important part of the Welsh literary canon.

Llwyd's visions, of course, would not come to pass. The puritan movement in civil war Wales was riven by differences both theological

and political, and the reformers' ambitions for religious emancipation were dashed by the Restoration of monarchy and the Established
Church. There was a series of clerical ejections in Wales between 1660
and 1662 which saw some 130 ministers removed from their livings
for nonconformity.[96] These ejections were concentrated in the south
and east of the country, places where the Propagation Commission
had been especially active. Some of the more violent puritans of the
previous decade, such as Vavasor Powell, found themselves in gaol; he
would die in the Fleet Prison in 1670 after years of incarceration. The
re-Establishment of the Church of England began a period of fitful
persecution for Welsh nonconformists under the Act of Uniformity
(1662) and the so-called 'Clarendon Code'. The Quakers, perhaps the
most troubling of the novel sects which sprang up during the interregnum, were particular targets for the authorities, but it would be
wrong to characterise this era as one of sustained and determined
repression. What soon became clear, however, was that although religious nonconformity was everywhere in a minority, it was now part of
the fabric of Welsh life, particularly in the south. It is also evident that
religious Independents and Congregationalists were the predominant
strain in Welsh nonconformist culture, and that this was a legacy of the
influential Llanfaches congregation and its progeny, the Propagation
Commission.[97]

The indulgence of sympathetic local gentry figures was often
important in determining the degree of toleration for local nonconformity. This was the case in Swansea, where a Dissenting school
was established which was 'countenanced by the leading men of
the country'.[98] Towns such as Swansea, Carmarthen, Brecon and
Haverfordwest were notable refuges for nonconformists after the
Restoration, while Glamorgan and Monmouthshire had the greatest concentration of Independent churches in the mid-1670s.[99]
Haverfordwest's town elders tolerated Quakers and the borough
even elected a dissenter, Thomas Owen, as its Member of Parliament
in 1679. Denominational boundaries were not hard and fast: members could move between different groups. That said, the Baptists
had significant concentrations in parts of Breconshire, Glamorgan
and later Pembrokeshire, while Quaker communities could be found
in Merioneth, Montgomeryshire and Radnorshire.[100] Merioneth's
Quakers, however, were severely compromised by the decision of some

2,000 of their number to escape Wales's persecution and establish the so-called 'Welsh Tract' in Pennsylvania in the early 1680s.[101]

The generation of dissenters who came of age during the 1660s and 1670s were significant in developing Morgan Llwyd's project of assimilating nonconformity more fully within Welsh culture. The press would be important in this process, and a crucial figure in this regard was Stephen Hughes of Meidrim, Carmarthenshire.[102] An old propagator, Hughes was central to the Restoration drive to produce religious texts in the Welsh language. He challenged those who maintained that it 'was unnecessary to print anything in the world of books in Welsh but that the people [of Wales] should learn English' to come to a knowledge of God, asking rhetorically, 'O Lord, how could this happen unless you were to make miracles?'[103] Hughes came to be associated with an ecumenical, though dissenter-inspired, venture called the Welsh Trust from the mid-1670s. The Trust, with Hughes's assistance, produced a new and affordable edition of the Welsh Bible in 1678, with some 8,000 copies printed, of which 1,000 were given away free of charge to the needy.[104] In this venture, Hughes was joined by another alumnus of the Propagation years, Charles Edwards, a scholar who, in the 1670s, would produce a classic of Welsh prose, *Y Ffydd Ddi-ffuant* (*The Unfeigned Faith*), which refashioned the history of Welsh Protestantism for dissenting sensibilities; this was Richard Davies without the surplice. In addition to his work with the Welsh Trust, Stephen Hughes was also a notable translator and publisher in his own right. He produced a Welsh translation of Bunyan's *Pilgrim's Progress* as well as editions of the popular Welsh religious verses of the cleric Rees Prichard which could be memorised and recited by the faithful. Hughes encouraged the expansion of literacy among the Welsh by adding to his texts the alphabet and instructions on how to read, in much the same way as Sir John Prise had done in 1546. Hughes's efforts provided important momentum for the Cambricising of nonconformity and its assimilation within Welsh-language culture.

The Toleration Act of 1689 provided freedom of worship for Wales's nonconformists (although not its Catholics) as long as they were licensed by the authorities. Although prejudice against them from the Anglican majority continued, dissenters now had a degree of peace and security. Nonconformists remained a minority of the Welsh population, however, and dissent was largely confined to the south, although Llwyd's Wrexham provided an outpost in the north. We should not, then, overstate Protestant nonconformity's influence in the principality at this time, nor should we connect it too readily with the later emergence of Methodism and the flowering of Welsh dissent in the modern era. However, it is clear that the mid-seventeenth century was pivotal in establishing nonconformity as a permanent feature of Welsh society. It was in 1648 that Walter Cradock famously told the Long Parliament that 'the Gospel is run over the mountaines between Brecknockshire and Monmouthshire as the fire in the thatch', and, once kindled, this was not a fire that could readily be extinguished.[105] This era was also crucial in imprinting a particular character on Welsh dissent which favoured forms of religious Independency and congregationalism. As we have seen, this period was also significant for nonconformity's movement away from English influences and bilingual centres into a more thoroughly Welsh milieu. The efforts of Llwyd and Hughes to naturalise nonconformity in Wales, to incorporate it within vernacular historical and linguistic cultures, would also prove influential. Although dissent did not represent the 'national faith' of the Welsh by 1689, nonconformists of this period could nonetheless draw upon an increasingly influential set of ideas and arguments that located their faith within rather than against concepts of Welsh identity.

5

'The Communion of One Tongue': Language and Society

This chapter considers perhaps the most important aspect of early modern Welsh identity: language. The prevalence of the Welsh language is one of the most salient defining features of Welsh society in this period. It has been estimated that perhaps 90 per cent of the population were monolingual Welsh speakers at this time.[1] This, of course, had a profound influence on concepts of Welshness and on the dynamics of social and cultural change in an era defined by closer political, social and cultural ties with England. The Welsh language faced numerous challenges in this period, principally in the realms of law, politics and administration from which, following the 1536 Act of Union, the Welsh language was formally excluded. As we shall see, however, Welsh remained a necessary, albeit largely invisible, component in these domains across the sixteenth and seventeenth centuries. The Acts of Union also produced an unusual situation in which some Welsh-speaking communities found themselves placed within England, while English-language communities, some of long standing, some of more recent coinage, were to be found in Wales. This chapter reviews their experiences within this context of linguistic and social change.

An influential idea within early modern Welsh historiography concerns the process of 'Anglicisation' believed to have derived from closer ties with England through the Union. Historians and literary scholars have seen this as a socially differentiated process, with elites turning their backs upon their country and culture as they were seduced by cultural trends and social opportunities emanating from east of Offa's Dyke, while the lower orders remained monoglot and true to their cultural origins. This chapter argues that the speed and completeness of this process has been overstated, and that the early modern era should be understood as a period in which the gentry remained integral parts of their cultural and social communities. A countervailing force to the Anglicising drift in policy laid down by the Anglo-Welsh union was the provision for the vernacularisation of the Bible. As this has already been discussed in Chapter 3, the current chapter concerns itself more with what might be described as the 'secular' domains of language use, although such a distinction is highly artificial, given the presence of religion in all aspects of early modern life. This chapter argues that Welsh remained a key social and cultural referent for practically all the principality's inhabitants throughout the sixteenth and seventeenth centuries.

Welsh was the medium of most people's daily discourse and constituted an integral part of their social identities. A powerful suggestion of the close relationship between language use and identity comes from George Owen of Henllys in Pembrokeshire. In the 1590s he described a situation in his county where speakers of English (the descendants of old Norman and Flemish settlers in the south of the shire) and speakers of Welsh were divided into separate communities along an ancient boundary called the 'Landsker'.[2] He noted a parish which lay on the borders of these communities where one encountered 'a pathe waye parteinge the Welshe and Englishe, and on the on[e] side speaking all English, the other all Welshe'.[3] Moreover, Owen described these two communities as 'nations', suggesting how they operated as socially as well as linguistically distinct groups.[4] Owen was probably exaggerating the profundity of the separation between these linguistic communities, but his example does suggest how central language was to notions of identity in this period. As we have seen, the Welsh word for 'language', *iaith*, was also a synonym for Wales itself: the country was defined as the community of Welsh-speakers. As an important modern essay on the language in this period puts it, Welsh was 'not only the sole medium of communication for the bulk of the population but also the most tangible and significant badge of national identity'.[5]

Owen's discussion of English-speaking southern Pembrokeshire highlights the fact that, although the Welsh language was dominant in most parts of the country, there were areas where English was a significant presence. Pembrokeshire's 'Englishry' was the most extensive of these, but others were to be found in regions which had a long legacy of Anglo-Norman settlement, including the Gower peninsula and, the Vale in Glamorgan (although Welsh was making significant inroads here), as well as the eastern parts of counties such as Flintshire, Radnorshire and Monmouthshire which bordered England. In addition, there were zones, usually surrounding these Anglophone areas, where a bilingual culture prevailed.[6] English would also have been a significant presence in many of Wales's small towns, a number of which had their origins as English plantation boroughs in the Middle Ages. There was also a degree of English in-migration in parts of the country, which would have required a degree of bilingual adaptation, a notable example being the settlement of English men and women in western Montgomeryshire in the 1570s when lordships in the area were controlled by the Earl of Leicester.[7] Bilingualism in early modern Wales was also a product of class and occupation: the lay and clerical elites became increasingly bilingual in this period, while some facility in the English language would have been required for drovers who moved their cattle from the Welsh uplands into English markets, and also for traders in wools, butter and other commodities who had regular business with places like Shrewsbury and Bristol. Indeed, William Salesbury published a short guide on Welsh pronunciation in 1550 which was partly to cater for demand among English-speakers in the Marches who wished to acquire a knowledge of Welsh, 'eyther for their promotions and lyvynges, eyther els for trade of marchau[n]dice and other their affayres'.[8]

The presence of English was not the only discontinuity within Wales's linguistic landscape. Differences in dialect could also be significant. In his survey of sixteenth-century Wales, Humphrey Llwyd described the 'tongue' of Cardiganshire's inhabitants as 'the finest of all the other people of Wales', while people from the north spoke 'the purer [Welsh] without permixtion' which was 'nearest to the ancient British', but those of the south had the 'rudest and coarsest' language 'because it hath greatest affinity with strange tongues'.[9] A long history of interaction with English-speakers meant that borrowings and loan words appeared in the Welsh spoken in the south and along the English border. In 1672, Stephen Hughes, a Carmarthenshire man, requested readers to make allowances for what he called his 'poor Anglicised Welsh', which had a difference in vocabulary and word forms from the 'excellent Welsh they have in Gwynedd [that is, north Wales]'.[10] In 1551, William Salesbury apologised for writing his translation of the gospels in the north Walian dialect as he was unfamiliar with that of the south and thus, 'because we are different', he worried that some passages might sound foolish or unseemly to southern ears.[11] The 1567 translation of the New Testament was rendered in Salesbury's (rather idiomatic) north Wales dialect, but, tellingly, he included south Walian forms as marginal annotations to allow all Welsh people easier access to the gospels. The Book of Revelation in this edition, however, which was translated by Thomas Huet, precentor of St David's, was produced in the dialect of south west Wales, which caused problems of intelligibility for readers and auditors from other parts of the country.[12] The author of the Catholic text *Y Drych Cristianogawl* noted that he employed a mixture of southern and northern dialect words in his work so that 'ordinary people' from the 'two provinces' (*dwywlad*) might understand his text.[13] The main division was a broad and ill-defined difference between what was perceived as a purer and more prestigious Welsh of the north and a more corrupted and less valued Welsh in the south. These differences were real and fostered a degree of cultural separation, although the rift was not quite as great as Thomas Jones suggested in 1684, when he wrote that Welsh and Hebrew were more alike than the Welsh spoken in the north and south of the country.[14] Despite these dialectical differences, however, contemporaries recognised themselves as belonging to a common linguistic and thus national community. Indeed, because of the influence of print in this period, particularly the translations of the Prayer Book and the Bible, the significance of these differences was considerably reduced.

An often overlooked but nonetheless fascinating part of this linguistic community was those Welsh-speaking areas which the Acts of Union apportioned to England rather than to Wales.[15] The union legislation paid little heed to patterns of language use in drawing its administrative boundaries and, as a result, Welsh-speaking places like Clun and Archenfield ended up in Shropshire and Herefordshire and remained Cambrophone for many decades afterward. In his 'Description of Cambria', published as part of Powel's *Historie* in the 1580s, Humphrey Llwyd observed that 'the Welsh toong is commonlie used and spoken Englandward ... as in Herefordshire, Glocestershire and a great part of Shropshire'.[16] He went on to note the 'divers lord-ships which be added to other shires [that] … were taken heretofore for parts of Wales, and in most part of them at this daie the Welsh language is spoken', before enumerating several Welsh-speaking lord-ships which now fell on the English side of the 'border'.[17] A brief of 1608 concerning the jurisdiction of the Council in the Marches noted that, in the English shires which lay on the Welsh border, 'the Welch tonge even to this daie is as frequent and as usuall as in other shieres in Wales'.[18] We should recall Llwyd's 1573 map, *Cambriae Typus*, and consider that, although this was primarily his historical rendering of an expanded Wales, to a degree Llwyd's cartographic image also rep-resented this Welsh linguistic dimension. The Welsh culture of such areas can be seen in the personal names and patronymics that crop up in the wills of men and women which were proved in Hereford's consistory court and also in those parishes which, while a part of England, remained within the diocese of St David's.[19] Defamation cases involving words spoken in Welsh continued in the area well into the eighteenth century.[20] In Ludlow's town court, we hear Welsh slan-ders being thrown about and involving individuals with names like 'Sion ap Hoel Phylips'. The town clerks needed some assistance in such cases, and there is an endorsement on one court case from the 1590s which reads, 'I pray you Mr Roger Evans, lay downe thes Englishe words … in yo[u]r right Welshe phrase to be entred in declarac[i]on'.[21] The Shropshire borough of Oswestry (which lay in St Asaph dio-cese) retained a strongly Welsh character in the early modern era, with many patronymics and Welsh occupational names among its inhabitants. The churchwardens of Oswestry also paid money in the later sixteenth century for a Welsh Bible, psalter and common prayer book.[22] The Welsh bard Wiliam Llŷn lived and died here in 1580.[23] It would be intriguing to know more about these linguistic communi-ties, their histories in the sixteenth and seventeenth centuries, and the manner in which their members constructed their ideas of selfhood as Welsh-speakers in England. Like Llwyd's *Cambriae Typus*, their pres-ence renders problematic our confident and easy location of Wales's confines in this period by relying only on its administrative borders. This issue is discussed in greater depth in Chapter 9.

If the union legislation paid little heed to the linguistic contours along the Anglo-Welsh border, some scholars have argued that the so-called 'language clause' of the 1536 statute did considerable damage to the Welsh language's integrity and status. Given the overwhelming preponderance of Welsh throughout most of the principality, this provision in the union settlement might have represented a potentially serious blow to prevailing concepts of Welsh status and identity. As was discussed in Chapter 1, this clause provided that legal and administrative processes in Wales be conducted in English only, and that English-speaking individuals alone were to be admitted to local offices. Essentially the government of Wales was to be conducted wholly in English. Although an understandable provision in the unification of legal and administrative systems, this nonetheless relegated the position of the Welsh language in native society, effectively divorcing it from the structures of power: if you wanted to get ahead in Wales, you needed to speak English. Although it is clear that Tudor administrators were not attempting systematically to eradicate the Welsh language, this clause nevertheless ensured that Welsh was henceforward to be a second-class language, and that English was to be the tongue of power and authority.[24] The social and cultural consequences of this were profound, but we need to understand that, despite what might appear to have been rather dire consequences for the language, in practical terms the domains of law and administration could not function without Welsh having a robust presence.

At the outset, we should be careful not to overemphasise the break with previous practice represented by the 1536 language clause. There is considerable evidence that English was being employed more and more in the administrative and judicial bodies of Wales *before* the union.[25] A leading historian has written that in Wales, long before the union, English was regarded as 'the language of lordship and power, of social aspiration and economic advancement'.[26] In many ways, therefore, the union statutes merely made existing practice mandatory and institutionalised developments which were already being felt strongly throughout the country. It is also the case that many Welsh scholars, gentlemen and clerics were supportive of, or at least paid lip service to, the drift of Tudor policy for encouraging the adoption of English among the country's administrative class. The great humanist and Protestant reformer William Salesbury, for example, produced in 1547 a *Dictionary in Englyshe and Welshe*. Salesbury lauded the prevailing governmental ideology that a single language would help facilitate the

unification of Wales and England, and the licence he and the printer
John Walley obtained for this publication noted that it was intended
so 'our welbeloved subjects in Wales may the soner attayne and learne
our mere englyshe tonge'.[27] In the book's dedication to Henry VIII,
Salesbury lauded the union's intention of removing differences in laws
and language between the two countries, noting: 'what great hatred
debate & stryffe hathe rysen emongeste men by reason of dyversitie of
language and what a bonde and knotte of love and frendshyppe the
communion of one tonge is'.[28] This is a surprising statement coming
from the man revered for producing the Welsh translation of the New
Testament, but we should acknowledge that Salesbury was addressing Henry VIII, who had little time for cultural diversity within his
realms. Moreover, Salesbury's priority was to bring his countrymen
to a knowledge of the scriptures, which were then only available in
English. It is likely he was keen to encourage bilingualism among the
Welsh elite and heads of households rather than any replacement of
the Welsh language with English. Indeed, soon after Henry's death
Salesbury produced another treatise designed to instruct the English
how to speak and read the Welsh language, a volume which he reis-
sued in 1567.[29] Salesbury evidently came to reason that too many souls
would be lost waiting for the Welsh to learn English, and his pride
and confidence in the Welsh language's capacity to be the vehicle for
God's word shone through in his vernacularising efforts which were
discussed in Chapter 3. However, his comments in the 1547 dedication
alert us to the political and rhetorical environment which prevailed
for decades after the 1530s, in which lip service needed to be paid to
the superiority and authority of English over Welsh.

Despite the rather pejorative attitude towards linguistic minorities
emanating from the political centre, however, there was a significant
gap between theory and practice, and Welsh continued to have a significant, albeit unofficial, role in law and administration after 1536.[30]
It would be very difficult, for example, for the English common law
to function in a society where the vast majority of those who made
up the accused, the plaintiff and the witnesses in law courts could not
express themselves in anything but Welsh. The same applied to the
civil side of the court, where it is likely that arbitration of disputes
was conducted orally in Welsh. Although the judges of the great sessions were English appointees who usually spoke no Welsh, those

who populated their courts were not. Some among the authorities recognised this. In 1576, for example, the vice-president of the Council in the Marches, Sir William Gerard, discussed the appointment of justices to the great sessions, arguing that one judge on each circuit should 'understande the Welche tonge, for nowe the justice[s] … must use some interpretor, And therefore many tymes the evidence is tolde accordyng to the mynde of the interpretor.'[31] This was a remarkable admission from one of the most senior officials in Wales that the Welsh language formed an integral part of the legal process which was supposedly wholly Anglicised.[32] Even at the Council in the Marches itself, however, it is evident that use of interpreters was normal practice for witnesses 'not havinge the Englishe tounge.'[33] In dealing with a population which largely spoke only Welsh, we should not be surprised to discover that the language was present at many phases of the legal process. Another revealing insight was offered in 1634 by Timothy Tourneur, the Deputy Justice of north Wales. He wrote to Secretary Windebank about a high-profile murder case in Anglesey and noted that the prosecution had made an unusual request to have a jury which all understood (although not necessarily spoke) English. He observed, however, that this was 'noe legall challenge in a Welsh country where the witnesses speake Welsh and where English witnesses are interpr[e]ted in Welsh when it is required'.[34]

It seems certain that in many legal cases, initial statements and depositions from witnesses were taken in Welsh, although these were rendered into English when submitted to the court. In 1617, for example, Edward Griffith ap Ednyfed gave a deposition concerning the killing of some sheep to the Denbighshire great sessions court. His testimony is written entirely in English, but it ends with his statement that one William Rogers had spent the night in Llanrwst, 'as farr as this deponente understood him, for hee can noe Englishe, nor the other noe Welshe'.[35] So despite his English deposition, ap Ednyfed did not speak the language! One legal historian has argued that the unusual detail and richness found in depositions among the Welsh great sessions papers, material which contains a good deal of extraneous detail that was usually filtered out in English proceedings, was probably the product of the initial evidence being given in Welsh. This oral evidence was then rendered into English by a translator-scribe, and the need to remain faithful to the original testimony, rather than the legalistic summary which was characteristic of English assizes, produced a legal record which was subtly different to that found in the English courts.[36] Although this process could not be documented (all legal materials had to be in English), it seems that a parallel, almost invisible, Welsh-language system *had* to operate next to the English one to ensure the smooth execution of justice in the principality.

It is also worth noting that this issue of language and translation was most pressing for the higher courts, which had English justices, and was much less of a concern in the lower courts. In the quarter sessions, for example, the local gentlemen who were appointed as justices of the peace would have been fluent in both English and Welsh, and could depose witnesses and conduct the court's business in a mixture of the vernacular and the official English.[37] The prevalence of the Welsh language probably increased the lower down the legal hierarchy one moved. The monthly hundred court and local manorial courts, borough courts and courts leet, for example, concerned themselves largely with minor issues of debts, trespass and local disputes which were almost certainly conducted in Welsh, although the record obscured this fact under Latin and English administrative cover.[38] Such courts also dealt with interpersonal disputes that involved slander and, as was the case with the great sessions, quarter sessions and also the church courts, here we do occasionally find Welsh in the legal record as the specific words used were central to the case under review.[39]

The realities of operating in early modern Wales's linguistic environment also meant that the vernacular had a widespread, albeit unofficial, presence in the country's administrative structures too, despite the letter of the 1536 law designating this as an Anglophone domain. Remarkably, as late as the 1590s a claim could be made that one of Radnorshire's JPs, Thomas Vaughan of Llowes, had 'creapte into the comission of the peace where he … canne neither writ, reade and hardly speake any Englishe'.[40] The communication of official policy through such institutions and officials also seems to have been bilingual.[41] A lawsuit from south Wales in 1531 recorded that royal proclamations were made 'both in Englis[h] and Welshe to th'entent that no man shuld be therof ignoraunt'.[42] In 1603 in the town of Denbigh, James I's accession was proclaimed by Hugh Clough, an alderman, who 'p[ro]nownced . . . [the proclamation] a loude in

Englishe & the Bushoppe [of St Asaph, William Morgan] delivered the same in Welshe to the people, whoe well applauded the same'.[43] A directive of 1577 to appoint an overseer to help Merioneth justices maintain order in the parishes, meanwhile, was 'to be openly read & published' at the quarter sessions 'in the Welshe tonge', something apparently in contravention of the union legislation.[44]

Such practices necessitated the appointment of bilingual administrators, of course, and there is evidence that possessing a facility in Welsh was important in these roles. The sheriffs who would undertake duties such as holding the county court and disseminating the monarch's proclamations, almost undoubtedly needed to speak Welsh in most parts of the country. Certainly, the overwhelming majority of sheriffs appointed in this period were local men, and the wealth of material dealing with shrieval selection in the 1630s which survive among Lord President Bridgewater's papers, for example, demonstrate a concern that capable individuals with a close interest in local society were appointed.[45] Beneath this administrative level, it seems certain that the army of local officials who acted as high and petty constables, escheators, coroners, churchwardens and subsidy collectors would perforce be Welsh-speaking or bilingual. In 1622, for example, Hugh ap John Lewis requested exemption from sitting on Flintshire's grand jury because he was poor, illiterate and monoglot Welsh. Interestingly, the justice of the circuit, Sir James Whitelocke, directed that he be discharged, 'but not for want of the Englishe tounge'.[46] Presumably Whitelocke was aware that it would be impossible for court business to function if a precedent was set for discharging someone from this local office on account of lack of facility in English. In the military sphere, too, it was important that appointments reflected local linguistic realities. In December 1598, for example, Richard Gwyne wrote to the Earl of Essex about the forces which would be sent to fight in Ireland, noting, 'I presume your honor will appoint none to leade the Welsh [but] ... such as hath the language'.[47] Such examples demonstrate how the intentions of the 1536 legislation were watered down and compromised in practice; this was the reality of operating within a largely monoglot Welsh culture. Indeed, in rare instances we find semi-official documents produced in the Welsh language, such as the parish register of Penrhosllugwy in Anglesey or the Welsh wills of Hugh ap Sion Goch (Montgomeryshire, 1563) and Owain Gruffydd

(Caernarvonshire, 1600), with the latter's testament taken down by a graduate of the 1568 eisteddfod who 'could not write the same in Englishe'.[48] These few survivals show the Welsh language on the 'official' page from which it was usually erased, but behind which it seems to have had a significant presence.

The nature of the official record in law and administration is eloquent testimony to the fact that the union legislation had decisively entrenched English as the language of advancement and progress in early modern Wales. Ambitious individuals were required to learn and employ English if they wished to be a part of the burgeoning state apparatus. Although this had been the case even before 1536, the union gave added momentum to the adoption of English by Welsh elites. This dynamic speaks to the socially differentiated cultural effects of the union legislation which particularly affected the Welsh gentry. Any discussion of this 'Anglicisation' brings us into somewhat controversial territory as many modern scholars have been keen to emphasise the cultural betrayal wrought by the Welsh gentry following the Acts of Union. Such a view has derived from a historical perspective which portrays the Anglicised elite as alien exploiters of the common people, y *werin*, who, by contrast, are rendered as Welsh-speaking, nonconformist and (usually) radical torchbearers of a form of Welsh national spirit. The narrative of cultural decline is particularly prominent in studies of Welsh literature in which, highly problematically, the criticisms of the gentry by the Welsh bards are taken as a proxy for the linguistic and cultural abandonment of Wales by its leaders. Indeed, some influential commentators have claimed that the Welsh gentry were effectively English by 1640.[49] This is nonsense. While we should not deny the increasing attractions of England and its language and culture, the process of Anglicising the Welsh gentry was just that, a process; and it was a lengthy and a protracted one. The cultural and linguistic rift between the gentry and their communities was a phenomenon of the eighteenth century, and we should be wary of connecting the 1536 union too readily with this process.[50] Indeed, such a perspective is unhelpful as it reduces a complex and culturally diverse Wales into a value-laden binary of 'pure' Welsh and 'corrupted' English. Such a narrative is also reductively linear and eschews the early modern realities of accommodation and adaptation in the cultural and linguistic spheres. Moreover, the paths of change in this period are perhaps rendered more productively as 'Briticisation' rather than 'Anglicisation'. Indeed, it seems more helpful to consider the linguistic experience of the post-union Welsh gentry as an expanded one which incorporated Welsh and English (and Latin) as part of an enriched cultural landscape.

There certainly was something of a cultural reorientation and an adoption of new perspectives among elites across our period, but this is hardly surprising in a era of profound cultural change associated with the Reformation, the Renaissance and, of course, Wales's assimilation with an English, and later British, polity. Increased educational opportunities offered in English, Latin and Greek, but not Welsh, were an important part of this picture. There was an enormous growth across the early modern period in Welsh attendance at new grammar schools both within the principality and in England, and also at the two universities of Cambridge and, particularly, Oxford.[51] In 1571 the Brecon gentleman, Hugh Price (or Aprice) founded Jesus College at Oxford, and it soon became something of a beacon attracting young Welsh gentlemen. However, we should not see attendance at such an institution as a simple process of 'Anglicisation', for this cluster of Welsh squires in England fostered something of a centre for Welsh cultural particularism. Indeed, Jesus probably did more to transmit Welshness into Oxford than spread English culture in Wales.[52] When they arrived at university or the Inns of Court, Welsh students often gravitated to those Welshmen who were already there. Henry Wynn, for example, wrote to his father from the Inner Temple in 1619 that on his arrival 'Mr Lloyd … made me acquaynted with some of our cuntrymen that are students'.[53] Similarly, we are told that when the Caernarvonshire man and future Lord Keeper John Williams arrived at Cambridge in 1598, he was placed under the tuition of the Welshman John Gwyn at St John's College, and was 'much welcom'd … by the Old Britains of North Wales'.[54]

Nevertheless, Welsh cultural patriots could foresee problems with the cultural shifts that could accompany such an education. For example, Dr John Davies of Mallwyd, Merioneth (a Jesus graduate), in his *Dictionarium Duplex* of 1632, lamented those gentlemen who neglected their language in their pursuit of a university education.[55] The forces of cultural change which concerned him are sometimes illustrated by an oft-quoted letter of 1637 from the Merioneth squire

William Wynn to his fourteen-year-old son, Cadwaladr, at Oriel College, Oxford. William entreated his heir to

> speake noe Welsh to any that can speake English ... that therby you may attaine ... [the] Englishe tongue perfectly. I hadd rather that you shuld keepe company with studious, honest Englishmen than with many of your own countrymen who are more prone to be idle and riotous than the English.[56]

Such views about getting ahead by adopting English manners and acquiring the English language seem to have caused anxiety among more culturally traditional elements in Welsh society. However, it has been pointed out that this letter is rather more complex than it first appears. It seems clear that Cadwaladr was expected still to speak Welsh with those able to converse in that language, and that the thrust of the letter was concerned more with emulating models of behaviour rather than modes of speech.[57] Becoming fluent in English did not mean forsaking fluency in Welsh, and the letter points not to the abandonment of Welshness but rather to the adoption of an identity fashioned as a cultured and educated member of an Anglo-Welsh, or British, elite.[58] The aim of schooling, according to George Owen, was for the Welsh gentry to become 'good members in the commonwealth of England and Wales'.[59]

The process of education and integration within a wider British linguistic and social environment was thus not oriented towards the abandonment of the Welsh language by the gentry. Indeed, there was something of a cultural pluralism folded into the growing educational opportunities afforded to those who attended university during this period. It is important to note, for example, that those in the vanguard of the Welsh cultural Renaissance and who defended the Welsh language and lauded its values such as Sir John Prise, William Salesbury, William Morgan and, indeed, Dr John Davies himself, were products of an English university education which stressed the benefits of rhetoric and the importance of vernacular cultures. In many ways, in fact, Welsh participation in English higher education provided the intellectual tools for defending the Welsh language in the sixteenth and seventeenth centuries. It is also the case that there are many Welsh bardic odes from this period which praise gentlemen for their education and the refinement they acquired at university.[60] It might be added that seeing Anglo-Welsh relations as a zero-sum cultural game is highly reductive; such an approach renders our subjects as one-dimensional figures rather than as complex individuals who were capable of navigating the new cultural and linguistic opportunities which opened up after the union without necessarily turning their backs on their native culture and language.

It is difficult to determine the status of the Welsh language in the households of many of these gentry figures in the seventeenth century, although we may be confident that Welsh dominated among the lower social classes who comprised their servants and labourers, and it would have been necessary for the gentleman and his immediate family to employ the language in everyday conversation. Sir John Wynn of Gwydir in Caernarvonshire, for example, described his English daughter-in-law in 1607 as loving 'as [well as] beloved of the countrey, and will soone attayne the [Welsh] langwadge, which will serve her turne well and be no burthen'.[61] One high-born Welshman, Lord Herbert of Cherbury in Montgomeryshire, was sent to Denbighshire by his parents in 1591 to 'learn the Welsh tongue … believing it necessary to enable me to treat with those of my friends and tenants who understood no other language'.[62] In the 1620s in Glamorgan, William Gamage told his neighbour William Herbert, who lived in an English-speaking part of the county, that he needed to become better acquainted with the 'foundation of our countrey language', for 'it is not good for you … in that you are a gentlemen borne to good means in your native soyle, and therefore [you] should not … deale in your affaires by interpreters which are deceiptfull but rather … answeare all in their owne language'.[63] It seems clear that Sir Thomas Aubrey of Llantrithyd, who was employing Welsh poets for communal entertainment at Christmas time and had Welsh praise poems composed to himself and his wife, would need to be able to speak Welsh to communicate with the multitude of servants who appear in his household accounts.[64]

To describe this period simply as one of gentry neglect for the language is thus too simplistic, and Welsh evidently continued to play a significant role in many gentry households. Indeed, it is difficult to imagine that the gentry could have operated within Welsh society unless they maintained an ability to speak Welsh, and the process of 'Anglicisation', often suggests the incorporation of English social, linguistic and cultural modes into the gentleman's social repertoire rather than his 'abandonment' of Welsh language and culture. A more satisfying picture would be to imagine a bilingual Welsh gentry class which was becoming increasingly attracted towards English behavioural norms. Moreover, we should not consider this simply a process which affected the upper classes only. Thomas Jones, the author and publisher, in 1688 bewailed the common fashion in Wales of incorporating English words into spoken Welsh, noting that 'the Britains [are] enchanted with the Englishman's dialect insomuch that the Britains own language is now become as barbarous as their neighbours'.[65] We must also remember that any process of linguistic reorientation was not uniform throughout the country, and was most rapid in areas like Monmouthshire which had easy communication with England, and slowest in those parts of the north and west like Merioneth and Caernarvonshire which were more insulated from such forces by geography, although even this simple image is often subverted by the realities on the ground. For example, in 1683 in the parish of Castle in Montgomeryshire, which was 'not far out of England', it was noted that 'not a third part of ye people understands any Englishe'.[66] It seems, then, that until the eighteenth century Welsh was the language of all social classes in Wales and the 'Anglicisation' of the gentry order was a much more protracted and complex process than many accounts allow.

One of the problems in dealing with this question of gentry 'Anglicisation' is that much of the evidence marshalled against the elites comes from interested parties; namely the Welsh bards and poets, although, as we shall see, even their critical comments of their sometime patrons are often not as straightforward as they might at first appear. The Welsh bards are critical figures in the early modern history of the Welsh language. Professional bards had for centuries been the mainstays of Welsh vernacular culture, acting as the principal guardians of the Welsh language as well as the historical and literary traditions of Welsh society.[67] Poets undertook a lengthy apprenticeship before they were considered sufficiently skilled to itinerate around the houses of the *uchelwyr* (gentry), particularly at Easter, Whitsun and Christmas, when they were paid for their poetic compositions. These were complex oral performances which involved strict-metre verses and dense forms of internal rhyme, rhythm and alliteration. The bards would be commissioned to write verses of praise, and sometimes of lament after a death in the family. Some of these poems were satirical pieces of social commentary; some were love poems; some dealt with religious change and the benison of the Bible in Welsh; others dealt in prophecy and auguries of the future. This was, however, a professional and exclusive class which sought to exclude amateur versifiers who were seen to be corrupting a noble art and lowering standards. It was to regulate the bardic order and to provide licences for those deemed to be sufficiently skilled that *eisteddfodau* were held at Caerwys in 1523 and 1567. The commission establishing the 1567 meeting stated that 'vagraunt and idle persons naming theim selfes mynstrelles, rithmers and barthes, are lately growen into such an intollerable multitude ... that not only gentlemen and other[s] by their shameles disorders are oftentymes disquieted in theire habitacions'.[68] As a result, a certification process was to be established for those deemed worthy, while others were liable for apprehension as vagabonds.[69]

This effort at certification and the commission's reference to the proliferation of lesser poets, gestures towards the profound unease about the future and integrity of the bardic order and their craft which developed during the sixteenth century. Scholars agree that the poetic class which had flourished in the late medieval era was now facing a period of crisis. The output of the bardic order remained considerable, but there were concerns that their compositions were becoming matters of form; stock or conventional eulogies churned out for money. The *cause célèbre* highlighting this issue was the poetic debate between Edmwnd Prys, a humanist and author of the metrical psalms, and Wiliam Cynwal, a professional bard certified in 1567.[70] Prys charged that Cynwal and his associates were using old forms, tired flattery and excessive genealogical detail in their verses. Indeed, it appeared that the bardic order was failing to move with the times and represented something of a late medieval social institution struggling to come to terms with the cultural realities of a post-Reformation and post-union world. The poets themselves turned a good deal of their ire and frustration onto the gentry whose patronage was drying up.[71] The bard Edward Morus, for example, lamented in the later seventeenth century that 'a knowledge of English ensures respect and success. The refined language of Britain [that is to say, Welsh] is valueless and unrewarded'.[72] Morys Benwyn, a poet of Merioneth, one of the more

culturally conservative regions of Wales, sang in the early seventeenth
century that 'Cold is the reward in this age, / An age which offers no
status to the poets'.[73] The bards also faced challenges from the new
Renaissance learning appearing in printed books, which had a far
wider reach and impact than their oral performances. The prevailing
intellectual, social and economic forces of our period were not condu-
cive to the survival of a bardic art which failed to adapt to a changing
society. The Welsh poets railed against the disappearing communal
hospitality which had characterised Welsh traditional society and
which was central to their livelihoods, and criticised the increasing
emphasis on wealth and materialism. This sentiment pierces an elegy
of 1655 sung by Edward Dafydd, one of the last of the professional
bards of Glamorgan, who lamented that 'This world is not with
the poets'.[74]

Scholars have argued that the large corpus of Welsh poetic manuscripts which survive from this period, such as that collected by John
Jones of Gellilyfdy, Flintshire, represent not so much a flowering of
bardic culture as a recognition that the world was changing and that
there was a need to collect and preserve a venerable culture which was
falling into neglect and disfavour.[75] As the professional class of Welsh
bards withered, so their particular contribution to the Welsh language
and to Welsh national consciousness became less significant. This is
not to say that either the language or a sense of Welshness was dealt
a mortal blow by the decline of professional Welsh poetry, but rather
that the character of both was changed by the gradual constriction
and waning of the bardic class. We should, however, be careful not
overstate the rapidity of this decline or to exaggerate the estrangement
of the gentry from the bards' linguistic worlds. We should remain
somewhat sceptical of the bardic complaints about the constriction of
patronage, and remember that these were poetical forms which dealt
in elevated images and *topoi* as much as clear-eyed social commentary.
It is also problematic simply to read off gentry attitudes towards the
Welsh language as a whole simply from their engagement or otherwise
with formal poetic modes in a time of changing fashions. Moreover, it
is also the case that scholars have often overstated the decline of gentry
interest in professional bards. Gentry families continued to patron-
ise poets like Wiliam Llŷn, Siôn Tudur (the chief bard or *pencerdd*
of the 1567/8 *eisteddfod*) in the north and Lewys Morgannwg and

Dafydd Benwyn in the south. We also should consider the evidence of a squire like Sir Thomas Aubrey of Llantrithyd in the supposedly 'Anglicised' Vale of Glamorgan, who in 1623 recorded giving money to a 'proudeth'(*prydydd*), or poet, and again to a 'Welshe poett' in 1633.[76]

There is no doubt but that levels of bardic patronage were constricting by the Jacobean period, and the civil wars seem to have dealt a serious blow to gentry support for the bards in a time of political upheaval and financial belt-tightening. There seems to be no question but that the gentry families of north Wales were more committed to supporting the bardic order than those in the south. Professional bardic culture persisted in the north into the 1680s with figures such as Huw Morys, Owain Gruffudd and the remarkable Phylipes of Merioneth remaining active deep into the Restoration period. The final poet to have made his living as a professional bard was probably Siôn Dafydd Laes who died in 1695. It is also the case that in discussing the 'decline' of the bardic order, we are not dealing with the end of Welsh poetry. Rather, free-metre verse, carols, ballads and a dramatic form called 'interludes' (*anterliwtiau*) took the place of the older strict-metre verse. These were practiced and popularised not by professional bards but rather by amateurs of the middling sort: artisans and yeomen whose compositions could be sung in taverns rather than in the great halls of the elite. Nonetheless, despite this social shift, there is no reason to believe that the gentry could not enjoy these cultural forms as their ancestors had consumed the more highbrow poetic compositions of an earlier age. For example, one William Prees (or Price) in Glamorgan produced a Welsh elegy for Bussy Mansell of Briton Ferry at his death in 1699 as well as a Welsh song for the *crwth*, or Welsh lyre, in 1703 in praise of the Mansell family's hunting hounds.[77] In discussing the 'decline' of the 'bardic order', then, we are dealing with the product of complex social and cultural realignments *within* Wales, rather than simply the product of some problematically monolithic process of 'Anglicisation'.

Although confidence may have been waning in the viability and vitality of established bardic forms, the sixteenth and seventeenth centuries witnessed Welsh scholars defending the status and antiquity of the Welsh language and providing something of the intellectual scaffolding it required to take its place among the learned vernaculars of Renaissance Europe. In this they were taking inspiration from countries such as Italy and France where the Renaissance had sparked an enthusiasm for translation studies and for research into national vernaculars. It may be that in Wales such efforts were encouraged by educated gentlemen who recognised the potentially serious consequences for the status of the Welsh language following from the 1536 union legislation. These figures might also have wished to challenge the implicit and sometimes explicit characterisation by Tudor regimes that Welsh was a barbarous tongue compared with English and was only fit for the field and the tavern. William Salesbury, for example, argued in 1550 that 'the Walsh tong even as it is not now to be compared wyth the Engyshe language, so it is not so rude, so grosse, nor so barbarous as strau[n]gers beynge therein all ignorante and blynd do adjudge it to be'.[78] Welsh cultural patriots utilised the resources of a humanist education and the printing press to defend, and indeed to try to augment, the status and lustre of the Welsh language. Part of this process is discussed in Chapter 3, where the publication of Welsh bibles in 1588 and 1620 represented landmark moments in a concerted drive to affirm the value, worth and potential of Welsh as a language of faith and of erudition. This drive was accompanied by a parallel, albeit rather more heterogeneous and diverse, effort to provide scholarly support for the language in other domains.

Renaissance humanism was grounded on the analysis of classical languages, and its scholarly motivations and analytical techniques encouraged some scholars to investigate, more carefully and thoroughly than had been done hitherto, the origins and rhetorical structures of ancient tongues. And in Welsh, many scholars were convinced they had a language of remarkable antiquity and purity. Taking the language itself as their subject, these humanists produced texts which demonstrated how Welsh was deserving of a place alongside other major European languages. More broadly, these scholars also sought to augment and extend Welsh vocabulary and to educate the people in its potentialities and sophisticated usage. The cleric and psalmist Edward Kyffin in 1603 described such work as being 'for the glory of God and for the elevation of our language'.[79] Part of this wider educative project was several initiatives to produce Welsh dictionaries.[80] This was in keeping with developments in other countries where lexicographies of vernaculars emerged from the printing press such as the first German dictionary produced by Johannes Gutenberg in 1460. Subsequently, numerous bilingual dictionaries of European languages were produced, often providing definitions in the vernacular and in Latin as tools for encouraging and enhancing many forms of scholarship. The dynamic was slightly different in Wales, and the first published dictionary was produced by William Salesbury in 1547. His *Dictionary in Englyshe and Welshe* was designed ostensibly to assist the Welshman to learn English, but its very production made an implicit statement about the comparability, even the equivalence, of the two languages. Thomas Wiliems of Trefriw in Caernarvonshire spent decades compiling a Latin–Welsh dictionary in the late sixteenth century. He mentioned that several other scholars, including the historian David Powel, had plans to publish dictionaries of a similar kind, and that his own work was designed 'to preserve our language' and to induce respect for its qualities through the 'language common to the whole of Europe', which is to say, Latin.[81] Wiliems's patriotic hopes shine through in his declaration that he undertook his labours for his country, its 'natural mother tongue and my cherished countrymen throughout the whole of Wales', and also to dishonour those 'Judases' who wished any ill to this 'illustrious tongue'.[82]

Although Wiliems completed his manuscript, *Thesaurus Linguae Latinae et Cambrobritannicae* in 1607/8, it was never published in his lifetime. However, the formidable classicist and assistant to the biblical translators, Dr John Davies of Mallwyd, took possession of Wiliems's manuscript. Davies was working on his own Welsh–Latin dictionary and incorporated an adapted and abbreviated version of Wiliems's text as part of his own *magnum opus*, the *Dictionarium Duplex* of 1632. Davies's work was a monument of humanist scholarship; rigorous, precise and profoundly learned, it drew on a deep well of Welsh poetry which extended back centuries. Davies has been described as 'the most authoritative of all Welsh Renaissance writers in the field of language and literature'.[83] Wiliems and Davies were putting Welsh literally in dialogue with the language of European scholarship, and thus showing that the vernacular was also a vehicle for erudition, and was worthy of respect. Another notable publication in the field of Welsh lexicography comes at the end of our period with Thomas Jones's

The British Language in its Lustre, which was an extensive, although portable and fairly cheap, Welsh–English dictionary directed explicitly towards non-elites. Jones considered the project necessary to help ordinary Welsh and English men and women understand one another better, knowing full well that such a text was unnecessary for the Welsh gentry who were now universally conversant with English.[84]

Alongside the development of dictionaries, scholars also provided a closer analysis of the Welsh language through the publication of grammars. The first of these was produced by the Catholic exile Gruffydd Robert, who published the initial part of his *Gramadeg Cymraeg* (*Dosparth Byrr* or *Short Lesson*) in Milan in 1567. Written in the Renaissance form of a dialogue, the work explores the nature, grace and beauty of the Welsh language as it was currently used, and as it functioned in Welsh poetry. It was a learned text but one which was also directed towards general readers of Welsh with an accessible and innovative structure and approach to its subject. Another grammar produced by an author who may have been Catholic was Siôn Dafydd Rhys's *Cambrobrytannicae Cymraecaeve Linguae Institutiones*, which appeared in 1592. Written in Latin, Rhys's intention was to ensure that 'understanding about this language [Welsh] might be more easily spread to other nations'.[85] The most significant Welsh grammar, however, was again produced by John Davies of Mallwyd: his *Antiquae Linguae Britannicae … Rudimenta*, published in 1621. Unlike Robert's work, this was a text for scholars rather than the general reader, and it was based on an enormous amount of research undertaken in manuscript sources over the course of thirty years. It provided a descriptive analysis of the structure of Welsh grammar but also presented evidence of the language's antiquity, something much treasured in a Renaissance culture which revered the classical world. This question of Welsh's antiquity is discussed in a little more depth below. Modern scholars have praised Davies's grammar as a towering work of scholarship, perhaps the most impressive achievement of humanist authors in early modern Wales.[86] Through these dictionaries and grammars, Renaissance scholars provided a rich set of resources for future Welsh prose authors. They also, however, challenged the imperial cultural ethic which underpinned the 1536 'language clause' and which positioned the Welsh language as a barbarous and uncultured tongue. By contrast, these works assimilated Welsh into the pantheon of scholarly

Renaissance vernaculars. Although these authors were less influential than the translators of religious texts in terms of language use and vitality, their enduring place in Welsh-language scholarship should be acknowledged. Many English authors would, of course, continue to mock and deride Welsh speech as strange and uncouth, but the scholarly community in England and beyond was more disposed to accept that Welsh was a language of status and scholarship because of the works discussed here.

It is perhaps unsurprising that John Davies of Mallwyd, in addition to his research into the structures and origins of the Welsh language, was also heavily involved in the translation of the Bible into Welsh. These two strands of language use were not readily separated, and they also had a common interest in the antiquity, and thus the prestige, of Welsh. As was seen in Chapter 2, an emphasis on history and antiquity was a crucial component of early modern Welsh identity, and an important aspect of this can be found in early modern claims about, and pride in, the ancient origins of the Welsh tongue. In 1547, William Salesbury had expressed his conviction that the Ancient Britons had the Bible in their own language, and this idea became incorporated into the patriotic prospectus articulated by Richard Davies in his 'Epistol' of 1567. This view of Welsh as 'the Ancient British' tongue was a source of considerable patriotic pride. In his 1603 translation of the psalms, Edward Kyffin argued that the Welsh should cherish their language more than other countries, 'which God … has defended in the one place in this kingdom … amongst multitudes of nations … [which have] tried utterly to consume and destroy the language and her people'.[87] A year later, the author Robert Holland referred to the Welsh as a nation of great antiquity, 'keeping their countrey and contynuing their language so long a tyme inviolate without change or mixture'.[88] Protestants believed that the Welsh language had been preserved by Providence, a sign that God favoured not only the language but, by extension, the survival of its speakers as a national community. This was a powerful counterpoint to the stress on the pre-eminence and civility of English articulated in governmental circles during the sixteenth and seventeenth centuries.

In his 1621 *Rudimenta*, John Davies observed: 'Regarding the language, its outstanding distinction, in terms of honour and dignity, is its antiquity, which is often a matter of contest between languages; …

[and] Welsh ... need not be afraid of entering this arena along with most vernaculars'.[89] This emphasis on antiquity in the context of linguistic analyses led to the claim that Welsh had close affinities with the oldest of all languages, Hebrew.[90] In 1551, William Salesbury described Welsh as being 'sisterlyke wyth the holy language (The Hebrue tonge)', and this was taken forward by scholars like John Davies. In his *Dictionarium Duplex* of 1632, Davies observed:

> It appears to me ... that [the Welsh language] is too different from all European and western languages, at least as they are now and have been for many centuries past, for one ever to dream that it could be derived from them. And I am satisfied by the view of those who believe that it originated at Babel.[91]

Welsh was one of the original tongues of the world and thus a fit vehicle for the Word of God and for both religious and secular scholarship. This connection between Welsh and Hebrew remained an important touchstone of national pride throughout the early modern period. In 1676, the dissenter Charles Edwards produced a short treatise on this topic, *Hebraismorum Cambro-Britannicorum Specimen*, in which he maintained that Welsh was a dialect of the original Hebrew; he incorporated this discussion into his Welsh classic, *Y Ffydd Ddi-ffuant* a year later. Through this kind of linguistic analysis, the argument developed that the Welsh were descended from the children of Gomer, son of Japheth, and grandson of Noah.[92] An alternative to the Trojan origins of the Welsh discussed in Chapter 2, this reconceptualisation of the Welsh as descendants of Gomer was no less ancient or prestigious, of course, and formed the basis for one reading of Welsh national identity as it developed in the eighteenth century. As the scholar Paul Pezron observed in 1706, the Welsh were those who had 'the honour to preserve the language of the posterity of Gomer', a notion which was popularised by Welsh authors such as Theophilus Evans in his classic *Drych y Prif Oesoedd* of 1716.[93]

The Welsh language, then, remained a central component of Welsh life and Welsh identity for all social classes throughout the sixteenth and seventeenth centuries. It faced severe challenges during this period, however, especially from its selective proscription by the Acts of Union, although, as we have seen, Welsh continued to be a significant presence even in domains from which it had supposedly been excluded. There are indications, then, of an indulgence towards Welsh which was not found in English attitudes towards other languages in Britain such as Cornish or Irish Gaelic. This was not some kind of ready accommodation on the part of the English authorities, however, but more of a grudging concession when faced with the realities of overwhelming monoglottism in an era of Reformation. Social changes saw the decline of the traditional bardic order, but, conversely, there were important gains made in this period in Welsh prose publishing, which was the principal vehicle for scholarship about the antiquity and prestige of the vernacular. Despite scholarship which often argues to the contrary, the Welsh language remained an important cultural referent for all social classes in this period, although it was clear by the later decades of the seventeenth century that social cleavages were coming to be described increasingly in cultural and linguistic terms. The Welsh language thus remained the critical bedrock for Welsh identity formation in this period but it never became the vehicle for any form of national resistance or developed anti-Englishness (although some degree of cultural friction was a persistent presence).[94] This was principally on account of the accommodations made with Welsh in the religious sphere, but also crucial in this respect was the willingness to accommodate the language within the ordinary course of justice and administration; this helped enormously in reconciling the Welsh with their place within the British state system. No Tudor or Stuart monarch showed any particular interest in promoting the Welsh language, but their indulgence of projects such as biblical translation seems to have been regarded as important threads in the knot that tied England and Wales together. Despite their apparent indifference to Welsh cultural forms, Tudor and Stuart monarchs represented important cultural resources for the early modern Welsh people, and the next chapter examines Wales's relationship with the Crown in this period in more detail.

6

'A Prince of our Own Natural Country and Name': Welshness, Britishness and Monarchy

Fidelity to monarchy was an important part of early modern Welsh identity. Monarchism was a critical element that anchored Wales and the early modern Welsh within the wider polity and, moreover, it became an important component in the reconfigurations of their 'British' identity as it developed during the sixteenth and seventeenth centuries. Welsh attachment to the Tudors and the Stuarts was proverbial, but it was more than simply an emotional or sentimental connection. Loyalty to the institution of a naturalised ruling house constituted the best approximation of a national political credo in the absence of any specifically Welsh political institutions or an ideology of self-determination. Indeed, one reason why historians have found it difficult to deal with Welsh 'politics' in this period is because the anachronistic desire to locate an anti-English dimension to Welsh political life is doomed to failure; and this seems to be, in no small measure, because of the Welsh people's close association with monarchy.[1] This chapter, then, traces the history of this culturally inflected monarchism through the sixteenth and seventeenth centuries and explores the ways in which it helped shape and inform Wales's political identity. It will provide a broadly chronological discussion but will not offer an exhaustive reign-by-reign treatment of the subject. The chapter will also discuss the ways in which Welsh loyalties to the Crown were mobilised and politicised during the civil war when the principality became a notorious centre of royalist activism. Civil war parliamentarianism cannot be understood simply as anti-monarchism, but some Welsh opponents of the king needed to fashion an alternative set of allegiances separate from that of the Crown. The ways in which parliamentarians such as Morgan Llwyd articulated and conceptualised their republicanism is thus also discussed here. We begin, however, by moving somewhat beyond this book's chronological range to discuss the foundations of this close association with what might be described as a 'Cymricised' Crown in the accession of Henry, Earl of Richmond, or 'Harri Tudur', to the throne of England as Henry VII in 1485.

The accession of Henry VII was a critical moment for early modern Welsh culture and politics as the new king represented the fulfilment of the prophetic *Brut*, or British history tradition, which was discussed in Chapter 2. In the *Brut*, an angelic prophecy was given to Cadwaladr the Blessed, the last king of Britain, that a redeemer of his line, a *mab darogan* – or 'son of prophecy' – descended from the native line of princes, would return to liberate the Welsh from their oppressions and re-establish them as the rightful rulers of the island of Britain. Tales of the *mab darogan* were vital, sparkling and aspirational in the mouths of Wales's medieval bards.[2] These narratives of the promised deliverer were woven into Welsh poetry and song, and also into the minds of the Welsh people. The mantle of the supposed liberator fell on several different heads. In the fourteenth century, Owain Lawgoch, descendant of the ruling house of Gwynedd that had produced the last native Prince of Wales, was hailed as the *mab darogan* in some quarters.[3] There was an intense upsurge of interest in the *Brut* prophecy during the rebellion of a second Owain, Glyndŵr, in the early fifteenth century. Glyndŵr genuinely believed that he was the *mab darogan*, and his status in this respect formed an important component in his political programme.[4] The English also reflected on the potency of these prophecies in Wales, with one fourteenth century chronicler observing:

> the Welsh habit of revolt against the English is a long-standing madness ... And this is the reason. The Welsh, formerly called the Britons, were once noble crowned over the whole realm of England; but they were expelled by the Saxons and lost both name and kingdom ... But from the sayings of the prophet Merlin they still hope to recover England. Hence it is that they frequently rebel.[5]

This search for a Welsh hero, then, was a potent concept in Welsh culture and was significant for both popular and elite politics, and also for ideas of identity and selfhood. In the late fifteenth century this mantle of deliverer fell on a young exile from the Wars of the Roses, Henry, second earl of Richmond, who was also known, in Welsh circles at least, as 'Henry Tudor' or 'Harri Tudur'.[6] Henry's lineage and family history was of principal importance in establishing his Welsh credentials. The Tudor or 'Tudur' family were long established as figures in the social and political life of Anglesey and north Wales.[7] They were descended from Ednyfed Fychan, steward of Llywelyn the Great, but a crucial individual from this family line for our purposes was Owain ap Maredudd ap Tudur, who entered the service of King Henry V's widow, Catherine de Valois, whom Owain secretly married around 1430. He adopted the English style of a settled surname as Owain Tudor. Owain's grandson, Henry Tudor, was born in Pembroke Castle in January 1457. Thus, Henry was only a quarter Welsh by descent, and his grandfather was the only full-blooded Welshman in his immediate family, but his connections with an illustrious line of north Wales rulers were strong. Through his mother, a descendant of John of Gaunt, Henry inherited a claim to the throne of England. Although this claim was weak, Henry nevertheless pressed it home with his invasion of England and defeat of Richard III at Bosworth Field in 1485.

From his emergence as a potential candidate for the throne, the partisan poetry of the Welsh bards almost unanimously supported Henry's cause, while Richard III was vilified by them as a poisonous influence in the body politic. This remarkable outburst of political poetry, and the emotions and momentum which built up behind Henry in Wales, deserve some attention as the basis for better understanding the enduring connections he forged between the country and the Crown. The Welsh bards embarked on what can only be described as a propaganda campaign to whip up support for the anticipated 'deliverer'.[8] Although his connections with Wales might appear tenuous, such reservations did not register in the political climate of the late fifteenth century. Henry was a natural-born son of Wales with an elevated bloodline and a clear connection to the ancient prophecies. This was a mouth-watering prospect not only for those who sought to free Wales from punitive English overlordship, but also for those who saw opportunities for advancement under a 'Welsh' monarch. One poet, Robin Ddu of Anglesey, for example, wrote: 'This is the time for our deliverance, the time for our little bull [Henry] to venture forth … There is a longing for Henry, there is hope for our nation'.[9]

This propaganda campaign had important practical consequences. Henry's choice of landing place for his invasion, Milford Haven, was surely a response to the positive reception he had already received from the Welsh. Moreover, as he marched through the country his army was swollen by Welsh recruits who rallied around his banner.[10] Importantly, that banner incorporated the red dragon of Cadwaladr, a canny publicity move that probably resonated with the Welsh, fired as they were by tales of the last British king's blood flowing in the next British king's veins. Henry's victory at Bosworth provided the Welsh bards with much new material, and they sang how the world was much improved by the death of the usurper Richard. There was precious little concrete dividend for the country from the new 'Welsh' king's reign, although perhaps we should not expect too much in this regard.[11] The poets had pitched their eulogies in the most dramatic terms; declaring some kind of Welsh 'independence' or superiority was not realistic politics, however, and we should not be surprised that their fantasies did not come to pass. The historian John Davies's sardonic comment was probably not too far from the mark, when he observed that 'it was not a matter of the Tudors identifying themselves with the Welsh, but rather of the Welsh identifying themselves with the Tudors'.[12] Nevertheless, Henry did acknowledge his role as the 'deliverer', something recognised by a Venetian visitor at Court, who reported that 'the Welsh may now … be said to have recovered their former independence, for the most wise and fortunate Henry 7th is a Welshman'.[13] It is at this level of 'independence', simply through obtaining a 'Welsh' ruler, that the Welsh understood part of the *Brut* prophecy as having been fulfilled. Indeed, there was expectation that the true consummation of the prophecy would occur after the *mab darogan* had ascended the throne. Such expectations gave Henry's successors the opportunity to reap the rewards of this mode of thinking, as their 'gifts' to Wales – such as the Anglo-Welsh union, the advent of Protestantism and the printing of the vernacular Bible – were placed within a continuum of benefits bestowed on the country by a naturalised ruling house. The establishing of this critical emotional and cultural bond through Henry VII became a key reference point in Wales's future relationship with the English (or, more accurately for the Welsh, now the 'British') Crown. This nexus of ideas concerning monarchy, Britishness, blood, genealogy, prophecy, faith, emancipation and liberation, cohered powerfully around Henry and his successors. For the Welsh, these concepts helped structure a national narrative that the country's fortunes had been transformed with the coming of the Tudors, and that Wales thereafter owed the Crown its allegiance.

Henry VII played upon the Welsh/British element of his dynastic origins by calling his eldest son Arthur and, in 1490, making him Prince of Wales. Arthur was destined to die young, however, and it was another Henry who would join Wales with England and remove Welsh second-class legal status through the Acts of Union. Although the union was not particularly commented upon in the 1530s and 1540s, its provisions were fulsomely welcomed by later generations. Henry VIII, of course, also took the first steps towards bringing Protestantism into Wales, and while more traditional elements in society voiced their resentment at the loss of cherished traditions, the reformed faith became incorporated into a vision of Henry VIII having made good on the hopes and expectations of a ruling house descended from Cadwaladr's line. The bard Lewys Morgannwg praised Henry VIII as heir to Brutus and a second Charlemagne, while also lauding his policy of union which removed 'all the disorder of Wales'.[14] In the preface to their 1567 translation of the New Testament, Richard Davies and William Salesbury presented Henry VII as 'a most godly and noble David', and Henry VIII as a 'wyse Salomon', who 'released their [the Welsh people's] paynes and mitigated their intolerable burthens … by abandoning from them al bondage and thraldome'.[15] However, they maintained that Elizabeth I's gift of the vernacular Bible 'exceedeth that other so far as the soule doeth the bodye'.

Although Elizabethan authors gloss over the complexities and problems of union and Reformation, their commentaries are none-theless useful for understanding how the bonds between Wales and the Crown were reinforced by official policy. The Glamorgan gentleman, Rice Merrick, for example, in the 1570s looked back on the Anglo-Welsh union as something of a deliverance wrought by the Crown, turning Wales from a land of disorder and rapine into one of stability and sober government. The country, he wrote, was 'enabled' by 'the gracious King Henry VIII' with England's laws and was thus 'brought to a monarchy, which is the most sure, stable and best regiment'.[16] Even more fulsome than Merrick in his assessment of the connections between Wales and the Tudor line was the Pembrokeshire antiquarian George Owen, who composed his tract, 'Dialogue of the Government of Wales', in 1594. Owen described Henry VII as 'a prince of our own nation and born in our country', who was sent by God to assuage Wales's troubles.[17] Owen also dilated on Queen Elizabeth's descent from 'British blood, which is the most ancient progeny of this land', through her grandfather, and proceeded to recite Henry VII's connection, via Owen Tudor, to Cadwaladr. In another section of the treatise, Owen reviewed the early Tudor period and argued that before the union Wales was in a 'lamentable estate', but that Henry VIII, out of 'a special care for the benefit of his own nation and countrymen the Welshmen', reformed the country's misgovernment and the oppression of its people by overmighty governors, so that 'I find ourselves now in far better estate' than any other part of the realm.[18] These developments, Owen argued, 'tied the hearts of Wales to ... King Henry [VIII] and his posterity as never before did any Prince'.[19] He described the country as 'emancipated' by the government of the two Henrys, noting:

> No country in England so flourished in one hundred years as Wales has done since the government of Henry the Seventh to this time, insomuch that if our fathers were now living they would think it some strange country inhabited with a foreign nation, so altered is the country and the countrymen, the people changed in heart within and the land altered in hue without; from evil to good, and from bad to better.[20]

Owen framed these deliverances as part of the promised recompense from a naturalised monarchy, styling these benefits as rewards

> attained by the blessing of God in sending them Princes of their own nation to govern them ... we of Wales are bound and must need love our ... princes with a more natural affection than the rest of the realm, for that they of England do not know the sweet

that we of Wales do feel ... for they have never tasted of the sour as the Welshmen did continually for the space of 400 and odd years. This I say does make our hearts to leap for joy when we hear the names of our loving princes recited, being more like fathers than princes to the poor Welshmen.[21]

Although, of course, Owen was indulging in rhetorical flourishes in a text which would circulate among the elite, he nevertheless needed to deal in ideas and images which would be acknowledged and understood by his readers. He certainly was not representing every Welsh individual's attitude towards Tudor monarchy, but he nevertheless must have been articulating a widely recognised version of Welsh political culture. Indeed, we catch echoes of such positions in the poet Siôn Tudur's composition for Elizabeth I which lauds Wales's emancipation brought about by 'the man from Gwynedd [Henry VII]', while even as late as the reign of Charles II another poet, Edward Morus, could sing of Henry as 'a man of British blood' who 'free[d] us from the yoke'.[22] Such reverence for the Tudor line might also be glimpsed in the 'pictures of king Henry the Eight and of Queen Elizabeth', reproductions of Court originals, which adorned the walls of homes such as that of Lady Anne Morgan in Jacobean Monmouthshire.[23] This image of the early Tudors as liberators sprung from native stock was clearly an influential and durable one in Welsh culture.

Henry VIII's children could thus rely on this wellspring of affection from their Welsh subjects, although there were, of course, confessional allegiances which would cut across these ties.[24] Sir John Prise addressed Edward VI in his *Historiae Britannicae Defensio*, for example, expressing his pride that the king was descended not only from 'the most illustrious kings of England ... but also from the most ancient and distinguished stock of British kings'. He described how the 'old Britons [the Welsh] long for a king descended from their ancient princes, and in you they find that very person, one who according to law and by birth fully satisfied their yearning'. Prise then went on to trace Edward's ancestry to native Welsh ruling houses and back to Cadwaladr.[25] Queen Mary's short reign obviously provided fewer opportunities for such expressions of fidelity. Nevertheless, the more conservative Welsh religious commentators welcomed her as a Queen descended 'from the heart of Gwynedd', a reference to the

Tudors' origins in Anglesey, while poets in the south of the country also hailed Mary as heiress of the Tudors who bore 'the crown of the island'.[26] It was, however, during the reign of Mary's sister, the long-lived Elizabeth I, that the ties between the Tudor Crown and the principality were most meaningfully developed and articulated. It was under Elizabeth's rule that Rice Merrick and George Owen penned their paeans to Tudor monarchy, and it was, perhaps, in this period of relative stability that the benefits of union were able fully to be appreciated. It was also, of course, during Elizabeth's reign that the Scriptures were first translated into Welsh, a development that contributed profoundly to the ties that bound Wales and the Crown together.

As we have seen, Salesbury and Davies lauded Elizabeth I as surpassing the gifts bestowed on Wales by her father and grandfather in allowing the translation of the Bible. Their thanks were reiterated by William Morgan in his 1588 translation, which lauded the 'affectionate care your majesty has for your British subjects' as well as the 'most devoted affection of your British subjects for your majesty'.[27] Although we might expect such addresses in a Latin dedication to the queen, these sentiments were also to be found in vernacular culture, as seen in Huw Machno's poem which attributed the wisdom of allowing the translations to Wales having a ruler of their own descent: 'Cymraes o hil Cymro'.[28] Sion Tudur provided the queen with a eulogy that praised her grace and 'island empire', but also played on the familiar theme of her bloodline liberating the Welsh from bondage.[29] The grammarian Siôn Dafydd Rhys produced an elaborate pedigree for Queen Elizabeth showing her descent from Henry VII, native princes such as Llywelyn ap Gruffudd and Howell Dda, back to Cadwaladr and Brutus.[30] In 1594, Edward ap Raff, the Denbighshire poet, also penned an ode to Elizabeth, addressing her as a 'renowned Welsh lady' descended from the line of Tudur.[31] Indeed, the poets had their own affectionate Welsh name for the queen, 'Sidanen', or 'the silken one', and one of their number greeted her as 'Sidanen fawr o Frutus', or 'Great Silken One from the line of Brutus'.[32] In the 1570s, the Welsh courtier Lodowick Lloyd penned an English language ballad to 'Sidanen', praising her as descended from 'Brutus['] stemme' and 'Cambria['s] soile', and as being superior to a litany of famous female figures of classical literature. The ballad was printed and, although no print survives, at least nine manuscripts of this Welsh paean to Elizabeth I have survived.[33] Welsh-language poets took inspiration from Lloyd's evocation of 'Sidanen', but, importantly, they moved its context from that of classical literature to the world of the Tudors and native worthies such as King Cadwaladr.[34]

The cardinal points of Tudor government in Wales – a native ruling house, the legal and administrative reforms of the union, and the translation of the scriptures – were understood by the Welsh as cumulative benefits accruing to the country from the hands of a naturalised monarchy. We would expect, then, something of a crisis of faith and an ebbing of enthusiasm for monarchy when the child-less Elizabeth died in 1603 and was succeeded by the Scottish king, James VI, who became James I of England (and Wales). Surprisingly, however, the kinds of dynastic enthusiasm which had jointed Wales into the Tudor state endured under the Stuarts, and, indeed, were in some ways reinvigorated as James represented a refashioned embodi-ment of that most cherished Welsh concept: Britishness. James VI, as king of both England (and Wales) and Scotland came to the throne with ambitions for formulating a new political entity, 'Great Britain'.[35] While most of the English were deeply unenthusiastic about this pros-pect, the Welsh responded to James's proposals with patriotic ardour, seeing prospects of Britain's refounding in the king's plans, something which had been foretold by the vision given to Cadwaladr the Blessed. George Owen, for example, welcomed James as king of 'the whole ile of Brittaigne, never harde or reade of soe seethence the death of Brutus, first kinge of the whole, being nowe 2710 yeeres seethence'.[36] In James I's first Parliament, his project for styling himself as king of 'Great Britain' was enthusiastically supported by Caernarvonshire's MP, Sir William Maurice of Clenennau. When a bill for recognising James's right to the Crown was delivered to the House of Commons, Maurice requested that

> ther mighte be added to that bill the tytle of Emperore of Grate Brittayne, for that he did observe that an old provesee [prophecy] among the Welchmen was in the kinge in parte performed … and wished that it might be fully fulfylled hearafter. The pr[o]phesee as he pronounced it was; A kinge of Brittishe bloude in cradle crowned with lyones marke shall joyne all brittyshe grounde.[37]

Also noteworthy in this regard was a 1604 poem by Montgomeryshire's William Herbert, entitled *A Prophesie of Cadwallader, Last King of the Britaines*. Drawing on established Galfridian images, Herbert presented James's accession as the realisation of the *Brut* prophecy that a true British monarch would once more reign over a united kingdom. Herbert described how the pain of Elizabeth's death was assuaged by the 'present salve' of James's succession, so that 'Britaine is now, what Britaine was of yore'.[38] The particularly Welsh defence of the *Brut* and its legitimating role in monarchical succession comes across strongly throughout Herbert's poem, even to the point at which Herbert praises James's 'new empires' sprung from the consummation of British union. Although it might seem counter-intuitive to modern eyes, then, the accession of this Scottish king struck a patriotic chord among a Welsh population disposed to see 'British' monarchy as a key element in its own political identity.

This historical and psychological attachment to the concept of Britishness as embodied by James I was not fashioned only from the prophecies of the *Brut*. Native bloodlines, so prized by the early modern Welsh, were also seen to acculturate James as descended from the same lineage as Henry VII. A notable publication on the king's accession was the Pembrokeshire cleric George Owen Harry's *Genealogy*, which traced James's bloodline through Owain Tudor, Henry VII's grandfather, back to Cadwaladr and Brutus, showing his rightful title to 'the Principalities of Northwales and Southwales', as well as to 'the Kingdome of Brittayne'.[39] Like Owen Harry, Siôn Dafydd Rhys produced a genealogical treatise tracing James I's pedigree to Welsh princes, although his work remained in manuscript.[40] So it was that this Scottish monarch was 'Cambricised', naturalised as Welsh, in a manner which probably held little interest for the king or most of his English subjects,[41] but which was genuinely important for Welsh attitudes towards the new dynasty. These attitudes were reflected in Welsh poetry, as in Huw Machno's 1606 ode to a Caernarvonshire gentleman which referred to James I as the 'perfect gift' from Henry VII's stock, and described him explicitly as a new *mab darogan*.[42] Siôn Phylip similarly described James as the true successor of Elizabeth I, a 'young Brutus', and 'He who possessed the heavenly grace of Henry VII – a second Cadwaladr', while Rhisiart Phylip in 1603 lamented Elizabeth's demise but acclaimed the new king as a 'Welshman from Welsh seed'.[43] So James was readily assimilated within the lineage of 'Welsh' monarchy and lauded not simply for his reunification of Britain but because of the genuine belief that ancient British blood flowed in his veins.

Also important in effecting something of a psychological as well as dynastic bond between Wales and the House of Stuart was the fact that the new king had a male heir, Henry, who could be made 'Prince of Wales'. This title was important in the monarchical affections of the Welsh, although they had been denied such princely associations since the death of Prince Arthur in 1502.[44] The importance of the Princes of Wales is suggested by the fact that national histories, such as those produced by David Powel and Percy Enderbie, possessed separate sections tracing the histories of these princes 'of the blood royall'.[45] The arrival of Prince Henry, then, was the cause for a good deal of Welsh excitement and enthusiasm. As part of the publishing campaign in which George Owen Harry welcomed Elizabeth I's successor, another cleric, Robert Holland of Prendergast and Llanddowror, issued a volume that translated King James I's 1599 book of advice to his son, *Basilikon Doron*, into Welsh. This effort was disrupted by an outbreak of the plague in London in 1603–4, but an incomplete copy survives, and it is worthy of some comment. In his preface to the text, Holland informed James that his intention was 'to ... let your majesty see what interest this nation hath in you, being so oft & that of both sides descended from the kings, princes and nobles of our country'.[46] Holland went on that his countrymen celebrated the appearance of 'that precious iewell which ... our hearts much desired to see, a sweet & gracious Prince, whose presence amongst us would wonderfully reioyce all your highnesse subiects here'. Holland even suggested that Henry might obtain 'a taste of the tongue [i.e. Welsh]', which would allow him 'to speake unto his people and also to understand them speaking unto him without interpretors'.[47] This never came to pass, but Holland's address does reflect the particular passion in Wales for a new Prince, something which constituted an important component in a 'Cambro-British' discourse as it developed in the early seventeenth century.[48]

Although Henry would not be created Prince until 1610 (and then he only lived for another two years), the historical bond between the principality and the Crown through the Prince helped fortify the British-inspired enthusiasm of the Welsh for the Stuarts. The intermission since the last Prince was close to a century, and one commentator was desperate to welcome Henry 'to thy long empty seat'.[49] In a letter of 1603 to Sir Robert Cotton, Robert Holland's kinsman Hugh Holland anticipated that Henry's

> noble father will shortly kisse him and deliver him the verge of gold with his patent, whereby hee is entituled Prince of Wales. Which (though now high in nothing but mountaines) I hope one day shall be raised by his Grace's presence. In whom we claime a double interest, as well by Walter Stewarte as Owen Tudyr, both of them lineally descended from the most haught and magnanimous Princes of Wales.[50]

In his 1603 work, *Microcosmos*, John Davies of Hereford included a poem entitled 'Cambria' addressed to Prince Henry, in which he assured him that in Wales he would find 'Brutes venerable stocke / To love thee as the creame of their best blood', adding, 'We are thy people, and thou art our Prince'.[51] Henry's appearance as putative Prince in 1603 also struck a chord with Welsh bards such as Edward Urien, who looked forward to the 'elevation of the Welsh nation' under a 'kinsman' like Prince Henry.[52] The poets also mourned Henry's premature death in 1612, with Siôn Phylip lamenting that the land wished to see a Henry IX, 'But it was not to be / Wales is mourning'.[53]

Henry's younger brother, Charles, succeeded him as Prince of Wales, but he was not formally invested until 1616. This was a rather low-key affair compared with his brother's lavish creation in Parliament in 1610, and it elicited a more muted response in Wales. A small pageant was held at Ludlow, seat of the Council in the Marches, which produced a published relation entitled *The Love of Wales to their Soveraigne Prince* by Daniel Powel, son of the historian, David.[54] This muted celebration was probably in keeping with Charles's own predilections as a man averse to showy public relations. Nevertheless, it seems clear that at his accession as king in 1625, the bonds between Wales and the monarchy remained strong. Charles's reign, of course, saw the most severe test of loyalty to the Crown with the outbreak of civil war in which the king fought a protracted and bloody conflict with his Parliament. It is noteworthy, then, that Wales was notorious

for its royalist sympathies and its support for the king's party in men
and money; one correspondent described Wales in 1645 as the 'nursery
of the king's infantry' on account of the numbers of foot soldiers he
was able to recruit there.[55] A good deal of this loyalty seems to have
derived from an understanding that Charles, as head of the Church
of England, was protecting the more conservative and acculturated
form of religion which had become cherished in Wales. It is also true,
however, that the discourse of naturalised monarchy was significant
as well.[56] A suggestion of the forces at play comes from a visit the
Prince of Wales (since 1638), the future Charles II, made to Raglan
Castle in Monmouthshire in 1642. At the castle, Charles was treated
to an entertainment full of Welsh imagery and pride in British loyalty.
Speakers at the gathering assured the Prince that:

> It is the glory of the Britaines that we are the true remaining and
> only one people of this land, and we have alwayes been true in our
> affections to our king and countrey ... We know no sun that can
> with the influence of royall beames cherish and warme our true
> British hearts, but the sun of our gracious sovereigne ... In what
> true and ancient Britaines may serve you, you may command us
> to our uttermost strength, our lives and fortunes to be ready to
> assist you.[57]

It seems that the kinds of British, integrative monarchical politics
which had been cultivated and nurtured by Welsh gentlemen, clerics, writers and bards over the previous century had successfully been
politicised and mobilised when a call to arms had come. Royalism was
certainly not a universal response in Wales – as we shall see, there were
important dissenting voices – however, the solid and active royalism of
the principality during the upheavals of the 1640s is one of the more
striking elements of the political geography of civil war Britain.

The people of Wales rose up not once but twice in support of the
Stuarts, as both south and north Wales were prominent in the second
civil war of 1648 as they had been in the first.[58] English contemporaries acknowledged the fierce royalism of the Welsh people, with one
newsbook author in March 1648 observing that 'Loyalty run[s] so in
a bloud amongst the Welsh that it will be in vaine [for Parliament]
to attempt this last refuge of monarchy, which Providence seems to

have given in earnest for the restitution of the whole'.[59] This royalist resistance was in vain, of course, and the victorious Parliament executed Charles I at Whitehall in January 1649 and established a British republic. These developments were deeply shocking to most inhabitants throughout Charles's three kingdoms, and we find numerous examples of Welsh outrage and disgust about the parliamentarians' actions. There are several bitter Welsh-language elegies for the fallen king from poets such as Wiliam Phylip of Llanaber, Huw Morys of Llansilin and Rowland Vaughan of Caergai.[60] One copyist of Phylip's verse on the regicide enclosed the text within a decorative border and added a pedigree which traced Charles I's descent back to Llywelyn ap Gruffudd, the last Prince of Wales, a move which suggests how the king's martyrdom was interpreted within a Welsh cultural frame.[61] In addition to penning anti-parliamentarian verse, in 1650 Rowland Vaughan also began a Welsh translation of the king's best-selling work of martyrdom-cum-hagiography, the *Eikon Basilike*, although he never completed the text.[62] In his manuscript, Vaughan lamented that 'Talented Britain has been slain, crownless it has been made … The host of imbeciles murdered / her sole governor'.[63] Another Welsh elegy on the king, this time in a popular free metre often used for ballads, was penned in mid-Wales and it too drew on the imagery and arguments of the *Eikon*; the verse was apparently recycled by loyalist clergy in Monmouthshire.[64]

The sentiments which animated the political poetry of Vaughan and his ilk can also be seen in humbler contexts through prosecutions for seditious words during the republic. The Flintshire labourer Harry Hughes, for example, when apprehended on a warrant in 1658, said 'five tymes over', 'though I am a prisoner taken, Kinge Charles his right I will maintaine'.[65] In Pembrokeshire a few years before, one John Jones had too many drinks and was reported to the authorities for saying, '[I] hope that Charles Stewart, kinge of England and Scotland, would be in England before Christmas Daie'.[66] One the eve of the Restoration a Caernarvonshire sailor had a prescient wish for 'shipps … to fetch over King Charles', a sentiment he expressed as he also drank the king's health.[67] A few months before in the same county, one Ellis John Thomas was brought before the quarter sessions for saying that he 'should be gladd shortly to wipe the kings britch'.[68] These were examples of the resentful and restive royalist sentiment which

pervaded Wales in the 1650s.[69] Although the republic had adherents in
the principality, even its senior governors acknowledged that 'the generality of the people in those parts … have invenomed hearts against
the wayes of God and, we very well know, were the forwardest and
greatest promoters of the king's interest in the time of war'.[70] The
regicide would become a critical reference marker for Welsh politics
thereafter; a fracture point when the monarchical foundations of early
modern Wales were broken.

Given the principality's prevailing royalism, then, it is unsurprising that the Welsh warmly welcomed back their onetime Prince as
King Charles II when the republic collapsed in 1660. We know that
the streets of Montgomery ran with beer and wine and that guns
were fired at the proclaiming of Charles II's return, and we should
suspect that such a response was typical of many, if not most, Welsh
towns and communities.[71] In early June 1660, Sarah Wynn at Gwydir
in Caernarvonshire replied to her husband's letter from the capital
informing her of the king's return. She told him that his dispatch
'hath filled me with so unexpressable a joy, being it braught the news
of that compleate happiness wich wee have so long groned for', and
added that it was 'such a marcy that we canot a nufe [enough] prise it,
the Lord make us truly thankfull'.[72] Her sentiments were echoed in
a loyalist address to Charles II from the six counties of north Wales,
which recounted how its subscribers had 'suffered as much & repined
as little as any part of your … realme have done', and claimed that
'excess of joy hath oft strucke men dumbe, but wee who now car-
rie our hearts in our mouthes may as well live & not breath[e] as not
professe our selves enlivened by your majesties returne to us'.[73] The
published version of a similar address from the six counties of south
Wales is notable as it acclaimed Charles's restoration within a particularly Welsh context, recalling 'the great immunities and gracious
favours conferred upon our nation by your royal grandfather and the
glorious saint and martyr, your father'. The text also made reference to
the recent 'lamentable devastations and sacriledges perpetrated upon
the, once most glorious and antient Brittish Church'.[74] Heralds and
antiquaries such as David Edwardes and Percy Enderbie responded
to that distinctive impulse to associate Charles II with the bloodlines
of native Welsh royalty, drawing up genealogies connecting him to
Cadwaladr and the native rulers of Gwynedd.[75] The Welsh-language

poet Wiliam Phylip's ode to Charles II, composed soon after the Restoration, also articulated the relief and exultation felt in Wales at monarchy's return. Rejecting the religious fanatics who had brought the country into a raging storm, Charles's restoration, he said, now promised fair weather and the protection of the Church of England. 'God', Phylip wrote, 'preserve the king from line to line', and added, 'in the month of May [1660], faultless was the day, / and full of every gladness, / when Charles came … to Britain … God of Heaven by his power has brought / the bones of Cadwaladr home'.[76] In a very real sense, then, it seems as though commentators like Phylip and the south Wales petitioners considered that an essential aspect of Welsh political identity, government by a prince descended from the native rulers of Wales, had been absent for a decade. Just as royalist activism in the civil war signalled the especially close bonds between the Welsh and the Crown, so the tenor of the acclamation which accompanied Charles's return indicated that there was a distinctive dimension to the politics of Restoration in the country. Although to some degree this Welsh aspect was a rhetorical one, it nevertheless does appear that the return of the Stuarts was understood by many to represent a form of political continuity that was native and naturalised.

The restoration of monarchy was accompanied by the re-establishment of the Church of England, of course, and this provided a powerful propaganda vehicle for lauding and defending monarchy as God's chosen government on earth, but it was also a means of anchoring Charles II's rule in a Welsh milieu. At the Breconshire assizes in 1663, for example, Alexander Griffith preached to the large assembly that the 'distempers & disorders' in the region in recent years were attributable to the fact that 'We wanted a head, there was no king in our Israel'. He went on to acclaim the king's power to address these instabilities and described Charles II as 'God on Earth'.[77] Anniversary sermons commemorating Charles I's execution on 30 January, were occasions on which Welsh clerics could lambast usurpers and their anti-monarchical principles from the pulpit.[78] John Thomas, incumbent of Penygroes, produced a Welsh volume on the doctrine and efficacy of prayer and the prayer book in 1680, in which he recalled Charles II's flight (like David) from his prosecutors in the 1650s, but also the 'noisome' dissenters of the wars who drank Charles I's blood, a man who, Thomas continued, was 'oppressed on earth, but is now a saint and glorious martyr in heaven'.[79] When William Owen of Brogyntyn was buried on 30 January 1678 (the anniversary of Charles I's execution), the poet Huw Morys took the opportunity to pen an elegy tying the deceased gentleman and his monarch together in a mnemonic chain of loyalty: 'Let Wales remember that the renowned / was buried on the anniversary of the sharp shower / when the traitors cut off / the golden head of a king without need'.[80] Also in 1678, the cleric Thomas Jones published a text defending the Cambro-British origins of the Anglican Church, in which he also expressed his admiration for 'the wonderful Providence of our Brittish Restoration'. Interestingly, in his discussion of the Church, Jones rehearsed the familiar 'Welsh' monarchical timeline, although he added something of a novel twist. He noted that, although most people ascribed the beginnings of the Reformation to Henry VIII, in fact the

> day-break of our deliverance and reformation began in the mirac-
> ulous and fatal entrance of our great, and wise, and magnificent
> Prince, King Henry the 7th. For then properly was the Church
> restored according to ancient hopes and expectations, the Ancient
> Brittains were in him restor'd to their crown and countrey.

Furthermore, he added, providence had through the vicissitudes of recent history revealed how 'true religion, and the Brittish monarchy, like twins, have fallen and risen up together, hand in hand, being partners, by a kind of sympathy, in the wounds and prosperity of one another'.[81] As was seen in Chapter 3, the Church was an institution which had come to embody Welsh values in a profound manner by the mid-seventeenth century, and Jones here highlights how the monarch, as head of the Church, was also assimilated within this particularist matrix of hierarchy, stability and national identity; many considered British monarchy and the British Church to be indivisible.

These bonds were placed under severe stress, however, by the accession of the Catholic James II in 1685. Strenuous but ultimately abortive efforts had been made in Parliament earlier in the decade to exclude the king's brother from the line of succession. The king's bastard son, the Protestant Duke of Monmouth, an alternative candidate to James, had rallied support through a series of tours in the West Country in the early 1680s, but these were countered by a remarkable

Tory progress of Wales by its Lord President, the Duke of Beaufort, in 1684.[82] Intended to buttress royal authority, Beaufort carried a portcullis on his journey inscribed with the legend 'Altera Securitas', 'the one security', a symbol which had supposedly been used by Henry Tudor to generate support in his campaign for the throne, a telling addition in a tour designed to stiffen loyalist resolve in Wales. At Carmarthen, Beaufort was informed by the town's recorder, Richard Vaughan, that

> your Grace will still find our heads and our hearts inform'd and regulated by the same principle of loyalty which was our antidote against the poyson and infection of those treasonable doctrines and practices, which in the late dismal times of rebellion (like the frogs of Egypt) overspread the land round about us but were not able to blast or corrupt our vineyard.[83]

Vaughan continued that 'the best ornament man is capable of' was 'loyalty and affection to the king', and further informed Beaufort, who was a scion of the Welsh Herberts of Raglan, that he derived his loyalty from his Welsh ancestors, adding 'he must needs be a great stranger to our British annals that is ignorant of the aid they have constantly ministered to the Crown in its distress'.[84] This was a successful public relations exercise and, in the short term, helped ease the acceptance of James II's accession. It was also notable that when the Duke of Monmouth led an invasion force into the west of England in 1685 seeking to topple the Catholic monarch, no support for the rebels was forthcoming from Wales.[85]

James II had a genius for alienating his supporters, however, and in his short reign Wales would be placed in the unusual position of becoming estranged from the Crown. The king promoted Catholics and dissenters to positions of authority in the principality, as elsewhere, antagonising his natural supporters and threatening the position of the Church. A mood of sullen resentment rather than open revolt attended these developments, and the so-called 'Glorious Revolution' of 1688–9 was broadly accepted in Wales as a means of avoiding bloodshed and safeguarding the Protestant settlement with the installing of William of Orange and Queen Mary. In the Welsh Marches, the Catholic supporter of James II, John Stevens, attributed the 'generality of the people' being receptive to the Revolution to the efforts of William Lloyd, bishop of St Asaph, who had 'preach'd at almost every church & din'd at the houses of most gentlemen of any note ... to incense the people against the king [James II] & dispose them for what follow'd'.[86] It is worth noting, however, that Stevens considered this change in people's attitudes to have come about quickly and rather late in the day (he described 'so great an alteration [among the people] in so short a time'). Indeed, it seems telling that, despite the relative quiescence of the country in 1688–9, the idea of lineal succession within a naturalised ruling house remained strong in Wales. One contemporary noted that the Welsh gentry had always 'coveted to bee governed imediately by the King or the Prince'.[87] Support for the return of the exiled Stuart line, Jacobitism, was relatively strong in the country, with toasts being drunk to the 'king over the water', while ostentatious displays of support for the Stuart line were not uncommon.[88] It is also revealing that the Welsh Jacobites celebrated their Stuart Prince on the day of the country's patron saint, 1 March. Such impulses were counterbalanced by the importance of Protestantism and parliamentary supremacy, which combined to assuage doubts about the legitimacy of the Hanoverians after 1714. Nevertheless, the lingering emotional attachment to a line which could trace itself, without too many diversions and contortions, back to the blood of Cadwaladr, is suggestive of the force of Welsh loyalty to the Tudor and Stuart dynasties.

Early modern Wales was thus renowned as a bastion of royalist and monarchical sentiment. It would be foolish, however, to claim that unalloyed and unquestioning devotion to monarchy was universal among the Welsh people. The idea of a 'monarchical Wales' is a shorthand that captures a truth about the early modern period, but it does not describe the messier realities of dissent, sedition and alternative concepts of government which were conceived and articulated during this period. Space precludes a developed discussion of these themes, but the concluding section of this chapter considers some of these alternative voices.

Allegiance to the monarch, of course, was a position that could be undercut by alternative confessional loyalties such as those of the

Catholic or puritan, as was discussed in Chapter 4. Those Catholics who intrigued against the throne in the sixteenth and seventeenth centuries developed resistance theories and concepts of authority which placed their conscience and allegiance to Rome above that of the secular magistrate. Mostly, however, such individuals wished to replace the heretic monarch with another ruler, and we can catch glimpses of such positions in prosecutions for seditious words. In Montgomeryshire in 1590, for example, a widow, Elizabeth Badoe (or 'Badow') of Crugion was reported to the authorities for saying (in Welsh) that 'there was a newe king made ... That ys to saie a certen noble man', whom she named as the Catholic Lord Strange, future Earl of Derby.[89] Also in Montgomeryshire, we obtain a very different perspective from the panegyrics of George Owen Harry or Huw Machno on the accession of James I. At the new king's proclaiming in the county in 1603, one Rees ap John 'uttered in great bravery, clappinge of his hands' before a large crowd, crying, 'shall we have a Scott to [be] our kinge? We will have no Scott to [be] our kinge!'[90]

Outbursts such as Rees ap John's were probably less ideological than that of Elizabeth Badoe and may simply have been predicated on national prejudices. Both individuals, however, wanted a monarch, just a different one from that with whom they had been presented. Many of the puritans and parliamentarians who fought against Charles I in the civil wars thought similarly. A precocious parliamentarian such as John Poyer of Pembroke, for example, was clearly fighting to reform Charles I's policies rather than to remove the king altogether. Indeed, Poyer took up arms again in 1648 in the name of the king and the Prince of Wales *because* he felt that parliament was becoming too radical in its policies towards the defeated monarch.[91] There were others among the parliamentarian phalanx in Wales, however, who had come to accept that government by kings was iniquitous and who supported a republican settlement as the means of reforming Church and commonwealth. For men like the radical William Erbery, for example, Wales was not blessed because of some genealogical inheritance from the line of Owain Tudur; rather it was blessed by God's election of the Welsh as a chosen people who would destroy all forms of Church government. His position was shared by Morgan Llwyd of Wrexham, who articulated a republican vision which explicitly rejected the monarchical obsessions associated with his countrymen. In a Welsh tract, he described prestigious genealogies as nothing 'but a web woven by nature in which the spider of pride is lurking', observing, 'You are nothing if you come from the princes of Wales, unless you are of the seed of the prince of the kings of the earth'.[92] Llwyd placed his trust in spiritual forms rather than in earthly ones, seeing the institution of a republic as a necessary step towards realising God's dominion on earth. In 1649 he asked, 'Was not the late king delinquent in chief? And was not death the condigne punishment?'.[93] He later put these opinions into verse, with a composition tellingly entitled 'Charles, The Last King of Britain'. Its opening stanzas noted: 'The law was ever above kings / And Christ above the law / Unhappy Charles provokt the lambe / To dust hee must withdraw'.[94] His fellow propagator, the fiery Fifth Monarchist Vavasor Powell, wrote similarly that 'Of all kings I am for Christ alone, For he is king to us though Charles be gone'.[95]

The republic thus represents an important point of discontinuity in Welsh history when alternatives to monarchical government were not only dreamed but implemented and experienced. Such republican positions were, of course, only held by a tiny minority of the population – among those like Llwyd and Powell who believed that monarchical government was inherently corrupted – but they cast long shadows in the later decades of the seventeenth century. Expressions of anti-monarchical opinion which might previously have been considered intemperate outbursts, with tongues lubricated by too much alcohol, were now potentially situated within a republican ideological tradition. Indeed, for all the joyous acclamation of Charles II's Restoration, in several parts of Wales there was an undercurrent of violent republican opposition from figures like Powell and his associates, which caused the authorities deep anxiety.[96] Rumours of plots and the eruption of actual violence, as in the Fifth Monarchist Thomas Venner's rising in London in 1661, served to heighten the sense of apprehension and foreboding in the early Restoration. Thus the Denbighshire quarter sessions investigated loose talk such as Mary Glynne of Holt telling her serving maid who had asked to attend the proclaiming of Charles II at the town cross, 'I would yow weare soe willing to serve God as the devil'.[97] Even more troubling, however, was her husband's remark of a year before that 'this king would not be quiet till they had his head as well as his father's'.[98] That the couple were both conventicle-goers who refused to attend church, and had probably been associated with Morgan Llwyd, only served to sharpen the authorities' concerns.[99]

Worries about 'sectaries', 'fanaticks', 'schismatiques' and ex-parliamentarian soldiers continued to pepper gentry correspondence in the following decades. As the political temperature rose in the 1670s and 1680s, so lay and clerical governors in Wales listened more attentively to rumours of local involvement in seditious activities from those whose 'dangerous principles' could once again augur political chaos and the downfall of monarchy. These were figures such as John Jones of Llantrissent in Monmouthshire who, in November 1680, quarrelled with his local vicar over the payment of tithes, and said that 'there was noe good time since the kinge came inn & cursed the very time that the kinge came to England ... that there were good time before', adding that 'if the Lord Protector & his Uncle [the radical preacher Walter] Cradock lived still, there should be neither king, bishopp nor priest but godly learned men'.[100] Thoroughgoing republicans were few and far between, but the political heirs of the 'Good Old Cause', the radical Whigs, were lumped together readily enough with fire-breathing regicides in both popular and elite imaginations. Indeed, it is possible that the strident declarations of loyalty to the Crown emanating from Wales after the Restoration were partly attempts to assuage the nagging doubts in their authors' minds about the cracks beneath the image of the country's steadfast royalism.

The attacks on monarchy from the mid-seventeenth century should give us pause in accepting too unquestioningly the rhetorical presentation of the principality as uniformly loyal and royal. Nevertheless, this rhetorical image does capture something essential about the monarchical politics of the early modern principality. Although the civil wars shattered the image of a kingdom united under a single king, this tumultuous era enhanced rather than diminished Wales's reputation for loyalty to the Crown. Looking across the sixteenth and seventeenth centuries, it is evident that this reputation was predicated on the principality's allegiance to the Established Church; to the native traditions of royal prophecy in its popular culture; to the concepts of bloodlines and genealogy that placed the Tudors and the Stuarts within a lineage of Welsh native rulers; and to the discourse of

Britishness which drew on and appealed to particularly Welsh ideas of history and legitimacy that were focused on the Crown. Although we should remain alive to dissenting voices of Catholics, puritans and republicans, fidelity to a Cymricised vision of British monarchy was the prime focus of loyalty and a keystone of Welsh political identity during the sixteenth and seventeenth centuries.

7

Politics, Officeholding and Participation

The absence of a nationalist or separatist Welsh politics under the Tudors and Stuarts has caused problems for historians venturing into the sixteenth and seventeenth centuries seeking such phenomena.[1] The quest for a discrete national 'Welsh politics' is doomed from the outset as early modern Wales's political life operated within and possessed the characteristics of a British political culture. Welsh political norms of the late medieval period had been moving unremittingly towards assimilation with those of England; the Acts of Union were, in many ways, the culmination of that process. Although the union did not snuff out a Welsh sense of identity, it certainly inhibited any impetus, or even desire, for a separate national (or nationalist) politics. Early modern Wales did not possess any institutions which could help formulate, sustain or express a separate (or separatist) Welsh politics, and in this respect was quite different from Scotland and, to a degree, Ireland also. The only forum in which the political position of 'Wales' could be articulated or devised was in the Parliament which met periodically at Westminster. To acknowledge the lack of a nationalist politics in this period, however, is very different from saying that there was no political life in early modern Wales. This chapter explores some aspects of early modern Welsh politics but does not go hunting after the phantom snark of a political tradition that was different from that of England, although it does argue that there was a distinctive Welsh voice discernible within British political discourse.

The approach adopted in this chapter is informed by recent developments in the study of 'political history' which have moved away from understanding pre-modern political life simply in terms of monarchs and statesmen, and have instead argued for a broader understanding of 'the political' as involving disputes over resources, power and authority which were conducted at local, regional and national levels.[2] These shifts in perspective have been accompanied by a recognition of the growth in political literacy throughout early modern society as the 'public sphere' of politics expanded with the advent and expansion of political print, the circulation of news and rumour and the mobilisation of socio-political constituencies or 'publics' in support of a plethora of local, regional and national political causes.[3] We will touch on some of these elements in the following chapter, but will begin with a discussion of local Welsh politics as it was channelled and expressed through officeholding. This leads us to an examination of the politics of local faction and the manner in which regional disputes often became caught up in the patronage of national figures who straddled the divide between provincial society and Whitehall and Westminster. Parliament remained a key arena for Welsh political interests, and the chapter briefly discusses elections and the nature of Welsh activity in Tudor and Stuart Parliaments. It argues that, although we cannot locate a Welsh national politics in this period, we can nonetheless identify occasions when a distinctive constellation of Welsh political interests became animated in Parliament over matters affecting the principality. Although much of this discussion necessarily concentrates on the Welsh gentry, the chapter concludes by examining some of the ways in which political participation reached beyond the elites to involve those lower down the social order.

One of the reasons why the sixteenth-century union was welcomed by the Welsh gentry was because it regularised and widened their access to offices of local government (the native gentry already largely controlled local administration in the years before the union)[4] and created a plethora of new official positions to which they could aspire.[5] The gentry coveted these offices because of the power and prestige which flowed from holding positions such as justice of the peace, sheriff or deputy lieutenant, and also because of the status and honour these offices bestowed on the gentleman in his local community.[6] There were different levels of participation available to the gentleman within his locality, and these broadly corresponded with his status and wealth.[7] At the apex of local administration was the deputy lieutenant, of which there were between three and six in each county. Charged with overseeing local defence and mustering troops, they were also responsible for oversight of the other branches of local government; it was sometimes a burdensome office, but it provided considerable status and prestige. The next tier of administration involved positions such as the justiceship of the peace and the office of sheriff (the shrievalty), and perhaps between twenty and thirty landed families in each shire were nominated regularly for these positions. Below this stratum was a plethora of offices such as high and petty constable, escheator, coroner, bailiff, subsidy commissioner, churchwarden and others, which were discharged largely by the 'parish' or lesser gentry, figures whose social status often shaded into the realms of the yeomanry. Although a degree of political activity and consciousness was present at all of these levels, here we will concern ourselves principally with the best-documented upper levels of local government.

In post-union Wales, a gentleman's status rested on his lineage, landholding and wealth, but, alongside these elements, officeholding was recognised as a critical marker of rank and standing.[8] Active civic governorship through public office was part of the ideal of the Renaissance gentleman as that concept was elaborated in sixteenth-century Anglo-Welsh culture. Protection of one's community through military prowess was an important dimension of gentility in the late medieval Wales, but this morphed into the ideal of a stalwart governor protecting his community through the just exercise of the law and the power of the state. In the 1530s the bishop of Bangor noted the desire for such offices among the Welsh, commenting that it was 'the nature of a Walshe man … to bere office & to be in authoritie'.[9] We can trace the cultural shift towards local officeholding in the poems bards addressed to their gentry patrons, which praised their probity and justness as justices of the peace, sheriffs and deputy lieutenants. Whereas earlier the poets had lauded gentlemen for their influence in a traditional region or *gwlad*, by the second half of the sixteenth century the focus of such poems was more likely to be the sphere of the gentleman's administrative office, usually meaning the shire.[10]

The principal local office for most early modern gentlemen was the justiceship of the peace.[11] From the outset, it was clear that demand for this post in Wales was considerable. In October 1536, soon after the union, the Anglesey magnate Sir Richard Bulkeley wrote to Thomas Cromwell asking him to delay the making of justices of the peace (JPs) in north Wales because, he said, he knew of at least two Caernarvonshire gentlemen who 'will giff hym large money to be made iusticez [justices] of the peace'.[12] JPs met together quarterly as the county commission of the peace, the body of leading gentlemen in a shire.[13] In many ways the commission of the peace was a natural focus for local loyalties, and we often find representations to central government being made by the commission of the peace speaking on behalf of its county.[14] The justices who constituted this body enforced a growing body of statute law which ranged from prosecuting vagrants to policing Catholics. JPs were also charged with sometimes burdensome administrative duties such as licensing alehouses, ensuring that bridges and roads were kept in good repair and overseeing welfare relief for those disabled in national conflicts. This body of officers shouldered the main judicial and administrative burdens in Wales after the Tudor settlement, and there was a constant dialogue between these commissions and the organs of central government, often mediated through the Council in the Marches of Wales at Ludlow.

The number of justices stipulated by the union statutes for each county was only eight, suggesting that the Henrician legislators had a restrictive view of local government being confined to the greatest squires.[15] However, competition for office and the status it conferred ensured that there was a rapid inflation beyond this number. Lists of JPs in Welsh counties were topping twenty by the end of the sixteenth century.[16] In 1626, the bishop of Bangor complained that the small county of Anglesey should only have eight JPs, but that they had 'growen sanz number'.[17] A commission for Anglesey from this period records thirty-four names, although some of these were ex-officio members of the bench.[18] The reasons for this inflation are complex, but it seems clear that part of the increase was occasioned by demand and competition for places among the county elite. Growing numbers of gentlemen wanted the esteem, honour and authority associated with the office, and a good deal of local politics involved manoeuvring to obtain a position on the bench for oneself or one's family and allies; to improve one's precedence on the commission of the peace; or to block the appointment and advancement of one's enemies.[19] There was an intense competitiveness over rank and primacy which focused on the major county offices. Yet political calculations involving the commission of the peace could not concern themselves with the locality only, for each commission was linked intimately to the wider political world. The power of appointing justices lay with the Lord Chancellor (often at the recommendation of the Lord President of Wales, a local magnate or the judges of the great sessions courts) and, ultimately, the Crown. It was *central* rather than local connections which determined the composition of the local bench.[20] Officeholding was plugged into the politics of the court and the political centre. A gentlemen in Wales, therefore, needed to maintain favourable contacts with individuals in the corridors of power at Whitehall, as well as to the great and the good in his own backyard, to ensure his continued tenure on the bench. The issue of patronage was thus a key consideration in local politics.

We can see how such patronage ties operated by considering south-west Wales in Elizabeth I's reign. The family of Robert Devereux, second Earl of Essex and sometime favourite of the queen, hailed from this region, and the Earl wished to maintain a network of gentlemen allies there, and they, in turn, wished to benefit from his influence and approbation. Managing appointments to local offices, particularly to the local commissions of the peace, was one way of doing this. In April 1585, for example, Essex wrote to one of the justices of the local great sessions, John Puckering, who was also the queen's sergeant, informing him that he had recommended several gentlemen to the Lord Chancellor for appointment to the commissions of Carmarthenshire and Cardiganshire, observing, 'I am desirous to counteynaunce my frends and servaunts in the countrey as far forth as I am able'.[21] In June 1587 he once again forwarded candidates to Puckering who were 'very fit' for local commissions: 'I have in Carmarthen shire two gentlemen towards me', adding that 'except there were some cause to the contrary I wold be willing to geve them some credit in the cuntry'.[22] In 1594 Essex acknowledged in another letter to Puckering that he 'hath heretofore made me behoulden unto yow for manie others by placing theym in the commissions of the peace at my request', and asked that his uncle, George Devereux, be put into the commissions for Carmarthenshire and Pembrokeshire.[23] Some years earlier, George Devereux himself had requested a seat on the Carmarthenshire or Cardiganshire bench from Puckering, noting

that he hoped thereby 'to wine credit, which thinge I chiflie dessyre'.[24]
A document drawn up around 1587 listed ten 'serving men in lyverye'
for Essex in south-west Wales who were also justices of the peace.[25]
When an order against retainers serving as justices was passed in 1595,
which threatened the removal of Essex's liveried clients from their
commissions, the Earl was incensed. He wrote to Puckering:

> I am verie loth to leave the name of master to so manie honest
> gentlemen in Wales as out of their love, desire to serve and followe
> me and as hold the place of justices in those partes; yet I had rather
> geve them libertie and free them from retayninge unto me than
> that ... they should loose any jot of their former reputacions.[26]

The order evidently had little practical effect, however, and in 1598
one Susan Morgan of Whitland in Carmarthenshire complained to
Essex about his placemen's pervasive and disruptive influence in the
region: 'most of those that weares your honour's cloth [i.e. his livery]
in this country is to have your lordship's countenaunce ... and to be
made shiriffs, lieutenants ... subsedymen ... everything is fishe that
comes to their nett'.[27] Essex's patronage would come to extend into
Radnorshire and also into Denbighshire, where it severely destabilised
the county's political balance.[28] The question of gentry faction is dealt
with in greater depth in a moment.

A further glimpse into the fascinating world of patronage,
clientage and local officeholding is provided by the early seventeenth-
century case of the Wynn family of Gwydir in Caernarvonshire and
their relative, John Williams. The Wynns were prominent members
of several county benches in north Wales and diligently sought to
monitor and influence their composition. The head of the family,
Sir John, received dispatches from relatives in London who infiltrated
the corridors of Chancery and obtained for him lists of commissioners as well as information about who was in and who was out.[29] In
1610, Sir John paid £10, 'beynge his promysed rewarde', to a cousin in
London for his labours in trying to get Wynn's relatives placed onto
local commissions.[30] The Wynns' efforts to shore up their presence on
the north Wales benches received a significant boost with the political
advancement of their kinsman John Williams. A Caernarvonshire
native, Williams was a bishop whom, in 1621, King James I also

advanced to the position of Lord Keeper, the official who oversaw JP appointments. One of Sir John Wynn's sons, William, was a member of Williams's staff in Chancery and was thus well placed to influence his decisions in populating Welsh commissions. The Wynns were involved at this time in a bitter rivalry with another group of gentry families in Caernarvonshire, and in July 1621 William Wynn wrote to his father that he had been at a meeting with the Lord Keeper about 'makinge of iustices of peace'. William reported that he had managed to get three of their enemies ejected from the subsidy commission (which assessed and collected parliamentary taxes) and had tried to eject three more from the Caernarvonshire commission of the peace, but Keeper Williams 'would not condiscend thereunto, because hee would not seeme too partiall of our side at first. But herafter, when the commission of the peace is to bee purged of unwoorthie men, I hope to purge them out, or my credit will fayle'.[31] He added that he had managed to get his brother Owen appointed 'if hee desire it'. To the Wynns' chagrin, however, Williams's desire to be seen as relatively impartial in local politics was not a passing fancy. In March 1622, William Wynn regretfully informed Sir John that the Lord Keeper would require a certificate from a justice of the local great sessions detailing the 'unwoorthines' of those Wynn hoped to see dismissed from the commission, as he was 'verie unwillinge to disgrace anie man in that kind without some good grownd'.[32] Although Keeper Williams was an enormously useful contact at the political centre, it was clear that it was he who was calling the shots about the composition of local commissions rather than his country cousins. The wholesale purge of the Wynns' enemies never transpired, although their own positions, and those of their allies, were safe while Williams remained in office. When Williams departed as Lord Keeper in 1625, however, the Wynns' enemies stepped up their efforts to turn the tables on their opponents by cosying up to a powerful patron of their own, the royal favourite, the Duke of Buckingham.[33]

As can be seen from the foregoing discussion, the holding of local office, such as that of JP, was bound up with issues of public reputation and honour. A contemporary term which often appears in this context is 'credit', which was, in some respects, the currency of much local politics.[34] Obtaining office or climbing higher in the scrupulously graded hierarchy of local positions bestowed status and honour; conversely, being ejected from office brought disgrace and shame. A good deal of local political life was thus about the relative standing and authority of gentlemen as measured by their offices and their precedence in those offices, and the effort to obtain an advantage in these domains was often the cause of intense local rivalry. As we have already seen, however, this arena of political life was far from simply a local and insular one (although it was partly that). Gentlemen needed networks and alliances which reached into the centre of political life, to the desks of great men such as the Earl of Essex or Lord Keeper Williams, to secure and retain their position on bodies such as the local bench, to advance higher in the *cursus honorum* or to stymie and frustrate the ambitions of their rivals.

Although local enmities could occasion a gentleman's removal from local office, dismissals could also be the result of national religious or political realignments which saw some Welsh gentlemen fall out of step with the interests and priorities of central government. This was particularly the case at times of heightened tensions or rapid political shifts, such as following Mary I's demise, during the during civil wars, the Popish Plot, or during James II's efforts to repeal the Test and penal acts. At such times political and religious ideology became critical variables in assessing a gentleman's fitness for local service. At the outbreak of the civil wars, for example, most Welsh local governors were committed royalists. As a result, the victorious Parliament was faced with potentially hostile and uncooperative commissions of the peace in Wales, which could obstruct or water-down their policies. Consequently, the period after 1646 saw many gentlemen purged from local commissions and replaced by parliamentary adherents. As the latter were in short supply, those appearing on county benches in the 1640s and 1650s were often more obscure gentlemen who had little experience of local government before the civil wars, but whose political reliability saw them entrusted with novel judicial and administrative responsibilities.[35] In the mid-seventeenth century, then, the social character of Welsh commissions altered, sometimes quite radically. Displacement from their traditional roles as local governors was, of course, deeply resented by the greater gentry, and the Crown effected another 'revolution' at the Restoration when Welsh commissions were once again extensively remodelled and established families repopulated these offices.

The Popish Plot and Exclusion Crisis of the 1670s and early 1680s saw local government in south-east Wales and the border region being used as an instrument in political and religious disputes which modulated the ideological convulsions of the national political scene.[36] The crypto-Catholic Henry Somerset, Marquis of Worcester, whose family had long-established links with Monmouthshire, was keen to secure like-minded supporters places on that county's bench and to purge his puritanically inclined opponents. Between 1674 and 1677 Worcester removed a dozen JPs from the commissions of south-east Wales.[37] A later pamphlet, which was hostile to the Marquis, described how he had 'secured the government of … Monmouthshire into the hands of his own creatures and servants by turning out of the lieutenancy and commission of the peace the most antient and chief gentlemam [sic: 'gentlemen'] of the country', and replacing them with what were described as his 'mercenary justices'.[38] Such manipulation of the local bench, particularly by individuals like Worcester who were suspected of Catholic sympathies, was connected closely to anxieties about arbitrary government and the loss of political liberty. One of Worcester's opponents, John Arnold, for example, asserted that Monmouth was 'governed by an arbitrary lord who pricks [chooses] mayors as the king pricks sheriffs'.[39] Although the county commissions were not representative bodies, their importance in the administration of local justice meant that there was an expectation that they should strive for a degree of impartiality rather than simply functioning as instruments of the Whig or Tory interest. In some respects, this was the ideological development of Lord Keeper Williams's desire to 'not seeme too partiall' in the composition of the local bench; but impartiality in the partisan politics of south east Wales during the Popish Plot was in very short supply.

In March 1678, Sir Edward Mansell of Glamorgan and William Morgan, a Monmouthshire MP, informed Secretary of State Sir Joseph Williamson 'that severall gentlemen of good note & condition had of late [been] turned out of ye commission of ye peace' in their counties, and, after discussions with the Lord Chancellor, they discovered that this had been done at Worcester's 'instance'.[40] Williamson asked Worcester to explain why these men had been removed, and even indicated that the King himself wished to have an account of the business. One of those dismissed from the Monmouthshire bench in November

1677 was John Arnold, who was discussed in Chapter 4. A contemporary noted that Arnold was turned out of the Monmouthshire commission (along with Henry Probert) for affronts to the Catholic Duke of York (the future James II) and for misdemeanours in office.[41] Arnold, along with local allies including his fellow ejected JP Henry Probert, took their case to Westminster. Before the bar of the House of Commons they provided damning evidence about former and current JPs appointed by Worcester who were 'papists or suspected papists'.[42] Arnold, for example, informed the Commons of the case of Henry Milborne of Llanrothal (one of Worcester's 'mercenary justices'), who was a JP in four counties but who, Arnold claimed, 'kept papists for his clerks', one of whom had been indicted for speaking treasonable words. Moreover, Milborne was said to have dissuaded local constables from presenting recusants to the authorities and to have annulled an order from activist Protestant justices against some 200 local Catholics.[43] After this onslaught, Milborne himself was dismissed as a local justice,[44] while, at the height of the anti-Catholic backlash surrounding the Popish Plot in 1679, the excluded justices like Arnold and Probert were re-admitted to their positions.[45] As the political pendulum swung back Toryward after the hysteria of the Plot died down in 1680–1, however, so Probert once more found himself dismissed from the bench as Worcester reasserted his influence.

This political 'tuning' of Welsh commissions in a period of intense political partisanship was not restricted to Monmouthshire. Worcester, as Lord President (and Lord Lieutenant) of Wales, had extensive powers throughout the principality and was a sympathetic agent for executing the policies of the ultra-Tory court interest. In 1680, with Worcester at the helm, something of a coordinated purge of Welsh commissions removed some twenty-five magistrates.[46] These were men whom the regime considered sympathetic to the kind of whiggish and pro-exclusionist politics that had animated Worcester's antagonists in Monmouthshire. As one correspondent put it, Worcester wished to remove such figures of local authority and to appoint instead those who were the 'kings freinds'.[47] One of these unfortunates, Thomas Mostyn of Gloddaeth in Caernarvonshire, was ejected from his deputy lieutenancy as well as the local bench. He wrote plaintively to Worcester in June 1680 that his family, staunch royalists during the civil wars, had given many sufficient 'prooffes of its loyallty' to the Crown. Mostyn added that he himself was 'free from a disloyall thought, much more word or action', and assured Worcester that the king could not find a 'truer faithfuller subject'.[48] Clearly Mostyn considered himself touched in his honour by having his loyalty and political reliability publicly questioned in such a manner. This concerted remodelling of local benches illustrates how increasingly politicised the business of local administration became in a time of bitter partisanship. It also points to the potentially critical role of Wales's Lord President and the Council in the Marches, institutions which were alien to the political calculus of local appointments in England. The central government ultimately operated on information and knowledge about local candidates which came from trusted agents in the localities. When these were filtered through a powerful partisan intermediary such as Worcester, there was the potential to generate significant disquiet in the provinces over his partial dealing. Such a dynamic not only helped transmit ideological conflict into the provinces; it probably also intensified it.[49]

The ejections of 1680 were certainly not the last instance of 'tuning' local commissions by the central authorities. James II's short reign witnessed perhaps the most remarkable attempt to transform the composition of Welsh local government during the early modern era. In December 1687, the Duke of Beaufort (as Worcester had now become), summoned Welsh deputy lieutenants and JPs to Ludlow to answer three questions ahead of a prospective Parliament. These asked whether the gentlemen would vote to repeal the anti-Catholic penal laws and Test Acts; whether they would vote for candidates committed to repeal; and whether they would live quietly with people of all religious views. James wished to pack a Parliament that would support his attempts to bring in religious toleration, for Catholics such as himself, but also for dissenters.[50] The Anglican Tories, who comprised the majority of JPs in Wales, largely absented themselves from Ludlow, claiming infirmity, illness or the problems of travelling in the winter. Those who did attend were usually either evasive or outright hostile to the idea of toleration.[51] The justices of Merioneth (bar one) boycotted the meeting, claiming that Beaufort's letter had never reached them, although they did write a collective letter to the Lord President in which they described the Test Act as 'not to be abrogated, as being the sole support and defence … of the Established religion and Church, whereof wee are all members'.[52] In Caernarvonshire, Thomas Mostyn wrote that he and his fellows were 'bound indispensibly by our duty to God (whose religion is in so much danger) to ye establisht government (which is in no less) & to our neighbour whose life, liberty and estate is at stake', to elect individuals to the prospective Parliament who would not be tempted by court blandishments or support repeal.[53]

The disappointing responses to the three questions produced a determined effort by the regime to alter fundamentally the composition of local government. The king looked to remove those who had rejected his plans for toleration and to replace them with Catholics and, especially, dissenters.[54] This produced some radical and destabilising shifts in Welsh local government: forty-one justices were removed in the three counties of north Wales alone, for example, with leading figures such as Richard Bulkeley and Sir John Wynne (the head justice in Merioneth) displaced from their positions. In their room, the government intruded individuals who were variously described by one witness as 'a furious Independant', 'a drover of catle', 'Independants of no considerable estate or quality', 'a furious violent young man', as well as a number of Catholics and the son of a regicide.[55] Similarly, in Glamorgan the justices appointed by the Crown were of the most extreme puritan type, with old Roundhead captains and Baptists who previously had been involved in anti-government plotting.[56] These new JPs were described by one local satirist as 'old fellow traitors ... with their ... hott zeale for the Commonweale', and as 'maintainers of that Good Old Cause'.[57] Local communities were presented with an unpalatable choice between government by arbitrary Catholics or the potential dictatorship of sectarians; both groups conjured up the spectre of arbitrary rule, violence and civil conflict. The alienation of established Anglican local governors and the broad constituencies which supported them, helped ensure the collapse of James's regime in the localities and the 'Revolution' of 1688–9; a 'Revolution' which was once again, of course, accompanied by a remodelling of the Welsh benches. That story, however, is beyond the scope of this book.

As the foregoing discussion demonstrates, competition for status and precedence within local society produced tensions and rivalries among the county gentry. From the mid-seventeenth century onwards, these disputes often adopted overtly ideological forms such as Presbyterian against Independent and Whig against Tory. Indeed, such party allegiances could cause serious rifts on some county benches, as in Monmouthshire during the Popish Plot when the Privy Council chided the justices over their requirement to tender the oaths of supremacy and allegiance to recusants, describing how the JPs' return showed only 'the markes ... of great animosityes & differences amongst your selves'.[58] In the sixteenth century, although confessional politics played a role in some local confrontations, ideologically-grounded disputes were less prominent. Instead, struggles for power and precedence characterised by local factionalism were conducted through the aggressive use of the law, contests of rival entourages and competition for positions of authority.[59] However, as we have already seen, many factional disputes were not simply local struggles, but were inflected by the interests and patronage of powerful courtiers. Through such means, court politics and its priorities were imported into the Welsh shires, and faction became imbued with what Penry Williams has described as the 'subtle mixture of personal conflict and political disagreement'.[60]

A particular problem in early modern Wales was the issue of 'maintaining': that is to say, of powerful gentlemen having large bodies of dependants, or 'retainers', who wore their badge, colours or livery, and constituted something of a local factional 'party' which could be mobilised aggressively against their opponents. Given the power and precedence of the Welsh gentry in their shires, this form of 'family politics' was especially significant for the complexion of political life there. The problem of maintaining was discussed by the Monmouthshire lawyer David Lewis in a letter of January 1576 to Secretary of State Walsingham. Lewis wrote that disorders in Wales, especially in the south, 'have growen muche of late daies by retayners of gentlemen whome they muste after the maner of the countrey bere out in all actions be they never so badd'.[61] Retaining and the mobilisation of followers was a venerable Welsh tradition, but commentators like Lewis worried about the growth and abuse of maintaining in Elizabethan Wales and about the violence of recent factional struggles. Despite the rhetoric of the likes of George Owen, then, Wales was clearly not a tranquil and wholly peaceful country following the Acts of Union. Many examples could be offered of gentry confrontations involving retrainers, particularly from the archives of the Star Chamber court in which such riots and broils were prosecuted.[62] Although we must treat such evidence very carefully – 'Star Chamber stories' had their own narrative conventions and style – the number and detail of such suits, corroborated by witnesses such as Lewis, identify retaining as a very real problem. To cite one case by way of illustration, in a 1599 Star Chamber suit it was alleged that William and Thomas Morgan of Machen had brought some 300 retainers to Monmouthshire's quarter sessions to intimidate their adversaries on the bench. On this occasion Thomas was reported to have said, 'this sessions was wount to be a sessions of the peace, but I thinke yt wilbe a sessions of warre', while William had urged the Morgans' followers, 'stande by me and I will stande by you; I have money sufycyent to defray your charges'.[63]

While such confrontations were often limited to inter-gentry disputes within individual shires or regions, the influence of courtly patrons could alter the dynamics of local factional struggles. A notable example in this respect was the influence exercised in north Wales by Robert Dudley, Earl of Leicester, one of the most powerful figures at the Elizabethan court. Through a series of royal grants in the 1560s, Dudley had obtained a significant landholding interest centred on Denbighshire which gave him an enormous territorial presence in the area, and which also brought the promise of significant potential patronage for the local gentry.[64] Leicester's influence destabilised the balance of gentry power in the region, as his clients and dependants reaped the rewards of his largesse, while those who remained outside his charmed circle became disgruntled and frustrated. The gentry groups which were shaped by his patronage (and the lack of it) were arrayed behind prominent figures in the region: the pro-Leicester camp was led by the Wynns of Gwydir and the Salusburies of Lleweni, while the anti-Leicester group was associated with Sir Richard Bulkeley of Beaumaris. Thus, faction intruded itself into the politics of Elizabethan north Wales in a particularly vigorous manner during the period of Leicester's influence, as these figures, and the constellation of families and interests behind them, battled it out for access to the political and economic resources at Leicester's disposal. This was played out through appointments to local commissions of the peace, to bodies of inquiry which had the power to determine rights of tenure in the Snowdonia region, and also through Leicester's patronage and influence in elections to Parliament.

Early modern period aristocratic patronage could thus distort the nature of local politics. As we have seen, the second Earl of Essex was especially influential in south west Wales, but he also inherited Leicester's mantle in Denbighshire and other parts of the north.[65] In the south east, the Herbert Earls of Pembroke were enormously powerful, especially in Glamorgan, where the second Earl was described in 1579 as 'lord ... of the substance of the whole county', and where gentry feuds became a feature of political life in the late sixteenth century.[66] The Earls of Worcester were rival magnates in this area, although their sphere of influence centred principally on Monmouthshire.[67] As we have seen in the case of the Marquis of Worcester during the Popish Plot, by the later seventeenth century the dynamics of local faction had assumed more recognisably ideological dynamics, adopting the tactics and party labels of national politics. Precursors of such polarisation can be seen in the civil wars, when the power blocs of the Earls of Pembroke and of Worcester clashed in their respective support for the parliamentary and royalist causes. One historian has interpreted the outbreak and course of the conflict in this area largely in terms of a struggle between these two houses and their dependants which had assumed thoroughly politicised and ideological forms.[68] However, even before this point, we should recognise that factional politicking not infrequently butted up against ideological concerns. For example, the Earl of Leicester advocated an activist Protestantism and an interventionist stance in European confessional conflicts, and his expedition to the Netherlands in 1585–6, which was an expression of these political priorities, included a number of his followers from north Wales.[69]

Aristocratic patronage was also sometimes important in the election of Welsh MPs to Parliament. Leicester, for example, was a domineering presence in the election of MPs for Denbigh boroughs in the sixteenth century and he was furious when the town's authorities ignored his nomination for the seat in 1572.[70] The Earl of Essex, meanwhile, held considerable sway over elections in Pembrokeshire, Carmarthenshire, Radnorshire and Denbighshire.[71] In 1593, fully a quarter of Welsh MPs were returned through Essex's direct patronage.[72] The Earls of Pembroke were influential in the electoral politics of Glamorgan and Cardiff, and the borough Member in 1621, William Herbert of Grey Friars, reflected how he was 'bound to that noble earle' for his election, adding, 'my life and all that I have shalbe reddy to doe him service to the uttermost of my power, with as good a will as anie man that breathes'.[73] Parliamentary elections in the sixteenth and early seventeenth centuries were largely products of local power politics rather than matters of principle. Contested elections could be spectacular affairs as in the well-documented contests in Denbighshire in 1588 and Caernarvonshire in 1621, which involved the mobilisation of large numbers of partisan supporters, and the use of bribes, violence and threats of violence, corrupt returning officers (the sheriffs) and plenty of ale as inducements for support.[74]

As these examples suggest, ordinary freeholder voters were potentially important components of the electoral process, but they were far from free and independent actors. Indeed, we should abandon our modern view of 'elections' for much of this period, as on most occasions only one candidate stood for the honour of being returned. Deals were struck between interested parties beforehand as to who should stand for the county or borough seat, and often the election was rather an acclamation; it was not unusual for the candidates to be absent from the hustings which elected them.[75] As with so much else, however, matters were rather different following the political convulsions of the mid-seventeenth century. While the elections to the Long Parliament in Wales were relatively 'traditional' in returning moderate 'Anglican' gentlemen to Parliament, the civil conflict opened the door to more partisan and ideological electoral contests in which party interests could weigh heavily. The 'recruiter' elections of the mid-1640s, for example, often saw candidates returned who were identified with the Independent or Presbyterian factions of the parliamentary party. In Pembrokeshire in 1646, for example, local factions that were aligned with Parliament's Independent and Presbyterian interests battled one another for the county seat.[76] In Monmouth boroughs in the same year, one correspondent wrote of interested parties who hoped that 'there were an Independent put in'; the place did indeed eventually fall to the Independent New Model officer Thomas Pury.[77] Royalists and ex-royalists, of course, had no formal place in this scene. The situation was transformed by the Restoration and the elections to the Cavalier Parliament, when it was those with a history of loyal service to the Crown who now had the advantage at the hustings, while it was republicans and radicals who were considered beyond the pale.[78] Elections, and politics more generally, became increasingly fractious and fractured in the period of Exclusion between 1679 and 1681. The struggles over the three seats available in Monmouthshire and its borough showed the dynamics of the Marquis of Worcester's Tory patronage and the resistance to his nominees posed by the Whigs Sir Trevor Williams and John Arnold.[79] Such contests were not universal of course, and there were many seats where gentry leviathans could count on being returned without the indignity of having to face a competitor or having to appeal to an electorate.

Although they had their own peculiar dynamics, particularly in the shape of the contributory boroughs established by the Acts of Union,[80] parliamentary elections in Wales tracked closely those in England in their form and nature. Parliament itself was an important venue for Welsh political life; indeed, it was the only place in which one can imagine political interests from across the principality coming together in one place. Historians used to think of Wales as serving a parliamentary 'apprenticeship' in the decades after their admission to Westminster in 1542, but such an idea is flawed and should be rejected. Indeed, there is evidence that Welsh representatives were active and adept Members of Parliament from early on.[81] These Members used the assembly to defend local interests and to advance matters which could assist their constituencies, such as the building of local bridges or the securing of exemptions from parliamentary taxation. What role, however, did parliament play in framing some kind of Welsh national political identity in the early modern period? To what degree can we locate any Welsh ideological line at Westminster? The fact of the matter is that we should not expect such a diverse and dispersed entity, which had no real institutional coherence, to express any form of national politics; this would be to import an anachronistic and nation-based set of expectations into a historical context where they do not belong. Indeed, when we remember that Parliament was a body which sat only intermittently and was composed of a diverse set of individuals from regions which had little intercourse, we encounter the difficulty of identifying any coherent 'English politics' at this time. Having said this, however, there are occasions when an evanescent type of Welsh 'national interest' is discernible within our sources, and this may be said to reflect some form of corporate political identity on the part of the Welsh MPs at Westminster.

Welsh MPs participated, sometimes collectively, in a number of issues involving regional and economic concerns. For example, in the early 1620s Welsh cloth interests of the northern and eastern counties were involved in parliamentary initiatives to free up the selling of their wool, a critical part of the local economy, from the monopolistic activities of the company which processed their raw material, the Shrewsbury Drapers.[82] The Attorney General made a report after the 1621 Parliament in which he described how a bill for lifting the Drapers' restraint of trade was produced 'upon complaint of ye gentelmen & other inhabitants of Wales', a construction that was picked up by other interested parties in the matter.[83] Another economic measure which drew the attention of Welsh MPs on several occasions was the importation of Irish cattle, a practice which many believed threatened the Welsh trade in beef and dairy produce. This issue focused the interest of Welsh Members in Parliaments from the 1610s to the 1660s, and in 1621 Sir Richard Wynn spoke of a bill to ban the import of Irish stock as a matter 'which concerns our country wonderfull much'.[84] Lobbying for the measure continued into the Restoration and an Act was finally passed against importation in 1666, with all Welsh MPs nominated to the committee that considered the measure.[85] One north Wales correspondent could write to an MP involved in the bill, 'how glad shall we be to receive you when the Act against Irish cattle is passt'.[86] Glamorgan MPs were also forward in debates over the export of Welsh butter, a major product of the county, which had been threatened by Bristolian merchants.[87] There appears, then, to have been a sense of obligation to the interests of one's constituency, of the need to 'serve one's country' as contemporaries described it, when they put themselves forward for candidacy at election time. Although these instances reflect regional rather than national political dynamics, they nevertheless demonstrate how discrete Welsh interest groups engaged on behalf of their communities at the political centre and often adopted corporate forms of action to do so.

Over and above these economic causes, however, there were occasions when issues arose that affected the whole of Wales as a single entity, and in which the Welsh members could and sometimes did act as a unified group. Often these concerned what might be described as 'legacy' matters from the union legislation.[88] One arresting example of such corporate action is the pressure applied by the principality's Members in the early seventeenth century to repeal a section of the union legislation which allowed the monarch emergency powers unilaterally to make law in Wales without reference to Parliament, the so-called 'Henry VIII' clause.[89] Pressure for repeal appears to have been maintained by all of Wales's MPs, and a petition has survived from 1621 which referred to the efforts of the 'knights, burgesses & others of that cuntrey nowe chosen & assembled in parliament' as lobbying collectively on this issue.[90] A petition of 1610 had advocated repeal in the name of the 'subjects of Wales', while a contemporary observer wrote that addressing this issue was the 'generall desire of the knights & burgesses of the principallity'.[91] In the case of the Welsh woollens bill referred to above, the resultant Act regulating the sale of wool, noted that the restraint on the trade by the Shrewsbury Drapers caused the Welsh considerable economic damage, and continued that this was 'verefied by the generall voice of the knights and burgesses of the twelve shires of Wales and of the countie of Monmouth'.[92] Although the necessary evidence is lacking to make a definitive judgement, we may assume that there was a large degree of unanimity of support, and perhaps some more concerted Welsh lobbying, for the Act of 1563 for translating the Bible into Welsh. We know that it originated as a private bill and that Humphrey Llwyd was instrumental in seeing it through Parliament.[93] It would seem, then, that some kind of communal action by the Welsh Members in Parliament was possible, but generally this was only when the issue was of concern to them all, and few measures came before the House which fulfilled such criteria. Nevertheless, the possibility of corporate agency, alongside the tendency for matters of Welsh moment to be referred for consideration to all Welsh Members in committee, suggests that a kind of Welsh political interest group, albeit not a Welsh political tradition or a political identity, was a feature of the early modern parliamentary landscape.

To this point, our discussion of politics, Parliaments and office in early modern Wales has focused on elites. Indeed, historians have asserted that they were the only ones who mattered in this domain, claiming that 'politics and its practice were the preserve of rich men'.[94]

Recent scholarly developments have rendered such Olympian assessments untenable. Historians have increasingly come to emphasise the 'social depth' of early modern politics and have expanded their scope and understanding of 'the political' to encompass matters beyond elections and proceedings in Parliament, the Privy Council and the court. Indeed, when we think about political events such as Welsh elections in this period, we are confronted by numbers of participants which move us beyond the world of the greater gentry: consider, for example, the 322 men who witnessed Matthew Davys's return as MP for Cardiff boroughs in 1604;[95] the nearly 1,100 freeholders who participated in the 1620 Caernarvonshire election;[96] or the 1,800 voters who marched '5 or 6 ... abreast' at the contested Denbighshire poll in 1681.[97] Although these may have been freeholders responding to the entreaties (and ale and victuals) of the gentry, they were nonetheless involved in the political process, and were a group which the gentry sometimes felt unable readily to awe or control.[98] It is telling, for example, that in the 1620 election in Caernarvonshire, the Wynns of Gwydir poured scorn on voting freeholders as 'the meaner sorte of people' who were subject to 'base flatterie as their blynd fancie guides them', and berated their opponents' supporters as a 'company of barefoote beggers'. However, it was the Wynns who ended up on the losing side of the poll, with the head of the family ruing 'the greatest publicke disgrace that ever I had in my time'.[99] Moreover, in the rhetoric of responsiveness to the needs and interests of their constituents which we find in some Welsh Members' parliamentary records, there is a tacit and sometimes explicit acknowledgment that MPs felt a degree of accountability to those who sent them to Westminster.[100] In the early 1580s, for example, some Glamorgan gentry described their sense of outrage that their MP had furthered the cause of 'oure adversaryes' in sponsoring an expensive bill to rebuild Cardiff bridge, and that in doing so he had 'falsified his faythe to his whole contrey at the tyme he was retayned to serve the same trewlye'.[101] Although the terms of accountability may have been vague and pliable, there nonetheless remained a potentially powerful vision of a broad social community to which Members, ultimately, needed to answer.

It is also the case that discussion of politics and political matters was not restricted to the social elites of this period. Recent research has stressed the growing importance of the circulation of news and information in the political education of a wide social constituency. In Wales the gentry, clergy and parish worthies were well placed to influence the wider dissemination of this news as it needed to cross the linguistic barrier from English into Welsh for popular consumption.[102] However, there were still many opportunities for the transmission of news, debate and ideas into the vernacular via trade routes, the circulation of chapmen, carriers and hawkers. Such news made politics a relevant commodity for those who were excluded from the offices and institutions of government and administration. Indeed, our evidence from prosecutions for political speech in this era is eloquent testimony of the capacity for relatively humble individuals to participate in the national political discussion. John Freeman, a husbandman of Bosheston in Pembrokeshire, for example, evidently had his own view of the political situation in 1685, when he chided Henry Poyer for carrying arms for James II, maintaining, 'I would not pay thee nor noe one else a farthing for carrying armes for such a papish fellow as hee is [meaning King James II]. That for ought I knowe hee … will have our throates all cutt shortly, or doe us a worse shroud turne'.[103] Scabrous political poetry about figures such as Lord Treasurer Robert Cecil circulated in the Welsh vernacular in the 1610s, while some Welsh verse carried topical messages about the Armada and Gunpowder Plot.[104] The rise and growth of manuscript and printed news in the seventeenth century was essentially an Anglophone phenomenon, and these texts were consumed as voraciously by Welsh gentlemen as their English counterparts.[105] Although many of the illiterate monoglot Welsh might not have had immediate access to such materials, it seems highly likely their messages crossed the linguistic barrier through discussion with literate bilingual figures, such as clergymen, clerks and scriveners.

It is clear, then, that there was a degree of political awareness that penetrated the social bedrock of early modern Wales, and that the population was not simply a feudal mass, 'apolitical and utterly apathetic', as one historian would have it.[106] What, however, of popular political agency and the mobilisation of political opinion by those beneath the gentry order? Was there any active role for non-elites in the political world, or was political action the preserve of the upper gentry? On closer inspection it seems that there were indeed spaces in which ordinary individuals could participate in local and national politics, albeit in different modes and through a different register than the gentry, although it also seems such opportunities were episodic and discontinuous. One such opportunity involved the subscription of petitions and oaths which became a feature of political life from the early 1640s. For example, a petition to Parliament of February 1641 organised by Welsh puritans and requesting the abolition of episcopacy, contained some 300 signatures, a significant number assembled as means of demonstrating the breadth of support the measure enjoyed.[107] Such 'mass' petitioning had previously been thought unseemly, but the political breakdown of civil war encouraged and helped legitimise a popular politics of this sort. The royalists were not left behind in adopting these practices and, as has been mentioned in Chapter 4, a petition in favour of episcopacy was presented to Parliament in early 1642 in the name of 30,000 inhabitants of the six counties of north Wales.[108] Although this number was almost certainly an exaggeration, it is unlikely to have been entirely a fiction, and probably represented a serious canvassing effort.

We gain more insight into subscription politics from activity in the summer of 1642 as the struggle between Crown and Parliament to control the country's militia intensified. On this occasion another petition, this time expressing support for the embattled Charles I, was being drawn up in north Wales. Although a gentry initiative, canvassing for signatures was adopted as a means of giving the message greater legitimacy. On 21 July 1642, David Lloyd wrote to Sir Thomas Salusbury of Lleweni, sending him the 'subscription' of two Denbighshire parishes and advising Salusbury to return the petition to Llanfair 'for more hands which are very ready there'. Lloyd continued that two men in Derwen were 'both very forward to advance yt', and called on Salusbury to write to John Wynn to 'oversee the work' in three other parishes. He added that if Salusbury sent a servant to 'hasten yt, you shall receive many more hands at Lleweny on Sunday night'.[109] Two days later, John Lloyd of Berth, Denbighshire, sent Salusbury a schedule of the 'freehoulders & other men of qualitie & habilitie' in the parish of Llanbedr, adding that others could be 'subscribed to the originall peticion, being good freeholders'.[110] The loyalist petition was printed (albeit without signatures, as was common at this time) and presented to Charles I on 1 August.[111] Five days later Salusbury wrote to Thomas Bulkeley of Anglesey about a recent meeting at Wrexham at which the local gentry 'undertook to use theyr endeavors in pursuance of theyr peticion, more unanimously then subscribed (especially Flintshire) to defend his Majeties person, honour and legall prerogative together with ye protestant religion'.[112] Although our evidence for this petitionary activity comes from gentry sources, what is noticeable is the gentlemen's efforts to secure subscriptions as a means of demonstrating the strength of their support and also to provide legitimacy for its loyalist message. Unfortunately we do not possess the original signatures, but such evidence is suggestive of a greater social range of political engagement opening up during a time of crisis.

Petitioning and subscription became a feature of mid-seventeenth-century political life. There were some notable examples in Wales, especially the anti-Protectorate tract *A Word for God*, devised by Vavasor Powell in 1655 which possessed some 322 signatures, and Walter Cradock's *Humble Representation and Address* which answered it, trumping its subscription efforts by sporting 762 signatures.[113] Once more we do not know very much about the mechanics by which these petitions were circulated and subscribed, but we are clearly dealing with broad-based mobilisations that drew in figures from beyond traditional ruling elites. As was mentioned in Chapter 6, in 1660 Charles II was met by loyal addresses from north and south Wales; these were organised by the gentry, and it is unclear to what extent they sought a more socially inclusive endorsement.[114] The subscription impulse unleashed during the civil wars receded somewhat in the early years of the Restoration, partly on account of the Tumultuous Petitioning Act (1661), but it fired back into life with the Exclusion Crisis. We find many local communities in Wales formulating loyalist addresses supporting Charles II during the Exclusion Crisis 1680–1, and, although most do not record the number of subscribers, we know that the address from Brecon corporation alone was endorsed by more than 400 individuals.[115]

Perhaps the most remarkable example of a socially inclusive political mobilisation from this period, however, comes in the form of a petition presented to Parliament in 1689 in support of a parliamentary bill for abolishing the Council in the Marches of Wales.[116] Although the Council had been a relatively popular institution in Wales and the Marches, and had, indeed, been restored in 1660 after petitions from the English border counties which sported some 3,000 signatures,[117] its association with the Marquis of Worcester had tainted it with the brush of arbitrary rule.[118] As one hostile commentator from Caernarvonshire put it, the Welsh were as 'ill used as the French subjects' by the Council.[119] As part of the 'Glorious Revolution', therefore, a campaign was set on foot to abolish this body whose powers derived from the royal prerogative. A bill was prepared to this effect and moved through Parliament in May and June 1689. This was a gentry-led measure rather than any spontaneous plebeian initiative; some twenty-three Welsh gentlemen were prominent signatories when the measure came before Parliament, and they provided legal counsel who argued against the court in parliamentary committee.[120] However, the bill was supported outside Parliament by printed lobbying papers arguing the case for abolition.[121] As a part of this lobbying effort, a gigantic petition was also submitted to Parliament which had been circulated in Wales, and which argued that 'by long and wofull experience', the subscribers had found the court to be an 'insupportable grievance to all subjects in Wales'.[122] The petition argued that the Council's civil and criminal jurisdictions were more readily available through the great sessions, while it deemed proceedings at the Ludlow court to be 'illegal and arbitrary'.

Fascinatingly, this petition had been distributed in many communities across Wales as a blank, with a printed head beneath which individuals could provide their signatures. One Caernarvonshire gentleman wrote to the local MP, Sir Robert Owen, in early April 1689 that the petition had recently arrived in the county, and that he hoped Owen would circulate more copies of it to several local gentlemen and also to the Dean of Bangor, so that they might 'put people in mind'.[123] The correspondent also noted the popular nature of this initiative, however, predicting that the petition would 'have very many hands', and that 'the people are extreamly pleased that there is a likelyhood to pass' the bill. The people were right to be hopeful and, despite some 'rubbs' in its passage, presumably because the King initially wished to regulate rather than abolish the body, it was ultimately enacted and the Council was dissolved, as one contemporary put it 'to [the] subiects great satisfaction there'.[124]

There was indeed a popular groundswell of support for abolition and the petition supporting it.[125] The counties providing signatories included Breconshire, Caernarvonshire, Cardiganshire,

Carmarthenshire, Denbighshire, Flintshire, Merioneth, Montgomery-shire and Pembrokeshire. In total a remarkable 18,000 individuals witnessed this document, a figure larger than the famous 'Monster' London petition organised during the Exclusion Crisis in 1680.[126] The low social status of some of its signatories is indicated by the fact that perhaps a tenth of subscribers could not write their names but could only make marks. On several occasions the lists were accompanied by statements from vicars, curates and other parish worthies who testified to the fact that these marks were genuine and were made by those named alongside them; it seems that the parish church was an important venue for organising subscriptions, and local ecclesiastics were often the first names to appear on each sheet. In towns and boroughs, the sheets are often headed by the names of the mayor and aldermen. This was, then, a remarkable manifestation of popular political engagement which crossed geographical boundaries and social hierarchies. Although orchestrated by gentlemen from Wales and the Marches, the petition was not simply imposed on the lower orders, and the effort taken to gather signatures seems eloquent testimony of the need to display a genuinely popular support for the initiative, and was a recognition that people beyond the gentry classes would be able to engage with and understand the cause they were being asked to support. Twice the following intriguing statement occurs among the lists of signatories: 'if there be any exceptions, we are willing to come to a poll'.[127] This suggests that, in at least some areas, a democratic approach had been adopted through which endorsement of the petition was understood to be a reflection either of the community's unanimous position, or as a legitimate embodiment of its majority view. On the strength of evidence such as this, therefore, although the greater gentry remained in command of the levers of political power, it does not appear that Welsh politics in this period was only for 'the wealthy'.

In the early modern era, then, we encounter politics in Wales but little sense of a discrete 'Welsh politics'. In some ways this speaks to the success of the Henrician union in incorporating Welsh political life into that of the wider polity. The Welsh gentry were the principal political agents under the Tudors and Stuarts, and they fought for office, intrigued against their enemies and battled for the spoils of honour and prestige in much the same manner as their counterparts in England. There was a sense that their disputes, particularly those of the sixteenth century, relied more heavily than those in England on the mechanics of retaining and on what appeared, on the surface, to be an older, semi-feudal type of family politics which harked back to the personal retinues of the late medieval period. However, we should be careful of casting matters in such a light, and need to recognise that a good deal of our evidence for such confrontations comes from the law courts, institutions established to arbitrate disputes through the power of the state. However, it would be too simplistic to suggest that the law simply triumphed over older and more violent forms of gentry dispute: the mob actions of the Popish Plot in Monmouthshire, or, during the early eighteenth century, of the Sacheverell riots in north-east Wales, should make us wary of such comforting, but ultimately unhelpful, modernising perspectives.[128] Intimidation, violence and passion were components of Welsh politics throughout the early modern era, but the power and authority wielded by the greater Welsh gentry in their counties, relatively far from the supervising eye of London, does seem to have been particularly wide in scope and intense in nature.

The factional disputes in Wales constituted a form of politics which revolved around issues that were often highly localised in character. However, Welsh political life was not insular, nor was it divorced from the wider concerns of the realm. The nature of aristocratic patronage demonstrates how local politics sometimes reached into the court, and how court politics could filter down into the Welsh shires. Parliament was also an important institution connecting Welsh communities to the circuitry of national power. While attending at Westminster, MPs had the opportunity to represent their communities, to support measures which would benefit their constituents and, on occasion, to work collectively on measures which affected the whole of the principality. It seems correct to say that truly 'ideological' politics based on national party discourse becomes a feature of Welsh political life largely after the mid-seventeenth century. However, this statement needs to be qualified, as what went before was not apolitical. Throughout our period a pro-monarchical, pro-Established Church and anti-Catholic discourse, possessing a distinctly Welsh cultural character, formed what we might describe as the foundational assumptions upon which politics operated in this period. Mobilisations such as the pro-episcopal and pro-monarchical petitions of the civil wars, and, indeed, the widespread support for Charles I during the wars themselves, argue that, although the structures within which Welsh politics operated were essentially British in character, there was, nonetheless, a Welsh accent to early modern political discourse. The foregoing discussion has also suggested that the realm of early modern 'politics' was not entirely the preserve of the greater gentry. As electors, petitioners and subscribers, non-elites reveal themselves at certain moments in the historical record to be parts of this political machinery. They are glimpsed in the crowds attending elections, as witnesses to election returns and in the marks that accompanied the Council in the Marches petition of 1689. Although their names are not recorded in this book's index, they too are part of Wales's political history.

8

Women and Gender in
Early Modern Wales

This volume has considered different aspects of identity in early modern Wales as revealed through topics such as history, language, religion and politics. However, little has been said about perhaps the most fundamental form of self-hood, that of gender, and the book's pages thus far are populated with precious few mentions of women. These imbalances and omissions reflect the nature of a text which examines what we might describe as 'public' visions of early modern Wales and Welshness. Yet they are also the product of an academic literature in which women and gender have not featured prominently. And here we arrive at something of a quandary. Scholarship on gender and on women's experiences in early modern Britain has exploded in the past two decades to become one of the period's most vibrant, and indeed most influential, research areas. However, discussion of these topics in early modern Wales remains relatively limited (although this situation is changing rapidly) and is thus difficult to integrate into a synoptic text such as this one. A path-breaking volume of collected essays on women and gender in early modern Wales which was published in 2000 has yet to be followed up by a comparable conspectus, although much excellent work has appeared in essay form and in unpublished theses.[1] There are many reasons for this relative lack of coverage: the basic fact of the smaller numbers of scholars who work on early modern Wales and who are familiar with the source material is an important issue. It is also the case that the scholarship which has emerged in this field, much of it very impressive, has tended to focus on the periods preceding and following that covered in this volume.[2] There is a further question to be raised as to whether a single chapter in a book such as this (and written by very much a non-gender specialist at that!) smacks of chauvinism or tokenism and little more. This is a valid concern, but I have decided to proceed with the discussion of this subject because it is such a crucial topic and because it will, I hope, stand in a fruitful dialogue with the other chapters dealing with questions of identity and culture in early modern Wales.

Because of these issues regarding coverage in the secondary literature (and perhaps on account of the author's limitations also), the approach adopted in this chapter is rather different from that of the others in the volume. Instead of providing a synthesis or overview of this enormous, multifaceted and complex topic, the chapter proceeds instead through four case studies which are designed to illustrate and explore particular themes of Welsh women's lives and identities in the sixteenth and seventeenth centuries. It is hoped that this approach will allow a mix of gentry and non-elite perspectives to emerge, as well as providing vivid and engaging portraits of a variety of women's experiences which connect with and emerge out of the volume's broader themes and arguments. It is important to stress that these case studies have not been chosen to represent typicality. Rather they follow where some revealing source material and published historical scholarship leads; the reader should resist thinking of the individuals discussed below as archetypes of their gender any more than they are of their class or locality. These are individual and imperfectly rendered lives which, nonetheless, open up important dimensions of culture, religion, law, marriage, family life and politics as these are refracted through the prism of female experience in the sixteenth and seventeenth centuries.

Throughout the early modern period, certain gender assumptions informed attitudes towards women which framed, conditioned and circumscribed their lives in particular ways. Women were considered to be less emotionally stable and less capable of self-government than were men. As a result, they were expected to submit to male authority figures, whether that was their father, their husband or their master. The operation of a vigorous patriarchy thus shaped attitudes towards women. Contemporaries readily drew analogies between the household and the state in which obedience and submission of the subordinate members (the monarch's subjects on the one hand, women, children and servants on the other) was seen to promote stability, order and good government. Thus a disorderly household in which proper female submission to male authority was not observed, was seen as problematic not just for the individual household itself, but because ordered gender relations were understood to constitute the very fabric of stable government and civil society more generally. The public sphere of the state generally was considered to be an unnatural place for female agency, which was why the queenships of Mary I and Elizabeth I caused unease in some quarters, and why Elizabeth cultivated an image which stressed her masculine qualities: having 'the heart and stomach of a king', as she put it. The domestic, private sphere was conceived as a particularly female space in which women ensured the continuation of the family line by giving birth and raising children, and in which they oversaw the smooth functioning of the domestic economy. Women's reputations were rendered through ideals of sexual chastity and virtue within marriage, but also through their work and contributions to the household economy. As this question of reputation suggests, however, the public–private dichotomy of women's early modern lives obscures a good deal of the reality, for women, far from being simply private figures, were participants in, and were evaluated through, public modes of scrutiny. Attitudes towards gender thus produced inequalities and hierarchies of power and authority throughout the early modern social order. Although these attitudes prevailed generally in society, they were also complicated by matters of social rank, wealth and cultural background.

We begin our exploration of the operation of these gender dynamics among one of the wealthiest but also one of the most dysfunctional families of north Wales: the Bulkeleys of Anglesey. The travails of Mary Bulkeley in attempting to secure her inheritance highlight the problems many women faced following their husbands' deaths, when they became somewhat ambiguous figures in society as widows who had status and a degree of influence, but whose independence and authority were often constrained and circumscribed. A second section considers questions of language, culture and gender through a discussion of two poetesses, Alis ferch Gruffydd and Katherine Philips. These women offer very different prospects in terms of evidence and academic scholarship, but they both pose intriguing questions about the female voice in issues of marriage, love, politics and Welshness between the mid-sixteenth and mid-seventeenth centuries. Finally, the chapter considers the tragic case of Gwen ferch Ellis, the first woman to be executed for witchcraft in Wales in 1594. The unusually rich evidence surrounding her case offers some intriguing insights into the functioning of everyday life and the nature of popular customs beneath the level of the gentry elite. These case studies have, in part, been chosen because they provide interesting comparisons and contrasts in term of the source materials which we can use to access early modern Welsh women's lives. These range from letters and a contemporary family chronicle to poetry in both manuscript and print, to legal depositions before a court which had the power to determine matters of life and death. None of this material is conventionally 'biographical', but hopefully the following discussions will help demonstrate some of the ways in which narratives of female experience can be gleaned from a variety of different evidence, and that this chapter can constitute something of a composite frame within which we can approach the topics of women, gender and identity in early modern Wales.

MARRIAGE, WIDOWHOOD AND INHERITANCE: THE TRIALS OF MARY BULKELEY[3]

Our first case study examines the sometimes rocky terrain of marriage, inheritance and widowhood through the case of Mary Bulkeley. In the early modern era, the marriages of prospective brides among the elite such as Mary were arranged by their fathers (or, in their absence their mothers or guardians) to cement political alliances, to connect influential families and to secure a comfortable future for the daughter if she became a widow (a not uncommon eventuality in an era of high mortality). Marriage brought with it a host of responsibilities and expectations for the couple, but the necessity of producing children and ensuring the continuation of the line was paramount. Early modern gentlewomen brought to their marriages prospects of connections as well as money and often land too. However, upon marriage women's separate financial identities and resources were largely subsumed within those of their husbands through the principle of coverture. This left women in markedly subordinate positions with respect to their spouses, and the matter of their maintenance in the event of their husband's death was often a source of particular anxiety.

Such anxieties would be heightened if there were disputes within the family, children from a previous marriage, strained relations with the next heir or, most troublingly, if the heir was still a minor. All of these problems beset Lady Mary Bulkeley in the early seventeenth century.

Mary Burgh was the daughter of lesser nobility. Her father was William, Lord Burgh of Gainsborough in Lincolnshire, and she was the granddaughter of Edward Clinton, first Earl of Lincoln. In the 1570s these connections saw her become one of Queen Elizabeth I's maids of honour, a position of influence and prestige. Mary, then, was an attractive proposition for an elite marriage, representing as she did the opportunity for a union into a wealthy, influential and well-connected family. Another courtier, a man who had been appointed as one of the queen's gentlemen pensioners in 1568, was Richard Bulkeley of Beaumaris in Anglesey, the most powerful gentry family on the island. In January 1577 John Wynn of Gwydir, then living in London, wrote to his father, Maurice, that Bulkeley was to marry 'on[e] of the maeds of honor', that her grandfather, the Earl of Lincoln, was then in 'great favor', and that Elizabeth I herself 'wyll have the marriadge in the Court', so that the 'world shall know what was heire affectio[n] to thos her [ser]vants'.[4] Wynn continued that 'he [Richard] will bringe her hom[e] to Bomares [Beaumaris] in Lent as he tould me him selfe. Her name is Mary'. The queen knighted Richard on the eve of the wedding, which was held at Whitehall Palace.

So Mary was displaced from London and the court, taken from an English milieu and expected to be a wife and mother in the largely Welsh-language surroundings of Anglesey (although Beaumaris would have possessed a significant number of bilingual English- speakers).[5] She was also marrying a man who was substantially older than her and someone who was a widower and who already had some nine children. Sir Richard's first wife, a Cheshire woman, had died in 1573 while giving birth to Sir Richard's much-longed-for heir, another Richard.[6] Elite Welsh men, particularly the heirs to large estates like Sir Richard Bulkeley, not infrequently married English brides, particularly as they were, in general, from wealthier and better-connected families than those in Wales.[7] This was probably a disorienting time for Mary, but she was marrying into the relatively comfortable life of an individual who was already one of the most powerful figures in north Wales. Her situation was, however, far removed from the

splendours of the court, although we may conjecture that Mary probably accompanied her husband on his journeys to London and the
south east: Sir Richard certainly met the queen again at his house in
Lewisham in 1602 and Lady Mary penned some letters from there.[8]
Richard and Mary's marriage would last forty-four years and produce
two sons and five daughters, but whether it was happy and loving is
difficult to tell. It was, however, certainly not without incident.

Mary was an educated and literate individual who followed her
husband's affairs. In the late 1580s she wrote a letter to John Wynn in
a careful but non-cursive semi-formal italic hand similar in style and
orthography to that of many other educated women of the time.[9] She
addressed Wynn as 'good cosyn', and thanked him for a letter bringing
'joyfull news of Mayster Bulkleys good sucsese in hys busynes agaynst
that old vyper Lewes ap Owen',[10] and assuring herself that Bulkley
would 'so well governe hym selfe in hys afayrs as hys enemys shall
ever have the foyle amongs the wysest & best sorts & he the credyt'.[11]
She thanked Wynn for 'haveyng thys care of me in Mayster Bulkleys
absens'. This was the public face of a dutiful wife supporting her
husband's endeavours, but it concealed some domestic friction. The
family suffered a number of internal rifts beginning around the time
of Mary's letter, and Mary herself would be subject to the whims and
financial control of her irascible and often unpredictable husband. In
the mid-1580s, Sir Richard disinherited the children of his first marriage in favour of his children by Mary.[12] Sir Richard was outraged
because his eldest son by his first wife had married against his will,
and in a letter of 1604 he referred to 'the marriage of the youth they
calle my sonne to the cottagers daughter'.[13] His anger and bitterness
at his son (and indeed, at his deceased first wife) was profound, and in
1619 he recalled that the son was 'soe full of malice as when hee killed
any fowles with his peece [i.e. gun] hee would wishe I had beene in
the fowles place'.[14] Sir Richard's attitude shows the kinds of authority and control that many early modern gentlemen expected to have
over their children's marital destinies; Bulkeley denied his son any
allowance 'untill hee shall followe my direcc[i]on and doe as I shall
appoynt him'.[15] So Mary's children were now to inherit Sir Richard's
vast estate which ranged across Anglesey, Caernarvonshire, Cheshire
and Lancashire and which was worth many thousands of pounds
per year. The disinheritance was probably welcome news to Mary, as

her maintenance, support and wellbeing in the event of her husband's death could have been jeopardised if the estate was controlled by her stepchildren. Widows' fortunes were precarious, particularly when an alternative family from an earlier marriage was involved.

However, any stability or peace of mind about her future with the naming of her own son as Sir Richard's heir was short-lived as the Bulkeley familial discord deepened in 1607. At this point Sir Richard and Lady Mary's eldest son and heir was involved in the killing of Kent's under-sheriff who had apprehended the younger Bulkeley for outstanding debts. Probably because of Sir Richard's anger with this wayward son, who was described as a 'wild, effeminate & unthrifite man … a great hunter of women … [and] given to all extravagances',[16] it was his mother, Lady Mary, who stepped in to write to the king's chief minister as a 'most humbell and woefull suter', pleading for clemency for her son, and asking that 'the act of his servant … may not be pressed to tainte him'.[17] Sir Richard, however, now resolved to disinherit this son also, determining instead to pass his lands to his and Mary's infant grandson, (yet) another Richard Bulkeley.[18] In 1614 Sir Richard drew up his will (witnessed by William Burgh, presumably one of Mary's relatives) constituting the eight-year-old grandson as his heir, but also appointing Mary as the executor of his estate, a position of influence, and certainly evidence that Sir Richard trusted his wife.[19] However, Sir Richard's tendency to turn against members of his family must have made Mary anxious about the stability and enforceability of her marriage settlement, the legal provision which, if she became a widow, provided for a jointure (an annuity from lands shared by husband and wife) to be paid to her out of the Bulkeley estates in Cheshire.[20] Sir Richard's volatile attitude towards his family can be seen in the way he treated his sons, but also his deceased first wife, his comments on the latter causing the Privy Council, no less, to upbraid him for 'laying so fowle and scandalous an infamy upon her so long after her death'.[21] Moreover, Sir Richard had also twice revisited and revised the provisions for Mary's jointure in the light of the family's disputes.[22] His fickle nature seemed to be reasserting itself when another deed appeared shortly before his death, although it was never formally sealed, which revoked his wife's trust over lucrative Bulkeley leases in Anglesey. Although Mary's support as a widow should have been secure through her marriage settlement, the realities of male power and the disruptions within the Bulkeley family meant that she must have feared for the financial security of her widowhood. In the light of this deed and of rumours which were circulating about Sir Richard's intentions towards her and her younger son, Thomas, Mary decided to act. She encouraged Thomas to enter Henblas, the family's mansion in Beaumaris, as Sir Richard lay on his deathbed, and to seize his deeds and papers. This provoked 'great routes & riots' as Thomas and a company of rowdy young gentlemen allegedly used swords and pistols to secure the documents.[23]

Following Sir Richard's death in June 1621, Mary faced a difficult prospect as the executor of a huge estate which was riven by internal rivalries and gazed at hungrily by local gentry. Influential gentlemen across north Wales were lining up to secure a match with the young heir (her step-grandson) and, although Lady Mary was his guardian, the heir's mother, Lady Anne Bulkeley (Mary's stepdaughter-in-law) was still alive and herself trying to influence the disposition of the Bulkeley estates. Lady Mary apparently found it difficult to deal with these competing interests and ambitions. In October 1621 the Caernarvonshire gentleman Sir John Bodvel described a meeting with 'old lady Buckley' at the Beaumaris assizes, where she was probably anticipating defending the estate from lawsuits.[24] Mary requested Bodvel's 'advise and furtherance for the setting of hir things [that is, her trust over leases] ... in Anglezey'. However, although she promised to sell Bodvel a parcel of land, when the two met again, he found that she had promised instead to sell the land to John Griffith 'in regarde that his sonn did sollicite her buiseness for her at London'.[25] Presumably this was the recently-elected MP for Caernarvonshire, who was acting as her legal agent in London, defending her position in the multiple jurisdictions where challenges to her control and disposition of the estate would be made.[26] Disgusted at this rebuff over the land purchase, Bodvel scornfully recited to Sir John Wynn (a mortal enemy of the Griffith family) that 'I finde her a foolish unconstant woman and knoweth not who are her frends'.[27] Clearly the male authority figures of the region felt that they knew better than Lady Mary and were probably affronted that she was now in (a somewhat ambiguous) command over a major power bloc in north-west Wales. Sir John himself weighed in after receiving Bodvel's letter, writing to Lady Mary, 'I am sorie to heare how thinges stand with yow ... yow are bought and sould by a number of our cowntrey sharkers and leeches that envyron yow, which onelie ayme at their owne proffitt'.[28] He dissuaded her from a proposed match between her grandson and the Trevors of Flintshire, warning that they would 'gayne from yow by your graundchild all the leases and make yow ... [a] pensioner of theirs ... as sone as yow have once delivered the rod and authoritie out of your owne hands, yow shall first of all others be troden underfoote'. He advised her, in terms he would never employ when addressing a man, that if she 'caried anie common sence or feelinge of your owne good', then she should not make a match for her grandchild until she had 'setled his estate and your owne', adding: 'keepe this letter ... that yow may another day weepe over it when yow have refused my cownsell'. In their widowhoods, women were potentially subject to many competing pressures to secure their own futures as well as that of potential dependants. Moreover, widows like Lady Mary entered a world of law, politics and power which was suffused with patriarchal assumptions and norms, and which must have been daunting and challenging for a woman, who was necessarily inexperienced in such businesses during her husband's lifetime, to navigate. Moreover, this case was, as one court acknowledged, a matter which was 'very intricate and doubtefull'.[29]

Mary was not, however, as easily cowed or led as Bodvel and Wynn believed. Lawsuits against her as executor of the Bulkeley estate began to fly and she needed resolve and determination to meet these challenges in the local assizes, the Exchequer, the Prerogative Court of Canterbury, the Council in the Marches and the Court of Chancery.[30] The collateral branch of the family, the Bulkleys of Whatcroft in Cheshire, along with other Bulkeley daughters from Sir Richard's first marriage contested the will.[31] A leading north Wales lawyer brokered an arbitration in 1622 which would have split the estate, assigning much of Sir Richard's Cheshire lands to the Whatcroft family and placing the Welsh estates with Lady Mary's grandson. This was not to Mary Bulkeley's satisfaction, however, particularly as her jointure lands lay primarily in Cheshire, and she rejected the arbitration.[32] However, amidst these manoeuvrings, Lady Mary now became a victim of north Wales power politics which reached into the Jacobean court. In July 1622 the young Bulkeley heir, through agents unknown, was married to a kinswoman of the royal favourite, the

Duke of Buckingham, an event which caused the Wynns to rejoice that John Griffith, their mortal enemy and solicitor for Lady Mary, and his 'faction' were 'utterly quashed in their wicked projects to ruine that howse'.[33] Presumably the Wynns believed that Griffith sought to marry the young heir to their advantage. As the seventeenth-century family historian put it, although the grandson 'received noe portion by this wife, yett hee obteyned the favour & countenance of that great darling of king James'.[34] The match would prove disastrous for Lady Mary with her chief bargaining chip as a widow, control of the heir's marriage, now gone. The day following the grandson's wedding, the King ordered Lord Keeper Williams (a Wynn ally) to turn the Anglesey leasehold lands over to the sheriff so that the 'younge man [i.e. the grandson] may receive no prejudice in his estate untill the matter receave triall'.[35] These developments emboldened the young heir's mother, Lady Anne, and, along with supporters such as the Wynn family, it seems she went on the offensive, petitioning the Court of Wards for control of the grandchild's wardship in Cheshire, and probably helping to launch a Star Chamber case in November 1622 against Lady Mary and Thomas Bulkeley for their riotous actions when Sir Richard lay dying.[36] The powerful Duke of Buckingham also intervened in the matter, agreeing that the Welsh estates be taken from Lady Mary and turned over to 'my cosen', the young heir, who, Buckingham wrote, was 'under my charge'.[37] Unsurprisingly given this kind of pressure, the Court of Wards complied with Buckingham's request, sequestering the Anglesey lands and placing young Bulkeley in the trust of a group of north Wales gentlemen, which included Sir John Wynn and Sir John Bodvel, who were to defend his interests and act as administrators of the Bulkeley estate.[38]

Lady Mary's interests were now placed in opposition to that of her step-grandson (and also his mother) as she tried to secure title and support for herself.[39] She now pressed more suits and petitioned several courts, pursuing the heir in an effort to regain control of the extensive Anglesey leaseholds and to secure her jointure lands in Cheshire.[40] As part of these proceedings, Dame Mary claimed that she, as a widow, was owed more out of the Anglesey estate by the 'custom of north Wales'. This was a legal provision enshrined in medieval Welsh legal texts which endured beyond the Acts of Union, and, which, in some but not all cases, gave a more generous provision for widows than was usual: of a third (or even a half in some instances) of the husband's personal estate.[41] This was a prize worth pursuing: Sir Richard's personal estate (as opposed to his lands) was estimated by one contemporary to be a whopping £7,000–£8,000! One lawyer advising on the matter, however, noted that few cases brought on the custom of north Wales succeeded, and it is also the case that there were powerful forces arrayed against Mary Bulkeley's attempts to enforce such a settlement. Nevertheless, she ploughed on with energy and resolve, and, in 1624, she even sought to have the case determined in her favour by bringing a private bill before Parliament to secure her title, asserting that she had spent the huge sum of £2,000 defending her cause. As one commentator put it, 'the business grew soe hott & high that the grandmother would have made it a parliament business'.[42] However, this effort failed, partly because this was a private dispute which could be remedied in the ordinary course of law, and, one observer commented, if Parliament focused on such measures, it would have 'little leasure to attend to the publicke affaires for which they are assembled'.[43] In November 1624, the dowager Countess of Buckingham, a relative of the grandson's wife, composed a successful arbitration in Chancery between the parties in which Mary dropped her claims to the majority of the Anglesey estates in return for an annuity of £400, principally out of Cheshire lands, and a total annual sum of £640, which was considered a 'faire and ample revenew for the widdowe of soe worthy a husband'.[44] After the conclusion of these bitter and fraught disputes, Dame Mary retired to London, living on Cannon Row in Westminster until her death around 1639.[45]

Mary Bulkeley was a determined and tenacious opponent in trying to secure the best financial settlement for herself that she could manage out of the morass that was the interpersonal politics of the Bulkeley family. Although of course not a wholly typical one,[46] her case illustrates some important features about gentlewomen's social lives in this period. Mary, like most early modern women, was not in control of her marital destiny: she was matched with a courtier for social and economic reasons. Sir Richard's will to control his sons' as well as his daughters' marriages demonstrates how critical such alliances were, but also how they were dynastic rather than personal in nature. Lady Mary's case is also a graphic rendering of the struggles which widows sometimes faced in this period to secure their rights and ensure their livelihoods after their husband's death. Mary manoeuvred through a thoroughly patriarchal, indeed contemptuous, gentry culture which considered her as something of an aberration: an unmarried woman with power and influence. She was calumniated by men in terms that were distinctly gendered, with Bodvel's suggestions that she was a 'foolish unconstant woman' who was at sea in the power relationships of north Walian society, and Sir John Wynn's disparaging efforts to counsel her on how to proceed after Sir Richard Bulkeley's death: early modern 'mansplaining' at its worst. Owen Wynn fell back on gendered images of Lady Mary when she suffered a reverse in the Court of Wards, writing that 'shee stormes exceelinglie & falls a ray-linge'.[47] Mary was thus associated with forces of emotion and impulse rather than (masculine) reason and deliberation. There was also out-right contempt for her, as in Owen's later comment, 'if she will not bee ruled, let her cause faile'. In the final settlement of the dispute, Mary's agency was not acknowledged, but rather she was rendered as 'the widowe of soe worthy a husband'; even after Sir Richard's death, her public identity was defined by his.[48] Patriarchal forces were perhaps particularly influential in north Wales where customary practices still retained some force in giving the male kinship group influence over both widows and minors.[49] Mary nonetheless navigated the storms of a deeply dysfunctional family as best she could. Like other less high-profile widows, she sought to secure a stable and comfortable life after their husband's demise, but did so in a system in which, she was reminded, 'yow shall first of all others be troden underfoote'.

Her case also highlights some of the wider themes encountered in earlier chapters. These include the expanding marriage horizons of the Welsh gentry class and the increasing opportunities for court service in the wake of the Anglo-Welsh union. The plethora of legal venues in which the case was tried shows the close integration of Welsh social worlds (particularly at elite levels) with the machinery of justice and arbitration as it functioned on a British scale in the six-teenth and seventeenth centuries. These legal venues operated from the local assizes in Beaumaris up to the national Parliament sitting at Westminster. Indeed, one interesting aspect of the case is the manner in which Lady Bulkeley tried to mobilise, albeit unsuccessfully, one aspect of the particularist Welsh legal culture that survived after the Henrician union with the 'custom of north Wales'. The jockeying for control of the Bulkeley heir also highlights some of the contours of gentry factionalism in this area and the many means through which it was expressed and practised. The Bulkeley case also shows how local politics meshed with wider structures of national power and influence with the decisive intervention of the Buckingham courtly interest in securing the marriage of young Richard Bulkeley. This, then, was a parochial case about an elderly widow's jointure, but it was also much more than that.

LANGUAGE AND CULTURE: ALIS FERCH GRUFFUDD AND KATHERINE PHILIPS

Chapter 5's discussion of language and culture focused on figures such as the cleric William Salesbury, the scholar John Davies of Mallwyd and members of the bardic order. The domains in which these individuals operated were, of course, exclusively male. However, women were not isolated from the cultural currents flowing through early modern Wales even if they were almost entirely absent from the worlds of print and scholarly debate. This section will focus on two very different female poets who lived and worked in Wales at either end of our period. They have been chosen to illustrate women's agency and contributions in the fields of language and literary culture at these different points, but also so that through them we can explore some of the changing aspects of gender identity, female authority and cultural encounter across the early modern era. We begin with Alis ferch Gruffudd.

Alis was born around 1520 in north Wales, although this date is uncertain.[50] She was the product of two influential dynasties, and, importantly, these were also prominent literary families. Her father was Gruffydd ab Ieuan ap Llywelyn Fychan, who hailed from Llannerch in (what would become) Denbighshire and who was the head of a notable landed family in the region. He was also, however, a literary figure of some stature and was himself the son of a poet. Gruffydd not only composed his own Welsh verses but was also involved with assessing the bards at the first Caerwys eisteddfod in 1523. The Vale of Clwyd area in which Gruffydd lived and moved was receptive to new forms of Renaissance learning, and contemporaries spoke of his impressive library which he opened to figures such as his great-nephew, the biblical translator Richard Davies. On the other side of her family, Alis's mother was Janet (possibly Sioned), daughter of Richard ap Hywel, the man who first assumed the family surname of 'Mostyn', a dynasty which was a major power in the emerging gentry structure of north east Wales. Richard also presided at the 1523 eisteddfod and his family was closely involved in the bardic culture of north Wales. It is perhaps unsurprising that this background produced a generation committed to Welsh literary culture, but it was unusual in that this generation saw three sisters composing formal Welsh poetry: Catrin, Gwen and, the most prolific of them, Alis.[51]

There is, however, a degree of confusion over the small canon of Alis's poems which speaks to the theme of women's subordinate status in sixteenth-century Wales and also in its world of cultural production. The poems which have come down to us were, in the first instance, oral rather than manuscript compositions, and thus were somewhat evanescent.[52] In addition, Alis seems to have operated through a degree of collaborative authorship, so she is sometimes confused or conflated with other poets, including her sisters. This uncertainty about authorship suggests the relative lack of power and authority invested in the contemporary female voice as a distinct and distinctive one in the literary sphere.[53] Women were doubly barred from formal poetic circles, both by their gender and by their status as amateurs. Indeed, of the surviving poems by women writers from this period, most only have a single composition attributed to them, and not infrequently these attributions are uncertain and contested. It may have been on account of Alis's associations with the *male* poets of her family and their tradition of manuscript copying and circulation that her compositions have survived and obtained a degree of authorial security.[54] Nonetheless, Alis is unusual in having (a somewhat conjectural) eight poems attributed to her and to have been recognised as a 'poetess' in her own time.[55]

Alis wrote in traditional strict-metre forms which reflected both her gentry background and the types of elite literary culture which remained potent in north Wales during the mid-sixteenth century. As the child and grandchild of poets, she moved in a cultural context in which these poetic modes would have been familiar.[56] It also seems safe to argue that Alis and her work represent some of the educational opportunities that were opening up for women of the gentry order in the sixteenth century.[57] In 1552 Richard Owen translated into Welsh the Spanish humanist Juan Luis Vives's influential Latin tract on the education of women as *Dysgeidiaeth Cristnoges o Ferch* (*Education of a Christian Woman*), which he directed to 'all the women of this tongue who might read it … labour to read it, or hear it being read'.[58] Alis was probably among its target audience, and she was one of a small group of elite women from the period who had the learning, opportunity and status to compose traditional verse. Sixteenth-century women's poetry covered a wide range of topics, with a particular focus on religious and devotional subjects although, like their male counterparts, most avoided close or critical commentary on religious controversies. Some material of this kind was associated with Alis's sister Catrin, such as the praise poem addressed to Christ, 'Owdwl foliant i Grist', although some scholars believe that some of her religious verse was, in fact, produced by another Catrin, ferch Gruffydd ap Hywel, who came from a bardic family in Caernarvonshire.[59] It was this Catrin who spoke critically of the Reformation changes to religious practice in north Wales and was mentioned in Chapter 4.[60] These authorial confusions and uncertainties are eloquent of the problems of acknowledging and recognising the female voice in early modern Welsh literary culture.

Alis's work, by contrast with such religious verse, is much more secular and earthy, and is noteworthy for its playful and satirical view on some of the shibboleths of the female 'private sphere': sex, love and (re)marriage. While the case of Mary Bulkeley illustrates the financial and transactional nature of early modern gentry relationships, Alis's poems offer a valuable insight into their emotional dimension, an aspect of elite relations which, despite the claims of an earlier generation of historians, was an important component of marital and family life.[61] In her poem 'Y Gŵr Delfrydol' ('The Ideal Husband'), she responds to an enquiry from her father about the sort of man she wishes to marry.[62] Alis describes the qualities of an ideal partner that the historian will not find in the (male) gentry correspondence of the period. She says that she wants a man who is beautiful, skilful, brilliant and brave, and also willing to deal a blow (perhaps to defend her honour) if this was required. Strikingly, she also focused on her prospective husband's physical qualities: he should be young, strong and someone with 'the finest body possible'. Alis then turns to her father's apparently cold, transactional, reply that she should best love 'a repulsive man', but one, presumably, who has money and connections. As a result, she laments that, contrary to her father's wishes, her 'heart yearns for a handsome young man'. This is a fascinating, and quite subversive, perspective on marriage in elite families. The contrast between the social and economic conventions of gentry marriage transactions and the desires, perhaps drawn from literary romances but also, surely, from everyday life and experience, is arresting. Although there was probably a satirical edge to her juxtaposition of the rules of her heart with the rules of her class, the effect is nevertheless to place a woman's emotional voice into the discussion of elite marriage; a voice that is wholly absent, for example, in any account of Mary Burgh's match with the Bulkeley family. In another poem, Alis bemoans the fate of a woman who was required to marry an old man, but acknowledged the father's powerful influence in such matters, noting (with poetic hyperbole one hopes) that '[he] will kill me if I stepped out of place'.[63]

Alis also breaches our usual impressions of the strict patriarchal structures of this society in an *englyn* (a short, formal poem) to her father, playfully reproving him for remarrying a much younger woman after his first wife's death.[64] The tone of the poem is mocking but also surprising in dealing with sexual themes across the generations. Alis chides her father by alleging that he should reflect on marrying such a young bride because, old man that he is, he struggles to get from the floor to the bed. In reply, her father asserts that his virility matches his wife's age. While Gruffydd did indeed have five children by his second wife, this exchange strikes the modern reader as distinctly odd, but it deals with the gentry priority of continuing the family line, and we should also recognise the relative commonness of wealthy widowers remarrying younger women in this period; Sir Richard Bulkeley and Mary Burgh being a case in point.[65] Alis herself was married to David Lloyd ap Rees of Wigfair in Denbighshire, by whom she would have four children.[66] However, whether this was a union based on love and affection we cannot know from our surviving sources. Alis produced another poem in which she discussed how she wept when her companion had a dalliance with a 'light woman'.[67] Although this seems to have been before her marriage, the composition again points to the emotional and affective attachments which were part of an elite culture that discussions of 'jointures' and 'marriage settlements' obscure from us. Alis emerges from this material as a sensitive and cultured, but also bold and playful figure, who was willing to challenge some of the assumptions and priorities which restrained the young gentle-woman at this time. Indeed, her very act of composing poetry might be seen as something of a transgressive act in the mid-sixteenth century, but her light-hearted engagement with her father suggests that her creative energies were allowed, perhaps even encouraged, within his poetic household. However, as one scholar has pointed out, we cannot identify compositions which date from after her marriage.[68] It may be that her husband, or the conventions of a patriarchal society, frowned upon independent poetic expression once Alis has become a respect-able householder and mother, and once her actions reflected upon his rather than simply her own public reputation.

By way of contrast, in the mid-seventeenth century we find another female poet living in Wales who operated in a very different milieu from that of Alis ferch Gruffydd. This was Katherine Philips, also known to posterity as 'the Matchless Orinda'.[69] Philips was not Welsh by birth but rather hailed from a family of wealthy London cloth merchants. She was born Katherine Fowler around 1632 in St Mary Woolchurch. Her family had puritan leanings and was connected to prominent parliamentarians of the mid-seventeenth century revolu-tion, among them the poet John Milton. Katherine was well educated at home, being 'mighty apt to learne', and able to copy sermons ver-batim when she was only ten years old; her parents then sent her to a school for girls in Hackney.[70] In the mid-1640s, her mother, who was already twice widowed, married the Pembrokeshire parliamentar-ian Sir Richard Phillipps and she, along with her daughter, moved to Wales. A year or so later, at the tender age of sixteen, Katherine was married to James Philips (although his surname, properly, was 'Philipps') of the Priory, Cardigan, her stepfather's relation, and the couple took up residence in Cardigan.[71] James Philips was a moderate parliamentarian who became a powerful figure in south west Wales and who sat in Parliament throughout the 1650s. His wife, however, although raised in a puritan household, was a royalist sympathiser who articulated her political sympathies in several of her poems.

Katherine Philips, then, was akin to Mary Bulkeley as an English woman brought into Wales through marriage (albeit initially that of her mother), and her spouse, like Mary's, was already a widower, but for Katherine there was no male heir to contend with from this first marriage. By contrast with Mary Bulkeley, however, these marital connections were formed through ideology, politics and religious affiliation; it is difficult to see how the Philipses and Fowlers would have come together but through their overlapping religious and political networks forged through a common Presbyterianism. Katherine was a precocious poet and a woman connected through the networks of manuscript circulation of her verses and letters (which is sometimes referred to as 'coterie publication') with cultural circles within Wales but also in London and, later in her life, in Dublin too.[72] Her husband was probably away in London as an MP for a good deal of their early life together, and it is unclear whether he took his young wife with him. The emotional dimension of their marriage is difficult to recover through her poems and extant letters. She allotted sobriquets to her friends in her work: she was 'Orinda' and her husband was 'Antenor', and in the 1650s Katherine penned a verse 'To my dearest Antenor, on his parting'. This poem articulates genuine bonds of affection in its image of Philips as 'the guardian of my heart', and argues that 'Absence can do no hurt to souls combin'd'.[73] It seems likely, however, that such sentiments were fashioned for a literary image rather than reflecting faithfully the couple's domestic lives, but the poem none-theless speaks to a foundation of friendship, association and mutual respect which, as in the case of Alis ferch Gruffudd, suggests some of the emotional foundations of early modern marital unions. Katherine and James had two children, Hector and Katherine. Hector died at just over a week old and Katherine composed a poignant and moving poem for this 'lovely boy': 'I did but see him and he dis-appear'd / I did but pluck the rose-bud and it fell'.[74] Clearly, early modern motherhood was not simply a cold and calculating matter of producing heirs and ensuring the continuation of the family line.

Perhaps the most striking element of Katherine Philips's verse, however, is its praise and construction of friendship, and particu-larly friendship among women. Katherine was at the core of a group branded a 'society of friendship', and especially important in this coterie were the Welsh gentlewomen Anne Owen of Orielton (Lucasia) and Mary Aubrey of Llantrithyd (Rosania). Philips addressed these women with a kind of passionate and eroticised verse that recalls some of John Donne's work. In one verse addressed to Owen, for example, Philips wrote:

> For thou art all that I can prize,
> My joy, my life, my rest.
> Nor bridegrooms nor crown-conquerors mirth
> To mine compar'd can be:
> They have but pieces of this Earth,
> I've all the world in thee.[75]

This kind of passionate address was usually found in contemporary verses directed by a man to his (female) lover.[76] Her verses to Owen and Aubrey deal in the tropes and images of love, jealously and desire and such evidence has led some critics to argue that Philips should be read as a lesbian poet, although others disagree and, beyond these necessarily ambiguous texts, there is no evidence to suggest that Philips had a physical relationship with other women. Nevertheless, the most intense emotional connection in her work is with women, and such evidence is suggestive of the importance of female sociability and companionship for women whose marriages were predicated on matters other than love.[77]

Although we have inherited an image of women as being absent from the public sphere of politics and political engagement, this was not the case with Katherine Philips.[78] As has been mentioned, her husband was a moderate Presbyterian and supporter of the interregnum regimes, but Katherine, despite her family's political background, was a rather different political animal. A royalist sympathiser, she wrote a poem 'Upon the Double Murther of K. Charles I', which answered what she described as a 'libellous copy of rimes' made by the Welsh Fifth Monarchist Vavasor Powell.[79] Interestingly, Philips makes sure that she presents herself as a demure and unpolitical woman at the beginning of the piece: 'I think not on the state, nor am concern'd / Which way soever the great helm is turn'd', but argues that she is forced to speak out of necessity in the unnatural silence produced by the regicide. Lamenting how Charles I continued to be traduced by his enemies, she appropriated Powell's language and turned it against him: 'Christ will be king, but I ne're understood / His subjects built his kingdom up with blood'. Philips also wrote a poem, 'On 3d September

1651', which commemorated the Battle of Worcester, 'when our gasping English royalty / Perceiv'd her period was growing nigh'.[80] She also produced commendatory verses to Charles II while he was in exile, wishing him to 'Hasten ... unto thy British Isles', and in 1660 praised the return of 'Great Britain's glorious king'.[81] We have seen in earlier chapters how this 'British' dimension of politics resonated particularly strongly in Wales and it seems that Katherine picked up on these ideas in her verse. Other political poems praised royal women such as the Queen Mother, the Princess Royal, the Queen of Bohemia (Charles I's daughter) and the Duchess of York who had requested some verses from Katherine.[82] She was also moved to involve herself in the local politics that concerned her husband when an enemy, 'J. Jones', the local parliamentarian official John Jones, who was pursuing her husband for financial impropriety, threatened to publish a paper by Katherine 'to his [James Philips's] prejudice'. Her 'paper' was evidently a piece of manuscript poetry that she had circulated, and she assured her husband that 'My love and life, I must confess are thine, / But not my errours, they are only mine'.[83] This is a striking statement which places Katherine apart and distinct from her husband's political body, a body that, in theory, should have incorporated her own following their marriage.

Katherine Philips's poetry, then, provides some stark contrasts with that of Alis ferch Gruffudd in its political engagement, emotional register and presentation of eroticised female companionship. It is also, of course, strikingly different in being written in English, having a definite attribution, surviving in many manuscript copies, being circulated via socio-literary networks throughout Britain, and, eventually, also appearing in print. Katherine came to the principality as something of a stranger, and scholars have seen her as an outsider who somehow did not belong in Wales or represent its cultural voice.[84] There are problems here in presenting Welsh-language material as the only 'authentic' Welsh voice of the period, but also with stressing Katherine's 'alien' status. In fact, Katherine represents a dimension of Welsh culture that was already, and would become increasingly, important: that of the Anglophone elite.[85] We should recall that this does not necessarily mean a monoglot English-speaking oligarchy, but rather a bilingual class which could negotiate the English-language cultures which reached across the British archipelago, and also interact with their monoglot neighbours and tenants. It is striking that Katherine herself wrote a poem commending 'the Welch Language'.[86] Although this clearly addresses the language as something of an outsider, it does so in terms of praise and respect for its antiquity which are reminiscent of the attitudes expressed by 'native' writers such as Humphrey Llwyd. Although Philips has been castigated by some as presenting the Welsh language as being in a state of decay, in so doing she was, in fact, assimilating and rehearsing similar arguments made by Welsh commentators who lamented the erosion of the bardic order and the decline of the language from some earlier uncorrupted state.[87]

It is also true that we should be careful of presenting Philips too readily as an 'English' interloper. She was, in fact, figured by contemporaries in terms of Wales and Welshness, and most of her short life was spent in Wales. Her close friend and correspondent Edward Dering called her 'the wise & learned druyde of Cardigan', while the poet Abraham Cowley mined her poem on the Welsh language for images which represented Philips after her untimely death in 1664 through Briticised concepts of Merlin and Boudica.[88] The Irish polymath and nobleman Robert Boyle addressed a poem to her which reflected that, 'If there be Helicon in Wales it is. / O happy country! Which to our prince gives / His title, and in which Orinda lives!'[89] Moreover, many of Philips's poems locate her expressly within a Welsh social context, particularly her elegies of local figures such as John Lloyd of Cilgerran (Pembrokeshire), Mary Lloyd of Bodidris (Denbighshire), Mrs Owen of Orielton (Pembrokeshire) and the royalist Sir Walter Lloyd of Llanfair Clydogau (Cardiganshire); and of the last she wrote: 'If those ancient bards had seen this herse, / Who once in British shades spoke living verse, / Their high concern for him had made them be, / Apter to weep, than to write his elegy'.[90] She also directed verses to the wife of the future Lord President of the Council in the Marches of Wales, the Countess of Carbery, 'at her coming into Wales', in which she spoke of 'our country', and was clearly using this phrase to refer to the principality.[91] We should also note that Philips was part of the literary circle that included Henry Vaughan 'the Silurist' of Breconshire, and that she wrote a poem commending his verses while he returned the compliment.[92]

It seems reductive either to claim Philips as 'Welsh' or to reject her as an English 'interloper'. Perhaps she is better seen as representative of the widening horizons available to and adopted by Welsh inhabitants, and particularly those among the elite, during the seventeenth century.[93] Philips's cultural circle was 'archipelagic' in scope, encompassing Wales, London and Dublin. Although she was somewhat unusual as a female poetess of such renown among male *littérateurs*, Philips's life and career also suggest the ways in which even a 'remote' county like Cardiganshire had, by the mid-seventeenth century, become part of a wider British social, political and cultural scene. That the cultural forces represented by her poetry were in a strained, problematic and sometimes destructive dialogue with the kinds of monolingual Welsh environments that produced a figure such as Alis ferch Gruffudd is undeniable. However, by dismissing Philips out of Wales and out of her Welshness, we would be missing a critical part of the principality's wider history in the seventeenth century.

WOMEN AND WITCHCRAFT: THE CASE OF GWEN FERCH ELLIS (1594)[94]

The majority of our discussion to this point has dealt with women from the social elite. It is such figures who leave behind most records that attract the historian's eye, but foregrounding their experiences necessarily distorts our understandings of the lives lived by most women in early modern Wales. To redress this balance somewhat we will briefly consider the more plebeian and parochial contexts of early modern Wales. One avenue into this world that has been adopted in recent times by social, cultural and gender historians is to utilise legal records to recover something of the experiences of 'ordinary' women who appeared before one of the multiplicity of the country's legal venues and left some trace of their lives on parchment and paper. Historians have explored women's experiences in the sixteenth and seventeenth centuries as they were disclosed through legal cases dealing with theft, slander, affray, homicide and sexual violence. This is a huge field which is opening up exciting avenues for research and discussion in early modern Wales. While we do not have the space to explore these matters in great depth, the final case study of this chapter offers a discussion of the intersection of non-elite women, gender and legal records by examining the first recorded prosecution for witchcraft in early modern Wales, that of Gwen ferch Ellis in Denbighshire in

1594.[95] Although I should reiterate that this is hardly a representative case for early modern women – witchcraft prosecutions were rare and there was no concerted witch-hunt in earl modern Wales[96] – nevertheless, the evidence thrown up by this case offers insights into the lived experiences of women outside the gentry order. Indeed, a good deal of witchcraft research is concerned as much with illuminating the contexts out of which accusations and prosecutions arose, and the social relations that they reveal, as it is with the matter of witchcraft itself. So it is with this investigation, and the case of Gwen ferch Ellis provides us with some fascinating evidence about gender, power dynamics and popular culture in late sixteenth-century Wales which generally can only be found in legal sources such as the ones under review here.

Gwen ferch Ellis was forty-two years old when she gave evidence before the bishop of St Asaph, William Hughes, at Rhyd in Flintshire in June 1594.[97] She was being examined about accusations concerning her troubling activities as a local soothsayer, cunning woman and alleged witch, but the story she told also looked back over her earlier life. Gwen was born in Denbighshire and moved around as a young girl perhaps because of her father's premature death. By the time she sat before Bishop Hughes she had been married three times, the first when she was in her early twenties, although her husband died only a couple of years later. Gwen then married a miller with whom she lived for eighteen years before he too died. In the midsummer of 1592, around the age of forty, she married again, this time to John ap Morrice of Betws-yn-Rhos near Abergele in Flintshire, although there is some ambiguity as to whether she was still living with him in 1594, because she is described as his 'supposed wief' in her examination, and no further mention is made of him during the case. Gwen informed the bishop that 'she getteth her livinge by spinninge and makinge of lynen cloth to be soulde', but also by making medicines ('plasters and salves') for sick and diseased animals. Gwen was not, then, representative of our typical image of a witch as an old, wizened crone who lived a solitary life on the margins of society. In fact, she was a married women of independent means who contributed to the local economy and needed to maintain good relations with the local people who bought her cloth and brought their animals to her to be treated.

In addition to this description of a typical modest householder of middling status, however, Gwen was also a dealer in charms and

a soothsayer. Such activities placed her in tricky territory at a time
when the boundaries between what had once been seen as harmless
practices of folk magic were being reinterpreted and redefined as
potentially nefarious acts of witchcraft. Witchcraft was a phenomenon that, before this point, was largely to be found outside Wales.
The reframing of forms of folk magic as 'maleficia' associated with the
devil and diabolism was an important development on the continent,
particularly in southern France and Germany, from the fifteenth century. Concern with witchcraft had penetrated England, with counties
such as Essex seeing relatively high accusations for witchcraft in the
sixteenth century and the passage of an Act against witchcraft in 1563.
However, as we have seen in earlier chapters, religious, intellectual
and cultural concepts in English culture were readily transmitted into
Wales, particularly following the Acts of Union, and this reframing
of witchcraft, it appears, was one such concept. It seems telling, for
example, that the word for 'witch' entered the Welsh language as
'wits' or 'witsh', a direct borrowing from the English, in the mid-
sixteenth century. Its first appearance was in William Salesbury's 1547
Dictionary where, troublingly for Gwen ferch Ellis, he offered up a
translation as 'wytche', but also an explanatory term of 'dewimwraic'
(*sic*: 'dewin-wraig'), or 'soothsayer' or 'charmer'; his definition was
also emphatically female.[98] As can be seen in Salesbury's definition,
but also in contemporary legal sources, the vocabulary of witchcraft
was imprecise and overlapped with older, non-maleficent, categories
of traditionally women's activity in charming and white magic. The
concept of 'witchcraft', then, was a relatively new one in Elizabethan
Wales, although Gwen's dealing in charms, prognostications and
soothsaying (practices which had been around for centuries) would fall
afoul of the authorities' licence to redefine these activities as potentially
harmful and illegal. Such an interpretation of her activities seems to
have come about because her work as a local 'cunning woman' came
up against the interests of a powerful local gentleman.

Gwen attracted the attention of the authorities because she discussed the magistrate and local gentry figure Thomas Mostyn of
Gloddaeth in Caernarvonshire with a woman from a relatively prosperous family, Jane Conway. Conway was apparently caught up in
a dispute involving the Gloddaeth squire, and, about a year before
Gwen's arrest, Conway had asked her whether Mostyn had any money

and also 'how longe he shold live'. Gwen maintained in her 1594 examination that she had responded that she did not know the answer to either of these questions, but it was obviously dangerous territory for two women to discuss the finances and possible death of a powerful local figure, especially when one of the parties was in dispute with him. Gwen was also asked under oath whether she had brought to Gloddaeth's parlour a 'written paper [which] contaigned (as it seemed) witchcrafte … Written to be re[a]d backwardes'. Gwen denied any knowledge of the offending paper but informed Bishop Hughes that she had spent a night at Gloddaeth two years before, although she did not expand on the reasons for her stay. She also noted that when the paper was found at Gloddaeth several people 'did counsaile her to get herself owte of the waie, and that Master Mostyn would punishe her for the same'. Despite the warning to flee, Gwen remained and was apprehended. At the end of her examination is the large signature of William Hughes, bishop of St Asaph, while Gwen makes a cross to witness that the words above, which she almost certainly could not read, were an accurate record of her examination. These marks on the record are eloquent of the power disparities operating in this highly gendered legal space.

While it seems that Gwen's misfortune in crossing the path of an influential local gentleman with practices that could be interpreted as 'maleficent' magic, or witchcraft, was the cause of her apprehension, at this point her case shifted away from the squire of Gloddaeth and towards her disruptive interactions with her neighbours. In July 1594 the local assize justices sent into Denbighshire to have witnesses produced and deposed against Gwen at the parish church of Dyserth. The witnesses convened here on 30 August 1594 before the local JPs William Wynn and John Lloyd. The eight witnesses (five men and three women) were drawn from the area around Gwen's house in Betws and included a bailiff, a tailor, a labourer, a gentleman and a widow. They told a story of neighbourliness gone awry and of Gwen's sometimes acerbic personality. A figure of some importance in the local community, the bailiff William Gruffith ap William, for example, informed the justices that he had heard 'by common report' that Gwen 'did use southsaying and charminge' and that 'diverse did resorte unto her for that purpose'. He thus, probably as a jest, sent word that he would come and drink in her house shortly and that, if she was a worthy soothsayer, then she would know at what time he would arrive without receiving any further warning. When he and a group of associates turned up at her home, she refused to give them any drink. One of their number angrily pushed her aside whereupon she swore that 'shee woulde revenge uppon them any injurye they should offer', and reluctantly gave them some ale. However, ap William reported that he saw a 'greate flye' ('about the biggnes of an umble bee') on the drink, which frightened the company, one of whom said, 'this is her … divell by the which she woorketh mischief'. Some days after they left her house, the man who had pushed her aside broke his arm 'without any faule [or] violence' but 'by the meanes of the … supposed witche', who, allegedly, confirmed that she had caused the break through dark magic. Ap William also deposed that he later found Gwen standing by his child's cradle in his house with no idea of how she got there, and his wife later asked him 'Whie that witche was in his house'. So the name of 'witche' was now in the air when people referred to Gwen. Although this was often a term of abuse – a term which appears in a number of Welsh slander cases from this period – it was also a legal category and one that could place Gwen in deep jeopardy.

Another deponent, Elin ferch Richard, who was around sixty years of age, recalled that about six years before her husband worked in the same mill as Gwen's second husband and that her family knew Gwen. At this time Elin's son, Lewis ap John, got into an argument with Gwen and hit her. Soon afterwards Lewis 'fell to be franticke', or mad, and several of her neighbours informed Elin that Gwen could cure him. However, when she pleaded with Gwen to help her son, she replied, 'it was to[o] late', and 'yf shee hadd come sooner and in tyme, shee could and would have holpen him'. Gwen then predicted the day on which Lewis would die of his affliction. Elin deposed to the justices that he did indeed 'departe this lief the verie daie that … Gwen beforre hadd appointed'.

These were disturbing tales of a revengeful woman who quarrelled with her neighbours and whose maleficent powers could explain their travails and misfortunes. Gwen was held in gaol until October 1594 when the Denbighshire great sessions court met. There three indictments for witchcraft were laid against her, one of which involved the murder of Lewis ap John. Her actions against Thomas Mostyn had fallen from view, presumably as these did not broach any particular legal category and no harm had come to the squire or his family. The trial jury, a group of twelve local men (women were not allowed to sit on juries, of course)[99] listened to the accusations laid against her, deliberated (probably only for a brief time) and came to a guilty verdict. At the end of the sessions Gwen was executed by public hanging.

Gwen was unusual in being presented as a witch – there were only some thirty-seven suspected witches brought before Welsh courts between 1568 and 1698 – and most accusations of witchcraft never reached trial. We should not, then, see Gwen's experience as typical. However, the voluminous papers surrounding her trial afford us a rare glimpse of a middling-status woman working at traditional trades of spinning and cloth manufacture which were critical domestic industries in many parts of Wales. She had also twice experienced the disruptions of widowhood and her uncertain marital status when she was deposed was probably representative of many separated couples at this time. Gwen was also part of a popular culture which we can otherwise only see through the jaundiced eyes of the Protestant reformers mentioned in Chapters 3 and 4. Introduced into her trial record, for example, was a Welsh-language charm, which she acknowledged using, that called on the Trinity to protect individuals from Satan in a manner that would have offended orthodox Protestants and Catholics alike, but which clearly had a currency at lower social levels. Although unrepresentative in many ways, Gwen ferch Ellis nevertheless leaves a haunting image of what a legal system configured by and for male elites could do to a humble woman at this time. We should not forget, however, that this same system also empowered Gwen's female accusers, and that it was a woman's evidence, that of Elin ferch Richard, which provided the material for Gwen's fatal indictment. Also foregrounded in this case, then, are the interpersonal disputes that operated within as well as across the gender divide in the parishes of early modern Wales.

These case studies hopefully provide some useful avenues into the wider subject of women's lives and experiences in early modern Wales. This chapter cannot hope to offer any kind of comprehensive coverage of this topic, but we can see in the above illustrations some of the gendered aspects of law, culture and society in early modern Wales.

Evidentially, women's identities were often subsumed into those of their husbands and there are often particular circumstances for their surfacing in the written record: as widows in a legal case; as poets in a printed text; as witches in a legal deposition. The gendered identities discussed here have particularly Welsh features, most obviously in Alis ferch Gruffudd's poetry, but also as seen in Mary Bulkeley's claim to the 'custom of north Wales' or Gwen ferch Ellis's Welsh language verse charm. However, we should not isolate Welsh women's lives from those in other parts of early modern Britain and Ireland, or see them as defined only by difference and distinctiveness. There are important indications in the foregoing discussions, for example, about early modern Wales's integration within a wider cultural, linguistic, marital, legal and political universe. For example, we could discuss the expanded marriage 'market' which brought Mary Burgh to Anglesey, the circulation of Katherine Philips's coterie publications which centred on the small town of Cardigan but reached through Wales and into the metropolitan centres of England and Ireland, or the appearance of the loan word 'wits' and the concept of maleficent witchcraft into Welsh-language culture. Welsh women's lives were often physically circumscribed, but they were also part of a society whose boundaries spilled beyond their local worlds, and the next chapter considers this theme further as it explores diasporas and the construction of Welsh identities beyond the country's borders.

9

'A Brittain by Nation Born':
Welsh Diasporas

At the beginning of the seventeenth century a yeoman's son, Rhys Evans, was born in Llangelynin in the county of Merioneth.[1] He developed into a strange young man who claimed to have the power to augur the future. As a child Evans, taught by his local curate, learned to speak and to read English 'perfectly, to the admiration of all that heard me'. When he was seven his father died and his mother remarried. He later moved to Wrexham in Denbighshire and became attached to a tailor in Chester where he served out an apprenticeship. Impressed by his wit and spiritual sensitivity, the tailor, a man of Welsh descent called Hugh Jones, named him 'Arise', and when any called him 'Rhys' or 'Rice', Jones reproved them, 'maintaining that they knew not the English of my name, giving me a charge not to answer any but such as called me "Arise"'. Having finished his apprenticeship, Evans moved briefly to Coventry in Warwickshire before settling in 1629 at lodgings in Creed Lane in London's Blackfriars district; he was about twenty-two years old. By 1633 he was living at Salisbury Court and listening to powerful sermons which, along with his study of the Bible, led him to experience visions and messages from God. These moved him to inform King Charles I about his dire predictions of the fate that was to befall the monarch. After returning briefly to Wales, where he married, Evans felt compelled to go back to the capital where, on one occasion, he was imprisoned for his dangerous political prophecies. However, he gained notoriety for his visions and his willingness to publicise them. Evans even gained access to Oliver Cromwell in the mid-1650s, warning the Lord Protector of the coming Restoration. His fame rests on the many books of political prophecy he published in the early 1650s. Evans petitioned the restored King for a pension in 1664 and died, probably sometime in the latter 1660s.

Although Evans's story is a diverting and engaging one which reveals something of the currency of religious zeal and prophetic counsel in times of political crisis, it also highlights important aspects of early modern Welsh migration, which is the focus of this chapter. Evans was born in one of the most thoroughly Welsh parts of the principality, yet he acquired facility in English as a young man. He was drawn to the border town of Wrexham and then to nearby Chester for economic reasons and to pursue training in a trade. To better assimilate with the English, he altered his name to a more Anglicised and pronounceable form. Eventually, like many of his Welsh contemporaries, he came to London and settled there. This theme of Welsh migration (sometimes, as in Evans's case, in several stages and with occasional returns to the homeland), often motivated by economic need, will be at the heart of this discussion. However, this phenomenon of an early modern Welsh 'diaspora' is considered here not just in terms of education and economics, but also to examine the way Welshness and connections back to the homeland were asserted and maintained by those who left Wales, and how ideas of selfhood were modified by contact with other cultures. This chapter, then, problematises any easy conflation of an early modern Welsh identity with a particular geographical or political space. It argues instead that forms of Welshness in the sixteenth and seventeenth centuries were fashioned and sustained beyond Wales's borders through bonds of positive association as well as through negative identification by those who were not Welsh. It is significant, for example, that when Evans wrote the biographical account of his life in 1652, he began by describing himself as 'a Brittain by nation, born in a part of it now called Wales'.[2] At this point he had lived in London for twenty-three years, but he remained highly conscious of his national roots and Welsh identity.

The chapter considers the Welsh diaspora principally in early modern England.[3] After an initial discussion of the background and nature of Welsh out-migration, it considers the Welsh in English border communities such as Bristol, Chester, Hereford and Shrewsbury. The chapter then moves on to the critical locus for Welsh settlement and society beyond the principality: the rapidly expanding metropolitan hub of London. An examination of Welsh movement to and interaction with the capital constitutes the bulk of this chapter. The discussion concludes by briefly reviewing Welsh involvement in the early iterations of the British empire and colonial expansion in Ireland, and finally the New World. The chapter thus examines the nature of Welshness as a 'transnational' phenomenon: a mobile and malleable concept which could be transported across geographical and political borders, but which changed, and was changed by, its encounters with different cultures. A common theme is the way in which Welsh migrants related to and interacted with one another when away from 'home', how they were sometimes defined as different and separate by indigenous groups, and also the migrants' efforts to maintain networks of association and connection that reached back into their *patria*.

Welsh migration was certainly not a novel phenomenon in the early modern era. Welsh travel to England, the continent and parts beyond had a long and rich history in the medieval period.[4] However, it seems clear that the scale and intensity of such migratory opportunities and impulses were given a significant boost by the Acts of Union and the removal of legal distinctions between Welsh and English communities. The Elizabethan George Owen wrote that since the reigns of Henry VII and Henry VIII, the Welsh were 'made free to trade and traffic through England', and had taken advantage of these opportunities to attend schools and universities in England and thus become 'good members of the commonwealth of England and Wales'.[5] The political and administrative reforms of the 1530s and 1540s thus encouraged the, often seasonal, economic migration into England of traders, drovers of cattle, sellers of woollens and cloth and hawkers of goods who could now more readily take advantage of the opportunities available to them, particularly in the communities which lay along the England–Wales border. As is discussed below, there was also an increase in the numbers of Welsh boys (and to a much smaller extent girls) who, like Arise Evans, went to England to be trained in various trades as apprentices. It also seems, however, that the sixteenth century witnessed a period of increased permanent Welsh settlement in England which lasted at least until the outbreak of the civil wars and probably down to the end of the seventeenth century. The reasons for such permanent settlement are complex but, for most settlers, they were initially economic in nature.

The sixteenth century saw the beginning of a lengthy period of population growth which placed increased pressure on land and resources.[6] This demographic expansion also produced price inflation for basic goods and foodstuffs (perhaps a sixfold increase between *c.*1500 and *c.*1640) while greater competition for land and leases drove up the price of rents. Growing complaints about wandering beggars from the sixteenth century highlight the unfortunates who were the victims of these social and economic trends. A view of Anglesey in the early Stuart period, for example, spoke of the 'infinite number' of beggars and vagabonds which troubled the island 'in heaps and troops … some men, some women; some old, some young; some weak, some strong'.[7] In the 1610s, the judge of the north Wales circuit, Sir James Whitelocke, castigated those 'who have noe trade to live on, wanderinge up and down, living upon the spoile without any lawfull course'.[8] Periodic dearth and near famine caused dreadful hardship, particularly in the late sixteenth and early seventeenth centuries, and these phenomena exacerbated the effects of inflation and land hunger, and thus encouraged some individuals and families to look beyond their locality for work and better prospects. Although England suffered from these hardships too, the economic trends tended to push individuals from the more marginal upland areas such as Wales into economically more secure and prosperous lowland regions like England. While economic migration was certainly not the only reason why Welsh men and women travelled and sometimes settled in England – there were also social and educational incentives among the upper classes, for example – it was certainly the most significant factor in the movement of Welsh populations at this time. And the first (and often the last) port of call for many, like Arise Evans, was the towns and cities of the England-Wales border.

Historians are apt to quote the 1567 comments of the grammarian Gruffydd Robert about the cultural effects of increased traffic between England and Wales. Robert wrote (in Welsh) that some men 'so soon as they see the River Severn, or the steeples of Shrewsbury, and hear the Englishmen but once say "Good Morrow", they shall begin to put Welsh out of their mind and to speak it in a most corrupt fashion'.[9] This is often read as some form of ready abandonment of a Welsh identity by migrants who were 'lured', 'tempted' or 'enticed' (such loaded terms are often employed in the academic literature) by England and Englishness. The fact that these words were written by a migrant exile from Wales is often ignored, while it is also the case that Robert's case is polemical and operates through caricature rather than constituting an accurate description of social realities. He does, however, describe a real phenomenon with the migration and settlement of significant numbers of Welsh men and women in England, although the cultural accommodations involved were more complex than he (and many historians) allowed.

The border towns and cities of Chester, Oswestry, Shrewsbury, Ludlow, Worcester, Hereford, Gloucester and Bristol were important settling points for many waves of Welsh out-migrants during this period, and all of these urban centres contained significant numbers of Welsh men and women.[10] These places were crucial hubs of regional Welsh economies which promoted trade and the movement of peoples; and in all of these locales there was a long history of Welsh settlement and community. In Chester, for example, Welsh migrants entered the city by the Bridgegate, which became known as the 'Welshgate', and settled nearby in the Bridge Street quarter.[11] Shrewsbury also possessed a 'Welsh Gate' and a 'Welsh Bridge' as well as a 'Welsh ward',[12] while in Bristol water-borne trade with south Wales saw an area on the northern quayside of the River Avon where the Welsh unloaded their cargoes christened the 'Welsh Back', a name it still retains, and one which recalls commerce and enterprise but also settlement and interaction.[13] Shropshire's Oswestry was quite Welsh in character, being christened 'Croesoswallt' ('Oswald's Cross') and described as the 'London of Wales' by a late fifteenth-century Welsh-language poet.[14] In the early Tudor era, some 30 per cent of Shrewsbury and Hereford's taxpayers had Welsh backgrounds, while in Bristol the figure was around 20 per cent, and the Welsh constituted about 10 per cent of Hereford and Worcester's taxpayers.[15] These were significant numbers and, although these populations were not concentrated in a single ghetto or district, they nonetheless suggest the scale of Welsh settlement and interaction in the English towns and cities of the border.

It appears that the more prosperous Welsh migrants moved slightly further from their homeland into Gloucester and Hereford, while those who were less wealthy favoured Shrewsbury and Chester, which were nearer the border: the Welsh ward in Shrewsbury, for example, had the highest concentration of the town's poor in a survey of 1640.[16]

Many of those Welsh men and women who ended up in these towns could be found working in their local trades; it has been estimated, for example, that around one-third of Shrewsbury's guild of shearmen in 1587 were of Welsh origin.[17] In a muster survey of the town in 1580, we find amongst the town's shearmen names such as Humphrey ap John ap Evan, William ap Rhys ap Ithel, Matthew ap Howell and John Tydder.[18] There must surely have been a Welsh flavour to that guild's feast days as well as to its everyday business. In Bristol, meanwhile, between 1532 and 1552, some 483 Welsh apprentices (including sixteen girls), mostly hailing from Monmouthshire, Glamorgan and Pembrokeshire, were indentured to Bristolian masters.[19] They entered a variety of professions, but constituted a significant proportion of Bristol's apprentice shearmen, shoemakers, tuckers, smiths, tailors and glovers. Notably, some 30 per cent of the masters to whom these young men and women were apprenticed themselves had Welsh names; this suggests that a national network reaching back into the principality was operating here. The apprenticeship records throw up illustrative cases, such as the three masters, Humfrey Jones, David Matthew and William Sutton, who took on more than half of Bristol's Welsh shearmen apprentices between 1532 and 1552. One historian has noted that while the Welsh in Bristol were not ghettoised, there were 'pockets of Welsh culture' in the city partly sustained by these Welsh master–apprentice ties.[20] We can catch a glimpse into one such cultural 'pocket' in a confession of 1549 made by one Jenkin Dee, a Bristol shoemaker, who described a conversation he had with the wife of a man named Barons who worked in the Bristol mint, which, he said, took place 'in Walshe, which she understandeth'.[21]

In such locales the Welsh identity of these migrants was modified by their encounter with England and Englishness. Such interactions were complex and multifaceted. There are certainly signs of what we might describe as 'Anglicisation' in our sources. For example, Welsh names, particularly those with traditional patronymics, must have

sounded difficult and alien to the English ear, and, like Rhys Evans's
shift to 'Arise Evans', we see cultural modifications and adaptations
taking place.[22] The Bristolian father and son of the early sixteenth
century, Thomas and William ap Howell offer some illuminating evidence in this regard.[23] Thomas was referred to in the city's records as
'ap Howell', but also as 'Appowell' and 'Apowell'. His son William,
however, was never referred to as 'ap Thomas', which would have
been usual practice in Wales, but was instead 'Appowell' and even
'a Powell', moving to an English-style surname albeit with a Welsh
twist.[24] This process of change reached its final stage in the 1530s when
he became simply 'William Powell'. We might see such instances as
evidence of Gruffydd Robert's cultural erosion and a simple process
of 'Anglicisation'. However, matters were far from this straightforward. Such adaptations were probably pragmatic responses to
operating within an Anglophone culture and were also the products
of an increasing bureaucratisation of local government and business:
it was simply easier for English scribes to deal with names that were
more familiar to them. For example, in Herefordshire in the early
1620s, a deponent in a case before the diocesean ecclesiastical court had
to explain that he knew James Pugh was the son of Hugh ap Bevan
('ap Evan'?), because 'in some partes of Wales the Ch[r]isten [sic]
names of the father are the surnames of the children, but are not generally soe, but more are named by their fathers surnames than by their
Christian names'.[25] In the same case, the curate of Churchstoke noted
that he did not know anyone called 'Richard ap John Griffith', but
that he did know a man 'whoe is comonly called and knowne by the
name of Richard Bishop ... and did affirme and sayeth his name was
Richard ap John Griffith'.[26] It seems that we should resist seeing these
kinds of cultural encounters as a simple shift away from 'Welshness'
to some form of 'Englishness' (categories which themselves were full
of regional variations and complexities, of course), and rather understand the process as one in which migrants adopted composite and
hybrid forms of identity: perhaps William was 'ap Howell' with Welsh
friends and neighbours, and 'Powell' before Bristol's council and
scribes. We can see indications of this kind of multiplicity in a tailor's
will from Much Wenlock in Shropshire, which was made in March
1641. In this document, the testator described himself as 'John David
ap Evan ap Mathew, sometimes called John ap David, and sometymes

called John Davis'.[27] It seems that these were simultaneous rather than conflicting versions of John's public self and cultural adaptation did not necessarily entail such individuals 'abandoning' their Welshness. It is notable, for example, that in the case of the Much Wenlock tailor, the testator continued the Welsh patronymic naming convention, calling his son 'David ap John'.

In this discussion of Welsh migration and settlement, we should also recall that the towns and countryside of the Welsh Marches contained significant communities of Welsh-speakers into the seventeenth century and beyond: migration into these regions was thus not always a move into an unfamiliar aural world. The town of Oswestry provided Welsh church services and bought Welsh prayer books for its congregants.[28] In Shrewsbury, the curate of St Chad's in the 1580s was the Welshman Thomas Price who ministered to the Welsh poor in the suburb of Frankwell. The town chronicler named him 'Prese', while the Shearmen's Company admitted him as 'Thomas ap Presse' in 1582. He donated to Shrewsbury School a copy of Davies and Salesbury's 1567 Welsh New Testament, and presumably used this text in his ministry in the town.[29] These Welsh-speech communities in the Marches were durable and long-lasting. In October 1642, for example, the parliamentarian soldier Nehemiah Wallington observed of the area around Hereford and Worcester that 'many here speake Welsh'.[30] Similarly, the cartographer Richard Blome in the 1670s noted that Shrewsbury was 'well inhabited by both the English and the Welsh who speak both speeches [i.e. languages]', while the publisher Thomas Jones established his press in the town in the late seventeenth century to produce Welsh-language texts.[31] In 1720 the parishioners of Whittington in Shropshire petitioned the bishop to be allowed a Welsh-language curate in their parish as the incumbent could not address the congregants in their principal tongue, while parts of west Hereford remained monolingual Welsh into the mid-eighteenth century.[32] We know too little about the sense of national identity in such Welsh settler communities and their inhabitants' connections back into the principality, but it seems likely that these areas would have been welcoming to Welsh migrants and that they sustained a distinctive cultural character throughout the sixteenth and seventeenth centuries. We should also remember, perhaps, that this border region produced authors such as Arthur Kelton and Thomas Churchyard, both 'English' writers from Shrewsbury who identified as Welsh and wrote commendatory verses on Welsh culture and antiquity.[33] The Anglo-Welsh border, then, was a distinctive region in which hybrid identities could be constructed, and in which there was a creative meeting of Englishness and Welshness rather than simply the 'erosion' or 'destruction' of the latter by the former, which is often the process described in the academic literature.

Welsh groups did not only associate together in the urban environments of the Marches but were also identified and constructed as different and distinctive by the English inhabitants of the border regions. In some instances, then, the Welsh were defined, often negatively, as an 'out-group' by English residents. We can see this dynamic operating on occasion in cases involving slander which were brought before local ecclesiastical courts. For example, in Leominster in Herefordshire in 1599, two women, Eleanor ferch Howell and Matilda Langford, were washing clothes at a well when they fell into a dispute; Eleanor had apparently asked Langford whether she had sent her husband to kill the Welsh woman's master. Langford hit Eleanor and called her 'hoore, Welshe hoore and hopped arsed hoore'. One husbandman related that Langford had spat at Eleanor, 'thowe liest like a Welshe hoore, I sent not my husband to kill thy master', to which Howell replied, 'if I am a Welsh hoore, you are an English hoore'.[34] It is fascinating to see national identifiers being thrown as insults between these women, but also to recognise that, although Eleanor was able to converse in English, she was still figured as Welsh and as being different by her neighbour. Mary Higges also called a neighbour, this time one Mary Pye, a 'Welsh whore' in 1624 at Sandford in Gloucestershire, and it seems relevant to note that when this term was spoken at her, Pye was in the company of individuals with Welsh names: John Powell and his wife Mary and also Thomas Griffyn.[35] Dorothy Roberts, a serving maid and deponent in a bastardy case in Somerset in 1656, is described fairly unconsciously as a 'Wellch wench' in the county quarter sessions records.[36] In Gloucestershire in 1601, one Mr Evans went to see a local man, Christopher Hornedge, to secure a tithe pig for a feast being held by the sheriff. When he found that the pig was too young to eat he refused to buy it, causing Hornedge to exclaim that Evans was 'a scuvy Welshe knave and swore godes woundes who would be trobled with such a Welshe roge?'[37]

This kind of language was even present at more elevated social levels and with individuals who were readily integrated into English society, as with Fulke Salisbury, an alderman of Chester who was descended from the Salusburies of Denbighshire, and who, in 1638 was derided by a fellow Cestrian as 'a Welch rogue'.[38] Although there is no sense of racial hatred here, it seems that when conflict arose, some individuals readily reached for an ethnic shorthand to characterise and identify their Welsh antagonists. During the civil wars, however, these tensions were sharpened and politicised so that the royalism of the Welsh and the parliamentarianism of some Marcher areas imparted a darker character of racial difference to the Welsh–English divide in these areas.[39] Although something of a transitory phenomenon, this too suggests that there was a sense of Welsh identity and of enduring difference in these (often quite substantial) communities of the England–Wales borderland.

Welsh men and women did not migrate only to the border counties of England, but can be found in many other English shires. At Stratford-upon-Avon, for example, Shakespeare's headmaster was Thomas Jenkins who, some argue, was the inspiration for the Welsh schoolmaster Sir Hugh Evans in *The Merry Wives of Windsor*. We can find Welsh settlers in other Warwickshire towns as well as Montgomeryshire women serving as maids in Cheshire, Welsh weavers in Berkshire and Glamorgan clothiers in Somerset.[40] We can also locate a smaller Welsh migration and settlement in counties of the south east such as Essex, Kent and Suffolk. The most significant destination for Welsh migrants in the sixteenth and seventeenth centuries, however, was the great metropolis of London. This was a period of significant growth for the capital, a growth which began in earnest at the opening of the sixteenth century, when the city's population was around 60,000. The number of inhabitants rose rapidly to around 200,000 by 1600 and to more than half a million by the end of the seventeenth century. London was by some distance the largest and most significant city in England and Wales, and a good deal of its demographic expansion was fuelled by in-migration from agrarian regions; most Londoners during this period were born outside the capital. And the Welsh contributed in no small numbers to this spectacular metropolitan growth. It has been estimated that approximately 5.5 per cent of London householders in 1582, representing perhaps more than 6,000 people, possessed a Welsh background.[41] Some of the Welsh migrants who arrived in London came directly from their mother country in search of work, while many more arrived in the capital from another English town (as in the case of Arise Evans). This phenomenon is particularly important as London was a crucial point of contact between lowland English and native Welsh cultures. London also formed a central hub for English culture, news, fashions and trends, and these were readily communicated back to their families in Wales by those who had made a more permanent residence in the capital.[42]

The Welsh who arrived in London did so for a variety of reasons, but the most significant of these, as with the settlement in the Marcher counties, was economic opportunity. Welsh immigrants in London occupied positions across the social spectrum, from serving maids and bricklayers to prominent merchants and city worthies; indeed in the early seventeenth century, London had a bishop who was born in Llŷn, Caernarvonshire, and a lord mayor from Denbighshire.[43] Many young Welshmen came to London to be apprenticed in the capital's prestigious guild companies which offered a route towards social advancement and possibly to London citizenship also.[44] Taking just four of the dozens of London Companies as his sample between 1600 and 1660, one historian has calculated that an impressive 1,375 Welsh men were apprenticed in these institutions.[45] This must represent only a small section of the many thousands of young men who entered the London Companies across the early modern period. Unsurprisingly, given the principality's involvement in the trade, the Clothworkers' Company was a particularly popular destination. Most of these apprentices came from eastern Welsh counties (some 69 per cent), with shires such as Denbighshire, Monmouthshire and Radnorshire being particularly prominent, although Caernarvonshire and Breconshire also sent many apprentices to the capital. It may be that prospective south Wales apprentices preferred the more readily available training in Bristol, while their north Walian counterparts were more inclined to make the journey to London. It is likely that these migrants already had a knowledge of English, but good communications networks such as those which ran through Shrewsbury and Chester also facilitated connections between the principality and the capital. Most Welsh apprentices in London were derived from yeoman stock (largely independent agricultural freeholders), while a smaller proportion were the sons of minor gentry, and some were the offspring of clergymen, craftsmen, artisans, traders and the like. Very few of these London migrants thus came from the lowest social groups. These young men went on to become clothworkers, goldsmiths, drapers, haberdashers, coopers, dyers, scriveners, and entered a host of other trades besides, with some of them returning to Wales to pursue their careers. One such was Roger Symonds who served an apprenticeship as a feltmaker in London before establishing his own shop in his home town of Ruthin.[46] Many apprentices, however, remained in London and assimilated into the great social hubbub of the capital and, for some, such as the fabulously rich haberdasher William Jones of Monmouth, realised the great prize of wealth and status.[47] As in border towns such as Bristol, in London we can see once again the pattern of Welsh apprentices seeking out Welsh masters, such as the seven young men from north Wales between 1606 and 1622 who were apprenticed to Denbighshire's Hugh Myddelton, a leading member of the Goldsmiths' Company.[48]

Elite families too, of course, were drawn to the capital for a variety of reasons, and London became an increasing draw for this group across the seventeenth century. Many socially aspirant yeomen and younger sons of the gentry were brought to the capital for legal training in the Inns of Court. It has been calculated that between 1540 and 1642 some 728 Welsh men were admitted to one of these institutions.[49] One Welsh diarist in 1610, with some exaggeration, noted that when a young Welsh gentleman, whose father was a noted lawyer, came before the King's Bench in a case for murder, some '500 gentlemen', most of them 'Welshmen' of the Inns of Court came to witness his arrival.[50] The royal court and the households of peers in London also drew in some notable Welsh figures. We might mention in this regard William Herbert, first Earl of Pembroke, who attended at the court of Queen Elizabeth, and Rowland Whyte (or Gwyn), who was secretary to the courtier Sir Robert Sidney. Wales's lack of urban centres and the absence of a separate fount of patronage and politics meant that gentle families had to look outside the country to take advantage of such opportunities. Indeed, one historian has claimed that in this period, 'London was Wales's only metropolis'.[51] Welsh gentlemen were also drawn to London to advance their business in the central law courts, to sit in Parliament, to connect with the great men of the realm, and simply to enjoy the shopping, luxuries and fashions of the capital. In 1637 John Rogers in London accompanied his letter to William Herbert in Glamorgan with 'poynts and gloves', which, he assured Herbert, were 'the newest fashion that are worne in London'.[52] Sir John Wynn in Caernarvonshire wrote frequently to his sons and relations in London about items he wanted purchased there, while the squire himself resolved in 1605 to 'spend the rest of my life for the winter and spring quarter in London'.[53] He did not make good on this resolution, but the attractions of London for the Welsh gentry were legion. In the 1580s William Mathew of Radyr near Cardiff possessed a London house (in Drury Lane), and residing in the capital for part of the year, taking part in the London 'season', became increasingly normalised, particularly after the civil wars.[54] The attraction to London's cultural offerings gave rise to accusations from the traditional bardic order that the gentry were 'abandoning' Wales and its culture. Although there is certainly some truth about their adoption of English fashions and forms and their neglect of traditional types of cultural patronage, few of these gentlemen before the eighteenth century resided permanently in London, and all continued to maintain close contacts with their localities.

At a much less elevated social level, of course, there were the thousands of young men and women who entered London to pursue unapprenticed 'menial' trades such as labouring or entering domestic service. We know little about the lives of such individuals, who are rarely recorded in subsidy lists or mentioned in correspondence. There certainly were many Welsh individuals who scraped a living in London, and also those who failed to do so. A tragic case was recorded in 1561 of a 'welch caryer', one Howell Aproberte' ('ap Robert'), who was alleged to have brought to London 'smale children' from Wales, likely prospective apprentices, but he abandoned them 'in the streates unprovided'. He then returned to the principality to pick up his next batch.[55] Numerous Welsh beggars, those who had failed to find gainful employment or had fallen on hard times, filled the streets of early modern London.[56] In 1582 the queen's coach was surrounded by 'rogues' in Islington which prompted something of a round-up of vagabonds in the capital, and one official noted that 'most were of Wales, Salop, Cestre [Chester], Somerset, Bowkingham, Oxford and Essex'.[57] In 1718 a Welsh Charity School was established in Clerkenwell by 'a few worthy public-spirited gentlemen of the Principality of Wales' to educate, clothe and apprentice the sons of impoverished Welsh parents in London and Westminster.[58] This initiative must have addressed a need that had been around among the Welsh settler community for decades, although the society of Welsh men and women who lived near to the margins of economic existence is difficult to recover from our current knowledge of the sources. We do know something about one of the somewhat better-off women in service, one Magdalen Lloyd, who was born in Denbighshire but who worked in a household in Tooting in the 1670s, and this chapter addresses her case in a little greater depth in a moment.

One author wrote in 1601 how the 'Welchmen, when they came to London were very simple and unwary, but afterwardes by conversing a while and by the experience of other mens behaviours they became wonderfull wise and judicious'.[59] He appears to describe how Welsh migrants melted into the background of the capital, and indeed it is difficult to locate any kind of Welsh 'ghetto' in London during this period. Welsh settlers appear to have assimilated relatively easily into the melting pot of the metropolis. They are often identifiable by their names and their patronymics, although we encounter shifts in these naming patterns like those found in the towns and cities of the English border. For example, when Gwyn ap Llywelyn (or as the scribe would have it, 'Lloellen') once of Nercwys in Flintshire, but in 1613 residing in St Saviours Southwark, died, he left bequests to his three sons, but, although they had taken his first name in a Welsh patronymic fashion, this had now become a (more scribably friendly) surname: John, Lewis and Evan Gwyn.[60] Another London Welsh gentleman in his will of 1584 described himself as 'David ap John ap John ap Edward, alias Davyd Jones'.[61] The smoothing off of Welsh edges was clearly necessary for this individual, a servant in an aristocratic household, to operate more freely and effectively in metropolitan society, although the fact that he related his lengthy patronymic in his will suggests that he still considered this to be an integral and important part of his persona.

Some commentators, however, argued that Welsh assimilation into London society was too ready and too rapid. John Owen, who hailed from Plas Du in Caernarvonshire and was educated at Winchester and Oxford, became a noted Latinist. He styled himself 'Cambro-Britannus' and was clearly proud of his Welsh roots and heritage – something he suggested was not shared by all London Welshmen. Around 1618 he produced a satirical Latin epigram on 'one called Davis', saying, 'You boast yourself of London lineage sprung / And say your father knew not the British tongue: / Your chiefest glory you would now disown / And spurn, and seek for ancestors unknown'.[62] Although Owen was doubtless charting a falling away from Welshness (and perhaps from obscure origins too) which could be seen in the city, matters of cultural adaptation and assimilation were usually more protracted than he suggests. As the discussion of the London Welsh that follows will illustrate, although the generational shifts towards a metropolitan identity was probably accurate enough for those migrants who lived and worked in London, the adoption of a plurality of non-conflictual identities, of being a Londoner *and* of being Welsh, rather than simply replacing one identity with another, probably captures better the gradual adaptations and accommodations of migrating to and settling in the metropolis. The Welsh immigrants could appropriate more than one identity as it suited them, that of the integrated and integral part of a bustling English metropolis and, when necessary, the Welshman or woman away from home who could recognise and associate with their fellow countrymen and women.[63]

One indication that the Welsh retained their distinctiveness in London is their frequent representation of the stock Welsh character on the London stage. This individual was often mocked for his naivety as something of an innocent newly arrived from the country. His most distinguishing feature, however, was his comic accent and mangling of English words with an invented Welsh dialect. This feature, which also crops up with some frequency in the popular broadside ballads of the period, suggests that the Welsh language, and a heavily accented version of English among first-generation Welsh settlers, was a readily recognisable feature of Tudor and Stuart London. Indeed, the contin-ued distinction drawn in the popular literature and drama of the day between Welshmen and others suggests that the Welsh constituted a readily identifiable group in London society. A kind of group visibil-ity bursts forth from an otherwise reticent record on the celebration of St David's Day in the city. On 1 March, the Welsh tradition of

wearing a leek in their hats made this group a highly visible and identifiable constituency in metropolitan society. This increased visibility
was also the occasion of some tensions between Welsh and English
communities. Samuel Pepys recorded in his diary for 1 March 1667
that he passed on Mark Lane 'the picture of a man dressed like a
Welchman, hanging by the neck upon one of the poles that stand out
at the top of one of the merchants' houses, in full proportion, very
handsomely done; which is one of the oddest sights I have seen a good
while'.[64] Somewhat later, on St. David's Day 1670, Lady Sarah Wynn,
a Welshwoman, wrote to her husband, Sir Richard, at Westminster
that she 'hopes he has passed St. David's Day well, and that none of
the enemies of Taffy have lost an ear for lack of reverence'.[65]

Such examples do not suggest that tension between the Welsh
community in London and others was usual, but they do demonstrate that there *was* such a community and that it could define itself
through ritual celebrations. As in the cases on the English border discussed above, we can also see traces of cultural difference between the
Welsh and other groups in London in allegations of slanderous words
before the ecclesiastical courts. For example, in 1589 Elizabeth Draper
allegedly said to Elizabeth Holborne, presumably in response to an
earlier insult, 'If I be a Welshe queane [then] thow art a Westminster
whore'.[66] A Welsh prostitute, masquerading as a landed heiress, was
one of the characters Thomas Middleton placed before London audiences in his 1613 play, *A Chaste Maid in Cheapside*. The language of
ethnic difference sometimes surfaced in moments of confrontation or
of potential violence; one old Londoner who was dumped in prison
in the late sixteenth century maintained that Bridewell's officers had
called him a 'Welsh dog'.[67]

The London Welsh retained some sense of collective identity
through the associations they maintained with other Welsh individuals, and they probably constituted a recognisable group on account
of their language, accent and common descent. During a manhunt for
a Welsh duellist and his brother in London in 1610, a London porter
interrogated before the local authorities told a story in which he had
met a man at *The Bull* at Temple Bar 'who seemed by his tongue to
be a Welch man'.[68] The poet William Llŷn maintained that William
Herbert, first Earl of Pembroke, insisted on speaking Welsh to his
countrymen at Elizabeth's court.[69] His kinsman and fellow courtier,

Sir John Herbert of Glamorgan, also used the language at court, with King James I making playful reference to 'his Welshe tounge'.[70] Use of Welsh was doubtless replicated much more readily at lower social levels, where a knowledge of English among first-generation migrants would have been sketchier. One wonders, for example, what Welsh conversations took place at the *Bosom's Inn*, where the carriers for the Denbigh post (such as Thomas ap Robert – see below) lodged on Thursdays, and also at *The Paul's Head* on Carter Lane, where the Monmouthshire carriers resided on Fridays.[71] The Welsh in London certainly retained group ties of various kinds with family and kin in the principality and would socialise with these visitors when in London, help them with favours in the capital, lodge relatives in their houses and provide them with loans and credit. In a letter of 1604, Sir John Wynn at Gwydir, who was trying to secure a match for his son in the city's marriage market, seems to have imagined the Welsh in London as something of a collective, advising his son (who was then in London) to make the acquaintance of Sir Robert Sidney's secretary, the Anglesey man, Rowland Whyte, 'who you are to respect as the most sufficient man of *our country* belonging to the Court'.[72] As Katharine Swett has argued, when a well-connected gentry family like the Wynns looked at London, they saw a constellation of Welsh associates, helpers, friends and kinsmen upon whom they could call for favours, for luxury goods and for advancing their businesses back in north Wales.[73] The Wynns used Welsh lawyers in their lawsuits, they patronised Welsh mercers, goldsmiths and haberdashers in the capital, they lodged with Welsh kinsmen and fostered networks of friendship and employment that were held together by connections that reached back into north Wales. Through such linkages a community of Welsh affiliation and affinity was sustained and supported in the capital.

Connections to the principality seem to have been important for many of London's Welsh migrant community. An excellent illustration of such links in operation can be found in the career of perhaps the most prestigious London Welshman of the period, Thomas Myddelton.[74] Myddelton was a native of Denbighshire but was apprenticed to a London Grocer in the 1570s, and when he acquired his freedom, he worked in Antwerp as agent for a group of London sugar bakers. Upon his return to London, Myddelton set up his own sugar house and diversified into other mercantile and trading businesses including cloth, blockwood and cochineal (as well as inheriting part of the family's Denbighshire estates) which made him a fortune. His was very much a London career, but, revealingly, he sustained an important regional dimension to his business which helped maintain and fortify kinship and familial ties in north Wales. Myddelton's access to ready cash made him an important source of credit, and he provided loans to members of his Denbighshire family, but also to other gentlemen from north Wales such as John Roberts of Denbigh, Roger Puleston of Emeral and Robert Wynn ap Cadwalader.[75] Myddelton, in fact, kept a separate book of what he described as 'Welsh deabts'. Myddelton's north Walian neighbours mortgaged their lands to him, apparently preferring a well-known source of Welsh credit in the capital to alternatives closer to home. Some of these loans could be quite small, such as the £10 mortgage Myddelton provided in 1589 for Thomas ap Robert, the Denbigh carrier who travelled between London and north Wales, and who probably also moved money and letters of credit for Myddelton.[76] He loaned the Denbighshire lawyer Peter Mutton £40 as a retainer, 'for the use whereof he geveth councell freely in all my cases what he can', and oiled the wheels by lending to his fellow north Walian Evan ap Howell, who also just happened to be a servant of the Secretary of State, Francis Walsingham.[77] When Sir Roger Mostyn of Mostyn asked Peter Mutton whether Myddelton would loan his kinsman John Wynn as much as £500 by way of mortgage, Mutton answered that it was better to deal with Myddelton personally than by letter in this instance, though 'such kynd of bargens were com[m]o[n] with him'.[78] In April 1597, Owen Vaughan of Llwydiarth in Montgomeryshire wrote to Myddelton, 'having occasion at this instant to use an hundred pounds'. He requested a loan via mortgage, emphasising their bonds of friendship but also stressing that he was 'one of your poor wellwilling kinsmen'.[79] This, then, was a letter of business but it was also a letter from home and a letter of affinity and kinship mixed with money that helped give a distinctly Welsh cast to Myddelton's money lending.[80] Myddelton, although residing in London and Essex, visited north Wales on occasion and, in the mid-1590s, he purchased the mansion house of Chirk Castle which was the core of an enormous estate covering some 30,000 acres in north Wales and the northern Marches. While he was clearly a London businessman and merchant of the first order, then, Myddelton was also, simultaneously, a Welsh magnate who fostered ties with his homeland and sponsored Welsh piety and culture: he loaned money for printing a Welsh metrical version of the psalms in 1603 and also funded the production of Y *Beibl Bach* of 1630.[81]

Myddelton stands at one end of the spectrum of London Welsh society, but at the other we find similar London Welsh connections and concerns, although this time through the remarkable survival of some correspondence from a Welsh maidservant from the 1670s and 1680s. This was Magdalen Lloyd, a woman who, like Myddelton, hailed from Denbighshire; indeed, she was connected to the Myddelton family through her 'cousin' Thomas Edwards who worked as an agent for the Chirk dynasty in north Wales. As a young woman in the mid-1670s, Magdalen migrated to London where she entered domestic service, passing through the Myddelton networks of influence and association to end up at Tooting Graveney in the London suburbs. This was the house of the Maynard family who, in the 1620s, had married into the Myddeltons. Magdalen's letters are a stark contrast with those penned by the formally educated men of this time, with a phonetic aspect to their spelling and a gossipy, intimate immediacy which takes us into Magdalen's life away from home. In one letter, Magdalen informed her cousin that she wrote of 'foolis[h] things ... onely to make you lafe'.[82] Lloyd was probably instructed in writing by a family member in Denbighshire such as Edwards, and one wonders whether she was composing these letters in a second language, English, which was, nonetheless, almost universally recognised as the language of literacy and correspondence.[83]

Magdalen's correspondence is much concerned with her finances, with fashion and with her employment. While in service, she once described herself as 'in a wors condison than a fatherless child'.[84] She wishes for more money to buy necessaries, but also for luxuries, and requests financial assistance and loans from her cousin back in Wales. In June 1676 she wrote from London thanking Edwards for his 'kind letter' and 'your care about mee'.[85] She informed him that her annual wage was £3 10s. and that one 'Mr [Morgan] Thomas', a mutual Welsh acquaintance in the sprawling Chirk Castle empire, had been very considerate of her in London. She included a letter to a female cousin in the country with the one she sent to Edwards as she had sent two 'to Denbis' (Denbigh) that were lost. So Magdalen is here maintaining connections with female as well as male relatives in Wales, and we may speculate whether this female cousin was literate or whether Magdalen's letters were read out to her. In one letter she asks, 'pray cos [i.e. 'cousin'] reed this letter to your frind'.[86] She requests financial help from Edwards on several occasions, maintaining that her wages were quite low and insufficient for her needs. This, at a much-reduced level, is something of an inverse reflection of Myddelton's linkages of credit between Wales and the capital. Magdalen also asks for her mother to send her some cloth she has spun, a prime export from Wales of course, so that she can make her own clothes.

Madgalen's correspondence is also closely concerned with the Maynard family for whom she worked, the health of herself and of her mistress, gossip about marriages and matches and rumours about misdeeds and reprimands among the service community. She is also, however, vitally concerned with her family and kin in Wales. She writes regularly about cousins like Howell Hughes and Meredith Williams as well as about members of Thomas Edwards's own family, such as his brother Robert, his mother (Magdalen's aunt) and associated kin such as the Prices and the Vaughans. Magdalen's letters speak of a homesickness for friends and relatives in Wales. She persuades Thomas Edwards to send her a horse so that she can 'sett out for ye contry'.[87] This 'contry' was the site of home, family and return, a place she clearly missed. On one occasion in November 1676, she wrote to Edwards, 'dear cos pray desire my mother not to dispaire but yt ye Lord will lend her of life soe long as to see me come down yet'.[88] In May 1679 she asked Edwards as soon as he could to 'let mee know how my mother is, if pleas God my mother and you bee a live [alive]'.[89] She was eager for news from home and mentioned one occasion when she was in the city but 'I had noe acquainttans for to enquire for ye drovers yf I might hear from Wal[e]s'.[90] By contrast with the Welsh landscape of family and affection, she figured 'this contry' around Surrey and London as 'soe proud yt nun [none] shall not have a good place [employment] except ye have good close [cloathes]', and that 'one must make good frinds afore ye can have a place'.[91] London and its environs for her were spaces of dislocation, of work and of different social values ('soe proud'). In October 1678, Magdalen described herself as being 'amungst straingers' in Tooting.[92] Hers must represent a common migrant experience of initial difficulty fitting in, of being an outsider and a stranger in a strange land. Over time such attitudes diminished, but Magdalen retained her sense of Welsh selfhood throughout her sojourn in and around London. Revealingly, her social circle while in England was largely composed of Welsh men and women, individuals with whom she could probably gossip and reminisce about their native communities, perhaps in the language Magdalen could not use with her mistress and fellow English servants.[93] She was, nonetheless, courted by an Englishman, Mr Tompson ('tormenting' her with 'flattering letters'), a widower whom she rejected with a startling phrase: 'if you intent to make a dying of it, be sure to leave a nuff [enough] for both your doughters to mourn for you. If you wo[ul]d dye for an Engliss woman you wo[ul]d have credit, but not for a Wells [i.e. Welsh] woman'.[94] Magdalen refers here to the perceived economic and social disparity between the Welsh and the English in London and, although she is adopting this conceit to use it as a weapon against an unwanted suitor, it nonetheless provides further evidence for her sense of occupying a position that was different and distinct from the English society in which she lived. Magdalen returned home to live permanently in Wales in the early 1680s, after having received a legacy under the will of Margaret Edwardes of Gallt-y-Celyn in Denbighshire, probably a relation of her cousin and correspondent Thomas Edwards, who became a party to executing the lease.[95] It is possible that she was the Magdalen Lloyd who married Peter Price, a distant relation from Cernioge in Denbighshire but the evidence is not conclusive.[96] As is so often the case with early modern women, Magdalen becomes less visible upon her marriage, but it seems that her London adventure was at an end.

England was not, of course, the only destination for Welsh migrants in the sixteenth and seventeenth centuries. Another important location for travel and sometimes for settlement was Ireland.[97] Racked as it was by frequent uprisings, rebellions and wars throughout the sixteenth and seventeenth centuries, many of the Welsh emigrants to the country were soldiers and commanders in British expeditionary forces. A significant number of these settled in the country, however, becoming part of the 'planter class' which morphed into the Protestant Ascendancy of the eighteenth and nineteenth centuries. Several leading figures balanced great estates in both Wales and Ireland, including the Bagenall family of Plas Newydd in Anglesey and Newry in County Down, and the Herberts of Montgomery and Castleisland in County Kerry. At more parochial levels, many Welsh soldiers also settled on Irish lands and became part of the bloody programme of conquest and colonisation. Initially these ordinary soldiers, often separated by linguistic difference, would settle together, usually on the estates of these great Welsh landlords. There was even a 'Welsh towne' planted in County Donegal on the estate of the Flintshire gentleman Robert Davies of Gwysaney.[98] The historian of Welsh settlement under the Tudors and early Stuarts has noted that 'Welsh networks of cooperation could span the Irish Sea, helping new Welsh migrants establish themselves in Ireland, and allowing established migrants to remain in contact with their home regions'.[99] We should not separate the Welsh from their wider context, however. They were part of a broader colonial community which was understood as 'British', although the Welsh element, perhaps particularly amongst its humbler constituencies, imparted a distinctive cultural dimension to this early imperial project of the Tudor and Stuart state.

The New World was also a destination for Welsh settlers. The most significant emigration in this regard was that of the Welsh Quakers, principally from Merioneth, in the 1680s to the so-called 'Welch Tract' in Pennsylvania. Under the leadership of figures such as John ap John and Thomas Wynne, perhaps 2,000 Friends emigrated by the close of the seventeenth century to the area north-west of Philadelphia where they left the imprint of their homeland in place names such as 'Merion', 'Radnor' and 'Haverford'.[100] This became an area full of Welsh speech too, and in 1681 William Penn agreed with these settlers that 'all causes, quarrels, crimes and disputes might be tried ... by officers, magistrates, and juries in our own language'.[101] The sense of an ethnically distinct Welsh community is also suggested by a document of 1690 in which Griffith Owen and other settlers referred to themselves as 'the inhabitants of the Welsh Tract ... in America, being descended of the Ancient Britains'.[102] Political and personal rivalries and antagonisms in the later seventeenth and early eighteenth centuries put paid to hopes of a self-governing 'Welsh barony', however, as their original grant was parcellated amongst others, although the Welsh cultural character of the area endured into the eighteenth century.[103]

One of the most intriguing encounters between early modern Wales and the New World was that mediated by the Carmarthenshire gentleman William Vaughan in the early seventeenth century.[104] Vaughan was a scion of the family from Golden Grove (Gelli Aur) in Carmarthenshire and was singularly exercised about the socio-economic problems blighting south Wales in the early seventeenth century. Vaughan came to believe that trade with and colonisation in the New World would provide a solution to these problems, and in 1616 he purchased territory on the Avalon peninsula in the south-west of Newfoundland, an area he rechristened as 'Cambriol' after his native country. Indeed, Vaughan maintained that his choice of Newfoundland was providential, for this land was divinely 'reserved … for us Britaines'.[105] Vaughan sponsored a colony there, transporting a number of settlers from Wales and Bristol. This effort was unsuccessful, however, and the colony collapsed in 1619, with some attributing its failure to the 'Welch fooles' who were ill prepared for the rigours of the venture.[106] Despite this setback, Vaughan's enthu-siasm for the project endured, and in 1625, upon King Charles I's marriage to Henrietta Maria, Vaughan, describing himself as 'Cambro-Britannus', published *Cambrensium Caroleia*, a volume of Latin verses which also included a map of Newfoundland drawn by John Mason, one of the colony's early settlers, which delineated the proposed settlement of 'Cambriola'.[107] In one of the Latin dedicatory verses in this text, John Guy, a Bristol alderman, merchant and colo-nist, referred to William Vaughan as 'Madocus' or Madoc. Madoc was the Welsh prince who supposedly sailed to America in the twelfth century.[108] This was part of the complex of ideas derived from Welsh history and myth which provided Humphrey Llwyd and John Dee with their justification for a 'British empire' and dominion over North America. The Madoc legend led some to believe that native Americans spoke a version of Welsh, and in 1608 one colonist at Jamestown, Peter Wynn of Flintshire, was asked by 'the gentlemen in our company … to be theyr interpretor', because his companions thought that the native language sounded 'very like Welch'.[109]

In 1626, Vaughan published another piece of colonial propaganda, this time in English, entitled *The Golden Fleece*. Mason's map made another appearance, and in this text Vaughan expanded in a prolix and circuitous way on his arguments for addressing contemporary

ills through colonisation in 'Cambriol ... for the generall and per-
petuall good of Great Britaine'. In his prefatory verses to this volume,
John Guy rendered Vaughan as 'New Cambrol's planter sprung from
Golden Grove, / Old Cambriaes soile up to the skies doth rayse'.[110] The
work is a rambling one, but it makes the case for the benefits of colonisation, particularly to 'my countrymen of Wales'. Vaughan's place
names for the new colony on Mason's map included 'Vaughan's Cove',
'Golden Grove', 'Cardiffe' and transplanted versions of all the counties of south Wales (Radnorshire excepted) as new settlements dotted
around the coastline. This was to remain a dream only, however, and
no Welsh colony was established; 'poor Cambriol's lord' died in 1641.

It seems fitting to end this volume where it began: with a map
describing a version of 'Wales' that was aspirational and imagi-
nary. Humphrey Llwyd's *Cambria Typus* drew on currents of Welsh
history to push the borders of the principality eastward; Vaughan's
map offered up a space in the New World in which Wales could be
reborn and reimagined. Although their images emerged from very
different circumstances, they underline the significance but also the
plasticity and capaciousness of concepts surrounding Welsh identity in
the early modern period. They remind us that ideas of Welshness were
relational and emerged from acts of imagination and association rather
than simply from statutes and governmental edicts. These images also
testify to the fact that Welshness was not bound to the geographical
spaces established by the Acts of Union. The materials which formed
the Welsh identities reviewed in this volume were drawn from history,
language, religion, gender, politics and geography. They constituted
shared spaces of association as well as fields for dispute and confrontation. The richness of this period can only be gestured at in these pages,
as Reformation, civil war and revolution reconfigured Welsh society
and, indeed, the very idea of the self. This era was transformative but
was not simply a transitional phase before the modern period or a time
when medieval legacies were being worked through. This was a distinct and distinctive era of Welsh history which deserves, indeed which
requires, more study and attention. This volume hopefully represents
a small contribution to that wider scholarly effort.

NOTES

CHAPTER 1

1 Abraham Ortelius, *Additamentum Theatri Orbis* (Antwerp, 1573), sig. 6C. See also, Philip Schwyzer, 'A Map of Greater Cambria', *Early Modern Literary Studies*, 4 (1998), 1–13, available at <*https://extra.shu.ac.uk/emls/04-2/schwamap. htm*> [accessed 19.05.21]; F. J. North, *Humphrey Lhuyd's Maps of England and Wales* (Cardiff, 1937). An interactive digital version of the map is available through the 'Inventor of Britain' project at <*https://queensub.maps.arcgis.com/ apps/webappviewer/index.html?id=e07ee87d03344562af2f90a3b3e6c6ae*> [accessed 19.05.21].

2 Philip Schwyzer (ed.), *Humphrey Llwyd, 'The Breviary of Britain' with Selections from 'The History of Cambria'*, MHRA Tudor & Stuart Translations, 5 (London, 2011), p. 98.

3 For this paragraph, see R. Geraint Gruffydd, 'Humphrey Llwyd of Denbigh: Some Documents and a Catalogue', *Transactions of the Denbighshire Historical Society*, 17 (1968), 54–107; Humphrey Llwyd, *Cronica Walliae*, ed. Ieuan M. Williams (Cardiff, 2002); *ODNB*: 'Humphrey Llwyd'; Schwyzer, *Breviary of Britain*, pp. 1–30.

4 David Armitage, *The Ideological Origins of the British Empire* (Cambridge, 2000), pp. 46–7, 52.

5 Bruce Ward Henry, 'John Dee, Humphrey Llwyd, and the Name "British Empire"', *Huntington Library Quarterly*, 35 (1971–2), 189–90.

6 For some provocative thoughts on this question of the ambiguous nature of 'Wales' at different points in its history, see Philip Jenkins, 'A New History of Wales', *Historical Journal*, 32 (1989), 387–93.

7 Gwyn A. Williams, *When Was Wales?* (London, 1982).

8 Williams, *When Was Wales?*, p. 194.

9 R. R. Davies, 'The Identity of "Wales" in the Thirteenth Century', in R. R. Davies and Geraint H. Jenkins (eds), *From Medieval to Modern Wales* (Cardiff, 2004), pp. 45–63; Huw Pryce, 'British or Welsh? National Identity in Twelfth-Century Wales', *EHR*, 116 (2001), 775–801.

10 R. R. Davies, *The Age of Conquest: Wales, 1063–1415* (Oxford, 1987), p. 12.

11 Philip Jenkins, *A History of Modern Wales, 1536–1990* (London, 1992), p. 4.

12 Jenkins, *Modern Wales*, pp. 5–8.

13 Although the concept of 'imagined communities' is derived from Benedict Anderson, for our purposes it is most fruitfully elaborated though his critics such as Anthony D. Smith and Adrian Hastings: Benedict Anderson, *Imagined Communities*, revised edn (London, 1991); Anthony D. Smith, *Myths and*

Memories of the Nation (Oxford, 1999); Adrian Hastings, *The Construction of Nationhood* (Cambridge, 1997). See also the useful discussion in Jason Nice, *Sacred History and National Identity: Comparisons between Early Modern Wales and Brittany* (London, 2009), pp. 17–19.

14 Davies, 'The Identity of "Wales"'.

15 Jenkins, Suggett and White, 'The Welsh Language in Early Modern Wales', p. 46.

16 Geraint H. Jenkins, Richard Suggett and Eryn M. White, 'The Welsh Language in Early Modern Wales', *WLBIR*, pp. 45–6.

17 Peter R. Roberts, 'Tudor Wales, National Identity and the British Inheritance', in Peter R. Roberts and Brendan Bradshaw (eds), *British Consciousness and Identity: The Making of Britain, 1533–1707* (Cambridge, 1998), p. 13.

18 TNA, SP14/37, fo. 109.

19 Garthine Walker, 'Modernization', in Garthine Walker (ed.), *Writing Early Modern History* (London, 2005), pp. 25–48.

20 *FMW*.

21 *SR*, III, p. 500.

22 Michael A. Jones, 'Cultural Boundaries within the Tudor State: Bishop Rowland Lee and the Welsh Settlement of 1536', *WHR*, 20 (2000–1), 227–53.

23 *RR*, p. 264.

24 *SR*, III, p. 427. See Steven G. Ellis, *Tudor Frontiers and Noble Power: The Making of the British State* (Oxford, 1995). The 1536 union Act referred to Wales as having always been united with 'the imperiall Crowne of this Realme': *SR*, III, p. 563.

25 *SR*, III, p. 563.

26 Peter R. Roberts, 'The Union with England and the Identity of "Anglican" Wales', *TRHS*, 5th series, 22 (1972), 53.

27 For a thoughtful and concise recent discussion, see Katharine K. Olson, 'The Acts of Union: Culture and Religion in Wales, *c.*1540–1700', in Geraint Evans and Helen Fulton (eds), *The Cambridge History of Welsh Literature* (Cambridge, 2019), pp. 157–75.

28 Gwynfor Evans, *Land of my Fathers* (Swansea, 1974), pp. 296, 370.

29 *RR*, p. 277. Cf. Peter R. Roberts, 'The "Act of Union" in Welsh History', *TCS* (1972–3), 50–1, 56–8.

30 *SR*, III, p. 567.

31 Mark Ellis Jones, '"An Invidious Attempt to Accelerate the Extinction of our Language": The Abolition of the Court of Great Sessions and the Welsh Language', *WHR*, 19 (1998–9), 226.

32 Tony Crowley, *Wars of Words: The Politics of Language in Ireland* (Oxford, 2005), pp. 12–15.

33 Llinos Beverley Smith, 'The Welsh Language before 1536', *WLBIR*, pp. 34–44.

34 Peter R. Roberts, 'Welsh Language, English Law and Tudor Legislation', *TCS* (1989), 28.

35 W. Llewelyn Williams, 'The Union of England and Wales', *TCS* (1907–8), 54.

36 Edward Coke, *The Fourth Part of the Institutes of the Laws of England* (London, 1644), p. 240.

37 Thomas G. Watkin, *The Legal History of Wales* (Cardiff, 2012), p. 126.
38 Representations in the sixteenth century generally subsumed Wales into England as 'Anglia', however: Ralph A. Griffiths, 'Wales', in Felicity Heal, Ian Archer and Paulina Kewes (eds), *The Oxford Handbook of Holinshed's Chronicles* (Oxford, 2012), pp. 679–80.
39 Although Saxton reproduced England and Wales under a united territory as 'Anglia' in his famous atlas, it is worth noting his production of a proof map of Wales around 1580 which might have been intended for publication but which never made it into print: D. Huw Owen and Julian J. W. Thomas, 'Saxton's Proof Map of Wales, 1580', *NLWJ*, 25 (1987), 124–30; D. Huw Owen, *Mapiau Printiedig Cynnar o Gymru: Early Printed Maps of Wales* (Aberystwyth, 1996), plates 1 and 4.
40 Thomas Watkin is unusual in acknowledging that post-union Wales 'retained a separate legal … identity': Watkin, *Legal History of Wales*, p. 143.
41 Gwilym Owen and Dermot Cahill, 'The Act of Union, 1536–43: Not Quite the End of the Road for Welsh Law', *Proceedings of the Harvard Celtic Colloquium*, 39 (2019), 217–50.
42 Jones, 'Abolition of the Court of Great Sessions', 226–64.
43 See below, pp. 161–3.
44 TNA, C219/35/2, fos 195–201.
45 Lloyd Bowen, 'Wales at Westminster: Parliament, Principality and Pressure Groups, 1542–1601', *Parliamentary History*, 22 (2003), 114–15; *PoP*, pp. 56–7, 114, 128.

CHAPTER 2

1 R. R. Davies, 'The Peoples of Britain and Ireland, 1100–1400: IV. Language and Historical Mythology', *TRHS*, 6th series, 7 (1997), 15, 23.
2 P. P. Sims-Williams, 'Some Functions of Origin Stories in Early Medieval Wales', in T. Nyberg et al (eds), *History and Heroic Tale. A Symposium* (Odense, 1985), p. 98.
3 Katharine K. Olson, 'The Acts of Union: Culture and Religion in Wales c.1540–1700', in Geraint Evans and Helen Fulton (eds), *The Cambridge History of Welsh Literature* (Cambridge, 2019), p. 169.
4 G. J. Williams, 'Tri Chof Ynys Brydain', *Llên Cymru*, 4 (1955), 235.
5 Brynley F. Roberts, 'Geoffrey of Monmouth and Welsh Historical Tradition', *Nottingham Medieval Studies*, 20 (1976), 29–40; J. Beverley Smith, *The Sense of History in Medieval Wales* (Aberystwyth, 1989); A. O. H. Jarman, *Geoffrey of Monmouth: Sieffre o Fynwy* (Cardiff, 1966), especially pp. 96–111.
6 Helen Fulton, 'Troy Story: The Medieval Welsh *Ystorya Dared* and the *Brut* Tradition of British History', *The Medieval Chronicle*, 7 (2011), 137–50; Laura Ashe, 'Holinshed and Mythical History', in Felicity Heal, Ian Archer and Paulina Kewes (eds), *The Oxford Handbook of Holinshed's Chronicles* (Oxford, 2012), pp. 153–70.
7 Sims-Williams, 'Origin Stories', p. 114.

8 Glanmor Williams, 'Prophecy, Poetry and Politics in Medieval and Tudor Wales', in his *Religion, Language and Nationality in Wales* (Cardiff, 1979), pp. 71–86; R. R. Davies, *The Revolt of Owain Glyn Dŵr* (Oxford, 1995), pp. 158–73.

9 Philip Schwyzer, 'Archipelagic History', in Heal, Archer and Kewes, *Oxford Handbook of Holinshed's Chronicles*, p. 599.

10 Henry Ellis (ed.), *Polydore Vergil's English History* (London, Camden Society, 36, 1846), p. 29.

11 Ellis, *Polydore Vergil's English History*, p. 33

12 John Rastell, *The Pastyme of People* (London, 1529), sigs. A1v–A2.

13 Roger A. Mason, 'Scotching the Brut: The Early History of Britain', *History Today*, 35 (January 1985), 26–31.

14 See, for example, John Bale's reference to 'thys our Englyshe or Bryttyshe nacyon': John Leland [and John Bale], *The Laboryouse Journey & Serche of John Leylande* (London, 1549), sig. B3v. Alan MacColl, 'The Construction of England as a Protestant "British" Nation in the Sixteenth Century', *Renaissance Studies*, 18 (2004), 582–608; Alan MacColl, 'The Meaning of "Britain" in Medieval and Early Modern England', *Journal of British Studies*, 45 (2006), 248–69.

15 Thomas Kendrick, *British Antiquity* (London, 1950), pp. 78–98. The term is a contemporary one and was used in prefatory verses to the 1573 English translation of Humphrey Llwyd's historical text: Philip Schwyzer (ed.), *Humphrey Llwyd, 'The Breviary of Britain' with Selections from 'The History of Cambria'*, MHRA Tudor & Stuart Translations, 5 (London, 2011), p. 47.

16 Leland, *Laboryouse Journey*, sig. D7v; Caroline Brett, 'John Leland, Wales, and Early British History', *WHR*, 15 (1990–1), 169–82; Cathy Shrank, *Writing the Nation in Reformation England, 1530–1580* (Oxford, 2004), pp. 65–103; Philip Schwyzer, *Literature, Nationalism and Memory in Early Modern England and Wales* (Cambridge, 2004), pp. 49–75.

17 For Prise (or Price/Pryse), see John Prise, *Historiae Britannicae Defensio: A Defence of British History*, ed. Ceri Davies (Toronto and Oxford, 2015); HPO (1509–58): 'Price, Sir John'; Glanmor Williams, 'Sir John Pryse of Brecon', *Brycheiniog*, 31 (1998–9), 49–63; *ODNB*: 'Sir John Prise [Syr Siôn ap Rhys]'; N. R. Ker, 'Sir John Prise', *The Library*, 5th series, 10 (1955), 1–24.

18 Prise, *Historiae*, p. 27.

19 Schwyzer, *Literature, Nationalism and Memory*, p. 89.

20 F. C. Morgan, 'The Will of Sir John Prise of Hereford, 1555', *NLWJ*, 9 (1955–6), 257.

21 Kelton's Protestant credentials are evident from his publications, but see also TNA, SP46/1, fo. 33.

22 Arthur Kelton, *A Comendacion of Welshmen* (London, 1546), sigs. A3v–A4.

23 Arthur Kelton, *A Chronycle with a Genealogie Declaryng that the Brittons and Welshemen are Lineallye Dyscended from Brute* (London, 1547), sigs. C3v–C4; William A. Ringler, 'Arthur Kelton's Contribution to Early British History', *Huntington Library Quarterly*, 40 (1977), 453–6.

24 Kelton, *A Chronycle*, sig. C7v.

25 Kelton, *A Chronycle*, sig. B4.

26 See below, pp. 198–203.

Notes to pages 25–31 • 223

27 Daniel Woolf, 'Historical Writing in Britain from the Late Middle Ages to the Eve of the Enlightenment', in Daniel Woolf et al. (eds), *The Oxford History of Historical Writing, Volume 3: 1400–1800* (Oxford, 2015), p. 476.

28 Humphrey Llwyd, *Cronica Walliae*, ed. Ieuan M. Williams (Cardiff, 2002).

29 Llwyd, *Cronica*, p. 82.

30 Llwyd, *Cronica*, p. 65.

31 For an influential thesis about British patriotism in this later period, see Linda Colley, *Britons: Forging the Nation, 1707–1837* (New Haven and London, 1992).

32 Llwyd, *Cronica*, pp. 64, 223.

33 Schwyzer, *The Breviary of Britain*.

34 Llwyd, *Cronica*, p. 56.

35 Philip Schwyzer, '"A Happy Place of Government": Sir Henry Sidney, Wales, and *The Historie of Cambria* (1584)', *Sidney Journal*, 29 (2011), 209–17; Jason Nice, *Sacred History and National Identity: Comparisons between Early Modern Wales and Brittany* (London, 2009), pp. 75, 84–5, 87, 89–93.

36 The other volume incorporated a Latin digest of Geoffrey of Monmouth's *Historia Britannica* along with Gerald of Wales's *Itinerarium Cambriae* and *Cambriae Descriptio*: [David Powel], *Pontici Virunii Viri Doctissimi Britannicae Historiae* (London, 1585).

37 David Powel, *A Historie of Cambria Now Called Wales* (London, 1584), sig. ¶5v.

38 Powel, *Historie*, sig. ¶6.

39 Powel, *Historie*, sig. ¶8v.

40 Powel, *Historie*, p. 239.

41 Peter Roberts, 'Tudor Wales, National Identity and the British Inheritance', in Peter Roberts and Brendan Bradshaw (eds), *British Consciousness and Identity: The Making of Britain, 1533–1707* (Cambridge, 1998), pp. 37–41; J. Gwynfor Jones, 'The Welsh Gentry and the Image of the "Cambro-Briton", 1603–25', *WHR*, 20 (2000–1), 615–55; Philip Schwyzer, 'The Politics of British Antiquity and the Descent from Troy in the Early Stuart Era', in Francesca Kaminski-Jones and Rhys Kaminski-Jones (eds), *Celts, Romans, Britons: Classical and Celtic Influence in the Construction of British Identities* (Oxford, 2020), pp. 79–96.

42 *PoP*, pp. 70–4, and see below, pp. 123–6.

43 BL, Royal MS 18 A. xxxvii, fo. 6v. Cf. John Lewis, *The History of Great Britain*, ed. H. Thomas (London, 1729); G. N. Griffiths, 'John Lewis of Llwynwene's Defence of Geoffrey of Monmouth's "Historia"', *NLWJ*, 7 (1951–2), 228–34.

44 [Robert Holland], *Basilikon Doron … Translated into the True British Tongue* (London, 1604); George Owen Harry, *The Genealogy of the High and Mighty Monarch, James* (London, 1604). Extended drafts of Harry's text can be found at NLW, MS 9853E and The Queen's College, Oxford, MS 43.

45 Wiliam Midleton, *Psalmae y Brenhinol Brophwyd Dafydd* (London, 1603), sig. ¶4v.

46 BL, Cotton MSS, Faustina E II, fos 258–272v; NLW, Peniarth MS 118, fos 731–864.

47 Ashe, 'Holinshed and Mythical History'; Patrick Collinson, *This England: Essays on the English Nation and Commonwealth in the Sixteenth Century* (Manchester, 2011), pp. 21–4.

48 William Camden, *Britannia*, trans. Philemon Holland (London, 1610), pp. 8–9.

49 William Lloyd, *An Historical Account of Church-Government* (London, 1684), sigs. A3–C3v.

50 E. D. Jones, 'Rowland Fychan of Caergai', *Llên Cymru*, 4 (1957), 228.

51 NLW, Wynnstay MS 12.

52 Percy Enderbie, *Cambria Triumphans* (London, 1661), p. 188.

53 Cf. Geraint H. Jenkins, *Literature, Religion and Society in Wales, 1660–1730* (Cardiff, 1978), p. 219.

54 William Wynne, *The History of Wales* (London, 1697), sig. A4. See R. T. Jenkins, 'William Wynne and the *History of Wales*', *BBCS*, 6 (1931–3), 153–9.

55 Wynne, *History*, sig. **3v.

56 Wynne, *History*, sigs. A2v–A3v.

57 Wynne, *History*, sigs. A2–A3v; Anon., 'Letter from William Wynne, the Historian to Bishop Humphreys of St. Asaph [*sic*]', *AC*, 3rd series, 1 (1855), 45–6; E. Gilbert Wright, 'Humphrey Humphreys, Bishop of Bangor and Hereford', *Journal of the Historical Society of the Church in Wales*, 2 (1950), 61–76.

58 Mary Chadwick and Shaun Evans, '"Ye Best Tast of Books & Learning of Any Other Country Gentn": The Library of Thomas Mostyn of Gloddaith, *c*.1676–1692', in Annika Bautz and James Gregory (eds), *Libraries, Books, and Collectors of Texts, 1600–1900* (New York and Abingdon, 2018), pp. 87–102; UBA, Mostyn Add. MS 9068, nos. 48 and 49; Mostyn Add. MS 9069, no. 46.

59 For Ferrar, see Andrew J. Brown. *Robert Ferrar: Yorkshire Monk, Reformation Bishop and Martyr in Wales* (London, 2000); Glanmor Williams, *Welsh Reformation Essays* (Cardiff, 1967), pp. 124–35; *ODNB*: 'Robert Ferrar'.

60 BL, Harleian MS 420, fo. 90

61 BL, Harleian MS 420, fo. 92.

62 Corpus Christi College, Cambridge, MS 114B, p. 503.

63 BL, Lansdowne MS 111, fo. 10.

64 Hatfield House, Cecil Papers 250/7, calendared in HMC, *Salisbury MSS*, X, p. 369.

65 Thomas Twyne, *The Breviary of Britayne* (London, 1573), sigs. ¶ii–¶iii; E. D. Jones, 'The Brogyntyn Welsh Manuscripts. XII', *NLWJ*, 7 (1951–2), 286, 304. He also defended a careful version of the Brut in print, chiding Vergil moderately for denying the British history, but also noting 'I find nothing so readie as errors in antiquities of countreys and in original of nations': Lodowick Lloyd, 'A Briefe for Britaine', in his *The Consent of Time* (London, 1590), pp. 710–22.

66 Alex May, 'Green Tights and Swordfights: *Edward I* and the Making of Memories', in Stewart Mottram and Sarah Prescott (eds), *Writing Wales, from the Renaissance to Romanticism* (Farnham and Burlington, VT, 2012), p. 67.

67 W[illiam] R[ichards], *Wallography* (London, 1682), p. 124; Lloyd Bowen, 'Representations of Wales and the Welsh during the Civil Wars and Interregnum', *Historical Research*, 77 (2004), 358–76.

68 Bodleian Library, Ashmole MS 1817a, fos 416–17, described in 'Early Modern Letters Online' at </tinyurl.com/y7ejrfyk> [accessed 01.06.21]. Some decades earlier Rowland Vaughan castigated Camden and his followers for their 'false teaching' in denying the Brutus story: Hughes, *Rhagymadroddion*, p. 119.

69 Elis ap Elis, 'Hanes y Cymru', in [Thomas Jones], *Newydd Oddiwrth y Ser* (Shrewsbury 1686), sigs. B1–B3.

70 Lloyd, *Historicall Account of Church-Government,* sig. a5v. Despite his scepticism of Geoffrey, Lloyd nevertheless claimed the Welsh 'live still in that country of which our ancestors were the first inhabitants', and lauded the antiquity of the Welsh language: Lloyd, *Historicall Account of Church-Government*, sig. a6v.

71 Daniel Defoe, *Tour Through the Whole Island of Great Britain* (2 vols, London, 1724–6), II, p. 102.

72 Sarah Prescott, *Eighteenth-Century Writing from Wales* (Cardiff, 2008); Prys Morgan, 'From a Death to a View: The Hunt for the Welsh Past in the Romantic Period', in Eric Hobsbawm and Terence Ranger (eds), *The Invention of Tradition* (Cambridge, 1983), pp. 43–100.

CHAPTER 3

1 Nicholas Tyacke (ed.), *England's Long Reformation, 1500–1800* (London, 1998); Dairmaid MacCulloch, *Reformation: Europe's House Divided, 1490–1700* (London and New York, 2003); David Lowenstein and Alison Shell (eds), 'Early Modern Literature and England's Long Reformation', a special issue of *Reformation*, 24 (2019).

2 The standard treatment for the sixteenth century remains Glanmor Williams, *Wales and the Reformation* (Cardiff, 1997), along with his discussion in *RR*, pp. 279–331.

3 For an authoritative judgement to this effect, see Williams, *Reformation*.

4 Prys Morgan, 'A Nation of Nonconformists: Thomas Rees (1815–85) and Nonconformist History', in Neil Evans and Huw Pryce (eds), *Writing a Small Nation's Past: Wales in Comparative Perspective, 1850–1950* (Farnham and Burlington, VT, 2013), pp. 97–111.

5 Philip Jenkins, *A History of Modern Wales, 1536–1990* (London, 1992), pp. 407–20.

6 Lloyd Bowen, 'Wales, 1587–1689', in John Coffey (ed.), *The Oxford History of Protestant Dissenting Traditions, Volume I: The Post-Reformation Era, c.1559–c.1689* (Oxford, 2020), pp. 224–6.

7 For some of this visual culture, see Madeleine Gray, *Images of Piety: The Iconography of Traditional Religion in Late Medieval Wales* (Oxford, 2000).

8 Nicholas Canny, 'Irish, Welsh, and Scottish Responses to Centralisation, c.1530–c.1640', in Alexander Grant and Keith Stringer (eds), *Uniting the Kingdom? The Making of British History* (London, 1995), p. 161; Felicity Heal, *Reformation in Britain and Ireland* (Oxford, 2003), p. 129.

9 Madeleine Gray, 'Change and Continuity: The Gentry and the Property of the Church in South-East Wales and the Marches', in J. Gwynfor Jones (ed.), *Class, Community and Culture in Tudor Wales* (Cardiff, 1989), pp. 1–38.

10 Williams, *Reformation*, pp. 309–37.

11 TNA, SP12/66, fo. 85.

12 Madeleine Gray, '"The Curious Incident of the Dog in the Night-Time": The Pre-Reformation Church in Wales', in Tadgh Ó hAnnracháin and Robert Armstrong (eds), *Christianities in the Early Modern Celtic World* (Basingstoke,

2014), pp. 52–3. Nicholas Robinson, the bishop of Bangor, in 1567 noted 'the most part of ye priestes are to[o] olde (they saye) now to be put to schole': TNA, SP12/44, fo. 62.

13 Here and elsewhere in the volume, 'principality' is occasionally used, for variety, as a synonym for 'Wales'. This is done where there is no chance of confusion with the medieval 'Principality', which is also distinguished by use of capitalisation.

14 Although matters could be different in urban environments such as Cardiff, Carmarthen and Haverfordwest. See the refreshing and challenging reinterpretation offered in Nia W. Powell, 'Rawling White, Cardiff and the Early Reformation in Wales', in Rosemary C. E. Hayes and William J. Sheils (eds), *Clergy, Church and Society in England and Wales, c.1200–1800* (York, 2013), pp. 121–37.

15 TNA, SP12/44, fo. 62. Robinson would later claim that he was 'in daunger of life' for suppressing pilgrimages, praying to images 'and such like errors of papistrie' in his diocese: TNA, SP12/153, fo. 133.

16 Richard Davies, *A Funeral Sermon Preached at the Burial of the Right Honourable Walter Earle of Essex* (London, 1577), sig. D2r–v. For earlier descriptions of unreformed and Catholic practices in the diocese, see TNA, SP1/113, fos 95v–96; BL, Harleian MS 420, fo. 111r–v; Thomas Wright (ed.), *Letters Relating to the Suppression of Monasteries* (London, Camden Society, 26, 1843), pp. 79, 183–6, 207–9.

17 TNA, SP12/66, fo. 81.

18 Katharine Olson, 'Religion, Politics, and the Parish in Tudor England and Wales: A View from the Marches of Wales, 1534–1553', *Recusant History*, 30 (2011), 527–36; Katharine Olson, '"Y Ganrif Fawr"? Piety, Literature and Patronage in Fifteenth- and Sixteenth-Century Wales', *Studies in Church History*, 48 (2012), 118–23.

19 See, for example, TNA, SP12/44, fo. 62; SP12/165, fo. 3.

20 Brendan Bradshaw, 'The English Reformation and Identity Formation in Wales and Ireland', in Brendan Bradshaw and Peter Roberts (eds), *British Consciousness and Identity: The Making of Britain, 1533–1707* (Cambridge, 1997), pp. 43–111.

21 P. L. Hughes and J. F. Larkin (eds), *Tudor Royal Proclamations, I: The Early Tudors, 1485–1553* (New Haven, CT, 1964), pp. 296–8.

22 Peter R. Roberts, 'The Welsh Language, English Law and Tudor Legislation', *TCS* (1989), 23.

23 Wright, *Suppression*, p. 207; TNA, SP1/113, fo. 97.

24 Anthony Fletcher and Diarmaid MacCulloch, *Tudor Rebellions*, 6th edn (London and New York, 2016), p. 154.

25 Nia W. Powell, 'Arthur Bulkeley, Reformation Bishop of Bangor, 1541–1552/3', *Journal of Welsh Religious History*, 3 (2003), 35–8; R. Geraint Gruffydd, 'Yny lhyvyr hwnn (1546): The Earliest Welsh Printed Book', *BBCS*, 22 (1969), 110–11; Williams, *Reformation*, pp. 145–7.

26 [Sir John Prise], *Yny lhyvyr hwnn* (London, 1546), digital copy available at *https://www.library.wales/discover/digital-gallery/printed-material/yny-lhyvyr-hwnn#?c=&m=&s=&cv=&xywh=-1076%2C0%2C4078%2C2844* [accessed 21.07.21]; Gruffydd, 'Yny lhyvyr hwnn', 105–11; Williams, *Reformation*, pp. 149–50.

27 *Tudor Wales*, pp. 117–18.

28 R. Brinley Jones, *William Salesbury* (Cardiff, 1994); Williams, *Welsh Reformation Essays*, pp. 191–205.

29 Hughes, *Rhagymadroddion*, pp. 10–12.

30 Williams, *Reformation*, pp. 188–215.

31 R. Geraint Gruffydd, 'Humphrey Lhuyd a Deddf Cyfieithu'r Beibl i'r Gymraeg', *Llên Cymru*, 4 (1956–7), 114–15.

32 *SR*, IV, p. 457.

33 Peter R. Roberts, 'Tudor Legislation and the Political Status of "the British Tongue"', *WLBIR*, pp. 142–4.

34 *SR*, IV, p. 457.

35 *SR*, IV, p. 457.

36 Lloyd Bowen, 'The Battle of Britain', in Ó hAnnracháin and Armstrong, *Christianities*, pp. 139–42.

37 *Tudor Wales*, pp. 121–2.

38 Sir John Prise, *Historiae Britannicae Defensio: A Defence of the British History*, ed. Ceri Davies (Toronto and Oxford, 2015), p. 45.

39 J. Gwynfor Jones, *Wales and the Tudor State* (Cardiff, 1989), pp. 238–9.

40 *Testament Newydd ein Arglwydd Iesu Grist* (London, 1567), sig. A1v.

41 Translation from Albert Owen Edwards, *A Memorandum on the Legality of the Welsh Bible* (Cardiff, 1925), p. 84.

42 Edwards, *Memorandum*, pp. 98, 103.

43 Glanmor Williams, *The Welsh and their Religion: Historical Essays* (Cardiff, 1991), pp. 173–229.

44 William Hughes, *The Life and Times of Bishop William Morgan* (London, 1891), p. 127. See the same argument articulated by his friend and translating assistant John Davies in 1621: Davies, *Rhagymadroddion*, pp. 116–17.

45 Prys Morgan, *A Bible for Wales* (Cardiff, 1988), p. 27.

46 Glanmor Williams, 'Unity of Religion or Unity of Language? Protestants and Catholics and the Welsh Language, c.1536–1660', *WLBIR*, p. 231.

47 These included William Morgan's revised translation of Salesbury's Prayer Book in 1599.

48 Thomas Parry, *A History of Welsh Literature*, trans. H. Idris Bell (Oxford, 1955), pp. 188–91; Sally Harper, 'Tunes for a Welsh Psalter: Edmwnd Prys's *Llyfr y Psalmau*', *Studia Celtica*, 36 (2004), 221–65.

49 Quoted in Cennard Davies, 'Early Free-Metre Poetry', in R. Geraint Gruffydd (ed.), *A Guide to Welsh Literature, c.1530–1700* (Cardiff, 1997), p. 91.

50 BL, Additional MS 70,106, fo. 156; Vavasor Powell, *The Scriptures Concord* (London, 1646), sig. A3r–v; M. G. Jones, 'Two Accounts of the Welsh Trust, 1675 and 1678', *BBCS*, 9 (1937), 72.

51 Williams, *Reformation*, pp. 219–20.

52 NLW, SD/CCCm/1.

53 Bodl. Lib., Tanner MS 30, fo. 124. For Lloyd's problems with an incumbent who claimed he could speak Welsh but who, in fact, could not, see Bodl. Lib., Tanner MS 34, fo. 31.

54 Bodl. Lib., Tanner MS 146, fo. 147. For earlier discussions of the Welsh language and sermons in Cardiff parishes, see NLW, Bute MS L3/7; TNA, SP1/114, fo. 26.

55 NLW, Great Sessions 4/16/3/6.

56 Williams, *Welsh and their Religion*, pp. 159, 222.

57 *PoP*, pp. 207–34.

58 W. N. Yates, *Rug Chapel, Llangar Church, Gwydir Uchaf Chapel* (Cardiff, 1993), pp. 10–19.

59 Judith Maltby, 'Petitions for Episcopacy and the Book of Common Prayer on the Eve of the Civil War', in Stephen Taylor (ed.), *From Cranmer to Davidson: A Church of England Miscellany* (Church of England Record Society, 7, 1999), pp. 103–67.

60 *The Humble Petition of the Gentry, Clergy and Other Inhabitants, Subscribed of … the Sixe Shires of Northwales*, in [Thomas Aston], *A Collection of Sundry Petitions Presented to the Kings Maiestie* (London, 1642), pp. 28–9.

61 Examples can be found at Bodl. Lib., shelfmark Arch. G.c.5(12); BL, shelfmarks 669, f.4(72) and 190.g.12(59); Society of Antiquaries Library, Lemon Broadsides no. 360.

62 Lloyd Bowen, 'Representations of Wales and the Welsh during the Civil Wars and Interregnum', *Historical Research*, 77 (2004), 367–8.

63 Bowen, 'Representations', pp. 373–4. For Griffith, see Lloyd Bowen, 'Preaching and Politics in the Welsh Marches, 1643–63: The Case of Alexander Griffith', *Historical Research*, 94 (2021), 28–50.

64 Lloyd Bowen, '"This Murmuring and Unthankful Peevish Land": Wales and the Protectorate', in Patrick Little (ed.), *The Cromwellian Protectorate* (Woodbridge, 2007), pp. 144–64.

65 Sarah Ward Clavier, '"Horrid Rebellion" and "Holie Cheate": Royalist Gentry Responses to Interregnum Government in North-East Wales, 1646–1660', *WHR*, 29 (2018), 69–70.

66 Gwynedd Archives, Caernarfon Record Office, XQS/1660.

67 Lambeth Palace Library, MS 930, fo. 33, emphasis added.

68 J. R. Guy, 'The Significance of Indigenous Clergy in the Welsh Church at the Restoration', *Studies in Church History*, 18 (1982), 335–43.

69 Thomas Jones, *Of the Heart and its Right Sovereign* (London, 1678).

70 Philip Jenkins, 'Church, Nation and Language: The Welsh Church, 1660–1800', in Jeremy Gregory and Jeffrey S. Chamberlain (eds), *The National Church in Local Perspective* (Woodbridge, 2003), pp. 265–84.

71 NLW, SA/MISC/1485. On Wynne, see below, p. 216.

72 NLW, SA/MISC/1438. For the efforts of encouraging catechising in St Davids in the 1670s, see Bodl. Lib, Tanner MS 146, fo. 138.

73 NLW, SA/MISC/1308.

74 NLW, SA/MISC/1405. For a contemporary Anglican Welsh-language poet of the parish, see *Dictionary of Welsh Biography*: 'Owen, Matthew (1631–1679)'. For Lloyd's upbeat report on the state of his diocese, based partly on the 'Notitiae', see Bodl. Lib., Tanner MS 30, fo. 124.

75 This was something Salesbury feared, describing how 'the Brythonic of Cornwall … became full of corrupt speech and well-nigh perished': Geraint H. Jenkins, 'Introduction', *WLBIR*, p. 14.

76 Williams, *Welsh and their Religion*, p. 229.

CHAPTER 4

1 *Testament Newydd ein Arglwydd Iesu Grist* (London, 1567), sig. A1v.
2 C. E. Long (ed.), *Diary of the Marches of the Royal Army* (London, Camden Society, 74, 1859), p. 208.
3 John Lewis, *The Parliament Explained to Wales* (London, 1646), p. 27.
4 Thomas Jones, *Of the Heart and its Right Sovereign* (London, 1678), p. 243.
5 William J. Sheils, '"Getting On" and "Getting Along" in Parish and Town: Catholics and their Neighbours in England', in Benjamin Kaplan, Bob Moore, Henk F. K. van Nierop and Judith Pollmann (eds), *Catholic Communities in Protestant Britain and the Netherlands, c.1570–1720* (Manchester, 2009), pp. 67–83.
6 Alexandra Walsham, *Church Papists: Catholicism, Conformity and Confessional Polemic in Early Modern England* (Woodbridge, 1993).
7 NLW, BR1632/104.
8 See above, p. 45.
9 BL, Lansdowne MS 111, fo. 10.
10 Colleen M. Seguin, 'Cures and Controversy in Early Modern Wales: The Struggle to Control St. Winifred's Well', *North American Journal of Welsh Studies*, 3 (2003), 1–17; Alexandra Walsham, 'Holywell: Contesting Sacred Space in Post-Reformation Wales', in Will Coster and Andrew Spicer (eds), *Sacred Space in Early Modern Europe* (Cambridge, 2005), pp. 211–36; Shaun Evans, 'St Winifred's Well, Office-Holding and the Mostyn Family Interest: Negotiating the Reformation in Flintshire, c.1570–1642', *Flintshire Historical Society Journal*, 40 (2015), 41–72.
11 BL, Lansdowne MS 111, fo. 10v.
12 TNA, SP16/151, fo. 21.
13 J. M. Cleary, 'The Catholic Resistance in Wales: 1568–1678', *Blackfriars*, 38 (1957), 111–25.
14 J. S. Brewer et al. (eds), *Letters and Papers Foreign and Domestic of the Reign of Henry VIII* (23 vols, London, 1862–1932), VII, p. 520.
15 *Tudor Wales*, pp. 121–2.
16 Nia W. Powell, 'Arthur Bulkeley, Reformation Bishop of Bangor, 1541–1552/3', *Journal of Welsh Religious History*, 3 (2003), 39–41; C. Charnell-White, 'Barddoniaeth Ddefosiynol Catrin ferch Gruffudd ap Hywel', *Dwned*, 7 (2001), 93–120.
17 Peter Marshall, '"The Greatest Man in Wales": James ap Gruffydd ap Hywel and the International Opposition to Henry VIII', *Sixteenth Century Journal*, 39 (2008), 681–704.
18 J. M. Cleary, 'Dr Morys Clynnog's Invasion Projects', *Recusant History*, 8 (1965), 305.
19 E. Gwynne Jones, 'The Lleyn Recusancy Case, 1578–1581', *TCS* (1936), 97–123.
20 Alexandra Walsham, 'The Holy Maid of Wales: Visions, Imposture and Catholicism in Elizabethan Britain', *EHR*, 132 (2017), 250–85.
21 Walsham, 'Holy Maid of Wales', 262.
22 R. Geraint Gruffydd, 'Dau Lythyr Gan Owen Lewis', *Llên Cymru*, 2 (1952), 44–5.

23 Longleat House, DU/II/53; Thomas Tanner, *Bibliotheca Britannico-Hibernica* … (London, 1748), p. 270.

24 Geraint Bowen (ed.), *Y Drych Kristnogawl* (Cardiff, 1996); an online version of the text can be found at <*https://www.library.wales/discover/digital-gallery/printed-material/y-drych-cristianogawl#?c=&m=&s=&cv=&xywh=-1186%2 Co%2C5479%2C3822*> [accessed 18.06.21].

25 Lloyd Bowen, 'Structuring Particularist Publics: Logistics, Language and Early Modern Wales', *Historical Journal*, 56 (2017), 759–62.

26 NLW, Great Sessions 4/6/2/24. They were also asked whether they knew any who resorted to the shrine at Holywell. For a similar drive in neighbouring Flintshire, see NLW, Great Sessions 4/970/5/19.

27 NLW, Great Sessions 4/5/4/7.

28 D. Aneurin Thomas (ed.), *The Elizabethan Catholic Martyrs* (Cardiff, 1971), pp. 191–3; TNA, STAC 5/W38/27. See also the case of 'a Welshe booke' containing 'certaine papisticall and erroniouse things' which one man who was seized in London claimed he had written out so that he 'thereby might learne to reade Welsh': NLW, Great Sessions 4/972/4/30–2.

29 NLW, MS 15,542B, fo. 254v.

30 [Robert Gwyn], *Gwssanaeth y Gwŷr Newydd (1580)*, ed. Geraint Bowen (Cardiff, 1970); James January-McCann, 'Robert Gwyn and Robert Persons: Welsh and English Perspectives on Attendance at Anglican Service', *British Catholic History*, 32 (2015), 159–71.

31 Bowen, 'Particularist Publics', 761–2.

32 T. H. Parry-Williams (ed.), *Carolau Richard White* (Cardiff, 1931); J. H. Pollen, 'The Carols of Richard White', *Catholic Record Society*, 5 (1908), 90–9; Thomas, *Welsh Catholic Martyrs*. See also John Penry's reference in 1586/7 to 'ungodlie Welsh songs and books' as a mainstay of popular religion in Wales: David Williams (ed.), *Three Treatises Concerning Wales* (Cardiff, 1960), p. 35.

33 NLW, Great Sessions 4/5/4/7–10; 4/6/2/19–20, 33; 4/6/4/101; Thomas, *Welsh Catholic Martyrs*.

34 Bowen, 'Battle of Britain', p. 146; G. Dyfnallt Owen, *Elizabethan Wales: The Social Scene* (Cardiff, 1964), pp. 218–19.

35 Williams, *Welsh and their Religion*, p. 152.

36 See, for example, Roland Mathias, *Whitsun Riot* (London, 1963); HMC, *Salisbury MSS*, XI, pp. 460, 498–9; XIII, p. 478; XVIII, p. 374; TNA, SP14/48, fo. 163v; BL, Lansdowne MS 167, fo. 25v.

37 J. M. Cleary, *The Barlow Family of Slebech* (Cardiff, 1956).

38 For anxieties about the Plot in Wales, see Hatfield House, Cecil Papers 191/69; NLW, MS 1595E, fo. 229; Great Sessions 4/974/6/55.

39 Thomas M. McCoog, 'The Society of Jesus in Wales: The Welsh in the Society of Jesus, 1561–1625', *Journal of Welsh Religious History*, 5 (1997), 1–27; Hannah Thomas, 'Missioners on the Margins? The Territorial Headquarters of the Welsh Jesuit College of St Francis Xavier at the Cwm, *c*.1600–1679', *Recusant History*, 32 (2014), 173–93.

40 Lloyd Bowen, 'Wales in British Politics, *c*.1603–42' (Cardiff University, PhD thesis, 2000), 468–503.

41 *A Discovery of a Damnable Plot at Ragland Castle in Monmoth-shire* (London, 1641).

42 *The True Informer* (Oxford, 1643), p. 30.

43 Philip Jenkins, 'Anti-Popery on the Welsh Marches in the Seventeenth Century', *Historical Journal*, 23 (1980), 279–80.

44 Jenkins, 'Anti-Popery', 275–93; E. T. Davies, 'The "Popish Plot" in Monmouthshire', *Journal of the Historical Society of the Church in Wales*, 25 (1976), 32–45; Julian Mitchell, 'Nathan Rogers and the Wentwood Case', *WHR*, 14 (1988–9), 23–52; Newton E. Key and Joseph Ward, '"Divided into Parties": Exclusion Crisis Origins in Monmouth', *EHR*, 115 (2000), 1159–83.

45 B. D. Henning (ed.), *Parliamentary Diary of Sir Edward Dering, 1670–3* (New Haven, CT, 1940), p. 70; *LJ*, XII, pp. 450–1; HPO (1660–90): 'Williams, Sir Trevor'; Harry Ransom Center, University of Texas at Austin, Bulstrode Newsletters, 26 May 1676.

46 *Memoirs of Thomas, Earl of Ailesbury* (2 vols, London, 1890), I, p. 30.

47 *CJ*, IX, pp. 466–70; Bodl. Lib., Carte MS 72, fos 382–3; John Arnold and John Scudamore, *An Abstract of Several Examinations* (London, 1680); W. J. Smith (ed.), *Herbert Correspondence* (Cardiff, 1968), pp. 219–21 (misdated). Although see the replies of some of those he accused in *A Letter from a Gentleman in Glocestershire to a Friend in London* (London, 1678), and Worcester's own claim in Parliament that these allegations 'were not true': Harry Ransom Center, University of Texas at Austin, Bulstrode Newsletters, 22 April 1678.

48 Folger Shakespeare Library, MS L.c.927; TNA, SP29/413, fos 186–7; *The Tryal and Condemnation of John Giles* (London, 1680); *An Account of an Attempt Made upon the Person of Mr Arnold* (London, 1680); *Clamor Sanguinis* (London, 1680).

49 TNA, SP29/416, fos 327–328v.

50 Folger Shakespeare Library, MS L.c.1275; Nicholas Luttrell, *A Brief Relation of State Affairs* (6 vols, Oxford, 1857), I, p. 291.

51 HPO (1660–1690): 'Arnold, John'.

52 Henry Foley (ed.), *Records of the English Province of the Society of Jesus* (7 vols, London, 1877–83), V, p. 901.

53 Foley, *Records*, V, p. 869. See also the anxieties of the Catholic Edward Petre in Flintshire: UBA, Mostyn Add. MS 9067, nos. 44–5, 47.

54 Philip Jenkins, '"A Welsh Lancashire"? Monmouthshire Catholics in the Eighteenth Century', *Recusant History*, 15 (1979), 176–88.

55 Glanmor Williams, 'Unity of Religion or Unity of Language? Protestants and Catholics and the Welsh Language, 1536–1660', *WLBIR*, p. 224.

56 *An Abstract of Several Examinations*, p. 6; *CJ*, IX, p. 466. For an earlier period, see Hatfield House, Cecil Papers 144/184.

57 For a more developed discussion of the ideas presented in this section, see Lloyd Bowen, 'Wales, 1587–1689', in John Coffey (ed.), *The Oxford History of Protestant Dissenting Traditions, Volume I: The Post-Reformation Era, c.1559–c.1689* (Oxford, 2020), pp. 224–43.

58 Hughes, *Rhagymadroddion*, p. 100.

59 For more on Myddelton as a London merchant and source of credit in Wales, see below, pp. 211–13.

60 Hughes, *Rhagymadroddion*, p. 124.

61 E[van] R[oberts], *Sail Crefydd Gristnogawl* (London, 1649), p. 2.

62 For studies of Penry, see *ODNB*: 'Penry, John'; William Pierce, *John Penry: His Life, Times and Writings* (London, 1923); Williams, *Three Treatises*; D. J. McGinn, *John Penry and the Marprelate Controversy* (New Brunswick, NJ, 1966); J. Gwynfor Jones, 'John Penry: Government, Order and the "Perishing Souls" of Wales', *TCS* (1993), 47–81; J. Gwynfor Jones, *Crefydd, Cenedlgarwch a'r Wladwriaeth: John Penry (1563–1593) a Phiwritaniaeth Gynnar* (Cardiff, 2014).

63 Williams, *Three Treatises*, p. 38.

64 Williams, *Three Treatises*, p. 30.

65 Williams, *Three Treatises*, p. 61.

66 John Penry, *Th'Appellation of Iohn Penri* (London, 1589), p. 16.

67 BL, Lansdowne MS 109, fo. 36; BL, Additional MS 48,064, fo. 184v. Cf. BL, Lansdowne MS 75, fo. 58.

68 *Dialogue*, p. 131.

69 Thomas Thompson, *Antichrist Arraigned* (London, 1618), sig. *4.

70 BL, Additional MS 35,331, fo. 74.

71 Geoffrey F. Nuttall, *The Welsh Saints, 1640–1660* (Cardiff, 1957), pp. 1–17; R. G. Gruffydd, *'In That Gentile Country ...': The Beginnings of Puritan Nonconformity in Wales* (Bridgend, 1976).

72 Lloyd Bowen, 'Wales and Religious Reform in the Long Parliament, 1640–42', *TCS*, new series, 12 (2005), 36–59.

73 BL, Harleian MS 4,391, fo. 90; BL, Additional MS 70,109, no. 69.

74 Stephen K. Roberts, '"One of the Least Things in Religion": The Welsh Experience of Church Polity, 1640–60', in Elliot Vernon and Hunter Powell (eds), *Church Polity and Politics in the British Atlantic World, c.1635–66* (Manchester, 2020), pp. 60–80.

75 Anthony M. Johnson, 'Wales during the Commonwealth and Protectorate', in Donald H. Pennington and Keith Thomas (eds), *Puritans and Revolutionaries* (Oxford, 1978), pp. 233–56.

76 *Severall Proceedings in Parliament*, 12 (14–21 Dec. 1649), p. 149.

77 Stephen K. Roberts, 'Propagating the Gospel in Wales: The Making of the 1650 Act', *TCS*, new series, 10 (2004), 72–5.

78 Stephen K. Roberts, 'Commissioners for the Propagation of the Gospel in Wales (1650–53)', in *ODNB*: <https://doi.org/10.1093/odnb/9780198614128.013.107961> [accessed 25.06.21].

79 Thomas Richards, *A History of the Puritan Movement in Wales* (Liverpool, 1920), p. 93.

80 *ODNB*: 'Powell, Vavasor'; R. Tudur Jones, *Vavasor Powell* (Swansea, 1971).

81 Edward Bagshaw, *The Life and Death of Mr Vavasor Powell* (London, 1671), p. 111.

82 Vavsor Powell, *The Bird in the Cage, Chirping* (London, 1661), sig. B1v.

83 Lloyd Bowen, '"This Murmuring and Unthankful Peevish Land": Wales and the Protectorate', in Patrick Little (ed.), *The Cromwellian Protectorate* (Woodbridge, 2007), pp. 144–64; Lloyd Bowen, 'Preaching and Politics in the Welsh Marches, 1643–63: The Case of Alexander Griffith', *Historical Research*,

84 Bodl. Lib., Tanner MS 146, fo. 138.

85 Powell, *Bird in the Cage*, sig. B3v.

86 Christopher Hill, *The World Turned Upside Down: Radical Ideas during the English Revolution* (London, 1972), pp. 192–8.

87 William Erbery, *Apocrypha* (London, 1652), pp. 2, 4–8.

88 *ODNB*: 'Llwyd, Morgan'; M. Wynn Thomas, *Morgan Llwyd* (Cardiff, 1984); Goronwy Wyn Owen, 'The Life and Work of Morgan Llwyd "of Gwynedd" (1619–1659)', *Welsh Journal of Religious History*, 3 (2008), 1–14.

89 TNA, SP29/41, fo. 3.

90 For the legacy of Wrexham separatism, see Bishop Lloyd's letter of January 1687: Bodl. Lib., Tanner MS 30, fo. 172.

91 Stephen K. Roberts, 'Religion, Politics and Welshness, 1649–1660', in Ivan Roots (ed.), *"Into Another Mould": Aspects of the Interregnum*, 2nd edn (Exeter, 1998), pp. 37–9.

92 Thomas, *Morgan Llwyd*, p. 11.

93 T. E. Ellis and J. H. Davies (eds), *Gweithiau Morgan Llwyd* (2 vols, Bangor and London, 1899–1908), I, p. 128.

94 The volume can be seen at <*http://hdl.handle.net/10107/4790765*> [accessed 24.06.21].

95 Ellis and Davies, *Gweithiau*, I, p. 129.

96 Eryn M. White, 'From Ejectment to Toleration in Wales, 1662–89', in Eryn M. White, David Appleby and J. Gwynfor Jones (eds), *The Great Ejectment of 1662* (Eugene, OR, 2012), pp. 125–81.

97 For the alternative history of presbyterianism, see Roberts, '"One of the Least Things in Religion"'.

98 Bodl. Lib., Tanner MS 146, fo. 138.

99 Philip Jenkins, '"The Old Leaven": The Welsh Roundheads after 1660', *Historical Journal*, 24 (1981), 807–23.

100 For these groups, see Richard C. Allen, *Quaker Communities in Early Modern Wales* (Cardiff, 2007) and T. M. Bassett, *The Welsh Baptists* (Swansea, 1977).

101 See below, p. 216.

102 Geraint H. Jenkins, 'Apostol Sir Gaerfyrddin: Stephen Hughes, c.1622–1688', *Y Cofiadur*, 54 (1989), 3–23.

103 Stephen Hughes, *Tryssor i'r Cymru* (London, 1677), sig. A6v.

104 M. G. Jones, 'Two Accounts of the Welsh Trust, 1675 and 1678', *BBCS*, 9 (1937–9), 71–80; Geraint H. Jenkins, *Literature, Religion and Society in Wales, 1660–1730* (Cardiff, 1978), pp. 57–60.

105 Walter Cradock, *Glad Tydings from Heaven* (London, 1648), p. 50.

CHAPTER 5

1 Geraint H. Jenkins, Richard Suggett and Eryn M. White, 'The Welsh Language in Early Modern Wales', *WLBIR*, p. 46.

At top: 94 (2021), 28–50; Sarah Ward Clavier, '"God's Vigilant Watchmen": The Words of Episcopalian Clergy in Wales, 1646–60', in Fiona McCall (ed.), *Church and People in Interregnum Britain* (London, 2021), pp. 225–41.

2 Brian S. John, 'The Linguistic Significance of the Pembrokeshire Landsker', *Pembrokeshire Historian*, 4 (1972), 7–29.

3 *Description*, I, p. 40.

4 *Description*, I, p. 48. See also the description of the Welsh and English Catholics in the English College of Rome as 'nationem Anglicam' and 'nationem Britannicam': Jason Nice, 'Being "British" in Rome: The Welsh at the English College, 1578–1584', *The Catholic Historical Review*, 92 (2006), 2.

5 Peter R. Roberts, 'Tudor Language and the Political Status of "the British Tongue"', *WLBIR*, p. 122.

6 See, for example, George Owen's description of bilingual parishes on the boundary of the Welsh and English language communities in Pembrokeshire: *Description*, I, p. 48.

7 Murray Ll. Chapman, 'An English Settlement in Western Montgomeryshire during the Tudor Period', *Montgomeryshire Collections*, 87 (1999), 111–37.

8 William Salesbury, *A Briefe and a Playne Introduction* (London, 1550), sig. A3v.

9 Humphrey Llwyd, *The Breviary of Britain*, ed. Philip Schwyzer, MHRA Tudor & Stuart Translations, 5 (London, 2011), p. 122.

10 [Stephen Hughes], *Gwaith Mr Rees Prichard* (London, 1672), sig. A6 [second pagination].

11 Davies, *Rhagymadroddion*, p. 20.

12 Glanmor Williams, *Wales and the Reformation* (Cardiff, 1997), p. 244.

13 [Robert Gwyn], *Y Drych Cristianogawl* (Rouen [i.e. Rhiwledin], 1585 [i.e. 1586/7]), sig. B3v.

14 Thomas Jones, *Newydd Oddiwrth y Seêr* (London, 1684), sig. A2r–v.

15 For the Welsh language in these areas, see Llinos Beverley Smith, 'The Welsh Language before 1536', *WLBIR*, pp. 17–20; B. G. Charles, 'The Welsh and their Language and Place-names in Archenfield and Oswestry', in Henry Lewis (ed.), *Angles and Britons* (Cardiff, 1963), pp. 85–100.

16 David Powel, *The Historie of Cambria* (London, 1584), pp. 5–6.

17 Powel, *Historie*, p. 22.

18 TNA, SP14/37, fo. 109.

19 Michael Faraday (ed.), *Calendar of Probate and Administration Acts, 1407–1550 in the Consistory Court of the Bishops of Hereford* (Walton-on-Thames, 2008); the wills can be found in the St Davids and Brecon probate collections at the NLW. Also, see below, pp. 200–3.

20 Geraint H. Jenkins, Richard Suggett and Eryn M. White, 'The Welsh Language in Early Modern Wales', *WLBIR*, pp. 56–7.

21 Shropshire Archives, LB9/2/3/81. See also LB9/1/1/95–8.

22 Shropshire Archives, P214/B/1/1/1, fos 13v, 21v, 52v, 126v; Katharine K. Olsen, 'Counting Communities, Counting Cultures: Problems and Progress with Early Modern Churchwardens' Accounts in Western England and Wales', in Valerie Hitchman and Andrew Foster (eds), *Views from the Parish: Churchwardens' Accounts, c.1500-c.1800* (Newcastle, 2015), pp. 98–103.

23 NLW, SA1580/R3, fos 177v– 178.

24 Gillian Brennan, 'Language and Nationality: The Role of Policy Towards Celtic Languages in the Consolidation of Tudor Power', *Nations and Nationalism*, 7 (2001), 317–38.

25 Llinos Beverley Smith, 'The Welsh Language before 1536', *WLBIR*, pp. 41–4.

26 Llinos Beverley Smith, 'Welsh and English Languages in Late-Medieval Wales', in D. A. Trotter (ed.), *Multilingualism in Later Medieval Britain* (Woodbridge, 2000), p. 20.

27 John Fisher (ed.), *Kynniver Llith a Ban* (Cardiff, 1931), p. 170.

28 William Salesbury, *A Dictionary in Englyshe and Welshe* (London, 1547), sig. A2.

29 Salesbury, *A Briefe and a Playne Introduction*; Salesbury, *A Playne and a Familiar Introductio[n]* … (London, 1567).

30 Richard Suggett, 'The Welsh Language and the Court of Great Sessions', *WLBIR*, pp. 153–206.

31 TNA, SP12/107, fo. 28. Cf. *Description*, I, p. 40.

32 For an example of oral evidence being given in Welsh at the Montgomeryshire great sessions in the 1570s, see Murray Ll. Chapman, 'A Sixteenth-Century Trial for Felony in the Court of Great Sessions for Montgomeryshire', *Montgomeryshire Collections*, 78 (1990), 167–70.

33 NLW, MS 9057E/725.

34 TNA, SP16/276, fo. 173v. Cf. TNA, SP15/42, fo. 111. For an example from a later period, see NLW, Great Sessions 4/43/2/31, 33.

35 NLW, Great Sessions 4/16/4/17.

36 Information from Professor Garthine Walker. Cf. Suggett, 'Welsh Language and the Court of Great Sessions', pp. 168–70.

37 John Gwynfor Jones, *Law, Order and Government in Caernarfonshire, 1558–1640* (Cardiff, 1996), pp. 69–70.

38 See, for example, the evidence from a later period in Evan D. Jones, 'Court Leet Records', *Transactions of the Cardiganshire Antiquarian Society*, 11 (1936), 69–70.

39 Some examples can be found at B. G. Charles, 'The Records of the Borough of Newport in Pembrokeshire', *NLWJ*, 7 (1951–2), 44–5; Gwynedd Archives Service, Caernarfon Record Office, XQS/1630; NLW, Great Sessions 4/21/4/11; NLW, Bronwydd MS II/76.

40 TNA, STAC 5/B60/6.

41 Lloyd Bowen, 'Information, Language and Political Culture in Early Modern Wales', *Past & Present*, 228 (2015), 141–3.

42 TNA, STAC 2/18/234.

43 NLW, Plas Nantglyn MS 1, fo. 29.

44 Peter R. Roberts, 'Elizabethan "Overseers" in Merioneth', *Journal of the Merioneth Historical and Record Society*, 4 (1961), 7–13.

45 These are to be found among the Ellesmere MSS at the Huntington Library.

46 NLW, Great Sessions 4/978/3/14.

47 Hatfield House, Cecil Papers 178/58.

48 Anglesey County Record Office, WPE/53 (available online at *<https://www.peoplescollection.wales/items/8539>* [accessed 29.06.21]); John Fisher, 'Three Welsh Wills', *AC*, 6th series, 19 (1919), 187–92; NLW, SA1563/R1, fo. 39v.

49 Michael Hechter, *Internal Colonialism: The Celtic Fringe in British National Development, 1536–1966* (London, 1975), pp. 109–11.

50 See, for example, the collapsing of eighteenth-century examples into a discussion of cultural change in the seventeenth century in Jenkins, Suggett and White, 'The Welsh Language in Early Modern Wales', pp. 80–1.

51 W. P. Griffith, *Learning, Law and Religion: Higher Education and Welsh Society, c.1540–1640* (Cardiff, 1996); William P. Griffith, 'Humanist Learning, Education and the Welsh Language, c.1660–1811', *WLBIR*, pp. 289–315.

52 *FMW*, p. 60; Griffith, 'Humanist Learning', pp. 311–13; W. P. Griffith, 'Jesus College, Oxford, and Wales: The First Half-Century', *TCS*, new series, 3 (1997), 21–44.

53 NLW, MS 9056E/860.

54 John Hacket, *Scrinia Reserata* (London, 1693), p. 7.

55 Davies, *Rhagymadroddion*, pp. 125–6.

56 T. Jones Pierce (ed.), *Clenennau Letters and Papers in the Brogyntyn Collection* (Aberystwyth, 1947), p. 127.

57 Michael Roberts, '"More Prone to be Idle and Riotous than the English"? Attitudes to Male Behaviour in Early Modern Wales', in Michael Roberts and Simone Clarke (eds), *Women and Gender in Early Modern Wales* (Cardiff, 2000), pp. 271–4.

58 See also the comments, relating to Welsh gentlewomen, in Simone Clarke, 'The Construction of Genteel Sensibilities: The Socialization of Daughters of the Gentry in Seventeenth- and Eighteenth-Century Wales', in Sandra Betts (ed.), *Our Daughters' Land* (Cardiff, 1996), pp. 57, 67–8, 70–2.

59 *Description*, III, p. 56.

60 J. Gwynfor Jones, 'The Welsh Poets and their Patrons, c.1550–1640', *WHR*, 9 (1979), 263.

61 NLW, MS 9053E/430.

62 Sidney Lee (ed.), *The Autobiography of Edward, Lord Herbert of Cherbury* (London, 1886), p. 20.

63 NLW, Bute MS L3/7.

64 Lloyd Bowen (ed.), *Family and Society in Early Stuart Glamorgan: The Household Accounts of Sir Thomas Aubrey of Llantrithyd, c.1565–1641* (Llandysul, 2006).

65 Thomas Jones, *The British Language in its Lustre* (London, 1688), sig. A2v.

66 Bodl. Lib., Tanner MS 34, fo. 31.

67 G. J. Williams, 'Tri Chof Ynys Brydain', *Llên Cymru*, 4 (1955), 234–9.

68 HMC, *Welsh MSS*, I, p. 291.

69 Richard Suggett, 'Vagabonds and Minstrels in Sixteenth-Century Wales', in Adam Fox and Daniel Woolf (eds), *The Spoken Word: Oral Culture in Britain, 1500–1850* (Manchester, 2002), pp. 138–72.

70 Gruffydd Aled Williams, 'The Poetic Debate of Edmwnd Prys and Wiliam Cynwal', *Renaissance Studies*, 18 (2004), 33–55.

71 *RR*, pp. 442–9; D. J. Bowen, 'Y Cywyddwyr a'r Dirywiad', *BBCS*, 29 (1981), 453–95.

72 Jones, 'Welsh Poets and their Patrons', 277, n. 125.

73 *RR*, p. 448.

74 Ceri W. Lewis, 'The Decline of Professional Poetry', in R. Geraint Gruffydd (ed.), *A Guide to Welsh Literature, c.1530–1700* (Cardiff, 1997), p. 69.

75 Nesta Lloyd, 'John Jones, Gellilyfdy', *Flintshire Historical Society Publications*, 24 (1969–70), 5–18.

76 Bowen, *Family and Society in Early Stuart Glamorgan*, pp. 46, 104.

77 NLW, Penrice and Margam MSS 6369, 6593.

78 Salesbury, *A Briefe and a Playne Introduction*, sig. E1v.

79 Hughes, *Rhagymadroddion*, p. 107.

80 Mary Burdett-Jones, 'Early Welsh Dictionaries', in Philip Henry Jones and Eluned Rees (eds), *A Nation and its Books* (Aberystwyth, 1998), pp. 75–82.

81 R. Brinley Jones, *The Old British Tongue: The Vernacular in Wales, 1540–1640* (Cardiff, 1970), p. 35.

82 Hughes, *Rhagymadroddion*, pp. 111–17.

83 Branwen Jarvis, 'Welsh Humanist Learning', in Gruffydd, *Welsh Literature*, p. 140.

84 Jones, *British Language in its Lustre*, sig. A4.

85 Davies, *Rhagymadroddion*, p. 73.

86 See the assessments in Ceri Davies (ed.), *Dr John Davies of Mallwyd: Welsh Renaissance Scholar* (Cardiff, 2004).

87 Hughes, *Rhagymadroddion*, p. 105.

88 [Robert Holland], *Basilikon Doron ... Translated into the True British Tongue* (London, 1604), sig. B3 (mispaginated for sig. A1).

89 Quoted in Ceri Davies, 'Introduction', in Ceri Davies, *Dr John Davies*, p. 10.

90 Erich Poppe, 'John Davies and the Study of Grammar: *Antiquae Linguae Britannicae ... Rudimenta* (1621)', and Caryl Davies, 'The *Dictionarium Duplex* (1632)', in Davies, *Dr John Davies*, pp. 125–30, 135–7, 157–60.

91 Quoted in Poppe, '*Rudimenta*', p. 129.

92 Such ideas were given the imprimatur of John Davies of Mallwyd earlier in the century: Poppe, '*Rudimenta*', pp. 121–45.

93 Adam Coward, 'Exiled Trojans of the Sons of Gomer: Wales's Origins in the Long Eighteenth Century', in Lotte Jensen (ed.), *The Roots of Nationalism: National Identity Formation in Early Modern Europe, 1600–1815* (Amsterdam, 2016), pp. 167–81.

94 See, for example, BL, Harleian MS 6804, fos 94, 96; W. J. Smith (ed.), *Calendar of Salusbury Correspondence* (Cardiff, 1954), p. 207.

CHAPTER 6

1 See, for example, Philip Jenkins, 'Seventeenth-Century Wales: Definition and Identity', in Peter R. Roberts and Brendan Bradshaw (eds), *British Consciousness and Identity: The Making of Britain, 1533–1707* (Cambridge, 1998), pp. 213–35, which concludes that, because of Wales's close ties to the Crown, 'there was no such thing as Welsh politics in the seventeenth century' (p. 215). However, this conclusion seems derived largely from the fact that Jenkins's quest for 'Welsh politics' is framed exclusively in terms of a nationalist or separatist discourse. For an alternative view, see *PoP*.

2 For this topic, see Glanmor Williams, 'Prophecy, Poetry, and Politics in Medieval and Tudor Wales', in his *Religion, Language and Nationality in Wales* (Cardiff, 1979), pp. 71–86; Ceridwen Lloyd-Morgan, 'Prophecy and Welsh Nationhood in the Fifteenth Century', *TCS* (1985), pp. 9–26; Helen Fulton, *Welsh Prophecy and English Politics in the Later Middle Ages* (Aberystwyth, 2009); Philip Schwyzer, *Literature, Nationalism and Memory in Early Modern England and Wales* (Cambridge, 2004), pp. 13–48.

3 A. D. Carr, *Owen of Wales: The End of the House of Gwynedd* (Cardiff, 1991).

4 R. R. Davies, *The Revolt of Owain Glyn Dŵr* (Oxford, 1995), pp. 88–92, 158–73, 326, 355–7.

5 Quoted in R. R. Davies, *The Age of Conquest: Wales, 1063–1415* (Oxford, 1987), p. 436.

6 There is a real problem with using 'Tudor' as a label for the dynasty and for the period 1485–1603, as was pointed out by the late Cliff Davies. However, as he also noted, the Welsh were one of the few groups that *did* have some sense of 'Tudor' as a surname. He was also sufficiently sanguine to recognise that its usage in scholarship and popular culture is too entrenched to be abandoned readily: C. S. L. Davies, 'Reputation, Repute, Reality', *EHR*, 124 (2009), 1437–47; C. S. L. Davies, 'Tudor: What's in a Name?', *History*, 97 (2012), 24–42. Cf. Peter R. Roberts, 'The Welshness of the Tudors', *History Today*, 36 (January 1986), 7–13.

7 David Williams. 'The Family of Henry VII', *History Today*, 4 (1954), 77–84; Ralph A. Griffiths and Roger S. Thomas, *The Making of the Tudor Dynasty* (Gloucester, 1985).

8 W. Garmon Jones, 'Welsh Nationalism and Henry Tudor', *TCS* (1917–18), 1–59; David Rees, *The Son of Prophecy: Henry Tudor's Road to Bosworth* (London, 1985); Gruffydd Aled Williams, 'The Bardic Road to Bosworth: A Welsh View of Henry Tudor', *TCS* (1985), 7–31; Glanmor Williams, *Harri Tudur a Chymru/ Henry Tudor and Wales* (Cardiff, 1985).

9 Williams, 'Bardic Road', 23.

10 See the patriotic account in *Description*, I, p. 262.

11 J. Beverley Smith, 'Crown and Community in the Principality of North Wales in the Reign of Henry Tudor', *WHR*, 3 (1966), 145–71; T. Gwynn Jones, 'Cultural Bases: A Study of the Tudor Period in Wales', *Y Cymmrodor*, 31 (1921), 168, 190–2.

12 John Davies, *A History of Wales* (Harmondsworth, 1994), p. 219.

13 Charlotte Augusta Sneyd (ed.), *A Relation … of the Island of England* (London, Camden Society, 37, 1847), p. 19.

14 Peter R. Roberts, 'Tudor Legislation and the Political Status of "the British Tongue"', *WLBIR*, p. 130.

15 *Testament Newydd ein Arglwydd Jesu Christ* (London, 1567), sig. A1v.

16 Brian Ll. James (ed.), *Morganiae Archaiographia* (Cardiff, 1983), pp. 67–8.

17 *Dialogue*, p. 81.

18 *Dialogue*, p. 82.

19 *Dialogue*, p. 84. This was an influential formulation. As late as 1690 commentators were explaining how Wales was 'better reconciled to the English, King Henry the Seaventh being a Welch man': TNA, SP 8/6, fos 166v–167.

20 *Dialogue*, p. 96.

21 *Dialogue*, p. 97.

22 Enid Roberts (ed.), *Gwaith Siôn Tudur* (2 vols, Cardiff, 1981), I, p. 379; *RR*, pp. 244–5. Cf. J. Gwynfor Jones, 'The Welsh Gentry and the Image of the "Cambro-Briton", *c*.1603–25', *WHR*, 20 (2000–1), 617.

23 G. Dyfnallt Owen, *Wales in the Reign of James I* (Woodbridge, 1988), p. 148.

24 Peter R. Roberts, 'Tudor Wales, National Identity and the British Inheritance', in Roberts and Bradshaw, *British Consciousness and Identity*, pp. 8–42.

25 John Prise, *Historiae Britannicae Defensio: A Defence of British History*, ed. Ceri Davies (Toronto and Oxford, 2015), pp. 29–33.

26 Glanmor Williams, 'Wales and the Reign of Queen Mary I', *WHR*, 10 (1980–1), 336.

27 Albert Owen Edwards, *A Memorandum on the Legality of the Welsh Bible* (Cardiff, 1925), pp. 129, 134.

28 Glanmor Williams, *The Welsh and their Religion* (Cardiff, 1991), p. 223.

29 Roberts, *Gwaith Siôn Tudur*, I, pp. 378–81.

30 NLW, Peniarth MS 118, fos 580–93, 597–600, 722.

31 HMC, *Welsh MSS*, I, p. 159.

32 Williams, *Reformation*, p. 216.

33 Sally Harper, '"A Dittie to the Tune of Welsh Sydannen": A Welsh Image of Queen Elizabeth', *Renaissance Studies*, 19 (2005), 201–28.

34 Harper, 'Sydannen'; T. H. Parry-Williams, 'Caniadau Sidanen', *Canu Rhydd Cynnar* (Cardiff, 1932), pp. 373–80.

35 The literature on this is now very large, but see Sarah Waurechen, 'Imagined Polities, Failed Dreams, and the Beginnings of an Unacknowledged Britain: English Responses to James VI and I's Vision of Perfect Union', *Journal of British Studies*, 52 (2013), 575–96 and the sources cited.

36 *Description*, I, p. 263.

37 Christopher Thompson (ed.), *Obseruatyones of the Proceedinges in the Ple=mente held at Westeminster Ano Primoe et Secundo Jacobi Regis* (Wivenhoe, 1990), pp. 10–11. See also Maurice's draft letter to a cousin which attests to his belief that James was the deliverer who would restore Britain to 'the pristine estate': NLW, Clennenau Letters and Papers, no. 474.

38 William Herbert, *A Prophesie of Cadwallader, Last King of the Britaines* (London, 1604), sig. G4v.

39 George Owen Harry, *A Genealogy of the High and Mighty Monarch, James … King of Great Brittayne* (London, 1604).

40 BL, Cotton MSS, Faustina E II, fos 258–272v.

41 See the dismissive response of James's first minister, Sir Robert Cecil, to a correspondent who had traced his lineage back to ancient Welsh princes: 'I desire none of these vain toyes, nor to heare of such absurditys': Hatfield House, Cecil MS 191/135.

42 Jones, '"Cambro-Briton"', 649.

43 Jones, '"Cambro-Briton"', 649–50; HMC, *Welsh MSS*, II, p. 622.

44 Tim Thornton, 'Dynasty and Territory in the Early Modern Period: The Princes of Wales and their Western British Inheritance', *WHR*, 20 (2000–1), 1–33.

45 David Powel, *The Historie of Cambria* (London, 1584), pp. 376–99; Percy Enderbie, *Cambria Triumphans* (London, 1661), pp. 329–56.

46 [Robert Holland], *Basilikon Doron … Translated into the True British Tongue* (London, 1604), sig. A4v [irregular pagination].

47 [Holland], *Basilikon Doron*, sig. (a)iv [irregular pagination].

48 For this concept, see Gwynfor Jones, '"Cambro-Briton"', but also the rather more sceptical view of the label's currency in Philip Schwyzer, 'The Age of the Cambro-Britons: Hyphenated British Identities in the Seventeenth Century', *The Seventeenth Century*, 33 (2018), 427–39.

49 John Davies, 'Cambria', in his *Microcosmos* (London, 1603), p. 29.

50 Hugh Holland, *Pancharis: The First Booke* (London, 1603), sig. D6.

51 Davies, *Microcosmos*, pp. 30–1.

52 Jones, '"Cambro-Briton"', 648; Jones, *Concepts of Order and Gentility in Wales, 1540–1640* (Llandysul, 1992), p. 165.

53 Nesta Lloyd (ed.), *Blodeugerdd Barddas o'r Ail Ganrif ar Bymtheg* (Cardiff, 1993), pp. 74–7.

54 Daniel Powel, *The Love of Wales to their Soveraigne Prince* (London, 1616). The payments for these celebrations can be found in Shropshire Archives, LB8/1/138, fos 5–8, 17.

55 Bodl. Lib., Carte MS 14, fo. 609v.

56 *PoP*, pp. 240–61; Lloyd Bowen, 'Structuring Particularist Publics: Logistics, Language, and Early Modern Wales', *Journal of British Studies*, 56 (2017), 762–5; Bowen, 'Wales in the Civil War: The Last Refuge of Monarchy', *BBC History Magazine* (November 2012).

57 *A Loyal and Loving Speech … at Raglan Castle* (London, 1642).

58 Lloyd Bowen, *John Poyer, the Civil War in Pembrokeshire and the British Revolutions* (Cardiff, 2020).

59 *Mercurius Pragmaticus*, 28 (21–8 March 1648), sig. D4v; Lloyd Bowen, 'Representations of Wales and the Welsh during the Civil Wars and Interregnum', *Historical Research*, 77 (2004), 362–72.

60 Nesta Lloyd, 'Late Free-Metre Poetry', in R. Geraint Gruffydd (ed.), *A Guide to Welsh Literature, c.1530–1700* (Cardiff, 1997), pp. 121–2; Jerry Hunter, 'The Red Sword, the Sickle and the Author's Revenge: Welsh Literature and Conflict in the Seventeenth Century', *Proceedings of the Harvard Celtic Colloquium*, 36 (2016), 1–14.

61 E. D. Jones, 'The Brogyntyn Manuscripts. XIII', *NLWJ*, 9 (1953–4), 8.

62 Megan Ellis, 'Cyflwyniad Rowland Vaughan, Caergai, i'w Gyfieithiad o *Eikon Basilike*', *NLWJ*, 1 (1939–40), 141–44; J. Gwynfor Jones, 'Cyfieithiad Rowland Vaughan, Caer-gai o *Eikon Basilike* (1650)', *Studia Celtica*, 36 (2002), 99–138.

63 E. D. Jones, 'The Brogyntyn Manuscripts. X', *NLWJ*, 7 (1951–2), 166.

64 Luned Mair Davies, 'The Tregaer Manuscript: An Elegy for Charles I', *NLWJ*, 31 (2000), 243–70.

65 NLW, Great Sessions 4/985/5/2–4.

66 NLW, Great Sessions 4/789/2/18.

67 Gwynedd Archives, Caernarfon Record Office, XQS/1660/8.

68 Gwynedd Archives, Caernarfon Record Office, XQS/1660/3.

69 Lloyd Bowen, "'This Murmuring and Unthankful Peevish Land": Wales and the Protectorate', in Patrick Little (ed.), *The Cromwellian Protectorate* (Woodbridge, 2007), pp. 144–64; Sarah Ward Clavier, "'Horrid Rebellion" and "Holie Cheate": Royalist Gentry Responses to Interregnum Government in North-East Wales, 1646–1660', *WHR*, 29 (2018), 51–72; Sarah Ward Clavier, "'Round-head Knaves": The Ballad of Wrexham and the Subversive Political Culture of Interregnum North-East Wales', *Historical Research*, 91 (2018), 39–60.

70 Thomas Birch (ed.), *A Collection of the State Papers of John Thurloe* (7 vols, London, 1742), II, p. 256.

71 NLW, Facsimiles 893, fo. 17.

72 NLW, MS 9066E/2235. Her husband's letter is NLW, MS 9066E/2234.

73 NLW, MS 9066E/2272.

74 *The Humble Addresse of the … Six Counties of South-Wales, and County of Monmouth* (London, 1660).

75 Enderbie, *Cambria Triumphans*; College of Arms Library, Box 36/IX.

76 Jones, 'Brogyntyn Welsh Manuscripts. XIII', 8–10.

77 Folger Shakespeare Library, V.a. 616, fos 115v, 114v.

78 Geraint H. Jenkins, *Literature, Religion and Society in Wales, 1660–1730* (Cardiff, 1978), p. 19.

79 John Thomas, *Unum Necessarium* (London, 1680), p. 34.

80 E. D. Jones, 'The Brogyntyn Welsh Manuscripts. [I]', *NLWJ*, 5 (1948), 244.

81 Thomas Jones, *Of the Heart and its Right Sovereign* (London, 1678), pp. 373–4.

82 Molly McClain, 'The Duke of Beaufort's Tory Progress through Wales, 1684', *WHR*, 19 (1997), 592–620.

83 *The Speech of Richard Vaughan* (London, 1684), p. 2.

84 *Speech of Richard Vaughan*, p. 4.

85 A. H. Dodd, *Studies in Stuart Wales* (Cardiff, 1952), p. 217.

86 David Lewis Jones, 'The Glorious Revolution in Wales', *NLWJ*, 26 (1989–90), 28.

87 TNA, SP 8/6, fo. 169v.

88 P. D. G. Thomas, 'Jacobitism in Wales', *WHR*, 1 (1960–4), 279–300; P. D. G. Thomas, *Politics in Eighteenth-Century Wales* (Cardiff, 1998), chs 6–7; Sharon Howard, *Law and Disorder in Early Modern Wales* (Cardiff, 2008), pp. 165–70.

89 NLW, Great Sessions 4/134/2/89, 209.

90 TNA, STAC 8/122/6.

91 Bowen, *John Poyer*.

92 Stephen K. Roberts, 'Religion, Politics and Welshness, 1649–1660', in Ivan Roots (ed.), *"Into Another Mould": Aspects of the Interregnum*, 2nd edn (Exeter, 1998), pp. 38–9.

93 J. Graham Jones and Goronwy Wyn Owen (eds), *Gweithiau Morgan Llwyd o Wynedd. III* (Cardiff, 1993), p. 41.

94 Thomas E. Ellis and J. H. Davies (eds), *Gweithiau Morgan Llwyd o Wynedd* (2 vols, Bangor 1899–1908), I, p. 55.

95 Quoted in John Kerrigan, *Archipelagic English: Literature, History, and Politics, 1603–1707* (Oxford, 2008), p. 196.

96 Philip Jenkins, "'The Old Leaven": The Welsh Roundheads after 1660', *Historical Journal*, 24 (1981), 807–23.

97 NLW, Chirk Castle MS B16/c/34/1.
98 NLW, Chirk Castle MS B16/c/34/2.
99 NLW, Great Sessions 4/25/4/24, 26, 35; TNA, SP29/112, fo. 168.
100 NLW, J. Conway Davies Papers, Box 87/17.

CHAPTER 7

1 Philip Jenkins, 'Seventeenth-Century Wales: Definition and Identity', in Peter R. Roberts and Brendan Bradshaw (eds), *British Consciousness and Identity: The Making of Britain, 1533–1707* (Cambridge, 1998), pp. 213–35.
2 For an overview, see Lloyd Bowen, 'Political History', in Garthine Walker (ed.), *Writing Early Modern History* (London, 2005), pp. 25–48.
3 See Peter Lake and Steven Pincus (eds), *The Politics of the Public Sphere* (Manchester, 2012); Laura A. M. Stewart (ed.), 'Publics and Participation in Early Modern Britain', a special issue of *Journal of British Studies*, 56 (2017).
4 A. D. Carr, *The Gentry of North Wales in the Later Middle Ages* (Cardiff, 2017), ch. 2.
5 W. Ogwen Williams, *Tudor Gwynedd: The Tudor Age in the Principality of North Wales* (London and Bradford, 1958); W. R. B. Robinson, 'The Tudor Revolution in Welsh Government, 1536–1543: Its Effects on Gentry Participation', *EHR*, 103 (1988), 1–20.
6 Felicity Heal and Clive Holmes, *The Gentry in England and Wales, 1500–1700* (London and Basingstoke, 1994), pp. 168–77; Sadie Jarrett, 'Officeholding and Local Politics in Early Modern Wales: A Study of the Salesburys of Rhug and Bachymbyd, c.1536–1621', *WHR*, 30 (2020), 206–32.
7 *RR*, pp. 342–6; Michael J. Braddick, *State Formation in Early Modern England, c.1550–1700* (Cambridge, 2000), pp. 20–46, 347–52.
8 Heal and Holmes, *The Gentry*, pp. 168–75; J. Gwynfor Jones, *Concepts of Order and Gentility in Wales, 1540–1640* (Llandysul, 1992).
9 BL, Harleian MS 283, fo. 153.
10 Jones, *Concepts of Order and Gentility*.
11 For a local study, see J. Gwynfor Jones, *Law, Order and Government in Caernarfonshire, 1558–1640: Justices of the Peace and the Gentry* (Cardiff, 1996).
12 TNA, SP1/106, fo. 245.
13 Justices also had considerable legal and administrative powers outside these quarterly meetings, either as individual magistrates or in regular 'petty' sessions with a smaller number of colleagues.
14 See, for example, TNA, SP12/66, fo. 59 (Glamorgan JPs, 1570); SP14/130, fo. 131 (Anglesey JPs, 1622); SP16/376, fo. 302 (Flintshire JPs, 1637).
15 *SR*, III, p. 930.
16 J. R. S. Phillips (ed.), *The Justices of the Peace in Wales and Monmouthshire, 1541 to 1689* (Cardiff, 1975). See also the complaint of David Lewis in 1576 that the number of JPs in Wales should 'be abridged to viii according to the ordynances of Wales': TNA, SP12/107, fo. 8v.
17 TNA, SP16/11, fo. 83v.
18 Phillips, *Justices*, p. 9.

19 Heal and Holmes, *The Gentry*, pp. 168–72.
20 Alison Wall, '"The Greatest Disgrace": The Making and Unmaking of JPs in Elizabethan and Jacobean England', *EHR*, 119 (2004), 312–32; Norman Jones, *Governing by Virtue: Lord Burghley and the Management of Elizabethan England* (Oxford, 2015), ch. 4.
21 BL, Harleian MS 6993, fo. 116.
22 BL, Harleian MS 6994, fo. 74.
23 BL, Harleian MS 6996, fo. 96. Cf. BL, Harleian MS 6993, fo. 15. He was placed on the Pembrokeshire bench but not that in Carmarthenshire: Phillips, *Justices*, p. 208. For his uncle's ties to Essex on the commission, see HMC, *Salisbury MSS*, XI, pp. 92–3, 106.
24 BL, Harleian MS 6992, fo. 127. Devereux was duly appointed to the Cardiganshire bench: Phillips, *Justices*, p. 188. Essex also asked Puckering to help 'a coepell [couple] of my frindes in Cardyganshyere to be in commyssyone of the pease': BL, Harleian MS 6993, fo. 109.
25 BL, Lansdowne MS 53, fo. 182.
26 BL, Harleian MS 6997, fo. 74.
27 Hatfield House, Cecil MS 177/142.
28 A. H. Dodd, 'North Wales in the Essex Revolt of 1601', *EHR*, 59 (1944), 348–70.
29 NLW, MS 9056E/836.
30 NLW, MS 9054E/550.
31 NLW, MS 9057E/968.
32 NLW, MS 9058E/1011.
33 HPO (1604–29): 'Griffith III, John'; NLW, MS 9061E/1406; MS 9062E/1533
34 Anthony Fletcher, 'Honour, Reputation and Local Office-Holding in Elizabethan and Stuart England', in Anthony Fletcher and John Stevenson (eds), *Order and Disorder in Early Modern England* (Cambridge, 1985), pp. 92–115.
35 The classic study is A. H. Dodd, *Studies in Stuart Wales* (Cardiff, 1952), pp. 110–77.
36 For this topic, see E. T. Davies, 'The "Popish Plot" in Monmouthshire', *Journal of the Historical Society of the Church in Wales*, 25 (1976), 32–45; Philip Jenkins, 'Anti-Popery on the Welsh Marches in the Seventeenth Century', *Historical Journal*, 23 (1980), 275–93; Julian Mitchell, 'Nathan Rogers and the Wentwood Case', *WHR*, 14 (1988–9), 23–52; Julian Mitchell, 'Politics and Power, 1660–1702', in Madeline Gray and Prys Morgan (eds), *The Gwent County History, Volume 3: The Making of Monmouthshire, 1536–1780* (Cardiff, 2009), pp. 109–23; Molly McClain, 'The Wentwood Forest Riot: Property Rights and Political Culture in Restoration England', in Susan D. Amussen and Mark A. Kishlansky (eds), *Political Culture and Cultural Politics in Early Modern England* (Manchester, 1995), pp. 112–32; Newton E. Key and Joseph P. Ward, '"Divided into Parties": Exclusion Crisis Origins in Monmouth', *EHR*, 115 (2000), 1159–83.
37 HMC, *Finch MSS*, II, pp. 43–4.
38 Nathan Rogers, *Memoirs of Monmouth-shire* (London, 1708), pp. 106, 109.
39 HMC, *Beaufort MSS*, p. 106.
40 TNA, SP44/43, fos 97–8; SP29/402, fo. 50.
41 HMC, *Finch MSS*, II, p. 44. For these removals, see Phillips, *Justices*, p. 364.

42 *CJ*, IX, pp. 468–70.

43 *CJ*, IX, pp. 468–9; HMC, *Beaufort MSS*, p. 68. For Milborne's response, see *A Letter from a Gentleman in Glocestershire to a Friend in London* (London, 1678), pp. 13–21.

44 He was removed 'at the desire of [the] H[ouse] of Commons': HMC, *Finch MSS*, II, p. 43.

45 Phillips, *Justices*, p. 365.

46 HMC, *House of Lords MSS, 1678–88*, pp. 172–88; S. N., *A Catalogue of the Names of ... Justices of the Peace ... According to the Late Alterations* (London, 1680), pp. 33–4; A. H. Dodd, '"Tuning" the Welsh Bench, 1680', *NLWJ*, 6 (1949–50), 249–59.

47 NLW, Clenennau Letters and Papers, no. 783.

48 NLW, MS 3072E, no. 129; B. E. Howells (ed.), *A Calendar of Letters Relating to North Wales* (Cardiff, 1967), p. 177. Cf. UBA, Mostyn Add. MS 9068, no. 55.

49 Key and Ward, 'Exclusion Crisis Origins', p. 1182.

50 Dodd, *Stuart Wales*, pp. 221–3; George Floyd Duckett, *Penal Laws and Test Act, 1687–8* (2 vols, London, 1882), I, pp. 247–91.

51 Scott Sowerby, *Making Toleration: The Repealers and the Glorious Revolution* (Cambridge, MA, and London, 2013), pp. 207–8.

52 Bodl. Lib., Rawlinson MS A139, fo. 179, printed in Duckett, *Penal Laws*, I, pp. 290–1.

53 UBA, Mostyn Add. MS 9070, nos. 30–1.

54 Duckett, *Penal Laws*, pp. 443–50; NLW, MS 11,020E, no. 17; Clenennau Letters and Papers, no. 867; UBA, Mostyn Add. MS 9070, nos. 30–1.

55 The Record Office for Leicestershire, Leicester and Rutland, T322/DG7/Law 15.

56 Philip Jenkins, *The Making of a Ruling Class: The Glamorgan Gentry, 1640–1790* (Cambridge, 1983), pp. 131–2.

57 Philip Jenkins, 'Two Poems on the Glamorgan Gentry Community in the Reign of James II', *NLWJ*, 21 (1979), 176–8.

58 TNA, PC2/67, fo. 57v. Cf. TNA, SP29/411, no. 77.

59 The subject of Elizabethan faction in Wales is dealt with in Penry Williams, *The Council in the Marches of Wales under Elizabeth I* (Cardiff, 1958), pp. 229–48.

60 Williams, *Council in the Marches*, p. 229.

61 TNA, SP12/107, fo. 8.

62 For an illustrative example, see H. G. Owen, 'Family Politics in Elizabethan Merionethshire', *BBCS*, 18 (1959), 185–91.

63 TNA, STAC 5/M46/13. Cf. STAC 5/P46/16, 5/T27/28; HPO (1604–29): 'Monmouthshire'.

64 Simon Adams, *Leicester and the Court* (Manchester, 2002), pp. 235–309; Madeleine Gray, 'Power, Patronage and Politics: Office-Holding and Administration on the Crown's Estates in Wales', in Richard W. Hoyle (ed.), *The Estates of the English Crown, 1558–1640* (Cambridge, 1992), pp. 150–1.

65 Dodd, 'Essex Revolt', 348–70. Cf. Paul E. J. Hammer, 'The Earl of Essex and Elizabethan Parliaments', *Parliamentary History*, 34 (2015), 90–110.

66 Penry Williams, 'Political and Administrative History of Glamorgan, 1536–1642', in Glanmor Williams (ed.), *Glamorgan County History. IV. Early Modern Glamorgan* (Cardiff, 1974), pp. 163, 172–3, 177–91.

67 Stephen K. Roberts, 'Local, Regional and National Politics to 1642', in Gray and Morgan, *Making of Monmouthshire*, pp. 35–61.

68 Stephen K. Roberts, 'How the West Was Won: Parliamentary Politics, Religion and the Military in South Wales, 1642–9', *WHR*, 21 (2002–3), 646–74. Cf. Jenkins, *Making of a Ruling Class*, pp. 101–7.

69 Adams, *Leicester and the Court*, pp. 235–52.

70 HPO (1558–1603): 'Denbigh Boroughs'.

71 H. A. Lloyd, *The Gentry of South-West Wales, 1540–1640* (Cardiff, 1968), pp. 112–18.

72 Hammer, 'Earl of Essex', 95 n. 24.

73 NLW, Bute MS L3/84.

74 HPO (1558–1603): 'Denbighshire'; HPO (1604–29): 'Caernarvonshire'; J. E. Neale, 'Three Elizabethan Elections', *EHR*, 46 (1931), 212–19.

75 See the discussion in *PoP*, pp. 12–38.

76 Lloyd Bowen, 'Faction, Competition and Politics in Civil War Pembrokeshire, 1640–49', *EHR* (forthcoming).

77 Roberts, 'How the West Was Won', 667.

78 Dodd, *Studies*, pp. 194–5.

79 HPO (1660–90): 'Monmouthshire'; 'Monmouth Boroughs'; Mitchell, 'Politics and Power'.

80 See above, p. 18.

81 Lloyd Bowen, 'Wales at Westminster: Parliament, Principality and Pressure Groups, 1542–1601', *Parliamentary History*, 22 (2003), 107–20.

82 T. C. Mendenhall, *The Shrewsbury Drapers and the Welsh Wool Trade in the XVI and XVII Centuries* (Oxford, 1953); *PoP*, pp. 57–64.

83 TNA, SP14/131, fo. 49; Shropshire Archives, 1831/10; TNA, SP14/131, fo. 105.

84 NLW, MS 9058E/1096A.

85 Carolyn Edie, *The Irish Cattle Bills: A Study in Restoration Politics*, Transactions of the American Philosophical Society, new series, 40 (1970); *CJ*, IX, p. 37; *SR*, V, p. 597.

86 NLW, MS 9067E/2470. Cf. UBA, Mostyn Add. MS 9067, no. 46.

87 *PoP*, pp. 67–8.

88 Bowen, 'Wales at Westminster', 111–12.

89 Peter R. Roberts, 'Wales and England after the Tudor "Union": Crown, Principality and Parliament, 1543–1624', in Claire Cross et al (eds), *Law and Government under the Tudors* (Cambridge, 1988), pp. 111–38; *PoP*, pp. 75–80.

90 TNA, SP14/119, fo. 272.

91 TNA, SP14/55, fo. 141; NLW, MS 339F, p. 119

92 *SR*, IV, p. 1218. Cf. NLW, MS 9059E/1220, 1228.

93 See above, p. 49.

94 *FMW*, p. 152.

95 TNA, C219/35/2, fos 195–201.

96 NLW, MS 9057E/921

97 NLW, Chirk Castle MS E.558.

98 *PoP*, pp. 16–18, 28–30.

99 NLW, MSS 9057E/924, 942, 996.

100 *PoP*, pp. 35–7.
101 Alnwick Castle, Northumberland Papers, III, fo. 78; NLW, Penrice and Margam MS L.44. For the context, see Bowen, 'Wales at Westminster', 117–20.
102 Bowen, 'Information'.
103 NLW, Great Sessions 4/798/2/68
104 TNA, STAC 8/205/21; Bowen, 'Information', 148–9.
105 Lloyd Bowen, 'News Networks in Early Modern Wales', *History*, 102 (2017), 24–44.
106 *FMW*, p. 157.
107 BL, Additional MS 70,109, no. 69.
108 See above, p. 57.
109 NLW, Lleweni MS (Correspondence), no. 194.
110 NLW, MS 1959E, fo. 228. Cf. Shropshire Archives, MS 212/364/77.
111 *Two Petitions Presented to the Kings Most Excellent Majestie at Yorke, the First of August 1642* (York, 1642).
112 NLW, MS 9063E/1711.
113 A. H. Dodd, 'A Remonstrance from Wales, 1655', *BBCS*, 17 (1958), 279–92.
114 See above, p. 129.
115 *Vox Angliae* (London, 1682). Loyalist addresses were received from Abergavenny, Brecon, Breconshire, Cardiff, Carmarthen, Denbighshire, Glamorgan Merioneth, Monmouth, Monmouthshire, Montgomeryshire, Newport, New Radnor and Radnorshire.
116 I am most grateful to Prof. Newton E. Key for help with this document and for sharing his notes on the petition with me.
117 TNA, SP29/39, fos 85–125v.
118 Indeed, the 1689 measure seems to have been a revival of an earlier effort during the Exclusion Crisis to remove the Council: Parliamentary Archives, HL/PO/JO/10/2/18; HMC, *House of Lords MSS, 1678–88*, p. 261; *CJ*, IX, p. 708; *LJ*, XIII, pp. 721, 727.
119 NLW, Clenennau Letters and Papers, no. 879.
120 For these arguments, see HMC, *House of Lords MSS, 1689–90*, pp. 105–9; Suffolk Archives, Ipswich, EE2/K/2/2.
121 *The Grievances of His Majesties Subjects Residing within the Principality of Wales ...* (London, 1689); *The Case of their Majesties Subjects in the Principality of Wales in Respect of the Court Held Before the President and Council in the Marches of Wales* (London, 1689). See also the responses: *A Welshmans Answer to a Paper Entitled, The Case of their Majesties Subjects ...* (London, 1689); *An Answer to a Paper Entituled The Grievances of His Majesties Subjects ...* (London, 1689).
122 Parliamentary Archives, HL/PO/JO/10/1/408/80. An online transcription can be found at <*https://www.british-history.ac.uk/petitions/house-of-lords/1689#h2-0041*> [accessed 30.07.21]. The petition was considered by the Lords on 1 June: *LJ*, XIV, p. 230.
123 NLW, Clenennau Letters and Papers, no. 877.
124 NLW, Clenennau Letters and Papers, no. 880; TNA, SP44/97, fo. 87; *CJ*, X, pp. 34, 35, 43, 65–6, 68, 84–5, 96, 103, 111, 201; *LJ*, XIV, pp. 195, 209, 223, 230–1, 237, 255, 258–9, 294; *SR*, VI, p. 93; H. C. Foxcroft (ed.), *Life and Works of*

Sir George Savile, First Marquess of Halifax (2 vols, London, 1898), II, p. 210; HMC, *House of Lords MSS, 1689–90*, pp. 107–8; TNA, SP 8/6, fo. 168.

125 Although a counter-petition was organised by the town of Ludlow where the Council sat: HMC, *House of Lords MSS, 1689–90*, pp. 107–8; HMC, *Portland MSS*, III, pp. 432–3.

126 Philip Loft, 'Involving the Public: Parliament, Petitioning and the Language of Interest, 1688–1720', *Journal of British Studies*, 55 (2016), 8–9.

127 Parliamentary Archives, HL/PO/JO/10/1/408/80.

128 For the Sacheverell riots, see Sharon Howard, *Law and Disorder in Early Modern Wales* (Cardiff, 2008), pp. 175–7; *FMW*, pp. 139–41; TNA, SP34/12, fos 59–60; NLW, Great Sessions 4/40/1/9–12.

CHAPTER 8

1 Michael Roberts and Simone Clarke (eds), *Women and Gender in Early Modern Wales* (Cardiff, 2000).

2 See, for example, Deborah Youngs, '"At Hir Owne Discrecion": Women and Will-Making in Late Medieval and Early Tudor Wales', *WHR*, 29 (2019), 408–35 and Angela Muir, *Deviant Maternity: Illegitimacy in Wales, c.1680–1800* (London, 2020).

3 Generally for this section, see HPO (1604–29): 'Bulkeley, Sir Richard' and 'Bulkeley, Richard'; Katharine W. Swett, 'Widowhood, Custom and Property in Early Modern Wales', *WHR*, 18 (1996), 189–227, esp. 210–12; Christine Peters, *Women in Early Modern Britain, 1450–1640* (Basingstoke, 2004), pp. 37–40.

4 NLW, Add. MS 464E/80.

5 It is unclear whether this arrangement endured, however. Several of their children were baptised on the family estate in Cheadle, Cheshire, and a 1620s breviat of one of her lawsuits noted that Mary 'had not lived there [Anglesey] nor would not in her husbands life time': NLW, MS 9059E/1150A.

6 TNA, SP14/104, fo. 42; SP14/107, fo. 19.

7 See, for example, the numerous English marriages contracted by the Wynns of Gwydir in this period: Katharine W. Swett, '"In Love and Duty": Marriage Strategy and Family Relations among the Wynns of Gwydir, 1570–1670' (Stanford University, PhD thesis, 1991); Felicity Heal and Clive Holmes, *The Gentry in England and Wales, 1500–1700* (London and Basingstoke, 1994), pp. 64–8.

8 Hatfield House, Cecil MS 117/14; N. E. McClure (ed.), *The Letters of John Chamberlain* (2 vols, Philadelphia, 1939), I, p. 145.

9 Heather Wolfe, 'Women's Handwriting', in Laura Lunger Knoppers (ed.), *The Cambridge Companion to Early Modern Women's Writing* (Cambridge, 2009), pp. 31–5.

10 For this Anglesey gentleman and his dispute with Bulkeley, see HPO (1558–1603): 'Owen ap Meurig, Lewis ab'.

11 NLW, Add. MS 465E/382. The dating of this letter in the Wynn calendar is incorrect.

12 UBA, Baron Hill MS 22; TNA, SP14/104, fo. 42.

13 TNA, SP14/8, fo. 211. He later described him as 'a man that calleth himself my sonne, which I doe not allowe nor thinke him to be the same': TNA, SP14/104, fo. 42.

14 TNA, SP14/110, fo. 218.

15 TNA, SP14/8, fo. 211.

16 E. G. Jones (ed.), 'History of the Bulkeley Family', *Transactions of the Anglesey Antiquarian Society* (1948), 38, 60–1.

17 Hatfield House, Cecil MS 122/88. Cf. her earlier letter to the Earl of Salisbury apologising for her son's escape from Salisbury's bailiffs after his arrest for debt: Hatfield House, Cecil MS 117/14 (calendared in HMC, *Salisbury MSS*, XVIII, p. 223). Sir Richard later paid 'a power of money' to quiet the widow of the murdered man and to obtain a pardon for his child: TNA, SP14/34, fo. 140; Jones, 'History of the Bulkeley Family', 38.

18 UBA, Baron Hill MSS 33–4; Jones, 'History of the Bulkeley Family', 60–1.

19 TNA, PROB 11/138, fo. 9; Youngs, 'Women and Will-Making', 414–21.

20 UBA, Baron Hill MSS 285, 297; TNA, C78/330/2.

21 J. V. Lyle (ed.), *Acts of the Privy Council, 1618–19* (London, 1929), p. 402.

22 UBA, Baron Hill MSS 29, 297.

23 NLW, MS 9057E/963; TNA, STAC 8/76/3; Jones, 'History of the Bulkeley Family', 31.

24 Shortly before the assizes, Lady Anne Bulkeley wrote to try and influence one Anglesey justice to be 'favorable in such differences as shalbe referred unto his iudgement': NLW, MS 9057E/976.

25 NLW, MS 9057E/980.

26 HPO (1604–29): 'Griffith III, John'.

27 Bodvel was, however, trying to secure a match between his own daughter and the Bulkeley heir: NLW, MSS 9057E/983, 988.

28 NLW, MS 9057E/981.

29 UBA, Bangor MS 1920/12.

30 TNA, C2/JasI/B23/13, 24; C2/JasI/B42/10; E112/144/89; E134/20JasI/Mich9, 31.

31 TNA, PROB 11/143, fo. 263r–v.

32 UBA, Baron Hill MSS 299–300.

33 NLW, MS 9058E/1027; Jones, 'History of the Bulkeley Family', 41.

34 Jones, 'History of the Bulkeley Family', 41.

35 Kent Archives and Local History, U269/1/OE387.

36 J. P. Earwaker, *East Cheshire: Past and Present, Volume 1* (London, 1877), p. 178; TNA, STAC 8/76/3.

37 Kent Archives and Local History, U269/1/OL6.

38 NLW, MSS 9058E/1050, 1120, 1126, 1130; Add. MS 466F/1061.

39 NLW, MS 9058E/1046.

40 NLW, MS 9054E/557; UBA, Bangor MS 1921, pp. 1–25; TNA, CHES 7/23.

41 Swett, 'Widowhood'.

42 Jones, 'History of the Bulkeley Family', 41.

43 NLW, 9059E/1150A; TNA, SP14/162, fo. 53; *CJ*, I, pp. 698, 758, 764; British History Online, Philip Baker (ed.), *Proceedings in Parliament, 1624: The House*

of Commons (2015–18), 8 and 13 April, 4 May; Parliamentary Archives, HL/
PO/JO/10/1/23.

44 NLW, MS 9059E/1150A; TNA, C78/330/2; UBA, Baron Hill MS 305; Jones,
'History of the Bulkeley Family', 41–2.

45 TNA, WARD 7/101/22. Legal disputes between her and her grandson continued
even after this settlement, however: TNA, C2/ChasI/B15/64, B51/43, B54/44,
B120/37, B140/14; UBA, Baron Hill MSS 53, 55.

46 Although not wholly untypical either: Heal and Holmes, *Gentry*, pp. 83–6.

47 NLW, MS 9058E/1046. See also George Owen's sardonic discussion of the decline
of widow's customary payments which, he said, would not endure 'except the
women of our country would erect an Inn of Court and study the law to defend
their common cause, wherein I think they were like to profit, for that there are
of them many ripe wits, and all ready tongues': Brian Howells (ed.), *Elizabethan
Pembrokeshire* (Cardiff, 1973), p. 7.

48 It is also the case that some bardic elegies of the period render widows as echoes
of their husbands' lives: E. D. Jones, 'The Brogyntyn Welsh Manuscripts. IV',
NLWJ, 6 (1949), 6.

49 Swett, 'Widowhood', 218–19.

50 For this section generally, see Gwen Saunders Jones, *Alis ferch Gruffudd a'r
Traddodiad Barddol Benywaidd* (Caernarfon, 2015); Gwen Saunders Jones,
'"A'r Galon Sydd yn Gofyn": Serch a Phriodas ym Marddoniaeth Alis ferch
Gruffudd (*fl*. 1540–1570)', *Dwned*, 18 (2012), 79–93; Cathryn Charnell-White,
Beirdd Ceridwen: Blodeugerdd Barddas o Ganu Menywod hyd tua 1800 (Swansea,
2005); Cathryn Charnell-White, 'Alis, Catrin a Gwen: Tair Prydyddes o'r Unfed
Ganrif ar Bymtheg. Tair Chwaer?', *Dwned*, 5 (1999), 89–104; Nia W. Powell,
'Women and Strict-Metre Poetry in Wales', in Clarke and Roberts, *Women and
Gender in Early Modern Wales*, pp. 129–58.

51 Jones, *Alis ferch Gruffudd*, pp. 23–33.

52 Ceridwen Lloyd-Morgan, 'Oral Composition and Written Transmission: Welsh
Women's Poetry from the Middle Ages and Beyond,' *Trivium*, 26 (1991), 89–102.

53 Cathryn Charnell-White, 'Problems of Authorship and Attribution: The
Welsh-Language Women's Canon before 1800', *Women's Writing*, 24 (2017),
398–417; Cathryn Charnell-White, 'Tair Chwaer?'

54 Lloyd-Morgan, 'Oral Composition and Written Transmission', 91.

55 Charnell-White, *Beirdd Ceridwen*, pp. 75–84.

56 Powell, 'Strict-Metre Poetry', p. 135.

57 On this, see Deborah Youngs, '"For the Preferment of their Marriage and
Bringing Upp of their Youth": The Education and Training of Young
Welshwomen, *c*.1450–*c*.1550', *WHR*, 25 (2011), 463–85.

58 Quoted in Powell, 'Women and Strict-Metre Poetry', p. 134.

59 Cathryn Charnell-White, 'Barddoniaeth Ddefosiynol Catrin ferch Gruffudd
ap Hywel', *Dwned*, 7 (2001), 93–120.

60 See above, p. 67.

61 Lawrence Stone famously maintained that affection had little place in elite relationships of the period, a claim that has since been widely refuted: Lawrence
Stone, *The Family, Sex and Marriage in England, 1500–1800* (Oxford, 1977).

62 Charnell-White, *Beirdd Ceridwen*, p. 77.
63 Charnell-White, *Beirdd Ceridwen*, p. 78.
64 Charnell-White, *Beirdd Ceridwen*, p. 79. His second wife was Alis ferch John Owen.
65 There are several other Welsh women's poems from the period on this theme: Charnell-White, *Beirdd Ceridwen*, pp. 366–7.
66 *Dictionary of Welsh Biography*: 'Alice verch Griffith ap Ieuan ap Llywelyn Fychan'.
67 Charnell-White, *Beirdd Ceridwen*, p. 80.
68 Charnell-White, *Beirdd Ceridwen*, p. 365.
69 For this section, see *ODNB*: 'Philips [née Fowler], Katherine'; Patrick Thomas, *Katherine Philips ('Orinda')* (Cardiff, 1988); Sarah Prescott, 'Archipelagic Orinda? Katherine Philips and the Writing of Welsh Women's Literary History', *Literature Compass*, 6 (2009), 1167–76; Sarah Prescott, '"That Private Shade Wherein my Muse was Bred": Katherine Philips and the Poetic Spaces of Welsh Retirement', *Philological Quarterly*, 88 (2009), 345–64; Sarah Prescott, 'Archipelagic Coterie Space: Katherine Philips and Welsh Women's Writing', *Tulsa Studies in Women's Literature*, 33 (2014), 51–76.
70 O. L. Dick (ed.), *John Aubrey's Brief Lives* (London, 1950), p. 242.
71 HPO (1660–90): 'Philipps, James'.
72 Catharine Gray, 'Katherine Philips in Ireland', *English Literary Renaissance*, 39 (2009), 557–85.
73 *Poems by … Mrs Katherine Philips, the Matchless Orinda* (London, 1667), pp. 76–7. It is worth noting that this is the first poem in the autograph manuscript of her verses: NLW, MS 775B, pp. 3, 5. Cf. Harry Ransom Humanities Research Center, University of Texas, Austin, pre-1700 MS 151, p. 1.
74 *Poems by … Katherine Philips*, pp. 148–9. See also the poem on his tomb: *Poems by … Katherine Philips*, p. 134
75 *Poems by … Katherine Philips*, pp. 51–2.
76 Hariette Andreadis, 'The Sapphic-Platonics of Katherine Philips, 1632–1663', *Signs*, 15 (1989), 34–60; Arlene Stiebel, 'Not Since Sappho: The Erotic in the Poems of Katherine Philips and Aphra Benn', *Journal of Homosexuality*, 23 (1992), 153–64.
77 For a general review of female sociability in a Welsh context, see Simone Clarke, 'The Construction of Genteel Sensibilities: The Socialization of Daughters of the Gentry in Seventeenth- and Eighteenth-Century Wales', in Sandra Betts (ed.), *Our Daughters' Land* (Cardiff, 1996), pp. 55–79.
78 Robert C. Evans, 'Paradox and Politics: Katherine Philips in the Interregnum', in Claude J. Summers and Ted-Larry Pebworth (eds), *The English Civil Wars in the Literary Imagination* (Columbia, MO, 1999), pp. 174–85; Catharine Gray, 'Katherine Philips and the Post-Courtly Coterie', *English Literary Renaissance*, 32 (2002), 426–51.
79 *Poems by … Katherine Philips*, pp. 1–2.
80 *Poems by … Katherine Philips*, pp. 13–14.
81 *Poems by … Katherine Philips*, pp. 2–5.
82 *Poems by … Katherine Philips*, pp. 5–13.

83 *Poems by ... Katherine Philips*, p. 47. Cf. *Poems by ... Katherine Philips*, pp. 45–6 and NLW, MS 775B, pp. 43–7: 'Upon a Scandalous Libell made by J. Jones'.

84 Kate Chedgzoy, *Women's Writing in the British Atlantic World* (Cambridge, 2007), p. 112.

85 Clarke, 'Genteel Sensibilities'.

86 *Poems by ... Katherine Philips*, pp. 131–2.

87 See above, p. 105–8.

88 John Kerrigan, *Archipelagic English: Literature, History and Politics, 1603–1707* (Oxford, 2008), p. 213; *Poems by ... Katherine Philips*, sig. C1v.

89 *Poems by ... Katherine Philips*, sig. B1v; Prescott, 'Archipelagic Orinda', pp. 1170–1.

90 *Poems by ... Katherine Philips*, pp. 42–4, 92–4, 152–3.

91 *Poems by ... Katherine Philips*, p. 16.

92 *Poems by ... Katherine Philips*, pp. 27–8; Patrick Thomas, 'Orinda, Vaughan, and Watkyns: Anglo-Welsh Literary Relationships during the Interregnum', *The Anglo-Welsh Review*, 26 (1976), 96–102.

93 See Prescott's reference to the 'expansive interactive Welsh context' revealed by Philips's coterie practice: 'Coterie Space', 53.

94 Generally for this section, see Richard Suggett, *A History of Magic and Witchcraft in Wales* (Stroud, 2008); Richard Suggett, 'Witchcraft Dynamics in Early Modern Wales', in Roberts and Clarke, *Women and Gender in Early Modern Wales*, pp. 75–103; Richard Suggett (ed.), *Welsh Witches: Narratives of Witchcraft and Magic from Sixteenth- and Seventeenth-Century Wales* (n.p., 2018); Sally Parkin, 'Witchcraft, Women's Honour and Customary Law in Early Modern Wales', *Social History*, 31 (2006), 295–318; Stuart Clark and Prys Morgan, 'Religion and Magic in Elizabethan Wales: Robert Holland's Dialogue on Witchcraft', *Journal of Ecclesiastical History*, 27 (1976), 31–46; J. G. Williams, 'Witchcraft in 17th Century Flintshire', *Flintshire Historical Society Publications*, 26 (1974–5), 16–37.

95 This case is discussed *in extenso* by Richard Suggett, and my account is based on his research: Suggett, *History of Magic and Witchcraft*, pp. 27–41; Suggett, *Welsh Witches*, pp. 40–69.

96 Suggett, 'Witchcraft Dynamics', pp. 76–8.

97 The documents from the case can be found at NLW, Great Sessions 4/9/4/8–15, 34 54–6, 94 and most are reproduced in Suggett, *Welsh Witches*, pp. 55–69, 189–90.

98 *Geiriadur Prifysgol Cymru*, s.v. 'witsh/wits'; William Salesbury, *A Dictionary in Englyshe and Welshe* (London, 1547), sig. Riiiv. He also defined 'witscrefft' as 'wytche-crafte'.

99 The names of the trial jurors can be found at NLW, Great Sessions, 4/9/4/34.

CHAPTER 9

1 This section is based on Arise Evans, *An Ecco to the Voice from Heaven* (London, 1652), but see also *ODNB*: 'Evans, Arise [Rhys, Rice]'; Christopher Hill, 'Arise Evans: Welshman in London', in his *Change and Continuity in*

Seventeenth-Century England (London, 1974); Bernard Capp, 'Healing the Nation: Royalist Visionaries, Cromwell, and the Restoration of Charles II', *The Seventeenth Century*, 34 (2019), 493–512.

2 Evans, *An Ecco*, p. 1.

3 For a valuable survey, see Glanmor Williams, 'The Welsh in Tudor England', in his *Religion, Language and Nationality in Wales* (Cardiff, 1979), pp. 171–99.

4 This has been captured in the recent volume, Patricia Skinner (ed.), *The Welsh and the Medieval World: Travel, Migration and Exile* (Cardiff, 2018). See also Ralph A. Griffiths, 'Crossing the Frontiers of the English Realm in the Fifteenth Century', in Huw Pryce and John Watts (eds), *Power and Identity in the Middle Ages* (Oxford, 2007), pp. 211–25; Peter Fleming, 'The Welsh Diaspora in Early Tudor English Towns', in Helen Fulton (ed.), *Urban Culture in Medieval Wales* (Cardiff, 2012), pp. 271–94.

5 *Dialogue*, p. 82.

6 An excellent summary of these economic developments can be found in *RR*, pp. 381–94.

7 Anon., 'Anglesey', *AC*, 4th series, 12 (1881), 50.

8 Longleat House, Whitelocke MS 21, fo. 111v.

9 *Tudor Wales*, p. 30.

10 Fleming, 'Welsh Diaspora'; Ralph A. Griffiths, 'After Glyn Dŵr: An Age of Reconciliation?', *Proceedings of the British Academy*, 117 (2002), 139–64.

11 Jane Laughton, 'Mapping the Migrants: Welsh, Manx and Irish Settlers in Fifteenth-Century Chester', in Catherine A. M. Clarke (ed.), *Mapping the Medieval City: Space, Place and Identity in Chester, c.1200–1600* (Cardiff, 2011), p. 171.

12 For the Welsh tenor of the ward's population in 1580, with half of those listed having patronymics and only three out of twenty-four having names which probably did not belong to men of Welsh descent, see William Philips, 'Papers Relating to the Trained Soldiers of Shropshire in the Reign of Queen Elizabeth', *Transactions of the Shropshire Archaeological and Natural History Society*, 2nd series, 2/2 (1889–90), 272. Cf. Thomas Churchyard, *The Worthines of Wales* (London, 1587), sig. K3.

13 Fleming, 'Welsh Diaspora', p. 289; Fleming, 'Identity and Belonging: Irish and Welsh in Fifteenth-Century Bristol', in Linda Clark (ed.), *Conflict, Consequences and the Crown in the Late Middle Ages* (Woodbridge, 2007), pp. 175–93.

14 Llinos Beverley Smith, 'The Welsh Language before 1536', *WLBIR*, pp. 18–19.

15 Fleming, 'Welsh Diaspora'.

16 William A. Campion and Alan Thacker (eds), *Victoria County History: Shropshire. VI. Shrewsbury* (Woodbridge, 2014).

17 T. C. Mendenhall, *The Shrewsbury Drapers and the Welsh Wool Trade in the XVI and XVII Centuries* (Oxford, 1953), p. 44.

18 Philips, 'Papers Relating to the Trained Soldiers of Shropshire', 261–4.

19 Spencer Dimmock, 'The Origins of Welsh Apprentices in Sixteenth-Century Bristol', *WHR*, 24 (2008), 119–20. Cf. Griffiths, 'After Glyn Dŵr', pp. 152–4.

20 Dimmock, 'Welsh Apprentices', 133.

21 Hatfield House, Cecil MS 150/92.

22 A dated though still useful discussion is T. E. Morris, 'Welsh Surnames in Border Counties of Wales', *Y Cymmrodor*, 43 (1932), 93–173.

23 Fleming, 'Identity and Belonging', p. 191.

24 He referred to himself as 'William Appowell' in a letter of 1533: TNA, SP1/78, fo. 97. Cf. Jean Vanes (ed.), *The Ledger of John Smythe, 1538–1550* (Bristol Records Society, 28, 1975), pp. 74, 142, 253, 255–6, 263–4, 315.

25 Herefordshire Archives, HD4/2/13, unfoliated.

26 Herefordshire Archives, HD4/2/13, unfoliated.

27 TNA, PROB 11/186, fo. 159.

28 See above, p. 95.

29 Barbara Coulton, 'The Establishment of Protestantism in a Provincial Town: A Study of Shrewsbury in the Sixteenth Century', *Sixteenth Century Journal*, 27 (1996), 322.

30 TNA, SP16/492, fo. 87.

31 Richard Blome, *Britannia* (London, 1673), p. 193.

32 Geraint H. Jenkins, Richard Suggett and Eryn M. White, 'The Welsh Language in Early Modern Wales', *WLBIR*, pp. 56–7.

33 See above, p. 25.

34 Herefordshire Archives, HD4/2/11, fos 297v, 308r–v, 310v–312.

35 Gloucestershire Archives, GDR/148, p. 292. For other contemporary examples of the use of the phrase 'Welsh whore', see Cheshire and Chester Archives and Local Studies, EDC 5/1622/20; B. H. Cunnington (ed.), *Some Annals of the Borough of Devizes* (2 vols, London, 1925), II, p. 12; A. W. Renton et al (eds), *The English Reports* (176 vols, Edinburgh, 1900–32), LXXIX, p. 996; LXXXII, p. 858.

36 Somerset Archives, Q/SR/95/281.

37 Gloucestershire Archives, GDR/89, pp. 69–70.

38 '575. Salisbury *v* Marten', in Richard Cust and Andrew Hopper (eds), *The Court of Chivalry 1634–1640*: British History Online, <*http://www.british-history.ac.uk/no-series/court-of-chivalry/575-salisbury-marten*> [accessed 18.08.21].

39 Mark Stoyle, *Soldiers and Strangers: An Ethnic History of the English Civil War* (London and New Haven, 2003), ch. 2.

40 G. Dyfnallt Owen, *Elizabethan Wales: The Social Scene* (Cardiff, 1964), p. 69.

41 W. P. Griffith, 'Tudor Prelude', in Emrys Jones (ed.), *The Welsh in London, 1500–2000* (London, 2001), pp. 10–11.

42 Lloyd Bowen, 'News Networks in Early Modern Wales', *History*, 102 (2017), 22–44.

43 These were Richard Vaughan and Thomas Myddelton, respectively.

44 There were also some formal apprenticeships for women such as that for Mary Griffin, who at sixteen was apprenticed to a London seamstress in the early seventeenth century: London Metropolitan Archives, DL/C/219, fos 145–6.

45 Jerry Luke, 'Welsh Apprentices in London, *c*.1600–1660' (Cambridge University, MPhil. thesis, 2015). I am most grateful to Jerry Luke for providing me with a copy of his dissertation.

46 Owen, *Elizabethan Wales*, p. 118.

47 W. M. Warlow, *A History of the Charities of William Jones* (Bristol, 1899).

48 Luke, 'Welsh Apprentices', pp. 2–3.

49 W. P. Griffith, *Learning, Law and Religion: Higher Education and Welsh Society, c.1540–1640* (Cardiff, 1996), p. 34.

50 Lloyd Bowen, *Anatomy of a Duel in Jacobean England: Gentry Honour, Violence and the Law* (Woodbridge, 2021), pp. 155–6.

51 Emrys Jones, 'The Welsh in London in the Seventeenth and Eighteenth Centuries', *WHR*, 10 (1981), 464. Cf. Jenkins, Suggett and White, 'The Welsh Language in Early Modern Wales', p. 95.

52 NLW, Bute MS L2/133.

53 Quoted in Emrys Jones, 'From Medieval to Renaissance City', in Emrys Jones, *Welsh in London*, p. 35.

54 TNA, PROB 11/71, fo. 102; Philip Jenkins, *The Making of a Ruling Class: The Glamorgan Gentry, 1640–1790* (Cambridge, 1983), pp. 241–4.

55 Paul Griffiths, *Lost Londons* (Cambridge, 2008), p. 106.

56 Griffiths, *Lost Londons*, p. 113.

57 Thomas Wright (ed.), *Queen Elizabeth and her Times* (2 vols, London, 1838), II, p. 166.

58 Sarah Lloyd, '"Agents in their Owen Concerns"? Charity and Economy of Makeshifts in Eighteenth-Century Britain', in Steven King and Alannah Tomkins (eds), *The Poor in England, 1700–1850: An Economy of Makeshifts* (Manchester, 2003), pp. 100–36.

59 Thomas Wright, *The Passions of the Minde* (London, 1601), sig. A4r–v.

60 TNA, PROB 11/123, fo. 333v.

61 TNA, PROB 11/67, fos 64v–65v.

62 J. Henry Jones, 'John Owen, *Cambro-Britannus*', *TCS* (1940), 140.

63 Katharine W. Swett, '"Born on My Land": Identity, Community, and Faith among the Welsh in Early Modern London', in Muriel C. McClendon et al (eds), *Protestant Identities: Religion, Society, and Self-Fashioning in Post-Reformation England* (Stanford, CA, 1999), pp. 249–65. My discussion is much indebted to Dr Swett's pioneering research.

64 <*https://www.pepysdiary.com/diary/1667/03/01/*> [accessed 18.08.21].

65 J. G. Ballinger (ed.), *The Calendar of the Wynn (of Gwydir) Papers* (Aberystwyth, 1926), no. 2578.

66 Loren L. Giese (ed.), *London Consistory Court Depositions, 1586–1611* (List and Index Society, 32, London, 1995).

67 Griffiths, *Lost Londons*, p. 144.

68 Bowen, *Anatomy of a Duel*, p. 99.

69 Jenkins, Suggett and White, 'The Welsh Language in Early Modern Wales', p. 79; J. Gwynfor Jones, 'The Welsh Language in Local Government: Justices of the Peace and the Courts of Quarter Sessions, c.1536–1800', *WLBIR*, pp. 190–1.

70 Hatfield House, Cecil MS 134/71 (calendared in HMC, *Salisbury MSS*, XVII, p. 121).

71 John Taylor, *The Carriers Cosmographie* (London, 1637), sigs. B2, B4.

72 Swett, '"Born on my Land"', p. 262, emphasis added.

73 Swett, '"Born on my Land"', p. 258.

74 The following paragraph is based on HPO (1558–1603): 'Myddelton, Thomas'; HPO (1604–29): 'Myddelton, Sir Thomas'; A. H. Dodd, 'Mr Myddelton, the Merchant of Tower Street', in S. T. Bindoff et al (eds), *Elizabethan Government and Society* (London, 1961), pp. 249–81; NLW, Chirk Castle MS F.12540.

75 NLW, Chirk Castle MS F.12540, pp. 62–3, 241 ('141'), 265 ('165'). See also Huntington Library, Ellesmere MS 1782h.

76 NLW, Chirk Castle MS F.12540, p. 43.

77 NLW, Chirk Castle MS. F.12540, pp. 44, 246 ('146'). For ap Howell as Walsingham's servant, see TNA, STAC 5/H49/32.

78 NLW, MS 9052E/300.

79 NLW, Chirk Castle MS E.490.

80 Vaughan received £200 by way of mortgage six months before: NLW, Chirk Castle MS F.12540, p. 225.

81 Dodd, 'Mr Myddelton'. pp. 276, 281, and see above, pp. 78–9.

82 NLW, Chirk Castle MS E.3676.

83 George Owen noted that Welshmen, 'allthoughe they usuallye speacke the Welshe tongue, yett will they writte eche other in Englishe, and not in the speache they usuallye talke': *Description*, I, p. 36.

84 NLW, Chirk Castle MS E..1347.

85 NLW, Chirk Castle MS E.6210.

86 NLW, Chirk Castle MS E.3730.

87 NLW, Chirk Castle MS E.3731.

88 NLW, Chirk Castle MS E.6211.

89 NLW, Chirk Castle MS E.484.

90 NLW, Chirk Castle MS E.6211.

91 NLW, Chirk Castle MS E.3352.

92 NLW, Chirk Castle MS E.3947. Cf. Chirk Castle MS E.6217.

93 NLW, Chirk Castle MS E.3730.

94 NLW, Chirk Castle MS E.5010.

95 NLW, Chirk Castle MSS. F.830, F.985, F.11822.

96 J. E. Griffith (ed.), *Pedigrees of Anglesey and Carnarvonshire Families* (Horncastle, 1914), p. 204. It is possible that she was the fairly substantial freeholder who made her will as 'Magdalen Lloyd, otherwise Price' in 1746: NLW, SA1746/80.

97 Our knowledge of this subject has been transformed by Rhys Morgan, *The Welsh and the Shaping of Early Modern Ireland, 1558–1641* (Woodbridge, 2014).

98 Morgan, *Early Modern Ireland*, p. 95.

99 Morgan, *Early Modern Ireland*, p. 156.

100 A. H. Dodd, 'The Background of the Welsh Quaker Migration to Pennsylvania', *Journal of the Merionethshire Historical and Record Society*, 3 (1958), 111–27; Geraint H. Jenkins, 'From Ysgeifiog to Pennsylvania: The Rise of Thomas Wynne, Quaker Barber Surgeon', *Flintshire Historical Society Journal*, 28 (1978), 39–61; Richard C. Allen, *Quaker Communities in Early Modern Wales* (Cardiff, 2007), ch. 7.

101 B. S. Schlenther, '"The English is Swallowing up their Language": Welsh Ethnic Ambivalence in Colonial Pennsylvania and the Experience of David Evans', *Pennsylvania Magazine of History and Biography*, 114 (1990), 201–2.

102 T. A. Glenn, *Merion in the Welsh Tract* (Norristown, PA, 1896), p. 52.

103 Richard C. Allen, 'The Origins and Development of Welsh Associational Life in Eighteenth-Century Philadelphia', *TCS*, new series, 15 (2009), 105–26.

104 For this section, see *ODNB*: 'Vaughan, Sir William'; E. W. Jones, 'Y Wladfa Cyntaf: Cambriola a Syr William Vaughan', *NLWJ*, 30 (1998), 231–68; Gillian T. Cell (ed.), *Newfoundland Discovered. English Attempts at Colonisation, 1610–1630* (Hakluyt Society, second series, 160, Farnham and Burlington, VT, 1982).

105 William Vaughan, *The Golden Fleece* (London, 1626), sig. Aaa3.

106 Cell, *Newfoundland Discovered*, pp. 13, 25.

107 For the maps, see Jones, 'Y Wladfa Cyntaf', 241–2.

108 Gwyn A. Williams, *Madoc: The Making of a Myth* (Oxford, 1987).

109 Paul E. J. Hammer, 'A Welshman Abroad: Captain Peter Wynn of Jamestown', *Parergon*, new series, 16 (1998), 62.

110 Vaughan, *Golden Fleece*, sig. b3.

SELECT BIBLIOGRAPHY

This bibliography is not a comprehensive review of the academic literature on early modern Wales. Instead, it provides a brief survey of major works, concentrating on accessible primary sources and on important scholarly books, chapters and articles published in recent decades. This selection is intended for the reader who wishes to delve a little deeper into the subjects covered in the foregoing pages. More detailed (albeit now somewhat dated) bibliographies can be found in Glanmor Williams, *Renewal and Reformation, Wales, c.1415–1642* (Oxford, 1993) and Geraint H. Jenkins, *The Foundations of Modern Wales, 1642–1780* (Oxford, 1987). Where library access allows, these can be augmented by the magnificent *Bibliography of British and Irish History Online*.

PRIMARY SOURCES

(i) *Modern Collections*

Two valuable collections of sources from sixteenth-century Wales covering topics such as politics, government, religion and social life were produced in the 1980s: Trevor Herbert and Gareth Elwyn Jones (eds), *Tudor Wales* (Cardiff, 1988), and J. Gwynfor Jones (ed.), *Wales and the Tudor State* (Cardiff, 1989). Unfortunately, no similar collection was ever produced for the seventeenth century.

Also noteworthy are two further collections which bring together the, often long and discursive, introductions to many early modern Welsh books. Garfield H. Hughes (ed.), *Rhagymadroddion, 1547–1659* (Cardiff, 1951) reproduces original Welsh introductions from texts such as William Salesbury's *Oll Synnwyr Pen Kembro Ygyd*, but retains their early modern orthography which can make the volume challenging to use. By contrast, Ceri Davies (ed.), *Rhagymadroddion a Chyflwyniadau Lladin, 1551–1632* (Cardiff, 1980), provides fine modern translations of dedications and introductions to early modern works by Welsh authors which were written originally in Latin.

(ii) *Online Resources*

Research on early modern printed texts has been transformed by the advent of digitisation and, in particular, scholars' use of *Early English Books Online* (*EEBO*) and *Eighteenth-Century Collections Online* (*ECCO*). These are, however, subscription services and affiliation to a research library is usually required to access their riches. Freely accessible, however, are some key Welsh printed texts of the period (such as the 1567 New Testament) which have been digitised by the National Library of Wales as part of their 'digital gallery' (*https://www.library.wales/discover/digital-gallery/printed-material*).

The National Library of Wales also provides free access to an extensive corpus of digitised early modern wills (*https://www.library.wales/discover/library-resources/wills*) as well as to some modern editions of contemporary texts produced by bodies such as the Cymmrodorion Society. The latter can be accessed through the Library's 'Welsh Journals Online' portal (*https://journals.library.wales/home*).

(iii) *Correspondence*

A crucial resource for the historian of early modern Wales is the correspondence of gentry families which provide important insights into many aspects of life and society during the sixteenth, and particularly the seventeenth, centuries. Of prime importance here is the voluminous correspondence of the Wynn family of Gwydir in Caernarvonshire, whose letters are summarised in John Ballinger (ed.), *Calendar of the Wynn (of Gwydir) Papers, 1515–1690* (Aberystwyth, 1926). Ballinger's calendar entries and digitised copies of much of the Wynn correspondence can now be accessed through the National Library of Wales's online catalogue (*https://discover.library.wales/primo-explore/search?vid=44WHELF_NLW_NUI*). Another extensive collection of correspondence from a north Walian family can be found in T. Jones Pierce (ed.), *Clenennau Letters and Papers* (Aberystwyth, 1947). Like the Wynn papers, these are fully reproduced and searchable through the National Library of Wales's online catalogue and, importantly, the catalogue also reproduces summaries from the Clenennau correspondence from the later seventeenth century which is not included in Jones Pierce's published calendar.

In the twentieth century the Board of Celtic Studies produced several important collections of early modern correspondence as part of its History and Law Series: W. J. Smith (ed.), *Calendar of the Salusbury Correspondence, 1553–c.1700* (Cardiff, 1954); W. J. Smith (ed.), *Herbert Correspondence: The Sixteenth and Seventeenth Century Letters of the Herberts of Chirbury, Powis Castle and Dolguog* (Cardiff, 1963); and B. E. Howells (ed.), *Calendar of Letters relating to North Wales* (Cardiff, 1967).

Published correspondence has concentrated on north Wales, but an important collection from a south Wales family of the late sixteenth century was printed as J. M. Traherne (ed.), *The Stradling Correspondence* (London, 1840); this is available online through the Internet Archive at *https://archive.org/details/stradlingcorrespootrahuoft*.

A good deal of Welsh correspondence, as well as a wealth of other material relating to politics, government, administration and religion in early modern Wales can be found among The National Archive's State Papers which have been calendared in J. S. Brewer et al. (eds), *Letters and Papers, Foreign and Domestic of the Reign of Henry VIII* (23 vols, London, 1862–1932), and also in the long run of volumes calendared by reign and collected together as the *Calendar of State Papers, Domestic*. This material is searchable through the British History Online website (*https://www.british-history.ac.uk*).

(iv) *George Owen*

A particular fount of information and commentary on sixteenth-century Wales was the Pembrokeshire gentleman and antiquary George Owen of Henllys. His writings were collected as *The Description of Penbrokshire*, ed. H. Owen (4 vols, London, 1892–1936) which is a rare publication today, but modern editors have made his most important works accessible as B. E. Howells (ed.), *Elizabethan Pembrokeshire: Evidence of George Owen* (Haverfordwest, 1973); Dillwyn Miles (ed.), *Description of Pembrokeshire* (Llandysul, 1994); and John Gwynfor Jones (ed.), *The Dialogue of the Government of Wales (1594)* (Cardiff, 2010). An excellent study of this many-sided figure is B. G. Charles, *George Owen of Henllys: A Welsh Elizabethan* (Aberystwyth, 1973).

(v) *Legal Sources*

Often difficult for non-specialists to use, legal sources are nonetheless of critical importance for understanding social relations in this most litigious age. Particularly useful, although now showing its age, is

I. ab O. Edwards (ed.), *Catalogue of Star Chamber Proceedings relating to Wales* (Cardiff, 1929). A fascinating narrative of an individual early modern Star Chamber case is provided by John Stradling, 'The Storie of the Lower Borrowes of Merthyr Mawr', *South Wales and Monmouth Record Society*, 1 (1932). An important publication relating to the institution and operation of local courts after the Acts of Union is W. O. Williams (ed.), *Calendar of the Caernarvonshire Quarter Sessions Records, 1541–58* (Caernarfon, 1956), while the wealth of Wales's great sessions records has been admirably served by Glyn Parry, *A Guide to the Records of Great Sessions in Wales* (Aberystwyth, 1995). Murray Chapman has produced several valuable volumes of transcriptions from Montgomeryshire's early modern great sessions records.

(vi) *Poetry*

There is a wealth of early modern poetry available in print, although these volumes are often rare and only available in major libraries. Valuable exceptions are Thomas Parry (ed.), *The Oxford Book of Welsh Verse* (Oxford, 1962); Meic Stephens, *The New Companion to the Literature of Wales* (Oxford, 1998); Nesta Lloyd (ed.), *Blodeugerdd Barddas o'r Ail Ganrif ar Bymtheg* (Swansea, 1993); and Cathryn Charnell-White (ed.), *Beirdd Ceridwen: Blodeugerdd Barddas o Ganu Menywod hyd tua 1800* (Swansea, 2005). An important resource and guide for this literature is Thomas Parry and Merfyn Morgan (eds), *Llyfryddiaeth Llenyddiaeth Gymraeg* (Cardiff, 1976).

(vii) *Urban History*

The survival of early modern urban records in Wales is poor. An exception, however, is the muniments of the Pembrokeshire borough of Haverfordwest, whose records are described in B. G. Charles (ed.), *Calendar of the Records of the Borough of Haverfordwest, 1539–1660* (Cardiff, 1967). Also of interest for urban historians is John Fisher (ed.), 'Historia Bellomarisei, or the History of the Town and Burrough of Beaumaris [*circa* 1669]', *Archaeologia Cambrensis* (Supplement), 6th series, 17 (1917), 275–306 (available at *https://journals.library.wales/view/4718179/4727519/293*), while material relating to Cardiff can be found in John Hobson Matthews (ed.), *Cardiff Records* (6 vols, Cardiff, 1898–1911) which is available through British History Online (*https://www.british-history.ac.uk/search/series/cardiff-records*).

(vii) *Autobiography and Life Writing*

Autobiography was a form that was in its infancy in the seventeenth century. However, a classic early example was produced by a Welsh aristocrat: Edward, Lord Herbert, *An Autobiography*, ed. Sidney Lee (London, 1888). Early modern Wales also possesses rich family chronicles in the form of Sir John Wynn, *The History of the Gwydir Family and Memoirs*, ed. John Gwynfor Jones (Llandysul, 1990); E. G. Jones (ed.), 'History of the Bulkeley Family', *Transactions of the Anglesey Antiquarian Society* (1948), 1–99; and Ralph A. Griffiths (ed.), *Sir Rhys ap Thomas and his Family* (Cardiff, 1993). Welsh diaries from this period include M. H. Lee (ed.), *The Diaries and Letters of Philip Henry, M.A., of Broad Oak, Flintshire, 1631–1696* (London, 1882); J. A. Bradney (ed.), *The Diary of Walter Powell of Llantilio Crossenny, 1603–1654* (Bristol, 1907); and H. Owen (ed.), 'The Diary of Bulkeley of Dronwy, 1630–36', *Transactions of the Anglesey Antiquarian Society* (1937), 26–173.

Individual biographies for Welsh figures from this period can be traced through the *Oxford Dictionary of National Biography* (*https://www.oxforddnb.com*); *The Dictionary of Welsh Biography* (*https://biography.wales/*); and The History of Parliament Online (*https://www.historyofparliamentonline.org/*).

SECONDARY LITERATURE

General Studies

The two volumes of the Oxford History of Wales series which cover this period remain indispensable guides: Glanmor Williams, *Recovery, Reorientation and Reformation: Wales, c.1415–1642* (Oxford, 1987), reprinted in paperback as *Renewal and Reformation, c.1415–1642* (Oxford, 1993) and Geraint H. Jenkins, *The Foundations of Modern Wales, 1642–1780* (Oxford, 1987). Valuable general studies include Philip Jenkins, *A History of Modern Wales, 1536–1990* (London, 1992); J. Gwynfor Jones, *Early Modern Wales, c.1525–1640* (Basingstoke, 1994); G. Dyfnallt Owen, *Elizabethan Wales: The Social Scene* (Cardiff, 1963) and his *Wales in the Reign of James I* (Woodbridge, 1988); G. E. Jones, *The Gentry and the Elizabethan State* (Swansea, 1977); W. S. K. Thomas, *Tudor Wales* (Llandysul, 1983) and his *Stuart Wales* (Llandysul, 1988).

Much of interest can be found in the Welsh county histories which cover the early modern period. These include Glanmor Williams (ed.), *Glamorgan County History. IV. Early Modern Glamorgan* (Cardiff, 1974); B. E. Howells and Elwyn Davies (eds), *Pembrokeshire County History, Volume 3: Early Modern Pembrokeshire, 1536–1815* (Haverfordwest, 1987); Madeleine Gray and Prys Morgan (eds), *The Gwent County History, Volume 3: The Making of Monmouthshire, 1536–1780* (Cardiff, 2009); and Geraint H. Jenkins, Richard Suggett and Eryn M. White (eds), *Cardiganshire County History, Volume 2. Medieval and Early Modern Cardiganshire* (Cardiff, 2019).

A wealth of scholarship in academic periodicals relating to all periods of Welsh history is freely available through the 'Welsh Journals' database hosted by the National Library of Wales (*https:// journals.library.wales/home*). More recent journal literature is often only available through library subscriptions.

CHAPTER BIBLIOGRAPHIES

Chapter 1: Locating Early Modern Wales

Brady, Ciaran, 'Comparable Histories? Tudor Reform in Wales and Ireland', in Steven G. Ellis and Sarah Barber (eds), *Conquest and Union: Fashioning a British State, 1485–1725* (London, 1995), pp. 64–86.

Jenkins, Philip, 'A New History of Wales', *Historical Journal*, 32 (1989), 387–93.

Jenkins, Philip, 'The Plight of Pygmy Nations: Wales in Early Modern Europe', *North American Journal of Welsh Studies*, 2 (Winter 2002), 1–11.

Jones, Michael A., 'Cultural Boundaries within the Tudor State: Bishop Rowland Lee and the Welsh Settlement of 1536', *WHR*, 20 (2000–1), 227–53.

Nice, Jason, *Sacred History and National Identity: Comparisons between Early Modern Wales and Brittany* (London, 2009).

Olson, Katharine K., 'The Acts of Union: Culture and Religion in Wales, c.1540–1700', in Geraint Evans and Helen Fulton (eds), *The Cambridge History of Welsh Literature* (Cambridge, 2019), pp. 157–75.

Kidd, Colin, *British Identities before Nationalism: Ethnicity and Nationhood in the Atlantic World, 1600–1800* (Cambridge, 1999).

Roberts, Peter R., 'Tudor Wales, National Identity and the British Inheritance', in Peter R . Roberts and Brendan Bradshaw (eds), *British Consciousness and Identity: The Making of Britain, 1533–1707* (Cambridge, 1998), pp. 8–42.

Schwyzer, Philip, *Literature, Nationalism and Memory in Early Modern England and Wales* (Cambridge, 2004).

Schwyzer, Philip, 'A Map of Greater Cambria', *Early Modern Literary Studies*, 4 (1998), 1–13.

Williams, Gwyn A., *When Was Wales?* (London, 1982).

Chapter 2: 'They Value Themselves Much upon their Antiquity': History, Myth and Identity

The key text for this subject is Huw Pryce, *Writing Welsh History: From the Early Middle Ages to the Twenty-First Century* (Oxford, 2022), esp. Part II, which appeared too late for its findings to be incorporated into this volume.

Bowen, Lloyd, 'The Battle of Britain: History and Reformation in Early Modern Wales', in Tadgh Ó hAnnracháin and Robert Armstrong (eds), *Christianities in the Early Modern Celtic World* (Basingstoke, 2014), pp. 135–50.

Broadway, Jan, *'No Historie So Meete': Gentry Culture and the Development of Local History in Elizabethan and Early Stuart England* (Manchester, 2006).

Davies, R. R., 'The Peoples of Britain and Ireland, 1100–1400. IV. Language and Historical Mythology', *TRHS*, 6th series, 7 (1997), 1–24.

Jones, J. Gwynfor, 'The Welsh Gentry and the Image of the "Cambro-Briton", c.1603–25', *WHR*, 20 (2000–1), 615–55.

Roberts, Peter R., 'Tudor Wales, National Identity and the British Inheritance', in Peter R. Roberts and Brendan Bradshaw (eds), *British Consciousness and Identity: The Making of Britain, 1533–1707* (Cambridge, 1998), pp. 8–42.

Schwyzer, Philip, *Literature, Nationalism and Memory in Early Modern England and Wales* (Cambridge, 2004).

Schwyzer, Philip, 'British History and "The British History": The Same Old Story?', in David Baker and Willy Maley (eds), *British Identities and English Renaissance Literature* (Cambridge, 2002), pp. 11–23.

Schwyzer, Philip, 'Archipelagic History', in Felicity Heal, Ian Archer and Paulina Kewes (eds), *The Oxford Handbook of Holinshed's Chronicles* (Oxford, 2013), pp. 593–607.

Williams, Glanmor, 'Prophecy, Poetry and Politics in Medieval and Tudor Wales', in his *Religion, Language and Nationality in Wales* (Cardiff, 1979), pp. 71–86.

Woolf, Daniel, *The Social Circulation of the Past: English Historical Culture, 1500–1730* (Oxford, 2003).

Chapter 3: 'Awake Now Thou Lovely Wales!':
The Reformation and its Legacies

Bowen, Lloyd, 'The Battle of Britain: History and Reformation in Early Modern Wales', in Tadgh Ó hAnnracháin and Robert Armstrong (eds), *Christianities in the Early Modern Celtic World* (Basingstoke, 2014), pp. 135–50.

Bowen, Lloyd, 'Preaching and Politics in the Welsh Marches, 1643–63: The Case of Alexander Griffith', *Historical Research*, 94 (2021), 28–50.

Bradshaw, Brendan, 'The English Reformation and Identity Formation in Wales and Ireland', in Brendan Bradshaw and Peter R. Roberts (eds), *British Consciousness and Identity: The Making of Britain, 1533–1707* (Cambridge, 1998), pp. 43–111.

Gray, Madeleine, '"The Curious Incident of the Dog in the Night-Time": The Pre-Reformation Church in Wales', in Ó hAnnracháin and Armstrong, *Christianities in the Early Modern Celtic World*, pp. 42–54.

Jenkins, Philip, 'Church, Nation and Language: The Welsh Church, 1660–1800', in Jeremy Gregory and Jeffrey S. Chamberlain (eds), *The National Church in Local Perspective* (Woodbridge, 2003), pp. 265–84.

Olson, Katharine K., 'Religion, Politics, and the Parish in Tudor England and Wales: A View from the Marches of Wales, 1534–1553', *Recusant History*, 30 (2011), 527–36.

Olson, Katharine K., '"Slow and Cold in the True Service of God": Popular Beliefs and Practices, Conformity and Reformation in Wales, *c*.1530–*c*.1600', in Ó hAnnracháin and Armstrong, *Christianities in the Early Modern Celtic World*, pp. 92–108.

Powell, Nia W., 'Rawling White, Cardiff and the Early Reformation in Wales', in Rosemary C. E. Hayes and William J. Sheils (eds), *Clergy,*

Church and Society in England and Wales, c.1200–1800 (York, 2013), pp. 121–37.

Williams, Glanmor, *Religion, Language and Nationality in Wales: Historical Essays* (Cardiff, 1979).

Williams, Glanmor, *Wales and the Reformation* (Cardiff, 1997).

Chapter 4: Alternative Visions: Catholicism, Puritanism and Dissent

Bowen, Lloyd, 'Wales, 1587–1689', in John Coffey (ed.), *The Oxford History of Protestant Dissenting Traditions, Volume I: The Post-Reformation Era, c.1559–c.1689* (Oxford, 2020), pp. 224–43.

Gruffydd, R. Geraint, *'In That Gentile Country …': The Beginnings of Puritan Nonconformity in Wales* (Bridgend, 1976).

Jenkins, Geraint H., *Protestant Dissenters in Wales, 1639–1689* (Cardiff, 1992).

Jenkins, Philip, 'Anti-Popery on the Welsh Marches in the Seventeenth Century', *Historical Journal*, 23 (1980), 275–93.

Jenkins, Philip, '"The Old Leaven": The Welsh Roundheads after 1660', *Historical Journal*, 24 (1981), 807–23.

Key, Newton E., and Ward, Joseph, '"Divided into Parties": Exclusion Crisis Origins in Monmouth', *EHR*, 115 (2000), 1159–83.

Roberts, Stephen K., 'Religion, Politics and Welshness, 1649–1660', in Ivan Roots (ed.), *"Into Another Mould": Aspects of the Interregnum*, 2nd edn (Exeter, 1998), pp. 30–46.

Roberts, Stephen K., 'Propagating the Gospel in Wales: The Making of the 1650 Act', *TCS*, new series, 10 (2004), 57–75.

Thomas, Aneurin (ed.), *The Elizabethan Catholic Martyrs* (Cardiff, 1971).

Thomas, Hannah, 'Missioners on the Margins? The Territorial Headquarters of the Welsh Jesuit College of St Francis Xavier at the Cwm, c.1600–1679', *Recusant History*, 32 (2014), 173–93.

Walsham, Alexandra, 'The Holy Maid of Wales: Visions, Imposture and Catholicism in Elizabethan Britain', *EHR*, 132 (2017), 250–85.

White, Eryn M., 'From Ejectment to Toleration in Wales, 1662–89', in Alan P. F. Snell (ed.), *The Great Ejectment of 1662* (Eugene, OR, 2012), pp. 125–81.

Williams, Glanmor, *Wales and the Reformation* (Cardiff, 1997).

Williams, Glanmor, 'Unity of Religion or Unity of Language? Protestants and Catholics and the Welsh Language, 1536–1660', *WLBIR*, pp. 207–35.

Chapter 5: 'The Communion of One Tongue': Language and Society
The essays contained in *WLBIR* are invaluable and should be the first
port of call for anyone approaching this subject.

Bowen, Lloyd, 'Information, Language and Political Culture in Early
  Modern Wales', *Past & Present*, 228 (2015), 125–58.
Bowen, Lloyd, 'Structuring Particularist Publics: Logistics, Language
  and Early Modern Wales', *Journal of British Studies*, 56 (2017), 754–72.
Brennan, Gillian, 'Language and Nationality: The Role of Policy
  Towards Celtic Languages in the Consolidation of Tudor Power',
  Nations and Nationalism, 7 (2001), 317–38.
Davies, Ceri (ed.), *Dr John Davies of Mallwyd: Welsh Renaissance Scholar*
  (Cardiff, 2004).
Evans, Geraint and Fulton, Helen (eds), *The Cambridge History of
  Welsh Literature* (Cambridge, 2019).
Gruffydd, R. Geraint (ed.), *A Guide to Welsh Literature, c.1530–1700*
  (Cardiff, 1997).
Jenkins, Geraint H., *Literature, Religion and Society in Wales, 1660–1730*
  (Cardiff, 1978).
Roberts, Peter R., 'The Welsh Language, English Law and Tudor
  Legislation', *TCS* (1989), 19–75.
Suggett, Richard, 'Vagabonds and Minstrels in Sixteenth-Century Wales',
  in Adam Fox and Daniel Woolf (eds), *The Spoken Word*, pp. 138–72.
Suggett, Richard, and White, Eryn M., 'Language, Literacy and
  Aspects of Identity in Early Modern Wales', in Fox and Woolf (eds),
  The Spoken Word: Oral Culture in Britain, 1500–1850 (Manchester,
  2002), pp. 52–83.
Williams, W. Ogwen, 'The Survival of the Welsh Language after the
  Union of England and Wales: The First Phase, 1536–1642', *WHR*, 2
  (1964), 67–93.

*Chapter 6: 'A Prince of our Own Natural Country and
Name': Welshness, Britishness and Monarchy*

Clavier, Sarah Ward, '"Horrid Rebellion" and "Holie Cheate": Royalist
  Gentry Responses to Interregnum Government in North-East Wales,
  1646–1660', *WHR*, 29 (2018), 51–72.
Davies, Luned Mair, 'The Tregaer Manuscript: An Elegy for Charles I',
  NLWJ, 31 (2000), 243–70.

Griffiths, Ralph A., and Thomas, Roger S., *The Making of the Tudor Dynasty* (Gloucester, 1985).

Harper, Sally, '"A Dittie to the Tune of Welsh Sydannen": A Welsh Image of Queen Elizabeth', *Renaissance Studies*, 19 (2005), 201–28.

Hunter, Jerry, 'The Red Sword, the Sickle and the Author's Revenge: Welsh Literature and Conflict in the Seventeenth Century', *Proceedings of the Harvard Celtic Colloquium*, 36 (2016), 1–29.

Jenkins, Philip, 'Seventeenth-Century Wales: Definition and Identity', in Brendan Bradshaw and Peter R. Roberts (eds), *British Consciousness and Identity: The Making of Britain, 1533–1707*, (Cambridge, 1998), pp. 213–35.

McClain, Molly, 'The Duke of Beaufort's Tory Progress through Wales, 1684', *WHR*, 19 (1997), 592–620.

Morgan-Guy, John, 'Arthur, Harri Tudor and the Iconography of Loyalty in Wales', in Steve Gunn and Linda Monckton (eds), *Arthur Tudor, Prince of Wales: Life, Death & Commemoration* (Woodbridge, 2009), pp. 50-63.

Roberts, Peter R., 'The Welshness of the Tudors', *History Today*, 36 (January 1986), 7–13.

Roberts, Peter R., 'Tudor Wales, National Identity and the British Inheritance', in Bradshaw and Roberts, *British Consciousness and Identity*, pp. 8–42.

Stoyle, Mark, 'English "Nationalism", Celtic Particularism, and the English Civil War', *Historical Journal*, 43 (2000), 1113–28.

Stoyle, Mark, *Soldiers and Strangers: An Ethnic History of the English Civil War* (New Haven and London, 2005), pp. 11–32.

Williams, Glanmor, 'Prophecy, Poetry, and Politics in Medieval and Tudor Wales', in his *Religion, Language and Nationality in Wales* (Cardiff, 1979), pp. 71–86.

Chapter 7: Politics, Officeholding and Participation

Bowen, Lloyd, 'Wales at Westminster: Parliament, Principality and Pressure Groups, 1542–1601', *Parliamentary History*, 22 (2003), pp. 107–20.

Gray, Madeleine, 'Power, Patronage and Politics: Office-Holding and Administration on the Crown's Estates in Wales', in Richard W. Hoyle (ed.), *The Estates of the English Crown, 1558–1640* (Cambridge, 1992), pp. 137–62.

Jarrett, Sadie, 'Officeholding and Local Politics in Early Modern Wales: A Study of the Salesburys of Rhug and Bachymbyd, *c.*1536–1621', *WHR*, 30 (2020), 206–32.

Jones, G. E., *The Gentry and the Elizabethan State* (Swansea, 1977).

Jones, J. Gwynfor, *Law, Order and Government in Caernarfonshire, 1558–1640: Justices of the Peace and the Gentry* (Cardiff, 1996).

Jones, J. Gwynfor, 'Government and Society, 1536–1603', in J. Beverley Smith and Llinos Beverley Smith (eds), *History of Merioneth, Volume II: The Middle Ages* (Cardiff, 2001), pp. 649–701.

Mitchell, Nathan, 'Politics and Power, 1660–1702', in Madeleine Gray and Prys Morgan (eds), *The Gwent County History, Volume 3: The Making of Monmouthshire, 1536–1780* (Cardiff, 2009), pp. 109–23.

Roberts, Stephen K., 'Local, Regional and National Politics to 1642', in Morgan and Gray, *The Making of Monmouthshire*, pp. 35–61.

Robinson, W. R. B., 'The Tudor Revolution in Welsh Government, 1536–1543: Its Effects on Gentry Participation', *EHR*, 103 (1988), 1–20.

Chapter 8: Women and Gender in Early Modern Wales

As mentioned in the text, the historiography of this subject, though quickly expanding, is somewhat limited. The starting point for any inquiry is the path-breaking Michael Roberts and Simone Clarke (eds), *Women and Gender in Early Modern Wales* (Cardiff, 2000).

Charnell-White, Cathryn, *Beirdd Ceridwen: Blodeugerdd Barddas o Ganu Menywod hyd tua 1800* (Swansea, 2005).

Charnell-White, Cathryn, 'Problems of Authorship and Attribution: The Welsh-Language Women's Canon before 1800', *Women's Writing*, 24 (2017), 398–417.

Chedgzoy, Kate, *Women's Writing in the British Atlantic World* (Cambridge, 2007).

Chedgzoy, Kate, 'The Civility of Early Modern Welsh Women', in Jennifer Richards (ed.), *Early Modern Civil Discourses* (Basingstoke, 2003), pp. 162–82.

Jarrett, Sadie, '"By Reason of her Sex and Widowhood": An Early Modern Welsh Gentlewoman and the Court of Star Chamber', in K. J. Kesselring and Natalie Mears (eds), *Star Chamber Matters: An Early Modern Court and its Records* (London, 2021), pp. 79–96.

Jenkins, Philip, 'Mary Wharton and the Rise of the "New Woman"', *NLWJ*, 22 (1981), 170–86.

Jones, J. Gwynfor, 'Welsh Gentlewomen: Piety and Christian Conduct, *c*.1560–1730', *Journal of Welsh Religious History*, 7 (1999), 1–37.

Muir, Angela, *Deviant Maternity: Illegitimacy in Wales, c.1680–1800* (London, 2020).

Parkin, Sally, 'Witchcraft, Women's Honour and Customary Law in Early Modern Wales', *Social History*, 31 (2006), 295–318.

Peters, Christine, *Women in Early Modern Britain, 1450–1640* (Basingstoke, 2004).

Prescott, Sarah, 'Archipelagic Orinda? Katherine Philips and the Writing of Welsh Women's Literary History', *Literature Compass*, 6 (2009), 1167–76.

Suggett, Richard, *A History of Magic and Witchcraft in Wales* (Stroud, 2008).

Swett, Katharine W., 'Widowhood, Custom and Property in Early Modern Wales', *WHR*, 18 (1996), 189–227.

Whyte, Nicola, '"With a Sword Drawne in Her Hande": Defending the Boundaries of Household Space in Seventeenth-Century Wales', in Bronach Kane and Fiona Williamson (eds), *Women, Agency and the Law, 1300–1700* (London, 2013), pp. 141–55.

Youngs, Deborah, '"For the Preferment of their Marriage and Bringing Upp of their Youth": The Education and Training of Young Welshwomen, *c*.1450–*c*.1550', *WHR*, 25 (2011), 463–85.

Youngs, Deborah, '"At Hir Owne Discrecion": Women and Will-Making in Late Medieval and Early Tudor Wales', *WHR*, 29 (2019), 408–35.

Chapter 9: 'A Brittain by Nation Born': Welsh Diasporas

Allen, Richard C., 'The Making of a Holy Christian Community: Welsh Quaker Emigrants to Pennsylvania, *c*.1680–1750', in Luda Klusáková and Tim Klerk (eds), *Cultural Conquests, 1500–2000* (Prague, 2009), pp. 45–61.

Bowen, Lloyd, 'News Networks in Early Modern Wales', *History*, 102 (2017), 22–44.

Dimmock, Spencer, 'The Origins of Welsh Apprentices in Sixteenth-Century Bristol', *WHR*, 24 (2008), 116–40.

Fleming, Peter, 'The Welsh Diaspora in Early Tudor English Towns', in Helen Fulton (ed.), *Urban Culture in Medieval Wales* (Cardiff, 2012), pp. 271–94.

Griffith, William P., *Learning, Law and Religion: Higher Education and Welsh Society, c.1540–1640* (Cardiff, 1996).

Jones, Emrys, 'The Welsh in London in the Seventeenth and Eighteenth Centuries', *WHR*, 10 (1981), 461–79.

Jones, Emrys (ed.), *The Welsh in London, 1500–2000* (Cardiff, 2001).

Morgan, Rhys, *The Welsh and the Shaping of Early Modern Ireland, 1558–1641* (Woodbridge, 2014).

Roberts, Michael, '"More Prone to be Idle and Riotous than the English"? Attitudes to Male Behaviour in Early Modern Wales', in Michael Roberts and Simone Clark (eds), *Women and Gender in Early Modern Wales* (Cardiff, 2000), pp. 259–90.

Swett, Katharine W., '"Born on My Land": Identity, Community and Faith among the Welsh in Early Modern London', in Muriel C. McClendon, Joseph P. Ward and Michael MacDonald (eds), *Protestant Identities: Religion, Society and Self-Fashioning in Post-Reformation England* (Stanford, CA, 1999), pp. 249–65.

Williams, Glanmor, 'The Welsh in Tudor England', in his *Religion, Language and Nationality in Wales* (Cardiff, 1979), pp. 171–99.

INDEX

A

Aberavon (Glam.) 18
Act of Uniformity (1662) 88
Acts of Union (1536–43) 2–3, 7, 8,
        9, 11–18, 19, 21, 22, 25, 26, 29,
        37, 42, 43, 47, 48, 49, 52, 53, 61,
        91–2, 94–6, 100–2, 104, 109,
        114, 118, 119–20, 122, 123,
        139–42, 151, 155, 157, 163,
        176, 178, 190, 197, 218
    see also 'Henry VIII clause';
        Welsh language, 1536
        'language clause'
Aequity of a Humble Supplication
        (1586) 79
After, John 55
alehouses 142
Alis ferch Gruffydd 169, 179–83
        passim, 184, 186, 188, 194
America 197, 216–17
Ancient Britons 1–2, 7, 21–2, 24,
        27–8, 30, 33–4, 36, 37, 42,
        50–2, 70, 80, 87, 93, 112, 116,
        121, 125, 127, 131, 196, 216,
        225 n. 70
    see also 'Britishness'
Anglesey 5, 58, 68, 69, 75, 98,
        100, 117, 118, 122, 142, 160,
        169–79, 194, 198, 211, 216
Anglica Historia (1534) 22
'Anglicisation' 10, 15, 47, 53, 61,
        91–2, 98, 101–8, 187–8, 196,
        199–202
    see also gentry, supposed
        'Anglicisation' of
Anglo-Welsh border 1–2, 8, 14, 17,
        82, 85, 92–3, 94–5, 147, 161,
        196–204 *passim*, 218

    see also Council in the Marches
        of Wales; Welsh Marches/
        Marcher lordships
Anglo-Welsh union, *see* Acts of
        Union (1536–43)
anterliwtiau see interludes
Antiquae Linguae Britannicae …
        Rudimenta (1621) 111
Antwerp 211
apprentices/hip 195–7, 200, 205–8,
        253 n. 44
Archenfield (Herefs.) 94
Armada, the (1588) 65, 159
Arnold, John 75–6, 147–8, 155
Arthur, King 20, 24, 25, 29, 34
Arthur Prince of Wales 119, 125
Athravaeth Gristnogawl, Yr (1568)
        69–70
Aubrey, Mary 184–5
Aubrey, Sir Thomas 104, 108
Augustine, Saint 52, 80
Avon, River 199

B

Badoe ('Badow'), Elizabeth 134
Bagenall family (Plas Newydd) 216
Bala (Merion.) 36
Bale, John 23, 25, 222 n. 14
ballads 35, 108, 122–3, 209
Bangor (diocese) 33, 34, 44, 141, 142
Bangor, dean of 162
Baptists 85, 88, 150
bards 2, 6–7, 10, 20, 21, 24, 35, 37,
        101, 103–8, 114, 116–18, 126,
        127, 141, 179–81, 187, 207
    see also Welsh language
Barlow family (Slebech) 73

Barlow, Bishop William 46–7
Basilikon Doron (1599) 125
Battle of Bosworth Field (1485) 117–18
Beaufort, Duke of *see* Somerset, Henry, 3rd Marquis of Worcester and 1st Duke of Beaufort
Beaumaris (Ang.) 152, 171, 174, 178, 260
beggars 198, 207
Beibl Bach, Y (1630) 55, 78–9, 213
Benwyn, Dafydd 108
Benwyn, Morys 106–7
Berkshire 204
Berth (Denbs.) 160
Betws-yn-Rhos (Flints.) 189
Bible(s) 2, 46, 49, 56, 59, 72, 78–9, 89, 95, 197
    Welsh translations of 2, 49–54, 61, 64, 78, 92, 94, 106, 109, 112, 118, 119, 122, 157
    see also Beibl Bach, Y (1630)
bilingualism 15–16, 50, 82, 90, 93, 97, 99–100, 105, 110, 159, 171, 186, 234 n. 6
Bishop, Richard *see* Richard ap John Griffith (*alias* Richard Bishop)
Blackfriars (London) 195
blacksmiths 200
Blaeu, Joan 17
Blome, Richard 202
Bodfari (Flints.) 60
Bodvel, Sir John 174–6, 178, 248 n. 27
Boece, Hector 23, 27, 36
Böheme, Jacob 86
Book of Common Prayer 41, 46–7, 49–50, 54, 56, 58–9, 78, 82, 94, 95, 130
    Welsh translation of 2, 49–50, 54, 56, 61, 78, 94, 95, 227 n. 47
Bosheston (Pembs.) 159
Bosom's Inn (London) 211
Boyle, Robert 187

Brecon 24, 30, 88, 102, 161, 246 n. 115
Breconshire 58, 64, 79, 88, 90, 130, 162, 187, 205, 246 n. 115
Breviary of Britayne (1573) 27
Bridewell (London) 210
Bridgewater, Earl of *see* Egerton, John, 1st Earl of Bridgewater
Bristol 5, 8, 83, 93, 156, 196, 199–200, 205–6, 217
Britain/British state 4, 8–9, 11, 19–21, 26, 28, 30, 31, 37–8, 114, 119, 123, 125, 139
'Briticisation' 102
British Antiquities Revived (1662) 31
'British empire' 2, 8
British History, the 1–2, 7, 10, 19–38, 47, 116
    popular appeal of 7, 33–7
    see also Brut chronicle; Llwyd, Humphrey; Prise, Sir John
British Language in its Lustre (1688) 111
Britishness 2, 4, 8–9, 20, 22, 26, 30, 52, 115, 123–6, 131, 136–7, 186
    see also Ancient Britons; Cambro-Briton/British; 'Great Britain'
Briton Ferry (Glam.) 108
Brogyntyn (Salop.) 131
Brut chronicle 20–3, 25–6, 30–7, 116, 118, 124, 224 n. 65
    see also British History, the
Brut y Brenhinedd 20, 23
Brut y Tywysogyon 26
Buckingham, Duke of *see* Villiers, George, 1st Duke of Buckingham
Bulkeley, Lady Ann 174–6, 248 n. 24
Bulkeley, Mary 169–79, 181–2, 183, 194, 247 n. 5
Bulkeley, Richard (d.1640) 173–9
Bulkeley, Richard (d.1704) 150
Bulkeley, Sir Richard (d.1547) 142
Bulkeley, Sir Richard (d.1621) 152, 171–8

Bulkeley, Sir Richard (d.1624) 171–2
Bulkeley, Thomas 160, 174, 176
Bull, The (London) 210
Bunyan, John 89
Burgh, William 173
Burghley, Lord *see* Cecil, William,
    Lord Burghley
butter 93, 156

C
Cadwaladr, King 20–1, 25, 26, 36,
    51, 116, 118, 120–4, 129–30,
    133
Caergai (Merion.) 31, 128
Caernarvonshire 12, 53, 59, 68, 84,
    104, 105, 110, 124, 128, 129,
    142, 144–5, 148, 154, 158, 162,
    172, 174, 181, 190, 205, 207,
    209
Caerphilly (Glam.) 82
Caerwys (Flints.) 106, 179
Camber 1
Cambrensium Caroleia (1625) 217
Cambria 1–2, 20, 26, 27, 94, 122
    see also Historie of Cambria, A
'Cambria' (poem) 126
Cambria Triumphans (1661) 32
'Cambriae Typus' 1, 3, 26, 95, 218
*Cambrobrytannicae Cymraecaeve
    Linguae Institutiones* (1592)
    111
Cambridge University 53, 79, 102
Cambriol *see* Newfoundland
Cambriola 217
Cambro-Briton/British 36, 38, 125,
    131, 209, 217, 240 n. 48
Camden, William 31, 36
Campion, Edmund 69
Cardiff (Glam.) 18, 56, 84, 153, 158,
    207, 226, n. 14, 246 n. 115, 260
Cardiff bridge 158
Cardigan 183, 187, 194
Cardiganshire 12, 143, 162, 187–8,
    243 n. 24

Carmarthen 34, 88, 132, 226, n. 14,
    246 n. 115
Carmarthenshire 89, 93, 143–4, 153,
    163, 217, 243 n. 23
carriers 159, 207, 211, 212
Carwr y Cymry (1631) 78
Castle (Mont.) 105
Catherine de Valois, Queen 117
Catherine of Aragon, Queen 11, 39
Catholicism 3, 39–40, 44–6, 49, 50,
    52, 60, 61, 63–77 *passim*, 81,
    94, 111, 131–4, 147–50, 151,
    193, 226 n. 16, 230 n. 28
    see also Popish Plot (1678–81)
Catrin ferch Gruffydd 180
Catrin ferch Gruffudd ap Hywel
    67, 181
cattle 93, 156, 197
Cavalier Parliament 154
Cecil, Sir Robert 35, 159, 239 n. 41,
    248 n. 17
Cecil, William, Lord Burghley 44,
    81
Cernioge (Denbs.) 215
Chancery, Court of 144–5, 175, 177
Chapuys, Eustace 67, 195
Charles I, King 57, 74, 83, 126–31,
    134–5, 160–1, 165, 185–6, 195,
    217
Charles II, King 59, 75, 76, 121, 127,
    129–30, 135–6, 161, 186, 196
Charles V, Emperor 67
Chaste Maid in Cheapside, A (1613)
    210
Cheshire 172, 175–7, 247 n. 5
Chester 5, 8, 195, 196, 199–200, 204,
    206, 208
Chirk (Denbs.) 73
Chirk Castle (Denbs.) 78, 212–13
Church of England 3, 4, 9, 41–3,
    55–61, 63, 73, 74, 77, 79–81,
    84–5, 87–8, 127, 130–1, 164
    'British' origins of 9, 43, 51–3,
    57–8, 80, 129
Churchstoke (Mont.) 201

churchwardens 55, 70–1, 95, 100
Churchyard, Thomas 202–3
civil wars 7, 9, 36, 39, 40, 55, 57,
        59, 74, 79, 83–8, 108, 115–16,
        126–9, 134, 136, 146, 148, 150,
        153, 154, 160, 161, 165, 184–6,
        197, 204, 207, 218
'Clarendon Code' 88
Clenennau (Caern.) 123
clergy 43–4, 55–6, 59–61, 64, 72,
        78, 79, 84–5, 93, 128, 136, 159,
        163
cloth trade see wool
Clothworkers' Company 205
Clough, Hugh 99–100
Clun (Salop.) 94
Clynnog (Caern.) 59
Clynnog, Morys 68, 69–70
Cnwclas (Rads.) 84
Coke, Edward Sir 16
College of St Francis Xavier (Cwm)
        73–4
Comendacion of Welshmen (1546)
        25
Commentarioli Britannicae
        Descriptionis Fragmentum
        (1572) 27
    see also Breviary of Britayne
        (1573)
Commission for the Propagation of
        the Gospel in Wales 60, 83–5,
        88, 89
commission(s) of the peace 142–50,
        243 n. 24
Commons, House of 52, 75, 123–4,
        148, 244 n. 44 of
    see also parliament
congregationalists/ism 82, 88, 90
constables, high 100, 141, 148
constables, petty 100, 141
Conway, Jane 190–1
coopers 205
Cornish language 47, 50, 61, 114,
        228 n. 75
Cornwall 50

coroners 100, 141
Cotton, Sir Robert 26
Council in the Marches of Wales
        13–14, 17–18, 27–8, 80, 95, 98,
        126, 142, 149, 161–3, 165, 175,
        187, 246 n. 118
    see also Egerton, John, 1st Earl of
        Bridgewater; Herbert, Henry,
        2nd earl of Pembroke; Lee,
        Rowland, Bishop of Coventry
        and Lichfield; Sidney, Sir
        Henry; Vaughan, Richard,
        2nd Earl of Carbery
Counter-Reformation 68–9, 77
    see also Catholicism
Coventry (Warw.) 195
Cowbridge (Glam.) 18
Cowley, Abraham 187
Cradock, Walter 82–4, 86, 90, 136
Croft, Bishop Herbert 75
Cromwell, Oliver 74, 85, 136, 195
Cromwell, Thomas 2, 12–13, 24,
        46, 142
'Cronica Walliae' (1559) 26, 28
Crugion (Mont.) 134
cultural imperialism 15, 50, 54, 96–7,
        111–12
Cwm (Herefs.) 73, 75
cyfran 16
    see also gavelkind
Cynwal, Wiliam 106

D
Dafydd, Edward 72
Dafydd, Edward (Margam) 107
David ap John 202
David ap John ap John ap Edward
        (Davyd Jones) 208
Davies, John (historian) 118
Davies, Dr John (Siôn Dafydd
        Rhys) 30, 54, 111, 122, 124,
        227 n. 44
Davies, Dr John (Mallwyd) 102, 103,
        110–13, 179

David Lloyd ap Rees 182
Davies, Rees (historian) 4, 19
Davies, Bishop Richard 45, 50–3, 55, 57, 64, 69, 70, 80, 87, 89, 112, 119, 180, 202
see also 'Epistol at y Cembru' (1567)
Davies, Robert 216
Davys, Matthew 18, 158
Dee, Jenkin 200
Dee, John 2, 217
defamation and slander 95, 99, 188, 192, 203
Deffynniad Ffydd Eglwys Loegr (1595) 55
Defoe, Daniel 37
Deheubarth 1
Denbigh 49, 56, 99, 153, 211, 212, 213
Denbighshire 2, 5, 13, 27, 45, 53, 56, 70, 73, 78, 98, 104, 122, 135, 144, 152, 153, 154, 158, 160, 163, 173, 182, 187, 188–91, 195, 204, 205, 208, 211–15, 246 n. 115
Derwen (Denbs.) 160
deputy lieutenancy 140–1, 147, 148
Devereux, George 143–4, 243 n. 23
Devereux, Robert, 2nd Earl of Essex 100, 143–4, 146, 153, 243, nn. 23, 24
Devonshire 5
'Dialogue of the Government of Wales' (1594) 120
dictionaries see Welsh language, dictionaries and grammars
Dictionarium Duplex (1632) 102, 110, 113
Dictionary in Englyshe and Welshe (1547) 96, 110, 190
Donegal 216
Donne, John 185
Donne Lee, Edward 79

Dosparth Byrr (1567) 111
Douai 68, 70, 71
Draper, Elizabeth 210
drapers 206
drovers 93, 197, 214
Drych Cristianogawl, Y (1586/7) 70, 94
Drych y Prif Oesoedd (1716) 113
Dublin 184, 188
Dudley, Robert, 1st earl of Leicester 70, 93, 152–3
Dyserth (Denbs.) 191
Dysgeidiaeth Cristnoges o Ferch (1552) 181

E
Ednyfed Fychan 117
Edward I (1593) 35–6
Edward I, King 12, 26, 35
Edward VI, King 39, 46, 48, 121
Edward ap Raff 122
Edward Griffith ap Ednyfed 98
Edwardes, David 129
Edwardes, Margaret 215
Edwards family (Chirk) 73
Edwards, Charles 89, 113
Edwards, Robert 214
Edwards, Thomas 213–15
Egerton, John, 1st Earl of Bridgewater 100
Eikon Basilike (1649) 128
eisteddfod/au (1523, 1567/8) 101, 106, 107, 179, 180
Eleanor ferch Howell 203
elections, parliamentary 18, 152–6, 158, 165
Elin ferch Richard 192
Elis ap Elis 36
Elizabeth I, Queen 35, 39, 45, 49, 52, 53, 55, 65, 68, 69, 73, 119, 121–3, 143, 169, 171, 206
see also 'Sidanen' (Elizabeth I)
Emeral (Flints.) 212
Enderbie, Percy 32, 125, 129

England and the English 2, 4, 7, 8,
    12, 13–14, 17–18, 21, 23, 27,
    34, 35–7, 45, 58, 65, 69, 71, 77,
    80–2, 91, 101, 112, 116, 120–1,
    164, 195–215
English language 1, 3, 5–6, 46–7,
    49–50, 53–4, 59, 84, 91–3,
    96–100, 103, 109, 186, 195–6,
    199, 202, 203, 205, 213, 234 n. 6
episcopacy 57, 59, 81, 82–3, 160, 196
'Epistol at y Cembru' (1567) 50–3,
    57, 64, 80, 112
    see also Davies, Bishop Richard
Erbery, William 82–3, 85–6, 134
escheators 100, 141
Essex 40, 190, 204, 208, 212
Essex, Earl of see Devereux, Robert,
    2nd Earl of Essex
Established Church see Church of
    England
Evan ap Howell 212
Evans, Arise 195–8, 201, 205
Evans, Captain 75
Evans, Gwynfor 14
Evans, Lewys 70
Evans, Fr. Philip 76
Evans, Rhys see Evans, Arise
Evans, Roger 95
Evans, Theophilus 113
Exclusion Crisis (1679–81) 147, 155,
    161, 163
Exchequer, Court of 175
Exhortation, An (1588) 80–1

F
Ferrar, Bishop Robert 34
Ffydd Ddi-ffuant, Y (1677) 89, 113
Fifth Monarchy Men 84, 87, 135, 185
Flintshire 60, 65, 66, 68–9, 73, 77, 85,
    93, 107, 128, 149, 161, 163, 175,
    189, 208, 216, 217, 230 n. 26,
    231, n. 53, 242 n. 14
France 109, 190
Freeman, John 159

G
Gaelic language 114
Gainsborough (Lincs.) 171
Gallt-y-Celyn (Denbs.) 215
Gamage, William 104
gavelkind 16
    see also cyfran
Gellilyfdy (Flints.) 107
gender and Welshness 10, 167–94
genealogy 7, 25, 30, 34, 35, 106, 117,
    119, 124–5, 129, 134–5, 136–7,
    239 n. 41
gentry 7, 8, 10, 11, 15–16, 43–4,
    70, 88, 92, 103–4, 111, 133,
    136, 140, 158–65, 171, 178–9,
    181–2, 206–7
    faction and 151–55, 174–9
    and officeholding 140–57, 163–5
    and Reformation 43–4, 47
    supposed 'Anglicisation' of
        15–16, 91–2, 101–8
Geoffrey of Monmouth and
        Galfridian tradition 20, 22–3,
        25–7, 30–2, 34, 36, 124
    see also British History, the
Gerard, Sir William 96
German 110
Germany 190
Glamorgan 5–6, 59, 64, 73, 88, 93,
    104, 107, 108, 119, 147, 150,
    153, 156, 158, 200, 204, 207,
    211, 246 n. 115
Gloddaeth (Caern.) 33, 148, 190–1
'Glorious Revolution', the (1688) 3,
    76, 132–3, 150, 162
Gloucester 199
Gloucestershire 1, 94, 203
glovers 200
Glynne, Mary 135–6
Golden Grove (Carms.) 217
Golden Fleece, The (1626) 217
goldsmiths 206, 211
Goldsmiths' Company 206
Gomer 113
Gower Peninsula (Glam.) 6, 85, 93

Grace ferch Ffrancis 59
grand jury 100
'Great Britain' 26, 30, 33–4, 37–8,
    123, 186
great sessions, courts of 13–14, 17,
    97–9, 130, 143, 145, 162, 174,
    175, 192, 235 n. 32
Greek 53, 102
Griffith, Alexander 58, 130
Griffith, John (Caefnamlwch) 174,
    176
Griffith, John (Llanddyfnan) 58
Griffyn, Thomas 203
Gruffydd, Owain 100–1, 108
Gryffydd ab Ieuan ap Llewelyn
    Fychan 179–83
Gunpowder Plot, the (1605) 65, 68,
    73, 159
Gutenberg, Johannes 110
Guy, John 217–18
Gwaedd Ynghymru yn Wyneb Pob
    Cydwybod (1653) 86–7
Gwen ferch Ellis 170, 188–94 passim
Gwen ferch Gruffudd ap Hywel
    180
Gwydir (Caern.) 104, 129, 144, 152,
    158, 171, 211
Gwyn ap Llywelyn 208
Gwyn, Evan 208
Gwyn, John 102
Gwyn, John (Southwark) 208
Gwyn, Lewis 208
Gwyn, Richard 71–2, 77
Gwyn, Robert 71, 77
Gwynedd 1, 12, 94, 116, 121, 129
Gwynne, Richard 100
Gwysaney (Flints.) 216

H
haberdashers 205, 211
'Hanes y Cymru' (1684) 36
Harley, Sir Robert 83
Harry, George Owen 30, 124–5,
    134

Haverford (Pennsylvania) 216
Haverfordwest (Pembs.) 88, 226
    n. 14, 260
Hay-on-Wye (Brecs.) 85
Hebraismorum Cambro-
    Britannicorum Specimen (1676)
    113
Hebrew 53, 94, 113
Hengwrt (Merion.) 31
Henrietta Maria, Queen 217
Henry V, King 117
Henry VII, King 12, 21–2, 37,
    116–20, 122, 124, 131, 132,
    197, 238 n. 19
Henry VIII, King 2–4, 11–13, 15,
    25, 39–40, 43–4, 46, 52, 67, 97,
    120–1, 131, 197
'Henry VIII' clause 157
Henry Frederick, Prince of Wales
    18, 125–6
Henry, Philip 85
Herbert family, earls of Pembroke
    153–4
Herbert family (Montgomery) 216
Herbert, Sir Edward, 1st Baron
    Herbert of Cherbury 104
Herbert, Henry, 2nd Earl of
    Pembroke 80, 153
Herbert, Sir John 211
Herbert, Sir Percy 74
Herbert, Sir Richard 16
Herbert, William (Glam.) 104,
    207
Herbert, William (Gray Friars)
    153–4
Herbert, William (Mont.) 124
Herbert, Sir William, 1st Lord
    Powis 74
Herbert, William, 1st earl of
    Pembroke 206, 210
Hereford 126, 196, 199–200, 202
Hereford (diocese) 95
Herefordshire 1, 7, 75, 86, 94, 201,
    203
Heylin, Rowland 55, 78

Higges, Mary 203
Historia Regum Britanniae 20
'Historiae Britannicae Defensio'
     24–5, 51, 121
Historie of Cambria, A (1568) 27–9,
     32, 94
History of Wales (1697) 32, 33
Holborne, Elizabeth 210
Holland, Robert 30, 112, 125
Holt (Denbs.) 135
Holywell (Flints.) 67, 76
Hornedge, Christopher 203
Howell Dda 122
Huet, Thomas 94
Hugh ap Bevan 201
Hugh ap John Lewis 100
Hugh ap Robert 207
Hugh ap Sion Goch 100
Hughes, Harry 128
Hughes, Stephen 89–90, 93
Hughes, Bishop William 189, 191
Humble Representation and Address
     (1656) 161
Humphrey ap John ap Evan 200
Humphries, Bishop Humphrey 33

I

Ieuan ap William ap Dafydd ab
     Einws 45, 66
Independents (religious) 60, 86, 88,
     90, 150
     see also congregationalists/ism
Independents (political) 151, 154
Inns of Court 102, 206
interludes 108
invasion, threat of 8, 12, 67–8, 74–5,
     118
Ireland 8, 9, 15, 39, 40, 50, 58, 69,
     74, 77, 100, 139, 194, 197,
     215–16
     Irish Rebellion (1641) 74–5
Irish cattle *see* cattle
Islington 207
Italy 109

J

Jacobitism 133
James I, King (and James VI of
     Scotland) 4, 30, 35, 37, 99,
     123–6, 134, 144, 176, 211, 239
     n. 37
James II, King (also as James, Duke
     of York) 75, 76, 131–3, 146,
     148, 149–50, 159
James V of Scotland, King 39
James, Edward 55
James ap Gruffydd ap Hywel 67
Janet ferch Richard ap Hywel 180
Jenkins, Thomas 204
Jesuits 69, 70–1, 73–7
Jesus College, Oxford 102
Jewel, John 55
John ap John 216
John ap Morrice 189
John David ap Evan ap Mathew
     (*alias* John ap David and John
     David) 201–2
John of Gaunt 117
Jones, Edward 73
Jones, Hugh 195
Jones, Humfrey 200
Jones, John (Gellilyfdy) 107
Jones, John (Llantrissent) 136
Jones, John (Pembs.) 128
Jones, Col. John 83
Jones, Thomas (printer) 36, 94, 105,
     110–11, 202
Jones, Thomas (cleric) 131
Jones, William 206
juries *see* grand jury; petty jury
justices of the peace (JPs) 99, 100,
     140–51 *passim*, 191, 242 n. 13

K

Kelton, Arthur 25, 202–3
Kenfig (Glam.) 18
Kent 204
Kerry 216
Kyffin, Edward 109, 112

Kyffin, Morus 55
Kynniver Llith a Ban (1551) 48–9

L

Lancashire 40, 172
Landsker 92
Langford, Matilda 203
Latin 1, 19, 23, 24, 25, 27, 28, 34, 36,
    47, 53, 99, 102, 110–11, 122,
    181, 209, 217
Laud, Archbishop William 56–7
Leicester, earl of *see* Dudley, Robert,
    1st earl of Leicester
Lee, Rowland, Bishop of Coventry
    and Lichfield 13
Leland, John 23
Leominster (Herefs.) 203
Lewis ap John 192
Lewis ap Owen 172
Lewis, David 151
Lewis, Fr. David 76
Lewis, Sir Edward 82
Lewis, John 30
Lewis, Owen 68–9
Lewisham (Kent) 172
Lewys, Huw 54
Lhuyd, Edward 36
Llanaber (Merion.) 128
Llanbedr (Denbs.) 160
Llandaff (Glam.) 56
Llanddowror (Carms.) 125
Llandudno (Caern.) 70
Llanfaches (Monm.) 82, 85, 88
Llanfair (Denbs.) 160
Llanfihangel Crucorney (Monm.) 75
Llangar (Denbs.) 60
Llangelynin (Merion.) 195
Llannerch (Denbs.) 179
Llanrothal (Monm.) 148
Llanrwst (Denbs.) 98
Llansilin (Denbs.) 31, 128
Llantarnam (Monm.) 73
Llantrisant (Glam.) 18
Llantrissent (Monm.) 136

Llantrithyd (Glam.) 104, 108, 184
Llanwyddelan (Mont.) 60
Lleweni (Denbs.) 73, 152, 160
Llowes (Rads.) 99
Lloyd, David 160
Lloyd, John (Berth) 160
Lloyd, John (Cilgerran) 187
Lloyd, Fr. John 76
Lloyd, Lodowick 35, 122–3
Lloyd, Magdalen 208, 213–15
Lloyd, Mary 187
Lloyd, Sir Walter 187
Lloyd, Bishop William 31, 36, 55,
    60–1, 133, 225 n. 70, 227, n. 53,
    228 n. 74
Llwyd, Humphrey 1–3, 7, 11, 17, 18,
    26–9, 31, 36, 49, 93, 94, 157,
    187, 217, 218
Llwyd, Morgan 83, 86–7, 90, 116,
    134–6
Llwydiarth (Mont.) 212
Llyfr y Tri Aderyn (1653/4) 87
Llywelyn ap Gruffudd 12, 26, 35–6,
    117, 122, 128
Llŷn Peninsula 68, 70, 205
Llŷn, Wiliam 95, 107, 210
Lollards 43
London 8, 74, 78, 83, 125, 135, 144,
    163, 164, 171, 172, 174, 177,
    183, 184, 188, 195–7, 204–15
    passim
Long Parliament 82, 90, 154
Lords President of Wales 13, 17, 27,
    80, 100, 132, 143, 148–9, 187
    see also Egerton, John, 1st Earl of
    Bridgewater; Herbert, Henry,
    2nd earl of Pembroke; Lee,
    Rowland, Bishop of Coventry
    and Lichfield; Sidney, Sir
    Henry; Vaughan, Richard,
    2nd Earl of Carbery
Lords Chancellor 143, 147
Lords, House of 52
Loughor (Glam.) 18
Low Countries 153

Ludlow (Salop.) 14, 126, 142, 149, 162, 199, 247 n. 125

M

mab darogan 21–2, 116–18, 124
Machno, Huw 122, 124, 134
Madoc, Prince 217
maintaining 151–2, 164
maleficia 190
    see also witchcraft
Mansell, Bussy 108
Mansell, Sir Edward 147
Mason, John 217
Mathew, William 206
Matthew ap Howell 200
Matthew, David 200
manuscript circulation 23, 24, 26, 33, 47, 66, 71–2, 77, 159, 180, 184, 186
Mary, Queen of Scots 39, 73
Mary I, Queen 14, 34, 39, 40, 49, 50, 121–2, 146, 169
Mary of Guise 39
Maurice, William 31–2
Maurice, Sir William 123–4
Maynard family 213
Meidrim (Carms.) 89
mercers 211
Merlin 34, 35, 116, 187
Merioneth 13, 54, 56–7, 61, 84, 86, 88, 100, 102, 105, 106, 108, 149, 150, 163, 196, 216, 246 n. 115
Merion (Pennsylvania) 216
Merrick, Rice 119–20, 122
Methodism 90
Middleton, Thomas 210
Midleton, Wiliam 30
Milborne, Henry 148
Milford Haven (Pembs.) 118
Milton, John 183
mises 18, 155
monarchism 4, 115–37
    see also royalism
monasteries, dissolution of 24, 44

Monmouth 73, 147, 154, 206 246 n. 115,
    see also Geoffrey of Monmouth
Monmouth, duke of *see* Scott, James, 1st Duke of Monmouth
Monmouthshire 5, 13–14, 65, 73, 74, 75, 77, 82, 88, 90, 93, 105, 121, 127, 128, 136, 147–8, 151, 153, 155, 157, 164, 200, 205, 211, 246 n. 115
Montgomery 81, 129, 216
Montgomeryshire 35, 60, 74, 88, 93, 100, 104, 105, 134, 163, 212, 235 n. 32, 246 n. 115
Morgan family (Llantarnam) 73
Morgan, Lady Ann 121
Morgan, George 73
Morgan, Susan 144
Morgan, Thomas 152
Morgan, William (Machen) 152
Morgan, William (Tredegar) 147
Morgan, Bishop William 53–4, 55, 100, 103, 122, 227 n. 47
Morgannwg, Lewys 107, 119
Morus, Edward 106, 121
Morys, Huw 58, 108, 128, 131
Mostyn family (Mostyn) 180
Mostyn, Ambrose 84
Mostyn, Sir Roger 212
Mostyn, Thomas 33, 148–9, 190–1
MPs (Members of Parliament) 13, 15, 18, 49, 75, 79, 123–4, 147, 153–8, 162, 164
    see also parliament; elections, parliamentary
Much Wenlock (Salop.) 201–2
Mutton, Peter 212
Myddelton, Sir Hugh 206
Myddelton, Sir Thomas 55, 78, 211–14

N

Neath (Glam.) 18
Nercwys (Flints.) 208
New Model Army 83, 154

Newfoundland 9, 217–18
Newport (Mon.) 246 n. 115
Newry 216
New Radnor (Rads.) 246 n. 115
news and information 158–60
north Wales *see* Wales, north

O

Oates, Titus 75
　see also Popish Plot (1678–81)
officeholding 140–57 *passim*
Oll Synnwyr Pen Kembro Ygyd (1547)
　48, 51
Olson, Katharine (historian) 20, 45
Orielton (Pembs.) 184
Ortelius, Abraham 1–2, 27
Orton, Elizabeth 68–9, 72
Oswestry (Salop.) 95, 199, 202
Overton (Flints.) 68–9
Owain ap Maredudd ap Tudur
　(Owain Tudor) 117, 120, 134
Owain Glyndŵr 4, 116–17
Owain Lawgoch 116
Owain Tudor *see* Owain ap
　Maredudd ap Tudur
Owen, Ann 184–5
Owen, George 81, 92, 103, 120, 122,
　123, 151, 197, 234 n. 6, 249
　n. 47, 255 n. 83, 259
Owen, Hugh 68
Owen, John 208–9
Owen, Richard 180
Owen, Sir Robert 162
Owen Thomas (Haverfordwest) 88
Owen, Thomas (Plas Du) 68
Owen, William 131
Oxford 208
Oxford assize circuit 14
Oxford University 2, 24, 27, 48,
　102–3, 209

P

Parker, Archbishop Matthew 34

parliament 2, 3, 13, 15–16, 31, 49–50,
　52, 69, 74, 79, 80, 82–4, 90,
　123, 126, 127–8, 131, 134,
　139–40, 146, 149–50, 152–4,
　155–7, 160–4, 177, 178, 183,
　207
　see also Cavalier Parliament;
　Commons, House of;
　elections, parliamentary;
　Long Parliament; Lords,
　House of; MPs (Members
　of Parliament); Rump
　Parliament; subsidy,
　parliamentary
parliamentarians/ism 58, 115–16,
　128–9, 134–5
Parry, Bishop Richard 54, 55
patronymics and naming systems 95,
　200–2, 208, 252, n. 12
Paul's Head, The (London) 211
Peele, George 35
Pembroke 117, 134
Pembroke Castle 117
Pembroke, Earls of *see* Herbert,
　Henry, 2nd Earl of
　Pembroke; Herbert, William,
　1st Earl of Pembroke
Pembrokeshire 5, 30, 67, 73, 75, 81,
　88, 92, 128, 143–4, 153, 154,
　159, 163, 183, 187, 200, 234
　n. 6, 243 n. 23
Pen-llin (Glam.) 73
Penn, William 216
Pennsylvania 89, 216
Penrhosllugwy (Ang.) 100
Penry, John 79–82, 230 n. 32
Penygroes (Caern.) 130
Pepys, Samuel 210
Persons, Robert 69, 72
petition against the Council in the
　Marches (1689) 17–18, 161–3
petitions against episcopacy (1641–2)
　82–3, 160
petition in favour of episcopacy,
　North Wales (1642) 57, 160–1

petty jury 98, 193
Pezron, Paul 113
Philips, Hector 184
Philips, James 183–4
Philips, Katherine 169, 183–8 *passim*
Philips, Katherine (da. of above) 184
Phillipps, Sir Richard 183
Phylip, Wiliam 128. 130
Phylips family (Merion.) 108
Pilgrimage of Grace (1536) 41
pilgrimages 45, 64, 66, 226, n. 15
Plas Cadwgan (Denbs.) 73
Plas Du (Caern.) 68, 209
Pontymeibion (Denbs.) 58
Popish Plot (1678–81) 75–7, 146–8,
    151, 153, 164
Powel, Daniel 126
Powel, David 26, 27–30, 36, 94, 110,
    125, 126
Powell, John 203
Powell, Mary 203
Powell, Vavasor 84–5, 88, 135, 161,
    185
Powis, Lord *see* Herbert, Sir
    William, 1st Lord Powis
Powys 1
Poyer, Henry 159
Poyer, John 134
'Prayer Book Rebellion' (1549) 41,
    47
Prees (Price), William 108
Prendergast (Pembs.) 125
Presbyterian/ism (religious) 40, 85,
    151, 154, 184–5
Presbyterian/ism (political) 151,
    154, 185
Price (Aprice), Hugh 102
Price, Peter 215
Price, Thomas (Thomas ap Presse)
    202
Prichard, Rees 89
Prerogative Court of Canterbury
    175
Prince(s) of Wales 14, 18, 57, 116,
    119, 125–7, 134

print and publishing 23, 25, 33, 36,
    46–8, 69–70, 77, 86–7, 89, 94,
    97, 107, 109, 114, 140, 159, 160,
    162, 179, 186
Prise, Sir John 16, 23–4, 29, 34, 36,
    47–8, 51, 89, 103, 121, 222
    n. 17
Prise, Richard 24
Privy Council 14, 34, 48, 151, 158,
    173
Probert, Henry 148
prophecy 20–1, 35, 106, 116–19,
    123–4, 136, 196–7
    see also mab darogan
*Prophesie of Cadwallader, Last King of
    the Britaines, A* (1604) 124
Protestantism 9, 20, 29, 34, 39–61
    passim, 64–5, 118–19, 161, 193
    see also Reformation
Prys, Edmwnd 54, 78, 106
Puckering, John 143–4, 243 n. 24
Pugh, James 201
Puleston, Roger 212
puritanism 40, 42–3, 56–7, 77–90,
    134–6, 150, 160
    see also religious nonconformity
Pury, Thomas 154
Pye, Mary 203

Q
Quakers 60, 86, 88, 216
quarter sessions 13, 99–100, 128,
    135–6, 152, 203

R
Radnor (Pennsylvania) 216
Radnorshire 30, 66, 84, 88, 93, 144,
    153, 205, 218, 246 n. 115
Radyr (Glam.) 207
Raglan Castle (Monm.) 74, 127, 132
Rastell, John 22–3
recusancy 45, 65–73, 76
    see also Catholicism

Rees ap John 134
Reformation 3, 9, 11–12, 23, 37,
      39–61, 63, 67, 78, 102, 119,
      131, 181, 218
   historiography of 42–3, 64,
      77–8
   see also Catholicism; Counter-
      Reformation; Protestantism;
      puritanism
Renaissance learning and scholarship
      3, 19, 22–4, 27, 33, 102, 107,
      108–14, 179–80
Restoration, the (1660) 58–9, 74, 85,
      88, 128–31, 135–6, 146, 154,
      195
religious nonconformity 9, 11, 42–3,
      63, 77–90 passim, 101, 149–50
   see also Baptists;
      congregationalism; Fifth
      Monarchy Men; Quakers;
      puritanism
retaining see maintaining
Rhyd (Flints.) 189
Rhysiart Phylip 124–5
Richard III, King 117–18
Richard ap Hywel 180
Richard ap John Griffith (alias
      Richard Bishop) 201
Richards, William 36
Robert ap Huw 58
Robert Wynn ap Cadwalader 212
Robert, Gruffydd 111, 198–9, 201
Roberts, Dorothy 203
Roberts, John 212
Roberts, Peter (historian) 46
Robin Ddu 118
Robinson, Bishop Nicholas 34–5, 44,
      45, 226 nn. 12, 15
Rogers, John 207
Rogers, Philip 60
Rogers, William 98
Roman Catholicism see Catholicism
Romans 20, 22, 25
Rome 68, 71
Rowlands William 36

royalism 57, 83, 115, 126–30, 133,
      153, 183, 185–6, 187, 204
   see also civil wars; Charles
      I, King; Charles II,
      King; monarchism;
      parliamentarianism
Ruabon (Denbs.) 27
Rûg (Merion.) 56–7
Rump Parliament 83
Ruthin (Denbs.) 205

S
Sacheverell riots 164
Salesbury, William 48–53, 56, 69, 70,
      71, 72, 93, 94, 96–7, 103, 109,
      110, 112, 113, 119, 122, 179,
      202, 227 n. 47, 228 n. 75
Salesbury, William (Rûg) 56
Salisbury, Fulke 204
Salisbury, Thomas 30
Salusbury family (Lleweni) 152, 204
Salusbury, Thomas 73
Salusbury, Sir Thomas 160
Sandford (Glos.) 203
Saxons 20, 50, 52, 67, 72, 116
Saxton, Christopher 17, 221 n. 39
schools and education 84, 102–3,
      196
Scotland 1, 4, 23, 26, 30, 37, 39–40,
      123–4, 128, 139
   see also James I, King (and
      James VI of Scotland)
Scott, James, 1st Duke of Monmouth
      131–2
scriveners 205
Severn, River 1, 198
Shakespeare, William 204
shearmen 200
sheriffs/shrievalty 100, 140, 141, 154
shoemakers 200
Shrewsbury 5, 8, 25, 36, 78, 93, 196,
      198–203, 205
Shrewsbury Company of Shearmen
      200

Shrewsbury Drapers Company 156–7

Shrewsbury School 202

Shropshire 1, 14, 94–5, 201–2, 208

'Sidanen' (Elizabeth I) 122–3

Sidney, Sir Henry 27–8

Sidney, Sir Robert 206, 211

Siôn ap Hoel Phylips 95

Siôn Dafydd Laes 108

Siôn Dafydd Rhys *see* Davies, Dr John (Siôn Dafydd Rhys)

Siôn Phylip 124

slander *see* defamation and slander

Slebech (Pembs.) 73

Somerset 5, 203, 204, 208

Somerset, Henry, 3rd Marquis of Worcester and 1st Duke of Beaufort 75–6, 131–2, 147–9

south Wales, *see* Wales, south

Speed, John 17

St Asaph (diocese) 31, 36, 54, 55, 60–1, 95, 100, 133, 189, 191

St Davids (diocese) 34, 44, 46–7, 85, 228 n. 72

St David's Day 133, 209–10

St John's College, Cambridge 102

St Mary Woolchurch (London) 183

St Mary's (Swansea) 55

St Winifred's Well 66–7, 76

see also Holywell

Star Chamber 68, 151–2, 176, 260

Stepney 81

Stevens, John 132–3

Stone, Lawrence (historian) 249 n. 61

Stradling, John 260

Stratford-upon-Avon (Warw.) 204

Stuart dynasty/Stuart line 123–33, 216

subsidies, parliamentary 18

subsidy collectors/commissioners 100, 145

Suffolk 204

Surrey 214

Sutton, William 200

Swansea (Glam.) 18, 55, 88

Swett, Katharine (historian) 211

Symonds, Richard 84

Symonds, Roger 206

T

tailors 191, 195, 200, 202

Temple Bar (London) 210

Test Act (1673) 146, 149–50

Thesaurus Linguae Latinae et Cambrobritannicae (1607/8) 110

Thomas ap Howell 201

see also William ap Howell

Thomas ap Presse *see* Price, Thomas (Thomas ap Presse)

Thomas ap Robert 212

Thomas, Ellis John 128

Thomas, John 130–1

Thomas, Oliver 78

Throckmorton, Job 79

Toleration Act (1689) 89

Tomas ab Ieuan ap Hywel 67

Tompson, Mr 215

Tooting Graveney 208, 213–15

Tourneur, Timothy 98

Trefriw (Caern.) 110

Trevor family (Plas Teg) 175

Troy/Trojans 20, 36, 113

see also British History, the

tuckers 200

Tudor dynasty/Tudor line 9, 21, 52, 117–24, 132, 133, 216, 238 n. 6

Tudur, Siôn 107, 121, 122

Tumultuous Petitioning Act (1661) 161

Turberville family (Pen-llin) 73

Twyne, Thomas 27

Tydder, John 200

Tyndale, William 46

U

union of England and Wales *see* Acts of Union (1536–43)

V

vagabonds 106, 198, 207–8
Vale of Clwyd 179
Vale of Glamorgan 5–6, 93, 108
Vaughan, Henry ('The Silurist') 187
Vaughan, Owen 212
Vaughan, Richard 132
Vaughan, Richard, 2nd Earl of
    Carbery 187
Vaughan, Robert 31, 32
Vaughan, Rowland 31, 128
Vaughan, Thomas 99
Vaughan, William 217–18
Vaughan, Sir William 9
Venner, Thomas 135
Vergil, Polydore 22, 24–7, 29, 32, 36,
    224 n. 65
Vikings 20
Villiers, George, 1st Duke of
    Buckingham 145, 176, 179

W

Wards, Court of 176, 178
Wales
    administrative divisions of 2–3,
        9, 12–14, 16–17
    concept of 'Welsh politics' in 115,
        139–40, 155–7
    customary law in 17, 176–9
    diaspora from 10, 88–9, 196–218
        passim
    economic and population
        pressures in 198, 217
    historiography of 3, 8–11, 42–3,
        59, 77–8, 91–2, 101–2, 114,
        155, 167–8
    history of 1–2, 7, 10, 19–38 *passim*
        see also British History, the
    internal divisions of 4–6, 201
    language divisions in 5–6
        see also Welsh language,
            dialects
    as 'Protestant nation' 48, 50–2,
        61, 77, 101
    religious conservatism of 10, 41,
        44–7, 55–61
    taxation in 18, 155
    see also Acts of Union (1536–43)
Wales-England border, *see* Anglo-
    Welsh border
Wales, north 5, 35, 37, 57, 66, 68–70,
    74, 83, 86, 93–4, 102, 105,
    107–8, 127, 129, 142, 144,
    150, 152–3, 156, 160, 161, 174,
    176–8, 180–1, 194, 205, 206,
    211–13, 259
Wales, Principality of 9, 12, 13, 226 n. 13
Wales, south 5, 64, 71, 74, 84, 88, 90,
    93–4, 107, 108, 127, 129–30,
    161, 199, 205, 217, 218
Walley, John 97
Wallington, Nehemiah 202
Walsingham, Sir Francis 151, 212
Walter, Henry 82
Warwickshire 79, 195, 204
Watkin, Thomas (historian) 221 n. 40
Welsh Back (Bristol) 199
Welsh Bridge (Shrewsbury) 199
Welsh Charity School (Clerkenwell)
    208
Welsh Gate (Shrewsbury) 199
Welsh language 1, 3, 5, 6–7, 24, 30,
    41, 42, 46–56, 59, 70, 84–5,
    89–90, 91–114 *passim*, 125,
    159, 179–83, 186–7, 192–4,
    199, 200, 202, 211, 216, 217,
    227 nn. 53–4, 235 n. 32
    1536 'language clause' 14–16, 47, 50,
        91, 96, 100–1, 109, 111–12, 114
    in administrative and judicial
        settings 96–101, 114
    as the 'British tongue' 1, 105,
        112–13, 225 n. 70
    communities in England 7, 91,
        94–5, 199–203
    dialects of 6, 93–4, 105
    dictionaries and grammars 110–12
    English attitudes towards 109,
        112, 203

Welsh language (continued)
poetry 7, 21, 45, 58, 67, 72, 86–7,
105–8, 110–11, 116–18, 124,
128, 179–83, 199, 260
see also bards; mab darogan
Renaissance scholarship and
109–13
use of interpreters and translators
95, 98–9, 125, 159, 217
see also bards; Bible(s), Welsh
translations of
Welsh Marches/Marcher lordships
9, 12–14, 93, 132, 161, 163,
202, 204, 205, 212
see also Anglo-Welsh border
Welsh towne (Co. Donegal) 216
Welsh Tract (Pennsylvania) 216
Welsh Trust, the 89
Welsh ward (Shrewsbury) 199, 200
Welshgate (Chester) 199
Westminster 2, 14, 139, 140, 148, 155,
158, 164, 177, 178, 208, 210
Whatcroft (Ches.) 175
Whitchurch (Glam.) 56
White, Richard see Gwyn, Richard
Whitelocke, Sir James 100, 198
Whitgift, Archbishop John 53
Whitland (Carms.) 144
Whittington (Salop.) 202
Whyte, Rowland 206, 211
widowhood 173–9
Wigfair (Denbs.) 182
Wiliems, Thomas 110
William III, King 132–3
William ap Howell 201
William ap Rhys ap Ithel 200
William Gruffith ap William 191–2
Williams, Glanmor (historian) 13,
15, 54, 61, 77
Williams, Gwyn Alf (historian) 3, 4
Williams, Lord Keeper John 102,
144–6, 147, 176
Williams, Penry (historian) 151
Williams, Sir Trevor 75, 155
Williams, William 60

Williamson, Secretary Sir Joseph
147
Windebank, Secretary Francis 98
witchcraft 170, 188–94
wool 93, 156, 157, 197
see also Shrewsbury Drapers
Company
women and gender 10, 167–94
passim, 203, 218
Worcester 199, 202
Worcester, Battle of (1651) 186
Worcester earls/marquises of 74, 153
see also Somerset, Henry,
3rd Marquis of Worcester and
1st Duke of Beaufort
Worcestershire 1
Word for God, A (1655) 161
Worthenbury (Flints.) 85
Wrexham (Denb.) 72, 83, 84, 86, 90,
134, 160–1, 195–6, 233 n. 90
Wroth, William 82–4, 86
Wye, River 2
Wynn family (Gwydir) 144–5, 152,
158, 211, 253
Wynn, Cadwaladr 103
Wynn, Henry 102
Wynn, John 160
Wynn, (Sir) John 104, 145, 171, 172,
174–6, 178, 207, 211
Wynn, Maurice 171
Wynn, Owen 145, 178
Wynn, Peter 217
Wynn, Lady Sarah 129, 210
Wynn, Sir Richard 156, 210
Wynn, William (Gwydir) 103, 145
Wynn, William 191
Wynne, Sir John 150
Wynne, Thomas 60, 216
Wynne, William 29, 31, 32

Y

Y Fan (Glam.) 82
Yny lhyvyr hwnn (1546) 47
Ysgeifiog 60

.